It is only recently that historians of the theatre in French Canada have turned their attention to playwrights active before the twentieth century. Their practice had been to trace the roots of theatre to the mid-1930s, to the appearance of Father Emile Legault and his troupe, the Compagnons de Saint-Laurent, dismissing what had gone before. In this innovative history, Leonard Doucette sets out to deal for the first time with all plays that have survived to 1867 and to link them with the evolution of politics, institutions, and culture in French Canada.

The study of theatre has often been handicapped also by the outdated practice of defining the literary-cultural history of a nation by identifying the masterpieces produced in specific periods and then defining other works in terms of what they are not. The surprisingly rich and varied history of theatrical forms in French Canada has just begun to receive the attention it deserves from scholars. Some of the texts and authors referred to in this history are identified for the first time: the materials cited and conclusions drawn are based upon original research in major Canadian libraries as well as the works of published critics and historians. The result is an excellent introduction to the various forms theatre has taken and the problems it has encountered in French Canada.

Leonard Doucette, of Acadian extraction, is Associate Professor of French at Scarborough College in the University of Toronto. He is the author of a previous book in the University of Toronto Romance Series, *Emery Bigot: Seventeenth-Century French Humanist*.

LEONARD E. DOUCETTE

Theatre in French Canada: Laying the Foundations 1606-1867

UNIVERSITY OF TORONTO PRESS
Toronto Buffalo London

© University of Toronto Press 1984
Toronto Buffalo London
Printed in Canada
ISBN 0-8020-5579-6

University of Toronto Romance Series 52

Canadian Cataloguing in Publication Data

Doucette, Leonard E. (Leonard Eugene), 1936-
Theatre in French Canada 1606-1867
(University of Toronto romance series, ISSN 0082-5336 ;
v. 52)
Bibliography: p.
Includes index.
ISBN 0-8020-5579-6
1. Canadian drama (French) – History and criticism.*
I. Title. II. Series
PS8177.5.Q4D68 1984   C842'.3   C84-098154-6
PQ3911.D68 1984

This book has been published with the help of grants from the
Canadian Federation for the Humanities, using funds provided by the
Social Sciences and Humanities Research Council of Canada, and from the
Publications Fund of University of Toronto Press, and with the assistance
of the Humanities and Social Sciences Division of the Research Board,
University of Toronto.

Contents

Introduction

This book examines the evolution of dramatic forms in French Canada from their earliest appearance to Confederation. There are three categories of such forms that it is useful to distinguish: the religious-pedagogic; the political; and what is here designated, for want of a more widely accepted term, as 'social' theatre: theatre intended for public performance with open access, and whose principal aim is the entertainment (as opposed to the edification, instruction, or politicization) of those for whom it is composed. This is not an attempt to characterize all theatre everywhere according to these three distinctions: they prove to be the most useful and most appropriate ones for the study of French-Canadian theatre.

The primary focus of this study is *written* theatre: the composition of plays, the history of each text, and (for those eventually staged) the record of public reaction to its performance. I do not apologize for that focus, for as the modern Quebec playwright, Paul Toupin, remarks, 'the only theatre which exists in Time, is the theatre one *reads*.' Where I have dealt with what is broadly defined as 'theatrical activity,' as in the period 1765-1825 in particular, I have done so in order to shed more light upon the forces affecting native dramaturgy, and because in this instance that is the period which has received the most intensive attention from researchers to date, exemplified in the careful monograph by Baudoin Burger, *L'Activité théâtrale au Québec (1765-1825)*, published in 1974.

This is, above all, a *history* of theatre. It is as little speculative and as highly factual as I could make it. I also evaluate, using traditional critical and esthetic criteria, the quality of each individual work described; but this, perforce, will prove to be the more ephemeral aspect of this undertaking. My evaluation is synthetic: where previous critical analyses of a dramatic text existed I have reported, compared, and contrasted them. It is also original, both in that respect and because I have also, where appropriate, added my own. And many of the texts examined were unknown or forgotten, others dismissed or misunderstood. This, I propose, represents the most complete corpus yet identified of extant dramatic and paradramatic texts from the period in question. It is hoped that future students and researchers will be able to refine the critical data and methodology I have used, thereby providing more and more sophisticated insight. I offer a well-anchored base on which future qualitative reassessment will, I hope, be based.

Inaugurated in 1606, sporadically flourishing in mid-century and proscribed at its end, almost invisible thereafter until the fall of New France, theatre has had to fight tooth and nail for its very existence for most of the past 300 years. Social theatre, in particular, has had to struggle, at various times, against a sincere but often intolerant attitude towards it on the part of the established Church; against economic and cultural colonialism, French and British-American; against serious problems of demography and geography; against public indifference as well as against recurrent attempts at politicizing it; and at times against its own apparent self-destructive urge. Historically, the very image of French-language theatre in Canada, and particularly that of the nineteenth-century, has suffered from a constant, if unconscious, distortion based upon a traditional European literary-critical approach which consists of identifying 'masterpieces' of the type discernible from the same period in French literature, and defining all other productions in terms of what they are not. A literature with no great universal summits, in other words, must have no plains, no valleys worth exploring! It is only in the last decade that the validity of this approach has been effectively challenged, in works such as that by Baudoin Burger already mentioned; in Etienne-F. Duval's seminal thesis and the *Anthologie thématique du théâtre québécois au XIXe siècle* (1975) which stems from it; in the disparate but highly useful fifth volume of the series Archives des lettres canadiennes, entitled *Le Théâtre canadien-français* (1976). An honest attempt is now being made to depict and to evaluate native dramaturgy and local theatrical activity on its own terms, and that attempt has proven productive and illuminating. One still perceives, however, a distinct bias in favour of 'social' theatre and against the instructive or the adversarial. This book attempts to correct that bias, for it insists that of the three categories of drama it portrays, the one which has had the most sporadic and the least vigorous history in French Canada, in the years which concern us, is precisely this 'social' theatre. And the reason is obvious, for it is the one most dependent upon factors external to it: a predictable and cohesive clientele, physical facilities, and religious or civic tolerance. I may appear, at times, in the course of this book, to be dealing with texts only remotely connected with the mainstream of drama as traditionally conceived. It is my hope that the reader will ultimately appreciate why, in tracing the evolution of written dramatic forms, such apparent digressions were necessary.

Composition of this work was originally undertaken in French, some years ago. Conversations with colleagues in various cognate disciplines soon convinced me that there is more need, at this stage, of a history of theatre in French Canada more accessible to that 'other' Canada – and particularly to that great portion of it which possesses little or insufficient French to explore this field on its own. In order to make this study useful to a broader public, while at the same time meeting legitimate demands of scholarly method, the body of the text is presented only in English, with the general, intelligent, interested but unilingual reader in mind. In the rare instances (Lescarbot's *Théâtre de Neptune*, Quesnel's *Colas et Colinette*) where an English version of a text already existed, I have generally used it for quotation. In all other cases the translations are my own. The notes provided, on the other hand, are intended primarily for the scholar, to help him or her pursue a reference to greater depth by suggesting sources worth checking, by pointing out conflicting views that may exist on details of a topic or incident, problems of deficient or contradictory information, and the like. Since it is obvious that any scholar intending to work in the history of Canadian theatre must possess at least a sound reading knowledge of French, the notes provide no translation of sources quoted therein. They also reproduce the French original of passages cited in the body of the text, in all cases where the original is inaccessible to the average researcher, working in proximity to a decent library (ie, in the case of manuscript materials and rare printed texts).

Finally, a bibliography is provided comprising all materials referred to in this book, along with a few others which, although perhaps not cited herein, have nevertheless proved useful in its preparation. This is not an exhaustive bibliography of theatre history in French to 1867: there is simply too much dross and too much repetition, particularly in journal articles, to make it worthwhile to commemorate it all. Readers interested in a fuller list are invited to consult the excellent bibliographies at the end of the fifth volume of Archives des lettres canadiennes and the first volume of *Dictionnaire des œuvres littéraires du Québec*.

The acknowledgments I wish to make are many, most of them directed towards a whole class of professional, expert, and irreplaceable people, those who staff the various archives, university, public reference, and microform libraries I have visited in Ontario and Quebec. I salute the intelligence, competence, and courtesy of those with whom I have dealt at the Archives du Séminaire de Québec; Archives Nationales du Québec on the Laval campus; Bibliothèque de l'Université Laval; Bibliothèque de l'Université de Montréal; Bibliothèque de l'Université du Québec à Montréal; Bibliothèque Nationale du Québec à Montréal; Bibliothèque de la Ville de Montréal, in particular those of the Collection Gagnon; of the Archives Nationales in Ottawa; the National Library, and especially the Chief of the Rare Book Division, Liana van der Bellen, and through her, M. Brillant of the Library of Parliament; of the Morriset Library at the University of Ottawa, especially those entrusted with the outstanding collection of the Centre de Recherche en Civilisation canadienne-française; of the Metropolitan Toronto Reference Library, particularly Heather McCallum; and last but not least, those of the various libraries of the University of Toronto. I have received courteous and prompt assistance in response to queries from John Hare of the University of Ottawa and Rémi Tourangeau of the Université du Québéc à Trois-Rivières. I wish to thank my colleague, David M. Hayne, as well as Lucie Robert of the Faculté des lettres, Université Laval, for invaluable help in locating some of the rare texts discussed in Chapter 4. And I owe special thanks to Dr R.M. Schoeffel of the University of Toronto Press for his invaluable encouragement and assistance in surmounting the many obstacles encountered on the way.

SCARBOROUGH COLLEGE, UNIVERSITY OF TORONTO
October 1983

Theatre in French Canada 1606-1867

Theatre in New France 1606-1760

THE THEATRE OF NEPTUNE IN NEW FRANCE

The history of theatre in French Canada begins in November 1606 with the performance of Marc Lescarbot's *Théâtre de Neptune en la Nouvelle-France*, upon the sheltered waters at the mouth of the stream the French called 'L'Equille' (today's Annapolis River, in northwestern Nova Scotia), within sight of Champlain's famous *Habitation* at Port Royal.

Lescarbot is better known as a historian (his *Histoire de la Nouvelle-France* remains even today a lively, legible source of information on the first attempts to establish a permanent French settlement in Canada) and minor poet than for this, his first and only foray into dramatic art. He wrote the work, which is more properly described as an aquatic pageant, and directed and participated in its performance in celebration of the delayed return of Poutrincourt, Champlain, and their men from an unsuccessful mission the former had led out of Port Royal along the coast of what is now New England, in search of a more promising base for the colony he and De Monts hoped to establish. Lescarbot had been left in charge of the base camp, and was no doubt concerned at the ten-week absence of his companions. 'After many perils,' he recounts, in the Erondelle (London 1609) translation of his *History*, 'Monsieur de Poutrincourt arrived in Port Royall the 14. day of Nouember, where we received him joyfully, and with a solemnity altogether new in that part. For about the time that we expected his returne (with great desire, and that so much the more, that if any harme had happened him, we had beene in danger to have confusion among our selves) I aduised my selfe to shew some jollity going to meet him, as we did.'[1]

As the author suggests, the little garrison left behind at Port Royal would indeed have been in serious straits, or 'great confusion,' if their leaders, along with their pilot, locksmith, surgeon, apothecary, and carpenter had not returned with their ship, supplies, and expertise. Lescarbot himself had been in the new land only a few months, having sailed from France in the spring of 1606; winter was coming on, and the fate of a previous attempt at wintering in that area would have been fresh in his and his comrades' minds, as they thought of the thirty-five Frenchmen dead from scurvy at Sainte-Croix, just across the bay, in the winter of 1604-5. His 'play' is, then, above all a heartfelt expression of joy at the return of friends and patron: the text shows this at every turn.

It comprises only ten pages in the Paris (Millot) edition of 1609, and is an unpretentious composition that even its author calls a mere *gaillardise*, or good-natured frolic. He begs the reader's indulgence for the lack of polish his verses display: 'If they are poorly clothed and in rustic garments, consider, Monseigneur, the country from which they come, uncultivated, shaggy with forests; and attribute to the company they have kept, and to the sea, their defects.'[2]

Fittingly for a transoceanic colony, the central focus is Neptune, god of the sea, patron of mariners. With long beard and flowing hair he sits, robed in blue, trident in hand, in a small boat decorated to resemble a chariot. This boat-chariot is drawn by six Tritons, half-fish half-men, attendants to Neptune. It flows smoothly out to meet Poutrincourt's landing craft or shallop and, in what must have been an arresting opening gambit (dictated no doubt by practical considerations as well), grapples fast to it. Neptune, perhaps played by Lescarbot himself, then begins his peroration:

> Halt, mighty Sagamo, no further fare!
> Look on a god who holds thee in his care.
> Thou know'st me not? I am of Saturn's line,
> Brother to Pluto dark and Jove divine...
> Neptune's my name. I, Neptune, rule the salt
> Sea waves, most potent under heaven's vault.[3]

Having thus identified himself, in case the improvised costume he wears did not serve to do so, Neptune then describes his own wide-ranging powers. Without him none of the great European explorations could have taken place; without him, in particular, Poutrincourt and his men would never have reached the shores of Acadia:

If I, in short, refused my aid and bounty,
No king would succor any brother king
Who dwelled beyond my Ocean's parting ring;
Thyself indeed despite thy deeds of daring
Had'st never sighted land, my sea-lanes faring,
Nor won the joy of landing on this coast
– Thou whose exploits thy fellows proudly boast!

A great peal of trumpets follows. Poutrincourt, with an obvious sense of
the occasion, draws and presents his sword for the second tableau where
the six Tritons address him in turn, commenting and refining upon their
master's speech in verses of 12, 10, and 8 syllables, sprinkling in a few
Souriquois (Micmac) words. They remind him of the great favour Lord
Neptune is bestowing upon him. The Fifth Triton, rather unexpectedly,
addresses the Frenchman in 'Gascon' (actually *occitan*, the language of
the Languedoc area of southern France, as recent scholarship has conclusively shown),[4] taking a playful swipe at his master's well-known erotic
ardours.

The next movement follows without delay: another boat takes the centre of this bobbing stage, containing four 'Indians' (ie, Frenchmen playing
the roles of Amerindians) who bring presents to Poutrincourt from the
land, after the sea's salute. They address him successively, each somewhat
better characterized than the Tritons, each offering feudal submission and
future co-operation. The quarter of moose and the beaver skins seem like
reasonable gifts for such an occasion, but the Micmacs and their legend-
arily aged leader, the great Membertou, reportedly present for the occasion, must have smiled incredulously if they understood anything of what
the third 'Indian' says. He claims to have been smitten by Cupid's barb,
for:

Cupid not alone in France,
    Love's captives leading,
Merrily with wanton lance
    Pricks hearts to bleeding.
Here on western shores as well
Sparkle eyes and bosoms swell,
    When Cupid's heeding.

And thus he hastens to offer his gift (ornaments made by his beloved's
own hand), so that he may speedily rejoin her. The fourth Indian has

even less to give, but promises to return soon with the product of a hunt-ing and fishing expedition he will undertake for Poutrincourt.

The fourth movement comprises an improvised speech by the latter (not recorded), thanking Neptune and all present for the graciousness of their welcome, and particularly the Micmacs, who are invited 'to come along to Fort Royal and partake of some *caracona*' (ie, bread), the 'circus' part of the performance now having finished. At which point the assem-bled company sings in four-part harmony, to a well-known air:

> Great god Neptune, send our fleet
> In safety o'er the waters,
> And bring us homeward all to meet
> Our loving wives and daughters.[5]

Then the cannons speak and the brass trumpets sound again, their echoes rolling through the hills and gentle slopes around Port Royal. With shouts of merriment and songs all set out for the *Habitation*. As they approach its gates, adorned for the occasion with the arms of France, of De Monts and Poutrincourt, they are saluted by a 'companion in a merry mood,' no doubt one of those destined to enliven the Order of Good Cheer which Champlain would found that very winter. The last tableau has the merry companion calling the kitchen staff to action as he issues a very Rabelai-sian invitation to all[6] to enter and start the traditional feasting:

> Up then, stewards, scullions, batmen!
> Hurry, lean, and scurry, fat men!
> Clatter out your pots and dishes,
> Roast your haunches, fry your fishes,
> Pour your flagons, fill our glasses,
> Drinks for everyone that passes.
> Let them swill all they can swallow,
> Throats are dry and bellies hollow...

And here the play ends, with one final summons to the company:

> Come my lords and noble red men:
> Here is wine to turn your head, men!
> But before you start your capers,
> Sneeze aloud to clear the vapours.
> This play's ended, that is certain;
> Naught remains but draw the curtain.[7]

Had theatre then gone on to flourish in New France, we might have claimed it was well begun with this piece. For the function it served on this occasion was faithful to the most ancient origins of the craft: a communal celebration, an act of participation that a modern theorist like Antonin Artaud would have approved, a sort of 'total theatre' with cannons, trumpets, costumes; with the fifty or so Frenchmen and a couple of dozen Micmacs all assembled in what splendour they could muster; and all this in a natural setting as spectacular as the Annapolis River basin, in Indian summer!

Obviously, this first play written and performed in French Canada is in no way a parthenogenetic phenomenon. The *Théâtre de Neptune* is firmly rooted in French cultural history, inside the academic context and outside it. In the better schools, such as the Collège de Laon in Paris which Lescarbot had attended, the custom had long existed of marking the occasion of an important visit with a semi-ritualized series of addresses or 'harangues' delivered to the visitor by designated members of the student body. The Jesuits, in particular, made frequent use of this type of mixed dramatic dialogue, called a *réception*, consonant with their use of dramatized dialogue in general as an essential pedagogical tool. They were soon to import that custom to New France, where we shall find evident bases of comparison with plays from 1658 and 1727, and where an enduring tradition of *théâtre de collège* would, time and again, serve as the wellspring for a resurgence of public theatre.[8] But Lescarbot's text belongs to another, quite different tradition as well, one that is representative of a broader segment of French society: the public masques and triumphal entries, the nautical extravaganzas and allegorical galas so integral to French (and English) courtly life since the Renaissance. The triumphal entries in particular, where the king's household received the corresponding cortege coming out from the town through which he wished to pass (a ceremony much more common in sixteenth-century France, when royalty had as yet no fixed home, as it would have later in Fontainebleau and Versailles), seem to have influenced Lescarbot's work. We know that he had been present for such a ceremony in his home town, Vervins, in 1598, upon the occasion of the signing of a treaty between France and Spain, and that he himself had prepared such a harangue, part of a *réception* for the papal legate.[9] He knew the format and its possibilities, as did his friend, patron, and compatriot, Jean de Biencourt de Poutrincourt.

In a broader sense, theatre was an integral part of the culture transported to French North America; and as the American critic Lewis P. Waldo has written, 'this work is exactly the type of entertainment which a cultivated Frenchman of the period would have prepared for such an occasion, whether in Old or New France.'[10] Certainly Lescarbot and Poutrin-court, steeped in Greco-Roman culture through the privileged education they both had received, would have felt at home amid Tritons, Neptune, and the otherwise recondite mythological allusions with which Lescarbot's poetry is replete. It is also true that, unlike many past and indeed future colonizing attempts, that of De Monts and Poutrincourt had enlisted a relatively high calibre of volunteered personnel, most of them, it is believed, of more than average education and skills. All of them were probably familiar with at least some of the types of theatre, public or aca-demic, I have alluded to.

It is, of course, a very different tradition from that which would evolve in Paris some thirty, fifty, sixty-five years later. At the turn of the century theatrical activity in the capital was somewhat limited, consisting mainly of farcical comedy, provided by the *bateleurs*, jugglers, tumblers, and small troupes of strolling players in the market-places of Saint-Laurent and Saint-Germain, living off their wits and an array of situational strategems. There were also occasional performances of tragedy as the French Renais-sance tended to conceive of it, emphasizing static lamentation still but already, thanks to Alexandre Hardy, moving towards that surer sense of its own identity which the next three generations would confirm. And of course there was the *comédie italienne* with its rich tradition behind it, uncertain perhaps as to the time and location of its next performance, but fairly fixed as to personnel and to general strategy: improvisation, within a well-practised framework, similar in its way to the extempore response Poutrincourt could so easily produce in the *Théâtre de Neptune*. In the provinces theatre was more widespread and more secure, free at least from the strictures imposed in Paris since 1548 by the Confrérie de la Passion.[11] All these currents are obvious in our short text, with the pre-ponderant influence being that of the triumphal entry.

It is ironic that this first dramatic production in a country which its author describes as 'uncultivated, shaggy with forests, and inhabited by wandering tribes' should stem from so courtly a paradigm, so stuffed with classical references mouthed by Greco-Roman divinities. But a clear attempt is also made to extend those classical mythological references, to counterbalance them with another, new, Canadian mythology. And the few Amerindian words introduced into the text (*caracona*: bread; *ades-quidés*: friend; *sagamos*: leader) evoke the colour and flavour of a wild, exotic Acadia. The performance became a true communal celebration end-ing, as good communal thanksgivings should, with bread, wine, and brotherhood. November 14, 1606 is a date that could annually have been celebrated as a more apposite Thanksgiving than our present one, one richer and older than the largely legendary sharing of the harvest by Pilgrim and Indian in that land of the Armouchiquois from which Poutrincourt and his men had felt so fortunate to return.

Finally, there is a political dimension to this play that must be underlined. As Harriette Taber Richardson has observed, in the introduction to her translation of Lescarbot's text, 'the playwright sensed a larger and more fashionable interest across the sea in the Palace of the Louvre, and wrote his slight verses to please the eye of Henry the Fourth.'[12] Poutrincourt was a personal friend of the king and dependent upon his wishes for renewal of the grant made to him and De Monts. Thus we know that here, as in his *Histoire de la Nouvelle-France* in general, Lescarbot was doing his best to make a case for more intensive colonization of the New World, under the aegis of the two gentlemen named. So when the Fifth Triton rhymes his suggestive allusion in 'Gascon,' one knows that the wink is for Henry, Henry the womanizing *vert-galant*, Henry of Navarre where the Gascon tongue prevailed. As I shall try to show, nothing is more typical of the extant dramatic compositions of French Canada than this 'political' aspect I here observe in passing.

THE DOUBLE PROGRAM OF 1640

But Lescarbot's pleading was in vain, for Port Royal was not destined to be the centre of a New France. His play remains an isolated exception, and it would be another thirty-four years before the next known performance in this country. It is reasonable to surmise that serious-minded colonists, after his day, made a point of acquainting themselves with his *Histoire de la Nouvelle-France* before crossing the Atlantic, as the Pilgrims apparently read the English translation of that work which appeared in the same year (1609) as the first French edition. But it is highly doubtful that his playful masque had any influence whatsoever on the evolution of theatre in North America until quite recently. There are many similarities with plays, especially *réceptions*, that come later; but this is due rather to a similarity of experience on their authors' part than to any attempt to use the *Théâtre de Neptune* as a model. Thus, when the City of Halifax chose 'Neptune' as the title of its permanent troupe's theatre in 1963, it recognized, not the birth of a continuing dramatic tradition, but the chronological primacy of Lescarbot's text on North American soil.

It was on 5 September 1640, that the next known dramatic performance took place, marking the second birthday of the child who would become Louis XIV, and whose ministers would, by help or hindrance, mould a lasting identity for the little colony. The program offered on this occasion was a heterogeneous one, comprising a *mistère*, enduring link with the High Middle Ages, and a tragi-comedy, a choice well representative of the trend in theatre in France at the time.[13] Yet the combination was resolutely 'Canadian,' the mystery play having been included at Governor Montmagny's insistence, and with the aim of hastening conversion of the native people also present on this occasion. The first, and by no means the last, instance where theatre was to be infused with a religious intention in French Canada!

We know of the performance of these two plays (or, if the mystery was somehow integrated *into* the other, of this mixed single offering) from the succinct reference to them in the *Jesuit Relations* which, along with the Jesuits' *Journal*, is the main source of information on such activity in the colony before the 1690s. The reporter on this occasion is Father Paul Le Jeune, Superior of the Jesuit Missions in New France from 1632 to 1639, and he mentions the first play only in passing, without condescending to inform us of the title of either. Even then, it is only by deduction that the first play is assumed to be a tragi-comedy, for the term Le Jeune uses is 'une action,' which, in the schools and religious communities, seems to be a generic word for any play which is not a *réception*; and most such plays were, in fact, in a fairly broad definition, tragi-comedies. Would it have been one of the type then prevalent in France, perfected by the great Corneille? So Le Jeune's apparent lack of interest in that part of the program might suggest: theatre, that is, for the social élite represented by Governor Montmagny and his staff. What does interest the Jesuit, and even more so the native audience, is the *mistère*. He describes its effect:

> We had the soul of an unbeliever pursued by two demons, who finally hurled it into a hell that vomited forth flames; the struggles, cries, and shrieks of this soul and of these demons, who spoke in the Algonquin tongue, penetrated so deeply into the hearts of some of them, that a Savage told us, two days afterward, that he had been greatly frightened that night by a horrible dream. 'I saw,' said he, 'a hideous gulf whence issued flames and demons. It seemed to me that they tried to destroy me, and this filled me with great terror.'[14]

From these few details, representing all that is known of the 'double bill' of 1640, one may observe that the combination of plays, one for the élite of this small society of some 400 Europeans, and one – or at least part of one – for the indigenous audience, was quite appropriate, and reminiscent of the *Théâtre de Neptune*. I deduce from its brief description that the *action* was performed, and probably prepared, by laity, since the governor's secretary, Martial Piraubé, is mentioned as having directed it and played the leading role. Similarly, from the use of 'we' in the quotation above, it seems certain that the Jesuits and/or their pupils prepared and performed the *mistère*. Montmagny's staff would not, in any case, yet have acquired the knowledge of an Amerindian tongue necessary for it. Which strengthens the speculation that the first play belonged to the category of *théâtre de société*, for the social élite.

The Jesuits, whose college in Quebec had been in operation for some five years, had long been in favour of using drama as an educational tool, as I have mentioned, and it was an integral part of the system in which Paul Le Jeune and his companions had been formed. As early as 1584 the manual for instructors in the Order had recommended the use of dramatic texts, often written by the Jesuits themselves, as a means of making studies more interesting for their pupils, as a way of instilling self-confidence and providing experience in public speaking for a student body that, by and large, was expected to provide intellectual, moral, and social leadership for its generation. The Ursuline nuns also, who had arrived in the colony just the preceding year, and to whom the education of young women was entrusted, made regular use of carefully chosen dramatic excerpts in their classes. As the anonymous chronicler of their history wrote, referring to the 1670s:

> In order to develop our pupils' memory, to furnish them with a useful store of edifying material, and in order also to teach them a certain grace of gesture and movement, it is customary in our classes to have them learn by heart some 'pastoral' or other religious play, for the occasion of certain annual feast-days, and above all at Christmastime. For this sort of exercise, each student takes on a role.[15]

Thus it is no surprise to see the Jesuits take a central part in the performance of the religious play of 1640. And indeed later, when drama was to undergo attack (as it frequently would) from the Church in Canada, that opposition rarely came from Jesuits or Ursulines.[16] It was no doubt fortunate for the early development of the stage that the former, until Laval was formally installed as Bishop of Quebec in 1674, were entrusted with general supervision of public morality in the country.

Father Le Jeune was certainly impressed with the quality of the performance on this occasion. 'I would not have believed,' he writes, 'that so handsome apparel and so good actors could be found in Kebec. Sieur Martial Piraubé, who had charge of this performance, and who represented the chief personage, succeeded excellently.' The governor, the clergy, and laity had all collaborated, in a spirit of communal interest reminiscent of the pageant at Port Royal in 1606. Perhaps theatre, with its high potential for interesting the Indian, for instructing the Frenchman, for edifying both, was about to take root in the soil of New France and produce a vigorous hybrid appropriate to that land? One might have thought so in the 1640s and 1650s, when various types of theatrical activity seem to have become surprisingly common there.

THE MID-SEVENTEENTH-CENTURY: CORNEILLE IN CANADA

Between 1640 and 1659 nearly half of all the known performances in the seventeenth century took place: four 'profane' tragi-comedies, three *réceptions*, one *action* serving dual function as a *réception*, and a mystery play.[17] For the 'profane' or social theatre, it was Pierre Corneille, then unchallenged at the summit of his craft in Paris, who was favoured also in Canada. It has frequently been remarked that his theatre was an obvious choice, with its emphasis on will-power, self-abnegation, and the 'virile' qualities of courage and fortitude, in a land where those very qualities were most in demand. One should not overlook also the fact of his being Norman, from Rouen, at a time when the religious government of New France emanated, legally, from that city.[18]

It is quite possible that his best-known work, *Le Cid*, was staged in Quebec as early as 1646, although this is likely to remain forever in debate. The confusion arises from the concision and the spelling found in the only source, the *Journal des Jésuites* for that year, written by Father Jérôme Lalemant. His report states in full:

> le dernier Iour de l'an on representa vne Action dans le magazin du sit, Nos Peres y assisterent p^r. la considerâon de Monsr. le gouu. qui y auoit de l'affection & les sauuages aussy scavoir les pp. de Quen, Lalement, & defretat: le tout se passa bien, & n'y eut rien qui put [mal?] edifier. ie prié Monsr. le gouu. de m'en exêpter.[19]

The centre of speculation is the phrase 'le magazin du sit.' As one may observe even in this short paragraph, Lalemant is quite inconsistent in his use of capitals (allocating one to 'Action,' refusing one to Father 'defretat,' ignoring even the convention of beginning a sentence with a capital), commas, and periods. And most historians of the theatre have concluded, as did the experienced translators of the *Journal* in the Thwaites edition, that the paragraph means:

On the last Day of the year, they gave a performance at the warehouse, Enacting the *sit*. Our Fathers were present, – in deference to
Monsieur the governor, who took pleasure therein, as also did the
savages, – that is, fathers de Quen, [Gabriel] Lalement, and defretat:
all went well, and there was nothing which could not edify. I begged
Monsieur the governor to excuse me from attendance.[20]

As to orthography, a word as exotic as 'Cid,' Spanish (from Moorish) in
origin, could easily be transcribed, especially by someone as uninterested
in literature as Lalemant was, as 'sit'; just as another Jesuit, writing in the
Journal in 1652, refers explicitly to a performance in Quebec of the
'tragédie du Scide de Corneille' (XXXVII, 94). An 'Action,' as we have
seen, generally means a tragi-comedy, and this would fit the description of
Corneille's play.

But more recently Beaudoin Burger, following the American critic Lewis
P. Waldo, argues with some conviction that 'sit' here means 'site, location'; that 'le magazin du sit' therefore means something like 'the local
warehouse'; and that the 'action' is thus not named in the *Journal*. More
convincing is another argument of his, based on the nature of Corneille's
play itself: would Catholic clergy attend, at this time, the performance of a
play with as dubious a moral message as *Le Cid*? Or if they did, would it
be reported (even by a priest who seems to make a point of the fact that
he declined to attend) that in the play 'there was nothing which would not
edify'? Professor Burger sums up his argument: 'It is difficult to believe
that the murder of Don Diègue by his future son-in-law is the token of
Christian virtue, especially since the Jesuits were quite fastidious on the
question of the morality of public spectacles.'[21]

And yet, to repeat, the same play was definitely staged in the same city
five and a half years later, on which occasion the fact was reported, without commentary, by Father Paul Ragueneau in the *Journal*. Surely there
had been little evolution in the Jesuits' attitude in the brief interval?
Moreover, where there is reference elsewhere to a warehouse or store-
house of the colony in the Jesuits' documents, it is never again called a
'magazin *du sit*.' One argument seems to counterbalance the other, and
this is why we shall probably never know with any certainty which play
was presented on 31 December 1646.

But this uncertainty should not be allowed to obscure the important
fact: on that day there was represented, under the auspices of the same
Governor Montmagny who had favoured the staging of the double program of 1640, a play, almost certainly a tragi-comedy, by and for the laity
of New France. Five years later, on 4 December 1651, the *Journal* reports, matter-of-factly, that 'There was a performance of the Tragedy of

Héraclius, by Corneille.' And four months after that, as we have seen, the succinct statement, 'On the 16th [of April 1652], there was a performance of Corneille's Tragedy, le Scide.'[22] From the phraseology of the bare report (there is no 'we' this time), as well as from the nature of these plays, it seems certain that they were again performed by laity, perhaps by officers and troops in the little capital, as was the case in 1693-4.

Héraclius, not listed among Corneille's major plays today, was none the less, from the point of view of popularity, one of the most successful of his entire career. Although it may not, therefore, be too surprising to see the miniscule colonial capital of New France emulate the metropolis in staging a play still in vogue there, it is impressive to see such an enactment take place so soon – a scant four years after its première and its publication in Paris. It is, furthermore, a demanding work to present, with its Middle Eastern setting and its cast of emperor, princes, princess, and nobles; with, also, its strong female character (Pulchérie), a role no doubt assumed by a man or a teenage boy.[23] *Le Cid* also requires a good deal of attention to staging, and is considered an ambitious undertaking by even an experienced theatrical company. Jean de Lauzon, during whose term (and no doubt at whose behest) the plays were put on, was obviously much interested in what was in fashion in Paris (his detractors might say that his interest was far too strong, in fact, for the good of the colony which was under his governorship), to which he was only too happy to return upon the completion of his Canadian service, in 1656. Other governors, until the time of Frontenac's second term, seem to have found more important interests to occupy them and their staff, and the two plays by Corneille are the last we know about before the winter of 1693-4. For theatre of this type, in the mother country as well, was decidedly for the very few, the *gratin* of society. In New France, if the governor was uninterested in the arts, if he was a provincial, or devout, no theatre appears to have been staged. This is no doubt the main reason why performances of social theatre in the seventeenth century tend to 'cluster,' to reach especial prominence under three governors: Montmagny, Lauzon, and Frontenac.

But one must be careful in making such an affirmation, since the major problem facing the historian of theatre in Canada under the French régime is that of documentation. Theatre was never considered an important aspect of the social and cultural life of the colony, at least by those upon whom we most depend for written information. The Jesuits, although espousing drama for pedagogic purposes, had serious misgivings about the appropriateness of performances accessible to the general public, and for its entertainment alone. And even though they never publicly opposed

theatre in Canada, they were certainly never *interested* in dramatic performances – at least, in those not offered under their own auspices. Theatre
was trivial: these resolute men had other, far graver tasks to fulfil. Thus
there was probably more – perhaps even a good deal more – theatrical
activity in New France than extant sources indicate. I shall return to this
question in my discussion of the plays staged in Quebec in the last decade
of the seventeenth century.

In the meantime, let us return to another type of drama, the *réceptions*
staged during that period. The first of these had taken place on 20 August
1648, to mark the accession of Louis d'Ailleboust to the governorship.
The *Relation* for that year reports:

> So soon as Monsieur the Chevalier de Montmagny became aware
> of the wishes of the King and Queen, and learned on the arrival of
> the ships [from France] that their Majesties had appointed Mon-
> sieur d'Ailleboust to the Government of the country throughout
> the whole extent of the River St Lawrence, he not only received
> the order with honor and respect, but he further manifested a gen-
> erous magnanimity by making, with much display, all necessary
> preparations for the reception of the new Governor. The latter was
> afterward received by all orders of the country, who paid him their
> compliments. Even the Savages wished to take part in it; and they
> delivered a short harangue to him through the mouth of a Reli-
> gious of our Society, who accompanied them.[24]

Although this is the full extent of our information on the event, one
can easily distinguish the identifying characteristics of the *réception*. Such
an occasion was, in essence, an opportunity for the various groups and interests in the colony to meet and to address their new civil leader, and the
whole ritual aspect merely clothes, in readymade rhetoric, that basic fact.
Despite the clear condescension of the reporter's tone (Jérôme Lalemant
again), it is perfectly natural that 'even' the native population, for whom
such ritualized 'dramatic' acts of formal submission, celebration, or solemn ceremony had been customary long before the arrival of the French,
understood the importance and the function of the occasion, and wanted
to be included in it.

A *réception* belongs to the general classification of dramatic art because
of its dialogue form and its role-playing. That is, one person usually em-
bodies or 'represents' a class, a group, a nation, and he strives to reflect,
through memorized speech and gesture, the interests of the larger estate
with which he identifies himself. This was the case with the *Théâtre de*

Neptune, as we have seen: despite its light-heartedness and certain eccentricities of form, Lescarbot's text conforms to the general description. For D'Ailleboust, it is safe to assume that all members of the various 'orders of the country who paid him their compliments' did not do so in person, but rather through a spokesman, just as the native people present were *represented* by the Jesuit who spoke for them on this day in 1648. The fact that no further information is provided is of no great consequence here: we have the complete text of an obviously similar *réception* for 1658, and we shall study it in greater detail.

But before that date there was one further such performance in Quebec, on 18 October 1651. Governor Jean de Lauzon was the dignitary fêted on this occasion: he had come to dine with the Jesuits in their refectory and, the *Journal* records, 'An hour after noon the pupils received Monsieur the Governor in our new chapel, – *latinâ oratione, et versibus Gallicis*, etc. [ie, with a speech in Latin, and verses composed in French]. The savages danced, etc.'[25] Again, no further information. But the basic structure of the exercise is clear and is traditional, apart from the formal address in Latin.

THE 'RÉCEPTION' OF GOVERNOR D'ARGENSON IN 1658

Let us examine that structure in the text composed for the next such occasion, the arrival of Pierre de Voyer, vicomte d'Argenson, as Governor of New France. His *réception* took place on 28 July 1658, seventeen days after his arrival in Quebec. On that day D'Argenson had come to the Jesuits' house to dine with them, as Lauzon had done. The *Journal*'s account: 'There he was received by the Youths of the country with a little drama in french, huron and Alguonquin, in our Garden, in the Sight of all the people of quebec. The sieur governor expressed himself as pleased with that reception.'[26]

We know the names of all the performers, whose ages range between ten and sixteen years, and the role each played, but we do not know the author's name. He was almost certainly one of the instructors at the Jesuits' college, and he would have had to rely upon his colleagues for collaboration, particularly when it came to the different native languages used in the text.[27] For this is a signal example of a communal ceremony, more so even than Lescarbot's play, since, after the expected addresses by the representatives of French interests in the colony, nearly three-quarters of the text is given over to pleas in four Amerindian tongues, and the French translation of those pleas.

The central figure, the 'master of ceremonies' for the occasion, is the 'Universal Spirit of New France,' and he is the first to speak. He presents each of the other actors in turn to the young governor, adding a curious touch of suspense at the end of his introduction:

> Those whom you see over yonder represent the élite of our little French Academy; the others over here represent the Algonquin and Huron nations who now, through the Christian Faith which they have embraced, form one single people with the French. The Spirit of these Forests will relay to you the words of the representatives of other nations who have as yet had no contact with Europeans. Finally, some unfortunate slaves will come forth to render you their homage, when they have managed to overcome to some extent the shame and fear which now keeps them in hiding, in the darkness of yonder wood.[28]

One visualizes the speaker, one Pierre Du Quet, impressively attired for the role, pointing solemnly to underline each French demonstrative (*ceux-cy*; *ceux-là*; *ces forêts*; *ce bois*), in a performance that was intended to inform the new governor, to impress him – and, one infers, to suggest skilfully the type of policies he should pursue in his dealings with the different Amerindian nations.

After the introduction, as announced, four 'Frenchmen' come forward in turn, to welcome and compliment the governor. Unlike the Universal Spirit of New France and the native spokesmen who will follow, they speak in verse. The time was a difficult and dangerous one for the inhabitants of the little colony of some 2000 souls. The Iroquois were fiercely hostile, and indeed held Quebec encircled. The very day after his arrival, D'Argenson had had to pursue an enemy force that moved in swiftly to carry off a woman working in the fields. The military-political 'hint' the third Frenchman delivers is thus not surprising:

> At last the Iroquois, swollen with pride
> Will no longer cast all his fears aside,
> Will no longer boast like a man deranged,
> Seeing this country now so changed,
> Seeing Your troops, colours held on high,
> Marching triumphant beneath the sky.

Then the Huron and Algonquin nations come forth to salute D'Argenson, bewailing their recent losses at the hands of the Iroquois, rejoicing in the new governor's advent and in the hope which the white man's religion will bring. Next, to underline the exotic setting, the Universal Spirit of New France presents the other tribes who address 'Onnontio' (a native word signifying 'Great Mountain,' applied originally to Montmagny, and frequently to his successors as governor) in turn, in their own language, with a second spokesman, the 'Spirit of the Forests,' translating as each 'native' finishes. This part of the program must have been intended to heighten the governor's opinion of the Jesuits' instructional skills since, to repeat, the native languages used were spoken by French-Canadian children in this instance.

Last come two of the freed captives mentioned at the end of the introduction, pleading also for the governor's prompt intervention. The second of these, from the nation of the Nez-Percé, whom the Iroquois have been harassing cruelly, has the clearest message of all: if Onnontio comes to their aid, there will be huge commercial profits for him (the natives had obviously had time to notice the self-enriching proclivities of almost all governors sent out from France): 'Each year the enormous wealth of our beaver pelts will come down the rivers to You; and in return Your zeal and Your charity towards us poor abandoned wretches will provide us with those people among you [ie, the Jesuits] who open unto us the treasures of eternal riches.'

The Universal Spirit of New France then brings an end to this ceremonial occasion with a final address to the governor, presenting him, on behalf of the released captives, symbolic weapons, fetters, and crowns, adding, 'In short, Monseigneur, they do homage to Your crown, offering you theirs, and resolving never to give allegiance to another but Your Grace, after God.'

It would be difficult to find anywhere a better example of the perfect symbiosis of theatre and society than this one. More even than the *Théâtre de Neptune* (which was, after all, intended primarily as a diversion), the bare text displays congruity of word, action and theme with a specific – and precarious – moment in time. Artistically, great theatre this is not. Nor is its action very dramatic. But it is *live, actual* theatre, the most representative piece to come out of New France, infused still with that sense of a moment when the very existence of European settlement in Canada was in doubt. Despite the clear signs of its ancestry in the *réceptions* staged in Jesuit schools in France, this dramatic form had taken on a local character all its own, perfectly appropriate to a country with no literary tradition, no printing presses during the entire period of French rule, and few books. Gone are the ornate allegories of Lescarbot's piece, the noble, love-struck savages, the fun and the feasting.

I must underline again the fundamentally political component of this play, a more salient trait than it had been in the *Théâtre of Neptune* and, as we shall see, a fundamental aspect also of the only other surviving text from New France, the *réception* composed and performed for Bishop Saint-Vallier in 1727.

AN 'ACTION' FOR BISHOP LAVAL: DRAMA IN THE SCHOOLS

The last of the plays I have identified for the period 1640-59 was enacted on 3 August of the latter year. Although there is room for some doubt, it appears to belong to the category of religious and pedagogic tragi-comedies usually associated with the term 'action,' frequently dealing with biblical themes. Father Jean de Quen, writing in the *Journal*, could hardly be more succinct in his reference to it: 'A representation was given in our chapel of quebec, in honor of Monseigneur the bishop of petraea. Everything went well.'[29]

Bishop Laval's ship had arrived on 16 June of that year, he had been received in formal celebration by the clergy the next day, and five days later 'gave a feast to the savages in our hall, and spoke to them very appropriately,' De Quen records. Thus he had already been 'received' by those orders of New France directly affected by his appointment: the play performed in the Jesuits' chapel on 3 August must not have been a *réception*, in its strict sense, for the new religious leader. This is confirmed by the language used in the *Journal*, which refers to the play as an *action*. I assume it to have been a dramatic composition of a traditional nature, similar no doubt to those so often performed in Jesuit schools with, in this case, a clear religious source or reference in order for its performance in the chapel to have been deemed appropriate. It would thus have been presented as part of the continuing welcoming ceremonies for the first bishop's arrival.

That the tradition of such *actions* was already established in the rudimentary school system of the colony seems confirmed by the next reference to drama less than two years later, again in the *Journal*, again involving Bishop Laval. It is obvious that the performance in question is not presented *in itself* as in any way anomalous. What is even more obvious is that the spirit of unanimity among civil, religious, and lay spokesmen which had characterized D'Argenson's reception in 1658 had already disappeared after the advent of the contentious Laval, ever preoccupied with the competition for power, in its fundamentals and its external symbols. On 21 February 1661, a formal, catechetical *action* took place:

Monsieur the Governor [D'Argenson] and Monseigneur the Bishop were present, and, as Monsieur the Governor had stated that he would not attend if Monseigneur the Bishop were saluted before him, we induced him to agree that the Children's hands should be kept occupied, so that neither the one nor the other would be saluted, both at the prologue and at the Epilogue. The Children were notified and commanded to do this; but the Children, who were Charles Couillar and Ignace de repentigny, instigated and persuaded by their parents, did just the contrary, and saluted Monsieur the Governor first. This greatly offended Monseigneur the Bishop. We tried to appease him; and the two children were whipped, on the following morning, for having disobeyed.[30]

Had it not been for the elbowing for prominence then going on between the two stubborn leaders of New France, would the Jesuits even have seen fit to mention this occasion? It seems hardly likely, and one feels justified in assuming that dramatized performances had become such a routine part of academic and religious life that their recurrence was not considered noteworthy enough to warrant mention.

Does the continuing friction between governors and bishop explain the apparent eclipse of all except religious and pedagogic theatre in the years between 1658 and 1693? Only three plays are known to have been performed in that interval, all of them clearly belonging to the classification of *actions*: two in 1668, one in 1691. Certainly it was the struggle between a governor (Frontenac) and a bishop (Saint-Vallier) over the projected performance of a 'profane' play that led to the formal prohibition against any form of dramatic activity within the colony, as we shall see.

A rare exception, we know both the title and text of the *action* presented in February 1668. The Jesuit François Le Mercier reports in the *Journal* that on the 7th and 9th of that month, 'The play of *Le Sage visionnaire* was performed with great success and to everyone's satisfaction. It was as well received the 2nd time as the first.'[31] This curious, baroque play enjoyed sufficient popularity in France to merit three editions in the 1640s and 1650s. An authority on French theatre for the period describes it as an 'allegorical and Christian tragi-comedy that resembles in many respects a morality play.' And the same critic continues:

Although the nature of the allegory is clear enough, a key is added to interpret most of the characters. The subject is the salvation of a youth, misled by sin, but saved, first by the thoughts of death, then by witnessing the drowning and condemnation of friends, impressions that bring the sinner to repentance. It was probably the popularity of the stage that induced the author to give his sermon dramatic form.[32]

The description is accurate, for a 'sermon in dramatic form' is indeed what we have in *Le Sage visionnaire*, with Truth, Sin, and Death personified; with a scene involving the Last Judgment, eerie recourse to a Death's Head, and abundant pithy (and not so pithy) moralisms. As one may deduce, the staging of the play must have been exceptionally demanding as well. Was it the Jesuits and their pupils who were responsible for it? It has always been assumed that they were, although there is nothing in the *Journal* to corroborate this assumption. What other group in New France would have had the resources and the interest necessary to undertake such an ambitious project? The governor, his administrative staff, and the officers of the military garrison of which he was commander-in-chief had the resources and the experience; but would the preparation of such an *action* have interested them? Moreover, Governor de Courcelle appears to have had no interest in theatre and his intendant, Jean Talon, had his hands too full defining his new position, in the face of conflicting demands of governor and bishop, to involve himself with the stage.

On 21 March another religious play was presented. The *Journal* reports, 'Master Pierson had a short latin play performed, on the passion of Our Lord; it was successful.'[33] The fact of its enactment in Latin should not surprise us, in this Lenten season of 1668, for Latin was basic to all serious study still, in New France as in France. One concludes, if such conclusion were necessary, that the performance was therefore for clergy and students, not for outsiders. But this is applicable to *théâtre de collège* in general, under the Jesuit system. Such exercises were prepared with the pupils', not the public's edification in mind.

The last *action* in the seventeenth century to which a specific date can be assigned took place on 1 April 1691 in the Ursulines' convent in Quebec. We have seen that such performances were a standard part of the nuns' pedagogical method, so much so that they elicit little further comment from the anonymous chronicler of the Order's history. But she does record for 1691 that: 'On Passion Sunday, which that year fell within the octave of the Annunciation, Monseigneur [Bishop Saint-Vallier] decided to attend the little *action* which our boarding-students presented in honour of the Mystery of the Passion. He declared himself very pleased with the performance.'[34] Jean-Baptiste de la Croix de Chevrières de Saint-Vallier, second Bishop of Quebec, may have been pleased with this particular performance, but it was his hostility to theatre in general, and most especially *théâtre de société*, which put an end to almost all manifestations of dramatic art in New France after the 1690s.

Before proceeding to the history of that conflict, let us look at the profile of theatrical activity in New France in the last decade of the seventeenth century. Was there really no theatre, apart from the little plays patronized by the Ursulines, between 1668 and 1691? Caution is again advised: it seems hardly coincidental that 1668 is the last year for which the Jesuits' *Journal* has survived, all succeeding reports having been lost or destroyed. And as the reader will have observed, this is the chief source of information for the period: of the eleven programs I have described as taking place between 1640 and 1668, all but two are known to us from the *Journal*, and only from it (the other two are from the *Relations*). But this is probably not the only factor. As the historian Margaret M. Cameron has aptly put it:

> All that we know of a period of several years is that the clergy of Quebec was becoming worried as the taste for worldly amusement became more and more marked in the colony. The first ball given in Canada, in 1667, was the occasion of a passage at arms between the representatives of the spiritual, and those of the temporal, powers; and we have reason to believe that the acting of plays was a second source of disagreement between the bishop on the one hand, and the governor and the intendant on the other, since the next time we hear of acting, in 1685, we find an allusion to disorders connected with amateur theatricals of which no record remains.[35]

As New France grew towards a surer sense of its own identity, the place it reserved for public entertainment seems to have become less and less generous. This was a country whose religious leaders vied with the lay leaders appointed by the crown for precedence, and who remained committed to a continental 'manifest destiny' for Christianity. They were frequently rigorous in the pursuit of that destiny. In particular, the area which would become the province of Quebec had been founded in a period of intense religious awareness. As it grew, strengthened by each challenge overcome, it could not avoid the effects of some of the central religious concerns of the century.

One of those central issues pitted Jesuit against Jansenist within the Roman Catholic Church, and managed to embroil almost all onlookers. The dynamics of their intermittent confrontation had many and diverse effects in France, and in Canada. One of those effects concerned the stage, which the Jansenist looked upon, in any of its forms, as a work of the Devil. Indeed, one of their most influential writers, Pierre Nicole of Port Royal had stated the case quite simply: 'A novelist or a playwright,' he affirms, 'is a poisoner of the public' (*empoisonneur public*). One has only to recall the many difficulties confronted by theatre in France, by authors (Molière, Racine) and actors (Molière, Poisson, Rosimond), to appreciate how that opposition, transposed to a far-off colony and distorted by the very distance travelled, could be stifling at times. Even those with no sympathies for Jansenism were forced to reconsider their own stance towards such things, in the face of the determined and eloquent attack led by some of the greatest writers of the century.

Another important factor in the developing antagonism against theatre on both continents was the increasingly pious tendencies of the royal court at Versailles, as the influence of the *dévote* Madame de Maintenon (whom Louis XIV had married secretly in 1683 or 1684) increased, with the consequence that zealous piety – in its *visible* manifestations, at least – became more and more in vogue. New France was always very much aware of what was in fashion in the mother country, and one would expect to see these two factors manifest themselves here.

LIVE DRAMA IN QUEBEC:
FRONTENAC, MOLIÈRE, AND SAINT-VALLIER

They were embodied, to different degrees, in the same individual: Bishop Saint-Vallier. He had been Confessor to the King at Versailles before receiving his appointment to Quebec, as Vicar-General to Bishop Laval, in 1685. Saint-Vallier was a tight-lipped, determined man of thirty-two on his arrival in the colony. Although rejecting the theological bases of Jansenism, he was a former pupil of the Jansenist Bernières, and managed, in the course of his career, to alienate a great many of the people with whom he came into contact. His own brother, captain of the King's Guards at Versailles, had had reason to complain of his sibling's *bigoterie*, and had at least once suggested to him that 'he would be better off shutting himself away in the Trappist monastery, so that nothing more should be heard of him.' More recently, an eminent historian has described him: 'The bishop was extremely stubborn, irascible, determined always to have his own way, and capable of believing anything of those who opposed him. His predecessor, Bishop Laval, soon came to regard him as a disaster likely to wreck the church in New France. Events were to prove this estimate to be not far removed from the truth.'[36]

He had been consecrated Bishop of Quebec in January 1688, and soon afterward found himself in conflict with nearly everybody in sight, including his own clergy. When Louis de Buade, comte de Frontenac, arrived in Canada the following year to begin his second term as governor, he was at first delighted to find such a convenient magnet to distract some of the attention of those who had been making life uncomfortable for him, and initially the two got along quite well. But inevitably the two would clash, and the occasion was, in a dual sense, theatre.

Frontenac, too, was a fiery man, impatient of opposition and easily carried to extremes in his reaction to it. His first term had been stormy (1672-82), highlighted by memorable quarrels with his intendant and with Bishop Laval; and he had a long memory. Numerous as those conflicts were, they seem to have had nothing to do with theatre. But considering his interest in that art, and in literature, one infers that he had probably had plays performed during that first term, if only for his private enjoyment.[37]

During the winter of 1693-4 the privileged among Quebec's small population had been entertained by the performance of plays at the governor's *château*. With his sponsorship, Corneille's *Nicomède* and Racine's *Mithridate* had been staged, with members of his staff and leading Quebec citizens as actors. There is no record of objection to these plays, both of which were currently enjoying something of a revival in Paris.[38] But trouble arose when word reached the bishop's ears that Frontenac's troupe was preparing a third and less acceptable play: Molière's *Tartuffe*.

By this time *Tartuffe* already had thirty years of controversy behind it, having been suppressed in its original version by the Archbishop of Paris in 1664; and, in slightly different garb (Molière had changed its resolution somewhat, and to ensure that there was no doubt about his attitude towards the lead character, had given it a new title, *L'Imposteur*) by the civil authority of the same city. Although the play had been tolerated, with some further revision, after 1669, it remained fraught with controversy. And in fact today, more than 300 years later, that controversial aspect remains, for it is still a matter of opinion as to what the author's real intent was. As the Canadian historian Séraphin Marion (a strong apologist for Saint-Vallier's actions in this circumstance) has remarked, whether Molière wished it or not, his *Tartuffe* has wound up being a powerful offensive weapon against the Church. Not only churchmen recognized the play's potential for social revolution: Napoleon, in exile on the island of St Helena, is quoted as having said that, if the play had been written in his day, he would not have allowed it to be performed![39]

Even before the ship carrying Jean Baptiste de Saint-Vallier had arrived in Quebec, he had had occasion to express his convictions on the subject of theatre in the colony. In his *Notice to the Governor and his Wife concerning their Obligation to set a good Example for the Common People*, apparently composed aboard ship for the edification of Governor Denonville, with whom he had made the passage from France in the summer of 1685, he had been forthright in his views on that topic, labelling theatre 'and other types of declamation' as dangerous for Christian principles as dances and balls.[40] The news of the projected enactment of *Tartuffe* was all the more alarming for the bishop, since rumour had it that there would be female actors taking part (as may also have been the case with *Nicomède* and *Mithridate*),[41] and – the crowning touch – that the production was to be directed, and the title role interpreted, by a protégé of Frontenac's, the very shady Lieutenant Mareuil, whose mottled background was already well known to everyone in the little town of 2000 inhabitants, only a year after his arrival in Canada. At this stage, it seems fair to say that any bishop, in France or in the colonies, would have had to react in the face of such rumours.

Whether they would have reacted as strongly and as stubbornly as he is a different question. Saint-Vallier fired the first round, issuing a *mandement*, or pastoral letter, against Mareuil, condemning him by name for offensive and blasphemous conduct, but not referring as yet to the play that was purportedly being rehearsed. Along with it, he had another episcopal directive disseminated, his 'Mandamus concerning *comédies*,' in which he decried the public performance of theatre in general, pointing out the long-standing opposition of the Fathers of the Church to such spectacles, even those 'which are decent in nature,' because even these 'can wind up being very dangerous because of the circumstances which surround them: the time and place, the individuals involved, the purpose of the performance itself; or because of the social activities which normally precede, accompany, and follow this sort of entertainment.'[42] And if these only apparently innocuous plays are to be condemned, what must he say of 'certain plays which subject piety and devotion to ridicule,' or which 'with the transparent pretext of amending public morality, only serve to debase it; and which, under the pretense of castigating vice, skilfully exploit it, rendering it subtly attractive to the audience; such a play as the *Comédie du Tartuffe*, or *The Impostor* may very well be, and others like it.'

The bishop was obviously ready for a fight, and he was pulling no punches. His *mandement* ends by affirming that no one can attend such performances without committing sin; wherefore 'We expressly forbid any member of Our diocese to attend, to whatever social class or condition he may belong.' This represents the first official denunciation by a churchman of theatre in New France. The issue, coincidentally or not, was also a heated one in France at that moment. It had been, on and off, for a generation or so; but there are many indications that the church's opposition to profane theatre was becoming more intense at this time, and resembling an organized campaign more and more. The court at Versailles, as mentioned, was displaying more 'official,' external piety, following the example of the aging king and his wife. Thus a well-known preacher, Father Soanen, had delivered, at the court itself, strong sermons specifically directed against theatre in 1686 and 1688. About this time as well, several eminent clergymen in France (the Bishop of Arras in 1689 and 1695; the Archbishop of Toulouse in 1702; the great Fléchier, Bishop of Nîmes, in 1708) issued directives condemning theatrical activity within their dioceses.[43] And in that very year which saw the sudden extension of the controversy to Quebec, Father Le Brun of the Oratory had published, in Paris, a resonant *Discourse against Theatre*.

But much more significantly, because of the stature – literary, religious, and political – of its author, this was the year of Bossuet's memorable confrontation with Father Caffaro on the subject of the morality of theatre in general. Bishop Bossuet, the 'Eagle of Meaux,' turned the full force of his oratory upon the unfortunate Caffaro because of a long (and, its author thought, private) letter the Theatine had written in defence of the works of the playwright Boursault, and of theatre in general. Bossuet's *Maximes* on the subject are a ringing condemnation of public theatre and the most eloquent of the various attacks directed against it in the seventeenth century.

Thus Saint-Vallier was very much in tune with many influential prelates in his homeland in his intense reaction against *Tartuffe* and the type of entertainment it represented. Similarly, Frontenac's tastes were very much those of the capital: Molière's play was undergoing a revival, and 1694 saw fourteen performances of it in Paris, making it the most popular of his plays that year, as in 1691 also.[44] The tiny colonial capital, in other words, was a perfect barometer of the pressure systems then operative in the metropolis: *Nicomède*, *Mithridate*, and *Tartuffe*, far from representing a 'retardation' of taste in Canada, reflected the current vogue in Paris; and the bishop's reaction could have been that of many a diocesan leader in France.

What is unfortunate for the development of theatre in New France is that, whereas in the mother country one episcopal see could follow a 'hard line' in its interpretation of the church's position, and another a more liberal one, thus maintaining some sort of overall equilibrium, no such possibility of balance existed in a colony with only one religious head. Saint-Vallier's word, or at least, his mandamus, was law – in matters under church jurisdiction, and sometimes beyond.

As it happened, blasphemy, the offence with which Mareuil, Frontenac's director and lead actor, was charged by the bishop, fell under the definition of a civil offence as well. So the bishop insisted that his case be brought before the Sovereign Council – of which, of course, Saint-Vallier himself was also a member. The Council was greatly embarrassed by the whole situation, and reluctant to take any action. But in anticipation of the outcome of this procedure, Mareuil had been excommunicated and imprisoned (15 March 1694). The bishop had now gone too far, and Frontenac had to do something or lose face. He objected strenuously to the whole manner of proceeding, and let it be known that he would not stand for this intrusion into the realm of civil authority, not to mention his own household (Mareuil had been living at the Château Saint-Louis, the governor's residence in New France). Charges and countercharges were hurled, and it looked as though the conflict could only escalate, with no solution in sight.

But the solution came swiftly, and with little credit to either side. Frontenac, out for a stroll with his intendant, Champigny, happened to meet the bishop, near the Jesuits' church in Quebec. After exchanging distant civilities, Saint-Vallier brought up the contentious issue of *Tartuffe*. These two direct men then came to direct terms: the bishop offered the governor 100 *pistoles* (probably equivalent to more than $5000, in 1984 terms) if he would forget about staging the play.

Frontenac accepted.

In fairness, as others have pointed out, this sum should not be considered so much a bribe, as compensation for the expenditures already incurred by the governor, if he had indeed undertaken to put on *Tartuffe*. Given contemporary tastes for costumes and props, a play was a very expensive proposition at this time, even for amateurs: Versailles had set a standard difficult to maintain, and the bishop, with experience of theatrical performances during his own years at the court of Louis XIV, must have been very aware of this. Frontenac, moreover, was in perennial financial difficulty with regard to his own affairs, as Saint-Vallier must certainly have known. That interpretation seems all the more probable in light of the bishop's subsequent actions, for he seems to have considered the 100 *pistoles* as some sort of reimbursable expense, even applying to appropriate governmental authority for their return.[45]

It was not quite the end of the *affaire Tartuffe*. Frontenac, concerned about the general denunciation of theatrical activity and, it seems, perplexed as to whether the plays already performed under his active auspices were included in the censure, asked the Sovereign Council to investigate whether there had, in fact, been any indecent or scandalous performances in Quebec to date. It is intriguing that, in bringing forward this request, he refers specifically to plays, 'tragedies and comedies which were performed during the *Carnaval* in previous years,' and even more generally, 'those which it has always been the custom to stage in this country.'[46] Let us not forget that Governor Frontenac, in 1694, had some fifteen years of experience in New France as its chief civil authority (considerably more time than Saint-Vallier had had), that he knew its social traditions as well as anybody, and that he was addressing a body which was in a position immediately to see through any misstatement of fact in this area. There seems, in other words, no reason whatever to question the basis of this assertion: theatre, even 'social' theatre, had a certain tradition behind it by 1694. I have already speculated elsewhere on the reasons why that activity is undocumented.[47]

When the ice broke up in the spring and navigation was again possible, the king's ministers eventually got wind of this whole complex case and were mortified by it. For this and other reasons (he was then squabbling with his seminary, with his own parish chapter, and with several other members of his clergy) Saint-Vallier was politely, but firmly, invited to come to France and explain his actions – and was detained there by a king reluctant to send him back, but with no intention of assigning him a diocese in France, where he might cause more immediate problems. The bishop remained in France until 1697. Mareuil, meanwhile, after a brief period of liberty procured by his own resources (he escaped from prison and managed, by his outrageous actions, to insult the bishop, infuriate the Council, and embarrass Frontenac), and another, longer one at the latter's orders, was hastily shipped off to the mother country in custody, and was never heard from thereafter.

As to the merits of the case, as Margaret M. Cameron succinctly observes, the King's Council 'ruled that the bishop was in the wrong but that the governor was not in the right,' and handed out reprimands to all concerned, including Champigny, the intendant, who was 'severely criticized for not having supported Frontenac with greater vigour in the latter's attempts to keep the bishop within bounds and so prevent his encroaching on the royal authority' (W.J. Eccles).[48]

In weighing the facts, 290 years later, a nagging doubt persists for the present writer: *did* Frontenac intend, even for a moment, to have this, the most provocative of Molière's works, staged in Quebec? All affirmative information comes, without exception, from people with a conflict of in-

terest in the case. The governor himself, in his correspondence with the
ministry in Paris, never indicates any such intention. He does not deny
accepting the proferred *pistoles*, admitting frankly to his relative, Pontchar-
train: 'As to the 100 *pistoles* which Monseigneur the Bishop gave me, the
whole thing is so laughable that I never thought it would ever be turned
to my disadvantage, but rather that those who heard of the affair would be
heartily amused by it.'[49] Why would the incident be matter for amusement
if he had in fact been dissuaded – nay, 'bought off,' from presenting a play
he really wanted to see staged? More perplexing still is the long, detailed
letter from another, admittedly controversial, protégé of Frontenac's.
Antoine Laumet (whom history – and General Motors – have preferred to
remember by the other name he seems to have concocted for himself, 'La
Mothe-Cadillac,' or simply 'Cadillac') wrote to the same minister on 28
September 1694. The writer's animus against Bishop Saint-Vallier is obvious, but he is curiously insistent also that Frontenac had had no intention
of staging Molière's play:

> In short, the worthy prelate was worried about the play *Tartuffe*,
> and had become convinced that the Count intended to have it per-
> formed, although that thought had never entered the latter's head.
> The Bishop strove long and hard against a stream of opposition
> which existed only in his own imagination. Once his vapours had
> settled, he realized that the whole thing was a joke, and that he had
> fallen for it because of rumours spread by some poorly informed
> person. None the less, either through determination to stick by his
> guns or in order to capture the public's attention, he arranged it so
> as to enter into conversation with the Count, in the presence of the
> Intendant, near the Jesuits' church; and there he took it upon him-
> self to offer the Count 100 *pistoles*, if he would not have *Tartuffe*
> enacted.
>
> The proposition didn't faze the Count at all: he perceived, as did
> many others as well, that the Bishop, having been too easily taken
> in by a rumour circulating in the town, and not knowing who was
> the author of that rumour, had examined his conscience and, re-
> cognizing his own mistake, now wanted to avoid the embarrass-
> ment resulting from it. That is why the Count laughingly promised
> him that, in exchange for the proposed sum, he would agree to the
> request and would intervene to prevent the fulfilment of that plan
> [to stage *Tartuffe*]. No sooner said than done: Monseigneur the
> Bishop signed a note for that sum, Monsieur the Count accepted it;
> all of which provided a good laugh for those present.[50]

Like Frontenac, Lamothe-Cadillac insists on the high comedy of the incident. But why is it funny *unless St-Vallier had in fact been duped or at least misinformed*; and unless Frontenac, at least when the money was offered, had no intention of having *Tartuffe* performed, what with spring on the way, fur-trade activity about to reach its peak, and little time for anyone in the colony to seek indoor amusement?

There is no doubt that the wildest rumours circulated, for a time, as to the governor's designs for the play. One of the first historians of French-Canadian theatre, Léopold Houlé, affirms solemnly that Frontenac had spread the word far and wide that he would have *Tartuffe* performed, not only at the Château Saint-Louis, but in the Quebec Seminary and in the religious communities. In making such an assertion he appears to have followed Bertrand de Latour, a century before, whose account of the affair is ludicrously distorted but who was responsible for some of those rumours, magnified by time and distance.[51]

Whatever the intent, the result remains the same: Saint-Vallier's mandamus against theatre, issued in January 1694 upon the heels of two forceful sermons against public theatre preached by chosen members of his clergy, remained in effect in Quebec for some 200 years.[52] That prohibition against public play-acting was reinforced by the bishop in 1699; at which time, as one weapon in a struggle he had undertaken against the Jesuits in New France for control of their schools, which he wished to hand over to his diocesan priests, he formally prohibited the former from any use of drama henceforth in their educational system.[53] This was the end of theatre, with the rare exceptions I shall now indicate, for the rest of the French régime in Canada.

THEATRE IN THE EIGHTEENTH CENTURY BEFORE THE CONQUEST

The first of these exceptions is the performance, at the official residence of Intendant Jacques Raudot, of something resembling a 'musical' or light opera, during the Lenten season of 1706, when memories of the *affaire Tartuffe* would still have been fresh in the minds of some residents of the colony. The work presented seems to have been entitled *The Four Seasons*, 'with a change of scene and costume for each act.'[54]

The Raudots (Jacques was officially intendant, 1705-10; he was assisted by his son, Antoine-Denis) had only arrived in Quebec in September the previous year, and may thus have been unaware of the severity of the local church's attitude towards such activity, since its head, the redoubtable Saint-Vallier, was at the time being held captive in England. If so, they were soon apprised of their error: Father Charles Glandelet (by no coincidence, the same priest had delivered one of the two major sermons

directed against theatre in January 1694, under orders from his bishop)
fulminated from his pulpit against this and like undertakings, thereby pro-
voking another confrontation – a minor one, this time – with Governor
Vaudreuil.[55] Glandelet, in his sermon, appears to have been particularly
disturbed at the social mingling of persons of both sexes at such performances, but he was suspicious also of the general disposition of these recent arrivals from the worldly metropolis, writing to Saint-Vallier that
'their attitude towards many of the clergy is not very deferential or courteous in the main; one would describe it, rather, as contemptuous.'[56]

There is no indication that the intendant or his son tried their hand at
theatre or opera again, in Canada. If they did, it was thereafter with a
good deal more circumspection than on this occasion.

Next is the year 1727, and a dramatic performance which poses intriguing questions. Strange to recount, the 'play,' of a type which the Ursulines
favoured and which they called 'pastorales,' was presented for, and at the
request of, that resolute opponent of all things thespian, Monseigneur de
Saint-Vallier! It was the young female boarding students at the Hôpital
Général, which he himself had helped to found in 1693, and in which,
shunning the relative magnificence of the Bishop's Palace in Quebec, he
had been living since 1713, who performed the work. It had been written
for the occasion by the former superior of the Jesuits in Canada, Father
Pierre de la Chasse. Saint-Vallier had proposed, with no great show of
modesty, that he be included in the work, depicted as the biblical Jacob,
'about to leave this world, asking his son Joseph to take care of his
remaining children.'[57]

The text of this little piece, which bears most of the characteristics of a
réception, was preserved at the Hôpital Général, and we can study it in
some detail. Seven girls from the boarding school participated in the performance, reciting, with appropriate gestures, versified sentiments of various length and form. Most of the performers returned to the stage three
times. Their recitations are, first of all, in the accepted tradition of the
réceptions we have seen, fulsome paeans to the many and obvious virtues
of the bishop. He is an 'august prelate'; he is the 'father of the poor,'
upon whom he has bestowed his kindnesses for the past forty years; he is
another Saint Paul; he is, as he had asked the author to portray him,

> Like Jacob of old, about to appear
> Before Him Who has granted all men their being.

But as with Lescarbot's masque, and especially with the réception for
D'Argenson of 1658, the basic political message of the performance soon
becomes clear. For if 'Jacob' is Saint-Vallier, then the 'Joseph' to whom

he would entrust his flock is the Marquis de Beauharnois, then Governor of New France, and Intendant Claude-Thomas Dupuy and his wife. They had been invited to the performance with that thought in mind: the bishop wanted their economic and political support for continuation of the hospital's humanitarian activities after his death. Thus young Angélique Guillimin, playing the role of the bishop, addresses her alexandrines directly to the political leaders of the colony. Again, just as Jacob had summoned Joseph,

> Illustrious Governor, and you, wise Intendant,
> I have invited you here to express that same intent:
> These my poor, most cherished of my flock,
> Found always in me the compassion of a true father...
> When I am gone, show yourself their guardians,
> Be the protectors, I pray you, of these orphans.
> Now, on the point of death, I recommend them to you:
> May your charity extend to them as well!

One assumes the topic had already been discussed with the two lay leaders, for their assent is assumed, as another girl follows Angélique with a response, 'To Monseigneur, in the name of the Governor and the Intendant,' in which she solemnly accepts the trust Saint-Vallier endows upon them. 'On both of them has been bestowed,' she says,

> By Nature, a heart too generous, too tender
>   To allow them to refuse
>   To respond to your wishes.

Then Mademoiselle Foucault, described as 'a very young child,' comes forward, touchingly, to beg the bishop not to desire death yet, for,

> If your life were to end so soon
> Alas! what would be the fate of us, your children!

There follows an invocation to the poor: they need not despair, for Saint-Vallier will bestow his continuing generosity upon them:

> Till now, he was able to provide you with peace, and with plenty;
> Beauharnois and Dupuy will follow his example
> And will heap their kindnesses upon you.

Mme Dupuy is then addressed: may she serve, in future, as the institution's mother. The nuns, too, are asked to rejoice at their past and future good fortune, assured by Saint-Vallier's devotion to them. And after all seven performers have sung another long hymn in praise of the bishop and his distinguished guests, little Charlotte Guillimin, in a manner charmingly reminiscent of the finale of Lescarbot's play, announces:

> Now the tables are set,
> The victuals already apportioned.
> Enough of speeches: now the poor are hungry,
> It is time, I think, that their feasting began,
> Time to leave off verse and music
> For it is more fitting now to provide them food.
> Let us serve them, reflecting on the extreme good fortune
> We enjoy, serving Our Saviour while serving them.[58]

There must have been something in the delivery of the text, for we are assured that 'there was not a dry eye among all those present.'

Even the most cursory analysis shows that this is no play, in the usual sense of the term, since there is no dramatic conflict, little interchange, no action, no real plot. What it most strongly resembles is a *réception*, of the type long practised in France and French Canada. The author, it is fair to say, demonstrates himself to be a far more skilful versifier than Lescarbot or the anonymous author(s) of the *réception* of 1658. But the verve and good humour of *Neptune* are absent, and the naïve vigour and immediacy of the second work sadly lacking here. The inclusion of music – for it is obvious that some at least of the passages recited were accompanied, and the ending from which I have quoted is explicitly choral – also separates this text from that of 1658 and brings it closer to the well-known 'school concerts' of our own day.

What about the problem of Saint-Vallier's interdiction against drama of any sort in New France? Here we must diverge from the majority of historians of theatre, who assume or affirm that the bishop's prohibition applied not only to public theatre and that of the Jesuits, but to the 'pastorales' of the nuns as well. There is not the slightest shred of evidence to corroborate this conclusion. We know why Saint-Vallier throttled public performances as a result of the *affaire Tartuffe*; and we know that, at least by 1699, he had prohibited all drama in the Jesuits' system. But that, it seems certain, was part of an all-out campaign he was then waging against the Jesuit order, recalcitrant to his wishes: it was a way of affirming his authority over all religious and pedagogic practices in the colony. The good bishop is known to have attended only two dramatic performances during his entire tenure in Quebec: this pastoral *réception* in 1727 and another, mentioned above, given by pupils of the Ursulines in 1691. I believe that in the interval the nuns had continued to produce their gentle pastorals, concerts, and *réceptions*, and that no special dispensation was necessary for the performance on 25 January 1727.

This is my last example of a complete text from New France, and its pedagogic-religious tone is the best guarantee of its acceptability in that society. For the rest of the period before the Battle of the Plains, there are references to only two more performances, both belonging to the category of 'social' theatre.

The first of these performances took place in Montreal in February 1749, and represents the first known staging of a play there. We know neither its title or its author. We do know that the person who mentions it (Mme Elisabeth Bégon, in her correspondence with her son-in-law), disapproves. She refers to the work as a 'comédie,' a general word for a dramatic performance in French. It was to be performed during the *carnaval*, as part of celebrations for the visit to Montreal of Intendant François Bigot, he who left a reputation for infamy with few parallels in the history of the colony. There were various public and private parties for the occasion, Mme Bégon reports, and dancing till dawn. 'I suspect,' she adds, 'that a good many among that lot will not be performing their Easter duty [ie, receiving Communion the requisite minimum of once a year, at Easter, in order to retain their standing as Catholics], especially those that are going to the play that's to be put on during the last three days of *carnaval*.'[59]

Brief as the reference is, it illustrates the sort of thought process a French-speaking Catholic might follow in New France when induced to associate 'theatre' and 'church.' Mme Bégon's implication seems to be that public carousing and mixed dancing – so strongly disapproved of by the Church in Canada – even all-night dancing, are not so scandalous as attending a *comédie*! But of course Montreal was then a long way from the diocesan seat in Quebec, especially in winter; and the bishops who succeeded Saint-Vallier were, in the main, much less rigorous than he in their interpretation of the Church's rules for public morality.

Before coming to the last reference to a performance in Canada during the French régime we must put to rest speculation concerning a sequence of fragmented dialogues found in the papers of a Canadian-born military officer, Louis Le Verrier. These dialogues, twenty-eight pages of them, presented a conundrum since their discovery by the historian R.-L. Séguin. Were they, as he assumed, original essays in dramatic fiction, jotted down 'out of dilettantism, to ward off boredom or kill time'?[60] Or were they, as Baudoin Burger deduces, notes and extracts from French plays Le Verrier was reading, about the time (1753) these pages are thought to have been written?[61]

The collection consists of a series of rambling debates on life, liberty, the existence of the soul, the status of women in life and philosophy, and the like. The debaters all have names of classical Greek origin: Théotime, Eusèbe, Sophrone, Philecous, Théophile, Eulalius, Timothée, Phèdre, Marcolphe. But of course so did many characters in classic seventeenth-century French drama. They converse in a manner directly reminiscent of philosophical methods going back as far in time as Plato, and favoured particularly by Thomists since the Middle Ages. But it is Professor Burger who is somewhat closer to the truth than Séguin: the final dialogue in the series (pp 27-8) is the key to the origin of the lot. This one bears a title (the others do not), 'On the Use of Fish' (De l'usage du poisson). The brief (400-word) text presents a butcher and a fishmonger debating the relative merits of the wares each offers, as they trade insults and predict ruin for each other's trade. The context seemed vaguely familiar to me, and it led eventually to one of the most widely-used manuals of the northern Renaissance, the *Colloquia familiaria* of Desiderius Erasmus of Rotterdam, the first collection of which was published in 1518. The colloquy in question is a later addition (1526), translated, in the best known of the English versions of these texts, as 'A Fish Diet.'[62] My discovery has since been confirmed, independently, in an excellent doctoral dissertation by David Gardner, in which, with the help of Professor John McClelland of the University of Toronto, he establishes beyond question that the other texts in the Le Verrier collection derive also from dialogues of Erasmus.[63] Far from being drafts of dramatic scenes, therefore, they appear to represent a valiant attempt at self-instruction by a forty-eight-year old (if 1753 is the right date) officer with time on his hands!

The last incident of dramatic activity we hear about before the Conquest is associated with the military as well, but this time the reference is genuine. It is reported by a major participant in the final military dénouement, the Marquis de Montcalm, in the *Journal* he kept during his campaigns in the New World from 1756 to 1759. This time the reference is to a genre with a future in French Canada and a glorious past in Europe: garrison theatre, a long-standing tradition for French and British troops immobilized by defensive posting in an area where more lively entertainment was not available.[64] General Montcalm records that under the auspices of Captain Pierre Pouchot, commander of the little fort at Niagara, the troops there rehearsed and presented plays for their own amusement. In the year

1759 they also composed at least one, which they entitled 'The Old Man Duped.' Baudoin Burger speculates that the work may have come from one of the many French vaudevilles of the time, and this seems an interesting possibility.[65] But from the meagre informatio supplied, one might also deduce that the play belonged to the long line of comedies and farces stretching back through the Middle Ages to antiquity, ridiculing the foibles of the elderly lover. For us, it would be useful to know whether a composition like this one constituted an isolated incident, or whether original garrison theatre was a normal cultural activity in New France at this time. Alas, the Marquis de Montcalm is one of the very few officers to leave any detailed account of his tour of duty, so all one can do is speculate.

One can only speculate, also, about the frequency of 'social' theatrical activity in Canada of the type we have seen associated with the Raudots in 1706, and with François Bigot's sojourn in Montreal in 1749. But, one must ask, in such an inauspicious era, would not the very guarantee of *privacy* be the best insurance against disruption by the Church, since the Church would not then hear of it? Unfortunately, of course, neither might we.

But we can be certain that theatre was not an important element in the fabric of this society, especially in the eighteenth century. The character of the nation was becoming more fixed, within the limits defined by the fiercely competitive commercial interests on the one hand, and a powerful, conservative, established Church on the other. As we have seen, since 1694 the latter had been the major force preventing normal evolution of theatre in Canada. But what of the absence of other literary genres, of poetry, prose fiction, the essay? What of the absence of journalism – indeed, even of printing presses? It is difficult to see the Church as responsible for the lack even of the mechanical means of disseminating the printed word. An astute foreign observer, the Swedish scientist Peter Kalm, tried to explain this cultural lacuna during a visit he made to New France in 1749-50:

> There is no printing press in Canada, nor has there formerly been any: but all books are brought from France and all the orders made in the country are written, which (as I have shown) extends even to the paper currency. They pretend that the press is not yet introduced here because it might be the means of propagating libels against the government and religion. But the true reason seems to lie in the poverty of the country, as no printer could make a sufficient number of books for his subsistence; and another reason may

be that France now has the profit arising from the exportation of books hither.[66]

Yet printing presses had been in operation in Mexico as early as 1536, and in the American colonies since 1639. It thus may be difficult to accept the poverty of New France as a major argument to explain their absence there. More convincing, given the general outlook of royal France towards its colonies, is Kalm's latter explanation: France brooked no competition in areas where its domestic economy was already committed.

Also convincing is the argument so ably advanced by the most professional historian of Canadian theatrical activity to date, Baudoin Burger, that the lack of a literary or dramatic tradition stems from a lack of commitment to the Canadian nation on the part of the nobles, administrators, and clergy who represented the only social and intellectual élite of the country. With the general exception of the latter, these were, almost by definition, transients who considered their stay in this country a necessary, uncomfortable interlude while they obtained the fortune or fame which would allow them to return to France and enjoy there the benefits of their energy. A transient class puts down few roots, particularly literary roots. That portion of the population which did consider itself permanent was unprepared (illiteracy was the rule for the *habitant*, and for most of the workers engaged in the fur trade), opposed (the clergy), and had in any case little leisure for literary or theatrical diversion.[67]

New Beginnings and New Trials
1760-1825

The hostility of the religious establishment of New France towards public theatre, and the effect of that hostility upon the attitude, conscious or unconscious, of French Canadians remained an important factor for most of the next century and a half.[1] But with the arrival of British garrisons, British and American entrepreneurs, and camp followers came a more relaxed attitude towards public drama, since the dictates of the Roman Catholic Church on that topic were more and more regularly breached by performances sponsored by Anglo-Saxons, and more and more regularly emulated by francophones. For most of the period in question there is a decided parallel in the history of English- and French-language stage in Quebec. But by 1825 the English stage in Canada would take a different, more professional, more secure path, while its French counterpart would remain resolutely amateur, cyclical, and ailing. We shall pursue that parallel to the extent that the fortunes of both stages, in their evolution, help to throw light upon the innate problems of theatre in French Canada.

NEWSPAPERS COME TO CANADA:
MOLIÈRE AND THE REBIRTH OF COLLEGE DRAMA

A new permissiveness is almost immediately apparent in the new political entity resulting from European conflict on the St Lawrence. Curiously, its manifestation, initially, is French. Only two years after the Treaty of Paris had made official the cession of France's interests on the North American continent to the British, we learn, via the newly established *Quebec Gazette/Gazette de Québec*, that an enterprising innkeeper by the name of Jean Roi (or more probably, 'John King') had engaged the services of one Pierre Chartier and his troupe, who would stage Molière's *Festin de pierre* for the public, almost certainly in the adaptation by Thomas Corneille. There was to be something in the program for everybody: refreshments would be served, and an acrobatic performance (*plusieurs tours d'équilibre*) would follow the play.[2]

There is enough irony in the situation to make us pause a moment: Molière, innocent cause of the disruption of drama in Canada for the preceding seventy years, returning in triumph as the first author whose plays were performed in Quebec City (as he would be the first in Montreal) after the Conquest! Not only that, the work chosen is at least as controversial as *Tartuffe*. Better known today as *Dom Juan*, the fascinating story of that cynical, philandering atheist based on Tirso de Molina's *Burlador de Sevilla* (1630) had had a stormy history in Molière's day, had been taken off the boards in France in his version (1665), not to return for regular performance in that country for 175 years thereafter. It was still in limbo in France, in other words, when it was being revived in Quebec, and where it would in fact be performed at least twice more that we know of, by 1804.[3]

The very fact that Chartier's troupe existed in Canada in 1765, and was capable of staging a demanding play in French, suggests at least some underground tradition of dramatic activity towards the end of the French régime. It is hardly likely that the players came from France. Speculation as to such covert activity is strengthened by the report of an impending performance by another francophone troupe in 1765. The play is entitled *The Village Festival*, written by one 'sieur Lanoux, famous Canadian poet' (his fame must have been very much localized, for this is the only reference to him anywhere), and, more curious still, it is to be presented under the auspices of a female group, 'Canadian village-women, new subjects of His Britannic Majesty, from a certain district of the Province of Quebec.'[4] Were it not for the staid *Gazette*'s general lack of whimsy, one would be tempted to see in the announcement some sort of hoax. Two plays, publicly announced and performed, in a single year, in Saint-Vallier's diocese!

Without the *Gazette*'s brief notices on these two programs, we would obviously not have known of their existence. Indeed, for the entire period, 1760-1825, newspapers and periodicals are the single most important source of information on theatrical activity in Quebec, assuming somewhat the role the Jesuits' *Journal* had for the seventeenth century. From a single one in 1764, these publications grew rapidly in number (many, it is true, lasting only a year or two), so that by 1825 no fewer than twenty-eight had sprouted to enduring or ephemeral existence.[5] The majority, eighteen of the twenty-eight mentioned, were directed towards the numerical minority in the province. French speakers would have to wait until 1806 for a newspaper founded and controlled by Canadiens, directed towards them, and called, appropriately enough, *Le Canadien*. But others, like the *Quebec Gazette*, carried articles and announcements in French, and there is plenty of evidence that the educated French Canadian did read and enjoy the new medium, even if its editorial stance frequently conflicted with his own perceived interests. Journalism had come to stay.

The history of theatre in these four decades is primarily the history of what those newspapers chose – or allowed – to have published. Much of this is merely factual information: 'such and such a play will be performed at such a time'; or 'has been, and here is a synopsis of plot, staging, and performance,' etc. But whereas we now have the newspaper, we no longer have the letters exchanged with the ministry in France, the correspondence between clergy in both countries, the diaries kept by French officers, or any of the other sources relied upon for the period before 1760. Just how defective a single main source is, is highlighted in the period 1765-89: were we dependent solely upon the 'English' (in language, ownership, and politics) newspapers, we would deduce that there was little or no theatrical activity in Quebec City during those years. Yet this is not the case, as is gleaned from other sources: the Archives of the Seminary of Quebec, the *Journal* of the same institution, the history of *Les Ursulines de Québec*. The newspaper, in other words, is the principal source of information after 1764; but it is incomplete, and sometimes unreliable.

There was, in fact, something approaching a rebirth of dramatic art in the institutions of secondary education in the province in that period: in the Seminary (which had replaced the Collège des Jésuites after the Conquest, when the Jesuit order had been officially suppressed); in the Ursulines' convent; in the new Collège Saint-Raphaël in Montreal. But the only reference in a newspaper is to one of the best-known manifestations of the rekindled interest, the program presented at the Seminary on 9 August 1775, in the presence of Sir Guy Carleton, less than a year after the beginning of his second term as governor.[6]

Although the setting sounds similar to that of the *réceptions* examined for the French period in Canada, the two plays presented on this occasion have nothing in common with that earlier genre, and were both imported from France. *Le Monde démasqué*, presented by the older students, written by Father Guillaume-Hyacinthe Bougeant, had been presented in Jesuit colleges in France in the 1730s and 1740s.[7] A moralizing comedy about the snares that await young graduands in the outside world, its message is not dissimilar to that of the tragi-comedy *Le Sage visionnaire*, staged, as we have seen, in New France in 1668.[8] The second play on the program was *Le Concert ridicule*, another comedy, written by David-Augustin de Brueys in collaboration with Jean Palaprat, first performed in France in 1689, seven years after Brueys had converted from Protestantism and four years after he had entered the Catholic priesthood. As one might deduce, this one-act prose farce has a well-developed moral message, as does *Le Monde démasqué*, and was in fact standard fare for college theatre in France.[9]

Although the performance was probably well attended, judging from the 800 copies of the program that were ordered from the printer,[10] this is of course not *public* theatre in the sense that the plays offered by Jean Roi, Chartier, and Lanoux were. Private also were the next two documents we shall consider, two manuscript plays from the Seminary, both dating from about 1780.

The first of these is complete, and is entitled 'Neglected Education' (L'Education négligée). We know that the text was completed by 1780 from a brief and quite unfavourable analysis of it written by the Director of Teaching (and later Superior) of the Seminary, Father Henri-François Gravé de la Rive.[11] Since these manuscripts are little known, and apparently no part of them has ever been reproduced in print, I shall here deal with them at more length than their intrinsic artistic merit might otherwise warrant, for where theatre is concerned they represent the ideals and the criteria then prevalent in French Canada.

Befitting its genesis and public, the first play focuses on a rustic nobleman, Count de Rudanière, and his two sons whose upbringing (*éducation*, in the broader French sense) has so far consisted in allowing them to do exactly as they wish. The elder son, the Marquis de la Nigaudière, is now nearly twenty, and his father has brought him from their home in Poitiers to Paris to decide what career he should now follow. The entire play, in best classical tradition, takes place at the home of one of the Count's two brothers, the magistrate Philémon, and turns around the decision to be taken concerning Nigaudière's future. A loosely connected sub-plot concerns the fate of the latter's younger brother, Dandinet, whose character and whose desires are designed as a counterfoil to those of Nigaudière.

His uncles soon discern that the Marquis is a hopeless case, and refuse their assistance. His father, after a vain attempt to teach him swordsmanship and dancing, decides to take him back to Poitou, to the life of mindless rustic indolence for which his neglected upbringing qualifies him. The younger brother, however, will remain to study in Paris.

The two most striking things about this play are its reliance upon Molière and its inexpert construction. The author must have kept a copy of *Le Bourgeois gentilhomme* at his fingertips, for there are echoes and obvious borrowings, structural and lexicological, throughout. He obviously knew Molière's *Les Précieuses ridicules* as well, and there are resonances of Regnard and of Jesuit college theatre.[12] Nothing is subtle, in word or deed, and the verbal and physical interplay is that of a farce. The construction is rightly criticized by Gravé de la Rive, for it is repetitive and centrifugal.

Despite all of which, there are a few scenes that would probably succeed on stage, especially in the first act, the first scene of which presents two cynical city valets, Mascarille and l'Espadille, in conversation with young Nigaudière's rustic man-servant, Roquille. Roquille is the traditional theatrical peasant, his speech recalling that of Molière's servants, particularly in his use of verbal forms such as 'je sommes' and 'je sçavons.'[13] His pungent expressions, his exclamations ('nenni-dà'; 'pargué'; 'margué') and his malapropisms ('les philosomies sont trompeuses,' he tells l'Espadille, meaning 'physiognomies' 'appearances are deceiving') are a sure and frequent source of easy comedy throughout the play. And the scene is effective introduction, for we acquire all the basic data on the main characters and their concerns. We are ready for Nigaudière's entry in Scene 2, and the caricatural exposition of his abysmal ignorance. In fact, the overall structure of this first act is reasonably sound: after the broad humour of Nigaudière's introduction two scenes are juxtaposed, the first involving his brother Dandinet and their tutor, Le Doux. Thus we quickly learn that the younger brother is quite different from the older, discerning enough to realize the deficiencies of their upbringing. 'I tell you, Monsieur Le Doux,' he says, 'you'll never get me to believe that dear papa did all he could to have me brought up properly. I'm not so dull as to have missed the fact that my dear uncles look upon me with pity ...'[14]

What Dandinet most desires is to stay on in Paris with his uncle Philémon and pursue a proper education. Le Doux agrees, as does Philémon: only the consent of the boy's father remains to be obtained. Neatly, then, the Count himself arrives for the next scene, along with the incomparable Nigaudière, and we are back to broad comedy again. As one would expect, Rudanière is a worthy parent to such a son, showing himself in his first few speeches to be vain, shallow, and a glutton. In the boy's absence, the adults get down to serious discussion of Nigaudière's future, and the two scenes in which this discussion takes place are lively ones indeed, revealing a nascent talent for dramatic finesse. For if the Count de Rudanière is an insensitive boor, his brothers are not, and do not wish to offend him by speaking out too candidly. Thus Philémon, in a sequence reminiscent of Molière's *Misanthrope*, first ascertains that his brother really wants to hear the truth about his son. Naturally, Rudanière insists on total frankness:

> I like people to speak their minds, to tell me what they think, openly and to my face.
> PHILÉMON
> You're quite right...
> LE COMTE
> And there's nothing I hate so much as false friends, the kind who never tell you what they're thinking!
> PHILÉMON
> On that point I agree with you entirely.
> LE COMTE
> The Law should put an end to that sort of thing!
> PHILÉMON
> That's the truth...
> LE COMTE
> I'd like to see half a dozen of them hanged, just as an example to others![15]

So Philémon hazards the suggestion that his nephew should take up, not the law as the Count proposes, but arms, as his profession. At which point their brother Colonel Straton makes his appearance and is asked *his* opinion – in total frankness of course! And the poor colonel hesitates but must finally confess he thinks the military calling is quite unsuitable for his brother's heir. What would he suggest? Why – the law!

Thus the two brothers, each fearing he will be left with the young lout on his hands, must explain in less and less equivocal terms why Nigaudière is not suited either for the law or the army. The Count, predictably is incensed. All one needs to know, to be an officer, is a bit of flashy swordsmanship and how to dance, so he announces he will summon instructors for that purpose, and his son will soon be as well equipped as any colonel.

Thus ends the first, long act: twenty of forty-five foolscap pages. It is, on the whole, successful: amusing and, as I have said, reasonably well constructed. It is a pity that the unknown author felt he should add two more, for Acts II and III are decidedly inferior. Act II does not advance the action at all. It begins with Straton and Philémon conspiring to have the young Nigaudière sent back to Poitiers. Straton, they decide, will talk to him and dissuade him from entering his profession by scaring him out of his wits. The scene that ensues is funny, but superfluous since the theme had already been exploited by Nigaudière's servant, Roquille, in the first act. The valet Mascarille returns to flatter the young ninny and persuade him that the court would be the best place for a man of his parts: he would be the king's favourite in no time. Whereupon the Count arrives, and, absurdly, father and son exchange two of the best-known lines from Corneille's *Le Cid*, that play which exalts physical and moral courage. This is all the more curious because we soon discover that the Count himself is under no illusion as to his son's fitness for bearing arms. 'I know what a coward you are,' he says. 'I know the only time you've ever drawn your sword was to frighten serving-maids; and I remember one day, when a young gentleman from our neighbourhood slapped your face, you went off to weep in the stable ... But here at last is your chance to show yourself worthy of a father like me!'[16]

This static act closes with the reappearance of Le Doux and Dandinet, pleading for the one favour we know they most desire. The author now ostensibly – and awkwardly – marshals his reader's sympathies against count and marquis (if any sympathy there had been) by having Rudanière first refuse outright, and Nigaudière display his mean side, taking obvious pleasure in counselling his father against Dandinet's wishes. But the Count decides to reconsider when Le Doux hints that Philémon is prepared to meet the expenses he and Dandinet might incur by staying on.

Act III begins (as one wishes II had) with the arrival of two instructors, Poussefort, the fencing master, and De La Gavotte, the dance instructor. The whole sequence is much too derivative, the parallels and the borrowings from *Le Bourgeois gentilhomme* abounding in every reply. These two instructors soon realize the impossibility of teaching the young oaf anything: Poussefort winds up whipping him with his sword blade and La Gavotte soon despairs, trips up the would-be courtier and takes to his heels. On hasty reflection, Nigaudière decides that courtly life is not the thing for him either. When all assemble for the final scene, the Count announces his decision: his elder son will return with him to Rudanière, and there they will remain. Dandinet and Le Doux beg again to be allowed to stay and the Count, entreated by his brothers, finally agrees. Thus all ends happily, and Philémon, addressing Dandinet, can end the play with its intended moral:

The best way of repaying me, dear nephew, is by working diligently for yourself. You see a good example of unfortunate consequences of neglected upbringing in your brother: he is unfit to enter the profession of law or that of the military without risking dishonour for his family. And there he is, reduced to spending the rest of his life in shameful obscurity. It was fortunate that Divine Providence brought you here, and thus inspired in me the resolution to prevent such dreadful consequences for you...[17]

Henri-François Gravé de la Rive, Director of Teaching at the Séminaire de Québec, had apparently been asked his opinion as to the suitability of the play. His response was unequivocal: 'I read this play, *L'Education négligée*, in 1780. It seems to me a rather pitiful effort: no plot, no dénouement, no dramatic interest.'[18] He found the character portrayal inept: 'A young man as intrinsically dull as Nigaudière is not capable of a proper education, and those involved should be congratulated for not having wasted time and money for such a purpose.' He found the style offensive, 'remarkable only for the base and popular locutions with which it is replete.' He continues: 'Tasteless and stale, such expressions are fit to draw laughter only from peasants. Moreover, I find these expressions much more characteristic of Canadian speech than that of Poitou.'

Here Gravé de la Rive's criticism becomes more interesting to the modern reader. It is true that a seminarian, and perhaps any reader sensitized by seventeenth-century neoclassical conventions, might object to some of the expressions used in the play: Nigaudière's 'je ne me mouche pas du pied'; Rudanière's 'le derrière à terre,' 'par la sanbleu,' and the like. Molière, of course, had used these, and much stronger ones; that would hardly be a point in their favour, for someone like Gravé de la Rive. Indeed, it seems improbable that the Director of Teaching had even a passing acquaintance with Molière's work, since the most striking part of his critique is what one does *not* find in it: any allusion to the very obvious plagiarisms from the plays I have mentioned. Most interesting of all, and a clue as to the probable nationality of the author, is the French-born priest's reference to the many 'Canadianisms' in the play. If he is right (to the present-day reader there is little that seems identifiably québécois: the 'je sommes' form is Acadian, and characteristic also of rural central France; the variants 'gagnît,' 'moquissiés,' for 'gagnât,' 'moquassiez,' are not confined to Quebec, or even the 'étou' and 'mitan' which Roquille uses), then the author was most probably a Canadian member of the Seminary. Surely the very structural defects bespeak, in addition, a student's effort. In which case it is a pity that the Director of Teaching did not paternally pass along his advice for improvement, instead of scuttling the whole play. His letter ends: 'I don't know who the author of this comedy is; and Monsieur Boivet, who copied the whole thing out, took more pains than the play deserves, etc. [sic].'

Before seeking a broader perspective on L'Education négligée and this criticism of it, let us pass on to the other surviving college play. It is incomplete, representing about half the length of the one just discussed, with a first act more or less finished and part of a long second with missing scenes and no ending. This is plenty, however, for the reader to discern the intended structure of the play and to reach an opinion about the author's aptitude. It seems certain the plot was not intended to go beyond this second act, given the stage the action had already reached by then.

Like L'Education négligée with its eleven male characters, and as with college theatre in general, we find a dozen personages in this text, all of them male. This would allow as many students as possible to participate actively, and no problems would arise from the representation of a female on stage for a private audience. The text is even more clearly influenced by the classical stage in inspiration and in form, as it is written in the rhymed alexandrine couplets so typical of French classicism. The action is simple: the main character, Pavane, who fancies himself a gifted writer and bel esprit, has recently arrived in Paris from the countryside, seeking recognition for the poetic genius with which, in his firm opinion, he is infused. He will not stoop to conquer Paris: when, in the first scene, Ariste (one of four other, rival poets seeking fame in the play) points out that 'in Paris everyone is motivated by self-interest,' and that he had better seek the friendship and support of his fellow artists first of all, Pavane responds, much in the vein of Alceste in Molière's Misanthrope:

> That would be the day, when I'd pay court to them!
> They wish to criticize me? Fine: I'll criticize right back!
> I'll retaliate, verse for verse and rime for rime,
> That's how I expect to acquire their esteem.[19]

Thus one can predict what misfortunes await him. By the end of the first scene we have a full depiction of Pavane's character: vain, insulting – and mediocre, as we learn from the poem of his own composition which, in another borrowing from Molière, he recites. By the end of the first act we also have a good idea of the outcome of the play, for Pavane's rivals have decided to conspire against him by feeding his self-delusions.

The first scene of Act II is missing and we begin with the second, in the middle of a stratagem involving De la Hablerie,[20] one of the rival poets who has purportedly just returned from the exotic land of Monomotapa, whose king wants Pavane to go there and found an Academy of Learning. Our poet swallows the bait and begins preparing for the king's ambassador and for his own journey to this wonderful land ruled by so perspicacious a monarch. All of which is greatly disturbing to Pavane's servant Frontin who, by long theatrical tradition, is much less of a fool than his master.

The 'ambassador' who then arrives is of course a fake, hired by the four poets. The scenes which have him mumble cacophonous nonsense, faithfully translated by De la Hablerie, are typical of schoolboy humour of every age:

FIERABRAS (*the 'Ambassador'*)
Carmagnol, clinquand verd
DE LA HABLERIE
He's asking you for a chair,
And offers you, as a present, a cork almanach.
This book is greatly prized in his country,
And is reprinted every year, at the King's orders.
PAVANE
I accept this present, with much gratitude.
FIERABRAS
Croc, broc, mouq, brouq, crac, brac
DE LA HABLERIE
He says that Knowledge is the highest good,
And that two verses from you are better than, in spring,
A hundred bushels of green peas.
PAVANE
He's too kind![21]

Soon the four poets arrive and plead with Pavane to be included in his New Academy. He consents, magnanimously, and here the text ends.

Apart from two minor personages, Frontin the valet and Georget (Pavane's elder brother, whose earthy common sense serves as a forceful contrast to his brother's vapidity, a tradition well established in Molière's work), there is no depth of character discernible. The verse is hackneyed and heavy, frequently deficient in rhyme and metre. Borrowings, although not as direct as in the previous play, are obvious and the whole setting is unoriginal. There is even less doubt than in the case of *L'Education négligée* that this is the product of a *collégien*'s pen, a conviction which is reinforced by the format of the manuscript itself.[22]

From these two manuscripts one may draw certain conclusions about attitudes towards theatre in French Canada about 1780. Here we have two (or more) authors who are very probably Canadian in origin and students at the Seminary, who are motivated to compose plays which are certainly not masterpieces, but which exhibit a working acquaintanceship with the rules and structural traditions of theatre. That knowledge must have come in part from the expurgated and carefully supervised theatre which had returned to the institutions of secondary education in Canada at least as early as the 1770s, as we have seen,[23] for Bishop Saint-Vallier's prohibition of such performances seems suddenly to have lapsed under the new régime. But would a program such as the one performed before Governor Carleton in 1775, comprising *Le Monde démasqué* and *Le Concert ridicule*, explain the pervasive influence of that irreverent genius, Molière, in these two manuscripts from the period?

It would be easy to overstate the point, since the ubiquitous influence of France's greatest comic playwright need not depend upon direct contact with his works.[24] Every dramatist working in the field of comedy in French since Molière has used, wittingly or not, some of his themes, structures, strategies, and ploys. Yet that influence seems particularly strong and direct, especially in the case of *L'Education négligée*, and one feels there was an external source of such inspiration, outside the careful supervision of Gravé de la Rive and his colleagues, in the public, 'social' theatre then being performed in both Quebec and Montreal, and which relied very heavily on the works of Molière.

'MOLIÈRE'S REVENGE': THEATRE COMES TO MONTREAL

I have mentioned the performance of Molière's *Festin de pierre* (or at least the adaptation of it by Thomas Corneille) in Quebec in April 1765. The first known performances of public theatre in Montreal after 1759 took place in 1774, when *Le Bourgeois gentilhomme* and *Le Médecin malgré lui* (The Mock Doctor) were staged there.[25] The fact which has long – and deservedly – impressed historians is that these two plays were performed in French, by the British troops in that city, and in the very building which had lodged the Jesuits. This modest dramatic activity must have evoked a responsive chord, for such performances soon become fairly regular, at least for a time. Since Montreal had no established newspaper before 1785, there are great gaps in our information, but it appears that, until 1786, the only theatre performed by or for the British garrison there was in French. This, however, is not as strange as it may sound, for such entertainment was generally arranged by officers, most of whom had a reasonably broad education; and at the time, French was very much a part of the education of the British gentlemen upon whom the officer class depended for recruitment. There we have 'Molière's revenge' for Saint-Vallier's suppression of *Tartuffe* in 1694, with its dire effects on the evolution of the stage: over a third of all the plays performed in Canada between 1765 and 1825 came from his pen.[26]

The newspapers did not report upon the performance of the Molière comedies I have just mentioned, since there was as yet no press in Montreal. They might not have done so in any case, for these plays represent a sort of borderline between public and private entertainment. But how could the press have missed the theatrical performances arranged by a young Canadian who, after a period of study in France, and upon his return to Quebec in 1787 or 1788 (the reporter is uncertain), 'immediately set about establishing a theatre, in order to stage French plays'?[27] This was certainly not a private dramatic club, for the Ursuline sister who records the fact goes on to remark that 'this theatre was attended by what was called the best society, at that time.' But not a word from another source. In fact, if one were to rely solely upon the *Gazette*, one would assume there were no French plays presented in the capital until 1791, apart from the double program I have mentioned in 1775. English-language plays, yes; and there is no doubt that these attracted some French-Canadians spectators.

Perhaps the history of theatre in Montreal at this time may supply some further clues as to the role of theatre in Canadian society. Between 1774 when, as we have seen, the first performances given there under British rule took place, and 1789, there was little French-language theatrical activity of a public nature. The only institution of secondary education, the Collège Saint-Raphaël, seems to have maintained a tradition of dramatic presentations from the time of its foundation, and we know of two programs presented there in the 1770s: first the tragedy, *Jonathas and David; or The Triumph of Friendship*, a play written by the French Jesuit Pierre Brumoy, and which had frequently been produced in France as well.[28] This was an ambitious undertaking, with its three full acts in verse. It was probably successful, however, for the text was honoured by a printed edition in Montreal that same year, the first edition of a play in Canada.[29] The theme is biblical, that of David wresting the throne from his childhood friend, Jonathas. And to ensure that nothing should distract from the edifying nature of the presentation, separate performances were arranged for male and female spectators, all of whom, as parents or close relatives of students of the institution, were to be admitted by invitation only. This seems to have been common practice with college theatre in French Canada until relatively recent times.[30] Two years later, in 1778, a play with analogous inspiration, *Le Sacrifice d'Abraham*, by an unknown

French author,[31] was enacted at the same school, this time in the presence of the newly appointed Governor Haldimand, who was pleased enough with the performance to present the college with a gift of 100 guineas.

Restricted though the repertoire, audience, and number of performances may have been on such occasions, they would have done their part to create and maintain a taste for the stage among the small intellectual élite of the country represented by the students, families, and staff associated with the Collège Saint-Raphaël in Montreal, the Grand and the Petit Séminaires, and the Convent of the Ursulines in Quebec. A less exclusive program was offered by a group calling itself the 'Young French-Canadian Gentlemen' (Les Jeunes Messieurs canadiens, at a time when 'canadien' referred only to French-Canadians), on 4 January 1780, when they staged Grégoire ou l'incommodité de la grandeur, according to the Gazette.[32] These young Canadians may have been independent of church or military, but their choice of this highly moralizing five-act comedy by the Jesuit Du Cerceau shows very clearly the direct and enduring influence of 'college' theatre in Montreal. More 'public' still were the performances arranged by the British troops stationed in that city, admission to which was apparently free. Thus we learn from a document authorized by Governor Haldimand, acting as Commander-in-Chief, in December 1780 that plays had been performed the previous winter in the Jesuits' residence in Montreal and that plans were under way to stage others, among them Molière's Fourberies de Scapin.[33] There must have been some level of collaboration between the Young French Canadian Gentlemen and theatre lovers among the troops commanded by General MacLean (it was he who had requested the use of the Jesuits' residents), since it was the Young Canadian Gentlemen who enacted Molière's play in January 1781.[34] The performance was public, and one of the young Canadiens who took part in it complains bitterly about the troupe's having to butcher the play 'by removing the female characters from it ... in order to obviate the Church's censure about mixing both sexes on stage.'[35] Yet chastened as the cast may have been, the personage of that resourceful rogue, Scapin, had to be included; and although he is less directly dangerous than a Tartuffe or a Don Juan, his appearance in conservative Canada at this time must surely have caused some alarm among the Catholic clergy, even if no record of their reaction now remains.

It is clear that Molière was much in vogue in French Canada at this time: indirectly, in the manuscripts composed at the Quebec Seminary about 1780; directly, in these performances by the military and by amateurs. The terrain was being prepared for more regular dramatic activity, and it was not long delayed. No doubt it is emulation of the success of these performances which explains the return of the same play two years later, as part of an ambitious plan for the *carnaval* of 1782, which would include dances and balls as well as the performance, by amateurs of tragedies and other comedies, and which would begin early in the new year. The same play reappeared on a program offered in Quebec in 1786 by another group of civilian enthusiasts, which included the painter and sculptor François Baillargé.[36]

English-language theatre had begun to grow roots as well.[37] It was in the mid-1780s that the first troupe of visiting actors, Edward Allen's American group, arrived, apparently from Jamaica, to perform in both Quebec and Montreal. Their tour met with considerable success, judging from the length of their stay and from the fact that the same company, divided into separate troupes (one for each city), returned in 1789 for another extended tour.[38] Their presentations were in English, but often included translations from French authors (especially Molière), and were accessible to that growing segment of French-Canadian society which, by interaction and emulation, had learned the conqueror's tongue and some of his cultural proclivities, to the scandal of some elements of francophone society. All of these factors, not excluding the initial lack of overt critical reaction by the Church, conspired to prepare the setting for the first attempt at something resembling a dramatic season, in 1789-90.

MONTREAL'S THÉÂTRE DE SOCIÉTÉ 1789-90: THE CHURCH'S REACTION

Between 24 November 1789 and 9 February 1790, eight separate plays were presented in Montreal, in five different double programs. Not only the number was unparalleled: so was the choice of authors and works, from the now predictable Molière (*Le Médecin malgré lui*) to the contemporary Florian (*Les Deux Billets*), but with emphasis on Regnard: three different plays by that author (*Le Retour imprévu*, *Les Folies amoureuses*, and *Le Légataire universel*, the latter performed on two different occasions).[39]

Regnard, bridging two centuries and less exceptional in his choice of themes than his predecessor, Molière, was a 'natural' for French-Canadian audiences, as the number of performances of his plays in the thirty-year period 1789-1819 attests (sixteen, as compared with fifty-one for Molière, of a total of approximately 150 known performances). But what of Florian, what of the less-known Beaunoir, author of *Jérôme Pointu*, staged and published in Paris only nine years earlier, enacted in Montreal on 4 February 1790?[40] We have a new factor at work here, and it is not difficult to deduce what it is.

This impressive dramatic season was due to the efforts of a small troupe calling itself a Théâtre de Société, a title and a concept directly imported from France, where such theatres had provided the liveliest and most innovative theatre the eighteenth century had known until the French Revolution. These 'Theatre Societies,' as Montreal's *Gazette* consistently translates the term, were essentially private, and in fact were generally established in direct opposition to public, paying theatre which, in the mother country, was going through a long period of semi-stagnation. By mid-century their vogue had become widespread, in Paris, at the court (where Mme de Pompadour had her own private theatre established), and in the provincial cities. Most self-respecting noblemen and many members of the upper middle class bowed to the trend, setting aside a room for such performances. And hundreds of plays were written with such intimate theatres in mind.[41] Thus we are not surprised to learn that two French-born, recent immigrants to Montreal were the chief movers in this local enterprise: Louis Dulongpré, a native of Paris who had fought for the Americans in their War of Independence and come to Canada soon after it ended; and Joseph Quesnel, born in Saint-Malo, now a naturalized citizen of Canada since his ship carrying contraband arms for those same rebellious Americans, had been captured off Nova Scotia in 1779.[42] The troupe had announced that its inaugural performance would take place on 24 November 1789, with a mixed program, Regnard's *Le Retour imprévu* (1700) and Florian's *Deux Billets* (1779), both comedies (as all plays presented by this company would be), but the latter, significantly, enlivened by songs and music, 'mêlée d'ariettes,' as so very many popular plays were in France at the time. This would be the trademark of Montreal's Théâtre de Société and Joseph Quesnel. Their next program, on 29 December of the same year, consisted of another comedy by Regnard, *Le Légataire universel*, plus a one-act *opéra comique*, *Les Deux Chasseurs et la laitière* (The Two Hunters and the Milkmaid), with text by Anseaume, music by Duni.[43] But of much more significance for us is their program the following month, on 14 January 1790, combining Molière's *Médecin malgré lui* with a short musical comedy written by Quesnel himself and entitled *Colas et Colinette*.

Before moving to this original work, and to the theatre of Joseph Quesnel in general, we must trace, briefly, the effects of this new troupe's activity upon Montreal's francophone population. On 22 November, two days before the first announced performance, the pastor of the parish of Notre-Dame, François-Xavier Latour-Déséri, mounted his pulpit to assail the project, its initiators, and theatre in general. He was particularly disturbed by the proposal to present comedies 'at night, with men and boys disguised as girls and women,'[44] and threatened to withdraw the sacraments from those misguided enough to attend. But Quesnel and company, less pliant than other members of the parish (perhaps because they were led by two transplanted Frenchmen, both world travellers), took up the flung gauntlet and decided to confront Father Déséri at the end of High Mass that day, 'to insult him and criticize his action, in their ill-considered zeal,' says our informant, 'since he was meddling in affairs which were no concern of his.'[45] But public reaction in general was far stronger than the priest expected, we learn, for 'poor Déséri is deprecated far and wide for it, and a lot of people are not displeased with that fact.' The reporter, Jean Brassier, Vicar-General of the Diocese of Quebec (to which Montreal still belonged at the time), after this résumé for his correspondent, Bishop Hubert, asks what his superior's counsel would be in this and similar instances. I shall now quote from the unpublished thesis of Marjorie Fitzpatrick, in which she has carefully studied the incident:

> Bishop Hubert's reply, in a private letter to Brassier dated November 30, 1789, suggested tactfully that Déséri had taken entirely the wrong approach to the problem. While the bishop concurred completely in Déséri's interpretation of the Church's position on *comédie*, he believed that a public attack upon such a venture when it was first proposed was ill-advised. He saw that the probable effect of Déséri's threat to withhold absolution would be to drive people away from the Confessional, rather than to inspire them to submit and repent. The bishop was obviously convinced that quiet persuasion was more likely to win over the proponents of theatre than public denunciation. This attitude, expressed also in another letter written by the bishop in 1795 [actually by his secretary, Desjardins, in his name, to the same Brassier], may explain why he issued no *mandements* against theatre despite his apparent conviction that it was evil and dangerous.[46]

There is confirmation from another source that public reaction was much stronger than the pastor of Notre-Dame intended: the press. Throughout that brief season, November 1789-February 1790, the *Montreal Gazette/de Montréal* kept the controversy alive with editorials, articles, and letters from readers in Quebec and Montreal. The Church's legal status in the conquered land was not yet solid enough, Bishop Hubert well knew, to risk this type of exposure – especially since theatre was bound to continue, if only that variety offered by garrisoned troops and by the British and American companies touring the country irregularly. His answer was to use a potentially much more effective organ: the confessional, since it was, by definition, the most private weapon available. 'You know as well as I do,' the bishop says, 'that the words of a confessor are generally more effective than those of a preacher.'[47]

This amended strategy on the Church's part allowed Quesnel's little company to continue its presentation of comedies and light opera during that winter of 1789-90, no longer facing broadside fire from the Church, but rather a debilitating campaign of attrition – which the amateurs would surely lose. In the meantime, Quesnel's new play was performed by the Théâtre de Société on two occasions during that season and received encouraging response from a public unaccustomed to such fare.

THE THEATRE OF JOSEPH QUESNEL

This first work, described by its author as an operetta, is a light comedy with frequent musical interventions, a genre which is the clear predecessor of today's musical comedies. *Colas and Colinette; or The Bailiff Confounded* is the first such work known to have been composed and performed in North America. But this type of musical entertainment had been exceedingly popular in France since mid-century, especially since the performance in Paris of Jean-Jacques Rousseau's *Le Devin du village* (1752), for which, exceptionally, the author had written both text and music. And when Favart assumed management of the Opéra-Comique half a dozen years later, a veritable invasion of such plays ensued. As an historian of the period observes 'comic opera becomes a true literary genre, and the musical element, in the form of ariettas, takes on an importance, in these new plays, that some considered inappropriate.[48] By the following decade lyrical dramas, even musical *comédies larmoyantes* were the rage, with Sedaine's *Le Déserteur* (1769) the best known and most successful example. 'The current taste for opéra-comique,' a contemporary complains, 'has destroyed this nation's former taste for the masterpieces produced by the human mind.'[49] Quesnel had imported an item in great demand in France and had found a responsive audience in Montreal.

Colas and Colinette is the only one of his works to have been performed or published in Quesnel's lifetime. It had been completed in 1788, according to a note appended to the original edition of the work, dated 1808; and it was probably with its performance specifically in mind that he had worked towards formation of the Théâtre de Société. When the play was revived in Quebec City fifteen years later (by the troupe calling itself 'Les Messieurs canadiens'), and again in 1807 in the capital, it proved to have lost none of its appeal. The printer John Neilson decided to publish it, with the author's approval and assistance. It is thus only the second play ever to have been printed in this country, and the first one written *and published* here.[50] Reprinted in its original form in 1968, it was performed and recorded for Radio-Canada in the same year, in Ottawa and Hamilton since then, as well as Milan. An even rarer honour for French-Canadian theatre until very recently: *Colas and Colinette* was translated into English and published in 1974.[51]

A measure of its importance is the fact that this work has frequently been emulated by later generations of Quebec dramatists, and as recently as 1942.[52] There is no doubt that this is the most successful play composed, staged, and printed in Canada before the 1860s. Yet there is nothing at all Canadian in its plot or setting. The action is situated in an unidentified village in France and only the description of the costumes to be worn by the actors suggests that the time is roughly contemporary to that of its composition. There are five characters, a fact which, as has been suggested, is probably tied in with the number of members in the original Théâtre de Société. The plot concerns the rivalry for the hand of a young country woman, Colinette, between the twenty-two-year-old peasant whom she loves, Colas, and the much older village bailiff (a magistrate with some judicial responsibilities under the Old Régime in France), who is not otherwise named. The latter takes advantage of his office and of the profound gullibility of Colas to have this rival suitor removed by enrolling him, without his knowledge, in a company of recruits being raised by the village *seigneur*, Monsieur Dolmont. Dolmont also happens to be the benefactor and legal guardian of the orphaned Colinette, so these four, with admirable economy of plot, are the principals in the play. Dolmont's rustic valet, L'Epine (who reminds one of the valet of identical name and similar personality in Florian's *Jeannot et Colin*, first performed in 1780), is a minor character whose pungent country speech vies with that of Colas and heightens the sense of class distinction in the text.

There is no attempt at providing either depth or subtlety in the depiction of any of these characters. In a tradition leading directly to the worst of nineteenth-century melodrama, the bailiff has no saving qualities, quickly laying bare his cunning and his unscrupulousness ('Any means is good,' he says, 'that leads to our proposed end').[54] Monsieur Dolmont, on the other hand, is the very exemplar of a humane *seigneur*: generous, paternal, concerned only for the well-being of his tenants. Colinette is not only young and pretty, she is resourceful, loyal, and far more intelligent than either Colas or the bailiff. As for Colas, he and L'Epine are very much a match, with scarcely a wit to rub between them. Their diction serves to underline this fact: upon the traditional (and probably obsolete) rusticisms from the age of Molière: the 'je sommes' form, for example, improperly used in this text) are grafted others that were no doubt inspired by Quesnel's ten years of Canadian experience, for many of them survive today in regional parlance in Quebec.[55] Yet Colinette, of identical social origin, speaks a 'correct,' standard French, perhaps because she has been housed for some time by Monsieur Dolmont. The inference is clear: rustic manners and speech are synonymous with dull, 'rustic' wit, and no imagination.

But of course the language of Colas and L'Epine is intended primarily as a source – an easy and traditional one – of humour in this operetta. Traditional also is the *quiproquo*, the verbal misunderstanding spun out to great length, used here to good effect in II, 8, where Colas thinks they are speaking of a marriage contract, while Dolmont is referring only to the army enrolment form Colas is about to sign with his 'X,' and only the bailiff and the spectator/reader are aware of the misunderstanding:

THE SQUIRE [ie, Dolmont]
But will you fulfil properly all the duties of the state into which you are about to enter?
COLAS (*with a smirk*)
You leaves that to me, sir.
THE SQUIRE
You must be in good health.
THE BAILIFF
He is quite healthy.
COLAS
Ne'er been sick a day in me life.
THE SQUIRE
You must have stamina.
THE BAILIFF
He is full of it.
COLAS
I's got lots, sir.
THE SQUIRE
Be able to resist the fatigue of the day.
THE BAILIFF
He is accustomed to it.
COLAS
I be used to it.
THE SQUIRE
Yes, but what about the fatigue of the night?
COLAS (*somewhat taken aback*)
If I gets too tired at night, I'll rests meself in the day.

THE SQUIRE

Oh! my friend, things are not so easily arranged, and there is often no rest, day or night.

THE BAILIFF

He is young, he will overcome all his fatigue

COLAS (*laughing*)

Ah, yes, that be our business![56]

One can well imagine the tittering sure to arise from such a sequence. One could imagine also the consternation that these sexual allusions would create for any clerical spectator, in the unlikely event that he would attend such a performance at that time! Colas, undaunted by intimations of the perils and fatigues he may be incurring, pushes on, a bit mystified as to why the squire wants to provide him with musket, knapsack, and cartridge pouch, but willing to go along with the thing, provided he gets Colinette's hand. As soon as he recounts the incident to Colinette, she realizes what the bailiff is up to, of course, and decides to entrap the villain and expose him by pretending to play along with his scheme to carry her off without her guardian's consent: that classic source of scandal for so many 'bourgeois' dramas, before and since Quesnel's time.

The rendezvous for their elopement is set, fairly predictably, for a wooded area, at night. Colas, at his beloved's instigation, collars the bailiff; Dolmont arrives, informed of all; the villain is totally confounded, justice and virtue triumph, Colas is released from his military engagement and the operetta ends with a fine vaudeville chorus sung by all five actors.

The night of its première, *Colas and Colinette* was to have been preceded by Molière's *Médecin malgré lui*, and in the advertisement for the performance which appeared in the *Montréal Gazette* on 31 December 1789, Quesnel had not mentioned who the author of the second work was – perhaps out of modesty, perhaps also to allow the author to remain unknown, if the play proved to be a fiasco. It did not, of course, and the combination offered (it was Regnard's *Retour imprévu* which opened the evening, according to the *Gazette*) was a happy one.[57] Furthermore, it gave rise to another 'first,' for the review which appeared in the *Gazette* on 21 January 1790 is the first dramatic criticism published in Canada. That report was highly laudatory (or at least was intended to be):

Each act is completely dependent upon the other two, and the interest aroused by the whole play is such that, as soon as one glimpses the first outlines of the plot, one has a burning desire to get to its resolution at once. Every character who appears seems appropriate, and is always consistent with his first portrayal. The audience's emotions are prepared in the first act, gripped in the second, transported in the third; at first the play causes pleasure, next it charms, then enchants. Virtue is painted in such attractive colours that it cannot help but appear appealing: M. Dolmont is virtue itself; Colas and his beloved are the personification of innocent, artless love; the Bailiff of ridiculousness ... The spectator's applause was justly deserved, and does credit both to the audience and the author. Another performance of this play is earnestly to be desired.[58]

A modern spectator or reader is less impressed by the static depiction of character and the utter predictability of the plot; but we must remember also that this is comic opera, and that the criteria applicable to this genre can be decidedly different from those we would use for straightforward theatre. Quesnel seems to have hit upon a recipe with proven success in France, and his formula deviates little, in ingredients and structure. The names of his title roles are second-hand, having already appeared, for example, in Sedaine's *Rose et Colas* (1764), in Grétry's opera, *La Double Epreuve, ou Colinette à la cour* (1782), in Mme de Beaunoir's *Fanfan et Colas, ou les Frères de lait* (1784). As Baudoin Burger has pointed out, the plot of Quesnel's play is well-nigh identical to Favart's *Annette et Lubin*, first performed in 1762.[59] Rural and pastoral settings, especially when the text was *mêlé d'ariettes* as in this case, were in vogue, from *Toinon et Toinette* by Desboulmiers and Gossec (1767) to Boutillier and Pouteau's *Alain et Rosette, ou la Bergère ingénue* (1777), Sedaine and Grétry's *Aucassin et Nicolette* (1779), Florian's *Jeannot et Colin* (1780) and *Blanche et Vermeille* (1781), to Gabiot de Salins' *Le Bailli bienfaisant ou le Triomphe de la nature* (1786). Quesnel's visit to France in 1788-9, when the taste for this sort of entertainment was still strong, must have given him ample material and inspiration for his own composition. Even the music is highly derivative, according to Willy Amtmann, who observes:

Quesnel was thoroughly French in his cultural manifestations; the pleasant and refined personality as which he is depicted in historic accounts remained imbued with the Gallic spirit to the end. And as he remained French in all artistic aspects he did neither adapt to the new country nor exert any influence on its literary or musical development. *Colas et Colinette* is French in spirit, in the story and its characters, it could not help but be French in the music as well, and if Quesnel in writing it looked for stimulus and motivation he found it not in his environment but in nostalgic thoughts about the country of his birth.[60]

One must, however, underline the importance of this unprepossessing work in a time and place where no theatrical tradition as such existed. With one concerted effort, over one modest season, Montreal's Théâtre de Société had brought repertory up to date; and its outstanding member had bridged the long gap between 1693 and his own age. Moreover, for French Canada in the uneasy years of the French Revolution, Quesnel's choice of a quaint, innocuous plot, well-tested form, and vague setting was a judicious one. Of all the forms still current in France, this was one of the most conventional and thus the one most likely to appeal both to its conservative author and to audiences in the British colony of French Canada.

The three plays attributed to Quesnel display amazing diversity of form, theme, and intent. For someone familiar with *Colas et Colinette*, it is difficult to believe that *The French Republicans* (Les Républicains français), the next of these, was written by the same man. Subtitled 'An Evening in a Cabaret,' it was composed before the end of 1801, and its setting is the Paris of that most fearful period of the recent French Revolution, the Terror of 1793-4, when the Committee of Public Safety kept the guillotine dripping with blood. *The French Republicans*, unlike Quesnel's first play, has inescapable political intent. It is a bitter satirical parody of a whole society, savaged through the portrayal of six of its members (seven, if the innkeeper is included) in the worst light the author can throw upon them and the political ideals they incarnate.

The characters in this one-act prose comedy are the old man Desvignes, a municipal functionary in the new order of things; Charlot, a citizen-soldier in the new National Guard; Monsieur Pincé, an attorney under the Old Régime, scrambling to conform and survive in this one; a lazy drunkard, Blaise; two women of peccable virtue, Javotte and Dame Catau; and the peripheral innkeeper. All the action takes place in one room of a cabaret or tavern, symbol of the base society Quesnel wants to portray. Visually, each character wears a clear symbol of his or her allegiance to the Revolution (a red, white, and blue cockade, if they haven't the right to wear a uniform, such as Charlot, or an official sash, as does Desvignes), and the only other visible action is the constant swilling of wine by all. Verbally also, the play is 'proletarianized' through the deformations in pronunciation, syntax, and vocabulary appropriate to the social origins of each; with the only partial exception being the former attorney, whose speech is studded with shallow clichés. Desvignes sets the tone in his invitation to the others ('Come, friends, let's amuse ourselves civically'), and immediately displays the clear intent of Quesnel's method: 'Let our every act be always for the Revolution, and let us drink together like true Republicans.'⁶¹ The characters, lest we had any doubt, are to be taken as representative.

In their ensuing conversation they delineate the aspects of the new revolutionary Constitution which they personally hold most dear. Of course these are the most obvious ones: liquidation of the nobility and of the clergy ('No king, no nobles, no priests: today we's our own masters'); sharing of wealth and opportunity; the new liberties for women, particularly in intersexual relations. With a mind to his French-Canadian audience and their traditional sensitivity on that subject, Quesnel develops this latter theme above all. Thus Pincé, despite his married status, is out to seduce Dame Catau; who, since she has been assured of her own liberty now, prefers the soldier Charlot, while Javotte would be perfectly happy with Pincé for the night, with the drunken Blaise – or anyone else, for that matter. This is what the noble aims of the drafters of the Rights of Man have been reduced to:

M. PINCÉ
Don't the Rights of Man give me the right to leave a wife that bores me, and find another that I like?
DAME CATAU
Me too! I want my choice, too, since that's the Rights of Man!

What does it matter if the country is in dire economic straits – there are compensatory advantages:

M. PINCÉ
It's true we've great poverty now, but the present famine is amply counterbalanced by the pleasures we now enjoy through our freedom to divorce, and other such advantages resulting from the Declaration of the Rights of Man.
JAVOTTE (*sneeringly*)
The Rights of Man! There's a law with a darned funny name! What do you think, Madame Catau?
DAME CATAU
No denying that there's one of the wisest laws ever made since the Revolution, especially the thing on divorce. Take the Old Régime, now: wasn't that a dreadful situation for a woman, to see herself bound for life to some grumpy fellow who, after nagging his wife all day, was only fit to snore at her side all night? Wouldn't you agree, Monsieur Pincé, that that's a sorry state of affairs for a young woman?

M. PINCÉ

I certainly agree! If the Revolution had produced no other benefit than the freedom to break such restrictive bonds, it would have been enough to endear it to all Frenchmen. Not that I have to confess to that type of deportment: I can truthfully say I never pestered *my* wife, and always took the greatest precautions so as never to interrupt her sleep.[62]

Not only marriage, the cornerstone of Quebec society, is endangered by the politics of revolt: religion would be suppressed, rights to property would disappear, drunkenness would prevail. Quesnel does not forget his English-speaking compatriots either, even if the praise the British receive comes from an odd source:

CHARLOT

Mademoiselle Javotte is still as proud as a Scotsman.

BLAISE

Sheems t'me it'd be a lot easier to deal with the English an' Shcots, than with the bad temper of shome gals...

M. PINCÉ

Don't even mention those people to me! Just the sound of their names interferes with my drinking, and takes all the fun out of it!

DESVIGNES

Hey, what do you mean by that?

M. PINCÉ

They're our enemies, aren't they?

DESVIGNES

Friends, let's not talk bad about 'em, even if they's our enemies. I heard it from lots o' people who knows em real good, an' who thinks like me: they's a brave, loyal an' generous lot. 'Tis true some folks can't stand 'em 'cause they's bloody heretics, y'see. But me, I don't hold it against 'em. They's good people, they is. They got good beer.[63]

As the play lurches towards its end, bottles pile up on the table, the characters get more and more intoxicated with words and wine, and it is soon time to end the party and the play, for the feared 'liberty patrols' will soon be scouring the streets to pick up anyone not in uniform. In the final scramble, Charlot winds up with Dame Catau, Pincé refuses the proffered favours of Javotte, and she is left alone with Blaise, dead drunk under the table. The parting message is a song to a well-known air, delivered offstage:

Gentlemen, if these few scenes
Are worthy of all of your sufferance,
If our grotesque Republicans
Have succeeded in entertaining you at all this evening,
Well then, don't be too critical, I pray you:
The author can applaud himself in private.
Laugh, laugh if you will
At the expense of the Republic!

We are not surprised that Joseph Quesnel, by this time a member of the seigneurial class of Lower Canada, should feel so strongly about the new tide which had carried away the France he knew, and probably the property and possessions of his relatives in that country. After his establishment in Canada he had returned only once to his native land, just before the Revolution. He had apparently not liked what he saw on the horizon, and the deterioration of the situation in France during the 1790s had only served to convince him more fully of the evils of popular government, of that 'democracy' he came to hate. Thus *The French Republicans* bears the visible stamp of the man, even though it is so dissimilar to *Colas and Colinette*. It bears evidence, too, of his continuing love of music, for the play is interspersed with comic opera songs, all of them composed to well-known and popular tunes, among them selections from La Chabeaussière and Dalayrac's *Azémia, ou les Sauvages* (1787), and from Mozart's version (1786) of Beaumarchais' *Marriage of Figaro*, another example of the important role Quesnel played in channelling contemporary European influences into Canada,[64] despite Amtmann's assertion. *The French Republicans* belongs to a hybrid genre whose closest connection is with the permissive *parades* that were so much a part of eighteenth-century theatrical tradition in France, a phenomenon closely connected with private Théâtres de Société, and which attracted authors as diverse as Nivelle de La Chaussée, Voltaire, and Beaumarchais, the latter's *Les Députés de la Halle et du Gros-Caillou* (date unknown: before 1775) exhibiting close parallels, in my view, with Quesnel's play, in its language, its quarrelling, and its characters. Baudoin Burger has also pointed out the influence of Destouches' *Le Tambour nocturne*, performed in Montreal by another Théâtre de Société in 1795, particularly upon the names of two characters, Pincé and Catau, their personality, and social positions.[65] And the music, to repeat, is all *vaudeville* in the precise meaning of that word at the time in France: popular melodies carrying interpolated words. Borrowed music, in short.

But the derivative aspect of situation, characters, words, and music is less significant here than elsewhere, for *The French Republicans* is above all an impassioned political statement in which esthetics and considerations of originality have little place. And to that extent it is representative of a genre that would be peculiarly popular in French Canada, for the most 'political' plays I shall examine from the nineteenth century use the same basic stratagem of a meeting attended by those whom the author wishes to attack, and who in fact denigrate their own image by their 'reported' words and actions. Indeed, this play is the most striking example of political theatre to have appeared until then. But it is by no means the first, as I shall show, for there already was evolving a tradition of using dramatic and paradramatic forms to convey one's own political convictions and to attack others'.

The last of Quesnel's completed plays, *L'Anglomanie, ou Dîner à l'anglaise* (Anglomania; or Dinner, English Style) has generally been assigned the date 1802, although internal evidence is convincing that the work was completed some time after March 1803.[66] At first blush, it would seem once again to have little in common with either of the two plays which preceded it. Its form, for instance: *L'Anglomanie* is written in rhymed alexandrine couplets, the other two in prose. There is no music or song, borrowed or original, in this third play. The setting, for the first time, is Lower Canada. And as to the theme, it is explicit in the title: the current mania among French Canadians for all things British, with the concomitant rejection of traditional French culture.

At the home of Monsieur Primenbourg, a *seigneur* with social ambitions, there is a good deal of stir as this one-act play opens: his son-in-law, Colonel Beauchamp, has just informed him that the Governor of Lower Canada will come to dine at Primenbourg's house the following day. The colonel is aide-de-camp to the Governor, and is the principal 'Anglomaniac' in the play. He has succeeded in communicating his passion for all things English to his father-in-law, and Primenbourg is properly appreciative for having been rescued from the Gothic night wherein he once dwelt:

> My wife, my house and furniture, my very clock,
> Even my table-settings: nothing was English.
> Everything about me was reminiscent of the Middle Ages.
> But I followed your counsel, responded to your efforts,
> Changed my dishes, had cutlery and serving-ware melted down,
> Exchanged my gold for copper, my silverware for pewter,
> And managed to introduce some taste into this household.[67]

Primenbourg's mother (referred to as 'The Dowager' in the text) arrives, and proves to be a counterpoise to the colonel's Anglomania. She is little dazzled by the customs and titles of the country's English masters, and sticks firmly to French manners and social graces. Thus she is not impressed with the news that the Governor is to arrive, particularly when she learns that her son, at the Colonel's urging, has decided to exclude several family members from the dinner, on the grounds that they are not quite 'cultivated' enough for the occasion. He can count her out, too, in that case!

Only Primenbourg's cousin, Vielmont, will ally himself with the Dowager and try to infuse some common sense into the family. The structural strategy of Quesnel's text consists of delineating the foolish Anglophile excesses of Colonel Beauchamp, M. and Mme Primenbourg, their daughter Lucette, and two minor, caricatural personages, the untalented poet François – an alter ego, curiously, of the author, and Doctor Pennkrève, a boorish quack of Germanic origin.[68] A brilliant bit of research by John Hare of the University of Ottawa reveals that all these characters (or at least the major ones, plus François and Pennkrève) are in fact based upon real, identifiable individuals in the small but influential society of Boucherville, close to Montreal on the other side of the river, where Quesnel lived from 1792. Hare points out also the careful strategy of the play, based on a real apprehension of the sociological danger at the time: least infatuated with Anglomania is the oldest generation, represented by Primenbourg's mother, the Dowager. Smitten, but ultimately curable, is the generation of Primenbourg himself; decidedly less so, the generation of his son-in-law, Colonel Beauchamp. And the most thoroughly Anglicized of all is the youngest segment, represented by Lucette.[69] Social dynamics are thus expressed most appositely in this internal family conflict, with good contrapuntal effect. Quesnel, by this time, seems to have acquired more skill in depicting a character through his speech, as when Vielmont, officer in a Canadian regiment (Beauchamp's commission is in a British one), uses ironic understatement to counter the Colonel's vapidity, making his interventions more effective and more credible. When he and Beauchamp report conflicting accounts of the outcome of the latest battle between English and French armies in Europe, for example, Primenbourg is indignant:

M. PRIMENBOURG

                                Really, Vielmont,
Sometimes you are as stubborn as an ox!
Do you actually purport to be as well informed
As my son-in-law, about the latest news of that sort?
You know what sort of position he has within the Government!

VIELMONT
I heard something about that. Apparently it is
A very lucrative post.
M. PRIMENBOURG
A very honourable one, as well.
VIELMONT
Is it true that all the left-over food from the Governor's
Table, on special occasions, belongs to you?
THE COLONEL
I should say so! That's the best part of my income,
Since it allows me to live well, without expense!
VIELMONT
Now that's what I would call a fine position!
Since you taste of all the Governor's food,
You certainly must know all his secrets, too.
In that case, when you announce political news, in future,
I'll be hanged if I'll even dare to reply![70]

Of course neither the Colonel nor Primenbourg perceives the irony of
such remarks, and both rush enthusiastically to prepare the great dinner,
English-style. But in an ending reminiscent of many a Molière play, the
legitimate head of civil and military authority in Canada proves to be a discerning, well-informed, and urbane leader who has realized the danger
inherent in excess. If Primenbourg's family cannot attend, he announces,
then his own visit is off, at least until the family recover from the various
indispositions they are reported to be suffering from. The Dowager then
has an easy time pointing out to her son and his wife what fools they have
been. And the Colonel, seeing which way the wind is now blowing, consents to go along with them for the moment in their too-sudden decision
to 'de-Anglicize' themselves. Primenbourg, after his instant conversion,
reacquires common sense as well, in the attitude towards the English he
will adopt henceforth:

I'm well aware of the advantages of being known to them;
I know how to appreciate them and their customs;
But I now see that, without forsaking our ancestral ways
We can obtain their respect for us, as well.
I admit, I was quite wrong in that respect;
But if I was wrong, it was you, Colonel, who deceived me!
First, according to you, our relatives were
Quite unfit to grace a dinner like this one;

Yet here we have His Excellency informing us now
That he wants to meet them, wants them to be invited!
So your idea of 'taste' has nothing to do with it;
But it's that 'taste' that's been ruining me and my household.[71]

Thus the problem posed in the play receives a solution of exemplary com-
promise: everyone will be invited, from both cultures, even the German
doctor. And the aping of English manners will henceforth cease: everyone
is to be him- or herself. This, one easily deduces, is also Quesnel's solution for contemporary Lower Canadian society: provided, of course, that
people like himself and Primenbourg retain their standing and their privi-
leges.

Although the work is a long way from being a masterpiece, *L'Anglomanie* is the most skilfully composed of Quesnel's three completed plays.
If Professor Hare's sleuthing is accurate, he also provides a convincing
reason why the play was never performed or published in the author's lifetime: if the characters it portrays were indeed copied from well-known
originals in the little society of Boucherville, it would have been most
unwise for anyone who intended to continue living there, to render those
unflattering portraits public. It is a pity the work remained little known,
for its topicality is unquestionable. And this was a theme the author took
to heart, judging from a short, unpublished piece in dialogue form preserved in the Archives of the Quebec Seminary, entitled 'The Disappointed
Rhymer' (Le Rimeur dépité). It presents, a poet clearly identifiable as
blood brother to the Monsieur François portrayed in *L'Anglomanie*, and
therefore to Quesnel himself. It excoriates the same excesses, just as thoroughly.[72] In a sense, Quesnel is himself a microcosmic model of the direction the evolution of French-Canadian theatre would take, in the progressive politicization and Canadianization his plays can be shown to take.

Aside from the composition of *Colas and Colinette* before 1789, most of
Quesnel's literary production took place during the last ten years of his life
(he died in 1809). By that time the well-publicized excesses of the French
Revolution had been followed by the advent of Napoleon and by the all-
out armed conflict with Britain which characterized the First Empire. It is
in this context too that we must understand the progression from the innocuous provincialism of *Colas and Colinette* to the sometimes strident
views he espouses in his subsequent works. The same evolution is evident
in his poetry, to which he turned more and more after 1799. His extant
poems range from the pompously pro-British to a tearful adieu to the
France he had known, while others affirm the importance of equal distri-
bution of power and opportunity for French-speakers in Lower Canada.[73]

What they all have in common in their fidelity to the literary and moral principles of seventeenth-century France (exception being made, of course, for *The French Republicans*). Those values are particularly evident in his didactic poem, 'Adresse aux jeunes acteurs' (Address to Young Actors), which appeared in the *Quebec Gazette/Gazette de Québec* on 7 February 1805, when *Colas and Colinette* was being revived in that city. His advice to the would-be thespian is to seek verisimilitude:

> Actor, to succeed here is a rule that's sure:
> Observe, imitate, and copy nature.

To eschew artificiality:

> In your pronunciation, avoid all affectation
> And speak as one speaks in normal conversation.

And to flee anything remotely redolent of immorality:

> If you choose the work of an indecorous author,
> You must excise all passages that may sound improper;
> But you'd be better off still, in my opinion,
> If you chose only the author who's decent and blameless.[74]

These are principles which owe as much to Boileau as they do to common sense.

Quesnel's most important role was that of a founder, and of a window upon a wider world. He was the catalyst in formation of the Théâtre de Société in Montreal, and the driving force behind its modest success. And through this group a link, albeit a tenuous one, had been re-established with a more modern French repertoire. Despite periods of retrogression, that is the path that would be followed henceforth. Despite the opposition of the Church, Quesnel and his little company endured for a time, establishing a precedent and a base upon which others would eventually build. As an author, his importance and influence are more open to question. *Colas and Colinette* certainly represents an important milestone on the way towards indigenous theatre; but we must remember that *The French Republicans*, *Anglomania*, and an unfinished operetta along the lines of his first play, to be entitled 'Lucas et Cécile,'[75] remained unpublished, uncirculated, and essentially unknown until the twentieth century. Their influence upon his contemporaries was nil.[76]

THE CHURCH TAKES A STAND AGAINST PUBLIC THEATRE

Let us return to the early 1790s, and to the first theatrical season in Montreal. Whether through the debilitating effects of an antistage campaign led
by the Church, via the confessional; whether through the lack of public
financial support that theatres in the province would long be heir to, that
season of 1789-90 was the last for Quesnel's troupe. Indeed, there appears
to have been no public theatre in French in Montreal before 1795, apart
from a benefit performance of some sort in February 1791. Instead, for
that period, the centre of modest francophone theatrical activity was Quebec, where ten public programs are known to have been offered between
January 1791 and December 1795. This activity is mainly attributable to
the indigenous group calling itself Les Jeunes Messieurs canadiens,[77] and
their preference was for Molière: of the eighteen performances of plays
represented by these ten programs, eleven were of his works, including
seven of the first nine. But the troupe also put on Beaumarchais' *Barber of
Seville* three times (the first known performances of his work in French
Canada), Brueys, Regnard, and Hauteroche, as well as Jean-Baptiste
Rousseau,[78] in an apparent attempt to maintain the interest of its public
with a degree of variety and relative modernity.

The Church was displeased with this attempt, and soon intervened as it
had done in Montreal just a little earlier. Despite the fairly frequent activity by English-speaking players, college students, and the occasional francophone amateur, there had been as yet no public dispute in the capital
between clergy and theatre-goers under the English régime. But oblique
references in the *Journal* of the Seminary about this time (an entry for 19
January 1789 records, for example, that there were 'deliberations concerning the conduct of a student who went to the theatre,' and that his case
would be referred directly to the Bishop)[79] suggest that the strings were
being tightened. And the first mention of public opposition is still indirect,
suggesting that the same tactic was being used in Quebec City as in Montreal: the confessional, instead of denunciation from the pulpit. The item
appears in the issue of the *Quebec Gazette/Gazette de Québec* for 20 January 1791, when the new troupe was presenting Molière's *Le Malade imaginaire* and *L'Avare*, and the impersonal French 'on' is used to refer to an
intervention which has already taken place:

> No one has ever imagined that there would be objections against
> the decent, honest entertainment that a few young Canadian
> Gentlemen of this town have undertaken to offer the public by per-
> forming a few plays ... An attempt is being made to persuade

people that theatre is dangerous for the young folk who attend it, which seems hardly likely. On the contrary, even the briefest reflection should convince us that actors and spectators as well could in fact be using the time they now devote to these performances, in much less commendable amusements that would be a good deal more prejudicial to morality, to their own best interests and their health, as well as to the edification of their neighbours.[80]

It has been assumed, with apparent good reason, that the man behind this opposition to public theatre was Father Joseph-Octave Plessis, then curate of the cathedral in Quebec, later coadjutor (1801) and bishop (1806-25), as resolute an opponent of public spectacles as any primate of Quebec since Saint-Vallier. Plessis, at this time, enjoyed the full confidence of Bishop Hubert, and we have already seen the strategy the latter preferred to employ in cases like this (pp 52-4 above). Thus there was no full, open conflict in this period. But of course there need not be, if available weapons were used properly. By 1795 the existing regulations, promulgated by Saint-Vallier a century before, had been infused with new life. We learn from a letter written in that year that 'Monseigneur has directed priests who hear confessions in the City of Quebec to refuse absolution to all those performing, aiding, or attending these sorts of performances.' But that directive was not issued publicly, for 'if the supporters of theatre win over proselytes, Monseigneur hopes that they will be won back through the confessional.'[81]

Nevertheless, for a time the new company continued and garrison theatre had apparently not ceased its activity, although reports of it are infrequent. Quebec was justly proud of its sophistication, relative as it was. The wife of Colonel John Graves Simcoe, spending the long winter of 1791-2 there before she and her husband proceeded to Upper Canada, of which he had been named Lieutenant-Governor, remarked to a correspondent in England upon the excellence and accessibility of public entertainment in the colonial capital. Her diary for Saturday, 18 February 1792, reports:

One of the Casmettes [ie, 'casemates' or fortified defensive enclosures in the wall] near Fort Louis Gate has been fitted up for a Theatre. Some Canadian [ie, French-Canadian] Gentlemen represented Le Medecin Malgré lui & La Comtesse d'Escarbagnas. I was surprised those people unused to see Theatrical Representations could perform so well as they did & I was much amused. The Fusileers are going to act Plays but as Coll. Simcoe does not like to see Officers so employed he does not intend to go to the Theatre again.[82]

From this report, one would surmise it was a mixed company: British officers and local francophones, probably using skills first acquired in the secondary educational system and little used since then. Mrs Simcoe was not the only one impressed with the abilities of these Young Canadian Gentlemen: The *Gazette* had praised their performance in Beaumarchais' *Barber of Seville*, given on 26 February 1791. When that play was repeated on 2 March, the newspaper had another glowing review:

> We have already observed how the Young Gentlemen who had offered this city, through their generosity, the pleasure of a few dramatic programmes, had merited the utmost applause. They gained that applause again in splendid fashion on Saturday, 26 February, in their performance of *Le Malade imaginaire* and *The Barber of Seville*, and once again in their presentation of the latter play on the 2nd of this month [March]. They distinguished themselves to a high degree in this performance, to the extent that the audience prevailed upon them to repeat a whole act. It is really astonishing that they staged this work to such a degree of perfection, since the plays appear to demand all the skills and experience of professional actors for their success. His Excellency General Clark honoured the performance with his presence, and seemed highly satisfied with it.[83]

Despite discreet interventions of the clergy, this company of amateurs, with occasional changes of name and personnel, continued to delight theatre-goers in the capital until April 1796, after which time stage performances in French seem to have disappeared completely until the autumn of 1804. In Montreal, programs continued to be presented in November 1796, and on 10 and 31 January of the following year, by an association still (or again) calling itself a Théâtre de Société and which appears to have included members of Quesnel's original company. Thereafter drama in that city was also eclipsed until late 1804. In other words, not a single play is known to have been performed in French in Lower Canada between 1797 and 1804, and the flame seemed to have gone out. Yet despite the discouragement of individual actors and troupe members, an interest in dramatic arts must have been maintained, for as early as 1802 a small group of devotees had been formed in Quebec in an attempt to create another society theatre. There were some influential members among them the printer John Neilson and Louis de Salaberry, an important member of the legislature, but it would be two years before they found a building appropriate for their plans. When the Théâtre Patagon opened its doors in October 1804, they were ready, and on 25 October they offered, predictably, Molière (*Le Mariage forcé*) but also, for the first known performance of one of Racine's works since the days of Frontenac, his comedy *Les Plaideurs*, proof of the literary education of those responsible for the program.[84] The next month they came back with a surer recipe: an evening of pure Molière (*Les Fourberies de Scapin* and *Le Médecin malgré lui*), the type of offering for which the French-Canadian élite had long shown their preference. But the high point of this first season came in the following January and February, when Quesnel's *Colas and Colinette* was revived, with great success, along with plays by Regnard (*La Sérénade*) and the more modern Destouches (*Le Tambour nocturne*, which quickly became a favourite).[85]

It is probably no coincidence that theatre returned to Montreal about the same time, and again through the efforts of a group of amateurs calling itself a 'society' (ie, 'upper' society) theatre. This group presented, on 29 November 1804, Thomas Corneille's adaptation of Molière's *Festin de pierre* and Brueys' *Avocat Patelin*, followed on 28 December by *Le Médecin malgré lui* (staged in Quebec a month earlier) and *Le Barbier de Séville*. It is curious also that a month later (25 January 1805) Montreal's Théâtre de Société offered *Le Tambour nocturne*, a month before its presentation in Quebec City. Was there collaboration between the two companies now, or was this a natural choice of program for Lower Canada at the time, given the international political situation?[86] No direct contacts between the two groups have yet been proven, but of course the information communicated by newspapers about projected performances would have been enough to suggest to one group that they try the other's repertoire.

After one more presentation on 22 February 1805 (Molière's *L'Avare* and Regnard's *Retour imprévu*), francophone theatre disappeared from Montreal for more than ten years. Plays continued to be staged in Quebec City every year until 26 November 1808, after which there was no known performance until the last day of 1814. But these seasons were short (only two performances in 1807, for example), and sometimes announced programs had to be cancelled for unspecified, but pressing, reasons. It is legitimate to suspect the clergy's hand in these curtailments, as the authors of a recent and highly informative study of the relationships between Church and stage in Quebec, Jean Laflamme and Rémi Tourangeau, have done.[87] We have an excellent example of the attitude of the Catholic hierarchy towards theatre about this time in a letter written by Bishop Plessis to Judge Jonathan Sewell in 1809, preserved in the Archives of the Seminary of Quebec. The communication deals with the case of one Joseph Tardy, who had apparently wished to attend or perhaps to participate in a dramatic program to be offered that evening 27 February during Lenten season, and who had been supported in his wish by the judge:

> Monsieur,
> Since I was afraid I could not find a free moment today to answer your letter, I have directed Jos. Tardy to follow his Confessor's instructions, since this is a case of conscience. I have just found a brief respite from my duties, and am now using that interval to present my respects to you.
>
> On your testimony, I am quite persuaded that the two plays to be performed at the theatre this evening are as expurgated as any plays can be: but they are still plays. Is it fitting that a Christian should attend them? Society folk will say, yes; the Fathers of the Church, and all Catholic theologians, ancient and modern, since their time, will say, no. Given this difference of opinion, whom should I follow, if not those who, by their very calling, are entrusted to lead men on the path towards Salvation?
>
> In the public instruction which it is my duty to offer, I have had occasion to condemn this type of entertainment as being against the principles of the Gospel. If I were now to permit an individual to do that which I have forbidden the multitude, I would be guilty of a high degree of inconsistency, and I am sure that you do not expect this of me. Thus, out of considerations of morality and consistency, I could not allow one of my flock to take part, even once, in the entertainment in question. In the present instance, the fact of our having just entered the season of Lent fortifies my conviction. Indeed, I am persuaded that the Clergy of your own Church would not decide otherwise, however disagreeable it may be for them, as for me, to differ in opinion with a person of your rank and merit.
> I am, Sir, yours (etc.).[88]

There is no doubting the sincerity of Bishop Plessis' conviction in the matter, and this is the man who held the authority and direction of the Roman Catholic Church in his firm grasp for a generation. Just as Joseph Tardy had to do what his confessor had told him, so it was for all those who desired to remain in communion with the Church in Lower Canada. A French Canadian's religious life was inseparable from his social.

But one way that francophone amateurs could still present an occasional play for the public was to do so in the presence, or with the official blessing of, the British governor. Montreal obviously had less access to that sort of patronage than did the capital, and this no doubt accounts to some extent for the more frequent performance of French plays in Quebec City during this period. Thus when theatre returned to Lower Canada after an eight-year absence, on 31 December 1814, the troupe presenting two plays that evening enjoyed the presence of the governor, Sir George Prevost. The works performed were from Molière and Brueys, so the Society of Young French-Canadian Gentlemen was daring neither in its choice of name nor plays.[89] There appears to have been no reaction from the Church on this occasion, and one suspects this was because of Prevost's implicit approval of the performance. The next year a more ambitious group, styling itself the 'Society of Young Artists,' set out to offer plays in both Quebec and Montreal. It too did not elicit any known, specific response from the clergy. Perhaps the reason this time was that the Young Artists were foreigners, with no roots in Lower Canada, and no apparent intention to remain there.[90]

Between 17 May and 14 October 1815, this troupe offered ten programs of one play each, seven in Quebec and three in Montreal. A summer season was something of a novelty, although the fact that seven of these performances were of Molière plays (*Le Médecin malgré lui*, *M. de Pourceaugnac*, *Les Fourberies de Scapin*) was not. But the young players experimented also with two much more modern plays, *Le Déserteur* by Sedaine and Monsigny, and Louis Carmontelle's *L'Enragé*. Whence the Young Artists came and whither they disappeared after their performance on 14 October is not known. Were they refugees from France, arriving in Lower Canada via England or the United States? Their manager seems to have been an anglophone by the name of Ingliss, and it has been speculated that others in the troupe may have been as well. Having no local roots, they would have been little susceptible to a campaign waged directly against them by Church authorities. But they disappeared in the fall of 1815 and no more is heard about them.

Significantly, a month after the Young Artists had proclaimed their intention of staying on to entertain Canadians throughout the winter, another and apparently quite different group, appropriating to itself the same title of 'Society of Young French-Canadians' as the company which had performed before Governor Prevost on 31 December 1814, was organized in Montreal. They immediately ran into stiff opposition from clerical and non-clerical sources, and one suspects that their choice of program accounts for much of the antipathy: Voltaire's *Death of Caesar* (La Mort de César), and Molière's *Amour Médecin* (Doctor Love), enacted on 24 November. *The Death of Caesar* is the first known play by Voltaire staged in Canada.[91] Even the Montreal *Gazette*, not generally concerned with such matters, published a stern letter from a critic signing himself

'Lentulus,' and taking the amateurs to task. The communication reads in full:

A frightful conspiracy, perfected for a month or more, was finally unveiled last Friday evening by a group calling itself 'Amateurs.' Julius Caesar was massacred, on this occasion, by new conspirators, more enthusiastic and more audacious than were Brutus, Caius, and their sworn allies in ancient Rome. It is amazing that this new assassination was not smothered in its infancy, though the magistrates of this city were well informed of its existence. Even Bonaparte would have been opposed.[92]

Articles and counter-articles then appeared, and many more were sent to the newspapers but suppressed without publication. There was considerable change of personnel within the troupe, most probably as a result of this public debate, and the performance of both plays was the last by that original group. But they persisted in their commitment to public theatre, and succeeded in enacting at least fourteen plays by the end of the following year,[93] all of them less reproachable than Voltaire's. Quebec City's stage, too, came to life for a time, due to a group styling itself 'Amateurs du Théâtre Français' (Lovers – or Amateurs – of French Theatre), offering a limited program leaning heavily towards Beaumarchais and Molière. The newspapers in both cities again provided a forum for those who felt strongly for and against dramatic activity of this sort. Montreal led the way, with ringing articles signed 'Argus' and 'Cato,' which delighted in sniping, through apparent discussion of drama, at the French-Canadian clergy. Naturally, sonorous voices were soon raised in their defence, the most notable appearing in the *Gazette* on 20 January 1817. It begins:

MR. BROWN [editor of the *Gazette*],
    It was not without great displeasure that readers of the latest issues of the *Sun* and the *Spectateur Canadien* have followed the comments signed 'Argus' and 'Cato,' which strive to ridicule various respectable members of the clergy of this town, in the full knowledge that there would be no response forthcoming from them. Without entering into a detailed refutation of their arguments in support of Theatre, I shall for the moment limit myself to stating to Argus that he is blind as a bat, despite all his eyes; and to Cato, that he is a very poor Censor; that it is quite untrue that St. Thomas Aquinas ever approved of Theatre; and that neither Leo X or any of his successors ever had a theatre, inside the Vatican or

elsewhere; and that the Popes have never authorized a public stage in any of the dependencies of the Holy See; that if such a stage was tolerated, along with other places of prostitution, it was only in order to prevent thereby some greater evil. Since one of these correspondents speaks a good deal about 'morality' in his communication, I shall ask every educated man if the plays performed by the players of this town on their Stage, such as *Le Médecin malgré lui, Le Tambour nocturne, Le Trésor caché, George Dandin, Le Malade imaginaire, Le Barbier de Séville* really impart lessons apt to improve public morals; or if they are not, rather, liable to corrupt them? Amorous intrigues; ridiculing of parents and guardians; scorn for the sacred bonds of marriage; low, coarse jokes; indecent language: there you have the common, base, comic material which these Gentlemen Actors have chosen in their quest to reform public morality and lead their audience towards Virtue; whilst the great Bossuet, the famous Rollin, the eloquent lawyer Boissy, several learned personages in England, nay even Jean-Jacques Rousseau, have all publicly decried Comedy and Theatre in their works, as being dangerous and more likely to pervert morals than to correct them. I feel there is no point in my quoting in my support the authority of the Church Councils, since that is a source which Catos and Arguses and their adherents would not recognize, and which they would make mock of in the same modest way they have treated the preachers of the Gospel who protested against that theatre which these Gentlemen call a *Théâtre de Société*, although the first comer is welcome to enter, if he has a dollar on him![94]

Exchanges of this sort continued to maintain interest in the theatre in 1817, but the interest was of the wrong sort. Defections from the troupe continued, with replacements coming from officers of the regular forces or the militia. The company was dissolved in May that year, and the stages in Montreal remained devoid of francophone activity until June 1819. Was the last program offered by this harassed association of amateurs, on 16 May 1817, intended as a Parthian shot at the forces which had made life so difficult for them? The plays offered were Dancourt's *Le Tuteur*, not likely to arouse particular opposition, but more significantly, Voltaire's *Le Fanatisme, ou Mahomet le Prophète*, a denunciation of intolerance in any form.

The determined amateurs of Quebec City, encouraged by the support of Governor Sherbrooke, held out a little longer. But French-language theatre there died out in January 1818, not to reappear, as far as is known, for another five and a half years. Wars of attrition favour the side with the stronger reserves, and the 'moralists' had only to be patient under the reign of Bishop Plessis. As Baudoin Burger observes with typical succinctness: 'For every, or nearly every new season, these amateurs had to re-establish a troupe, look for a theatre, attract an audience ... As a result of their efforts they were constantly at odds with the clergy and weakly supported by their subscribers, and had to abandon their projects.'[95] Thus theatrical activity was predictably cyclical, and the bottom of a cycle was reached in 1818. However, there was one interesting side effect of this busy period, 1815-18: the brief flowering of a third centre of activity, Trois-Rivières, where, with the help of the industrious nineteen-year-old Ludger Duvernay, later to make a mark in journalism and politics, five mixed dramatic programs were presented between December 1818 and April 1819. Offerings ranged from the predictable Molière to Bruey's adaptation of that medieval 'hit,' L'Avocat Pathelin, but also included Dorvigny's Les Battus paient l'amende (1779), Carmontelle's L'Enragé (1774), and Florian's Deux Billets (1779). Little is known about this brief season in Trois-Rivières, but it would be a long time before another was attempted.

When another attempt at establishing a viable theatre in Montreal and Quebec was undertaken in 1824-5, little had changed. Conditions, as Professor Burger has convincingly pointed out, scarcely evolved between 1789 and 1825. The enthusiasm and the capital pooled by daunted amateurs (notaries, journalists, members of the liberal professions for the most part) sufficed to energize a troupe for a season, a year or two. But the opposition in the 1820s was, if not as visible, as rigorous as it had been in 1694. 'In 1824,' the chronicler of the Ursulines reports,

> a certain number of young lawyers and doctors came up with the
> idea of re-establishing theatre [in Quebec City] ... Around the time
> of the carnaval they gave a performance which caused quite a stir,
> and then announced that after Easter they would stage another
> comedy, as a relief for people after their Lenten penance. But on
> Quasimodo Sunday [first Sunday after Easter] Monseigneur Plessis
> took to the pulpit and prohibited everybody from going to the the-
> atre; and such was his authority, that he was obeyed.[96]

Perhaps many did obey, but by no means all, for the performances in question (Molière's Fourberies de Scapin and Racine's Plaideurs) were given, on 24 April 1824. As often as the flame was beaten back, a spark survived somewhere, to smoulder and eventually kindle another cycle. Clovis Demers, in his thesis 'Musique et théâtre à Québec, 1764-1800,' remarks:

As soon as the Church's vigilance eased up a moment, a few plays were hastily staged ... and even young ladies fresh from their years in the Ursulines' convent school would go to the theatre, to the despair of their former teachers: '... The girls entrusted to us for their education, are brought up on these false principles. As soon as they receive their First Communion, they are withdrawn from our classes and brought to social gatherings and plays. One can imagine what misfortunes follow these disastrous pleasures' (*Les Ursulines de Québec*, III, 163) ... Then, once again, prohibitions would be imposed.[97]

The Church and the stage were nearing a stand-off: in any direct confrontation the former would surely win, but it could no longer, by formal, general interdiction, prevent that innate human instinct for the drama from seeking satisfaction. In fact, until after mid-century, it no longer tried to do so by direct intervention. When the intransigent Joseph-Octave Plessis died in 1825, his death represented, in a sense, the passing of an era.

ANGLOPHONE THEATRE IN LOWER CANADA TO THE OPENING OF THE THEATRE ROYAL (1825)

That year was an important one for the evolution of theatre in Canada for another reason: the opening of the first modern, full-scale building devoted exclusively to theatre in Canada, the Theatre Royal in Montreal.[98] Up to that point, there had been a distinct parallel observable in the evolution of English- and French-language theatre in Lower Canada. Let us now take a brief look at the anglophone stage until 1825, in order thus to throw more light upon French-language activity in the same period.

We have seen that British troops stationed in Lower Canada amused themselves and the public by presenting occasional plays from the classical repertoire, in French. This activity seems to have lessened after 1785, when the first English-language performances took place and a series of visits by American troupes led to a natural preference for their offerings.

The repertoire of these visiting professional companies was almost always more modern and topical than that of the amateur francophone troupes. Thus in Quebec in 1786 we have Allen's American Company performing, in Solomon's Dance Hall, *The Siege of Quebec; or The Death of General Wolfe*, some sixteen years after its performance in London. That play would be performed again frequently in the period. Similar in topic but less temperate in tone was the older *Liberty Asserted; or Canada Restored*, performed in the capital in February 1790, by another American troupe, that of Worsdale.[99] French Canadians, on the other hand, could never venture into the realm of politics or of recent history in their presentations. This necessity of avoiding all that might seem contentious was another factor militating in favour of the tried and true, the traditional and the inoffensive. What their reaction was to the performance of these chauvinistic British plays can only be surmised, in the continuing absence of any newspaper representing their interests. The fact of American actors performing such plays should not surprise us when we see that, in the full heat of the War of 1812, another American company performed Sheridan's stridently pro-British *Pizarro*, prefacing it with a stirring address entitled 'The Invasion; or Britons Strike Home.'[100] In certain cases, art does know no frontiers – especially when the artists' livelihood and safe-conduct depend upon the whim of the public.

But it was not only in the topicality of its offerings that English-language theatre had a clear advantage. The physical facilities available to them, although scarcely of a 'professional' level by today's standards, were none the less greatly superior in the main to those at the disposal of francophone actors, and continued to improve. At first, of course, the troops had their barracks; by extension, the Jesuits' residence and other such requisitioned buildings. As time went by and the civilian anglophone population grew, troupes had easier access to halls, lodges, and temples built by prospering British merchants and transformed, with variable success, into theatres. Not, initially, without frequent problems and concomitant financial risk: a patchy sequence of documents preserved in the Archives of the Quebec Seminary, involving three principals in an unnamed theatrical enterprise operating in that city in 1789, shows the seriousness of the legal difficulties one could encounter.[101] As amateur English productions became steadily eclipsed by touring American companies, those problems increased, sometimes with drastic results, witness the case of the transplanted Bostonian John Mills who arrived in Montreal in June 1810 with an eager troupe and great ambitions, but who by January of the next year was forced to abandon his lodgings and move with his entire family into the drafty theatre building (The Montreal Theatre) itself, in which sparse surroundings he soon contracted jaundice and died.[102] Then there is the largely legendary adventure of another company led by William Henry Prigmore which, in the dread Laurentian winter, set out in a great sledge from Montreal to Quebec City, all bravely cuddled in furs and blankets. The company, it is said, never reached its destination, and all, including horses, were assailed and devoured by wolves![103]

French-language troupes did not encounter dangers of that sort, one of the few advantages they enjoyed being the fact that they were all amateur, and thus all local, devoting spare time and funds to prepare and stage their plays. Discouragement, not financial ruin, was the worst eventuality they faced. To demonstrate the difference, one has only to recall the fate of the first company of touring French professionals to visit Canada, just after the opening of Montreal's Theatre Royal. This was a troupe led by one Scévola Victor, which ventured into Montreal (there was also a brief side tour to Quebec) between February and May 1827. They were doubly unfortunate, since their performances seem to have aroused the Church's hostility and very little public support. With bankruptcy imminent, Monsieur Victor himself disappeared, along with their meagre remaining funds, leaving the rest of the troupe to the charity of local citizens!

But by and large, English-speaking companies held decided advantages, not the least of which was official support from the administration, from the more and more prosperous anglophone merchant class, from religious, charitable, or social institutions (the Masonic lodges were particularly consistent in their support of such activity), from the newspapers and periodicals which often seized upon the occasion of an especially remarkable performance of an English play – or any overt attempt by the Catholic clergy to interfere with the performance of a French one – as an opportunity to condemn a society which allowed its religious leaders thus to interfere in such important cultural activity. The very frequency of their overstatement of the case makes it suspicious. As Baudoin Burger remarked, after a careful study of this type of intervention:

> When anglophone critics comment upon francophone performances, some of which are not even mentioned in French-Canadian newspapers, their aim is not so much that of stimulating these amateur performances themselves, as of opposing the French-Canadian clergy which has been attacking those productions. The most detailed commentary upon a French-language play was elicited by the performances of a play by Quesnel [*Colas and Colinette*]; and this was because those performances revived the whole question of the morality of theatre, whence the argumentation and quarrelling which found a forum in the newspapers.[104]

Professor Burger's statement may be amply corroborated from even a rapid sampling of the English press in Canada in this period. Here, from the *Canadian Magazine and Literary Repository* of 1823, is a fine example of the direction such 'criticism' could take:

> In Catholic countries, actors have always been treated with great contumely ... Such is priestcraft: they who reprobated stage-players

on the score of a vicious profession, preached the holiness and infallibility of Popes who committed incest and sealed their crimes with blasphemy. The latest instance of bigot zeal exerted against the inanimate body of a performer in France, was after the return of the Bourbons in January, 1815, when the funeral of Madame Raucourt, on arriving at the burying-ground of Père La Chaise, at Paris, was refused the rite of burial by the minister, who wished to restore, with the temporary, the spiritual customs of old times.[105]

Nor was this intermittent offensive directed exclusively against the 'papist' church and its 'benighted' ministers: theatre was clearly considered by some editors and correspondents as an important tool for Anglicizing reluctant francophones. This point was often made in the few years preceding the establishment of the Theatre Royal, when there was something of a campaign in English-language newspapers for such a venture. Thus the *Canadian Magazine* would write, again in 1823:

> Were it possible, by means of a well-regulated English Theatre, to draw some of the French Canadians to the representation of some of [Shakespeare's] best pieces, the effects would doubtless be salutary, by tending to impart those feelings so much in unison with British hearts. To encourage this attendance, and to promote these beneficial consequences, I would recommend that considerable attention should be bestowed on procuring scenery appropriate and striking. This will not appear insignificant or frivolous, if we once reflect, that the first objects of Canadian imitation have been our dress and external behaviour.

Unperturbed by the thought of French-Canadian readers (and there were some) of the magazine, our writer goes on to suggest including lots of music (probably fiddles for those foot-stomping yokels?), and then adduces the most telling argument of all:

> [W]ere the French Canadians casually drawn to our theatre, either by the love of novelty, or by the attraction of scenery and music, even though their knowledge of English were at first imperfect, they might there receive such a stimulus to improvement in our language, from the natural workings of curiosity, that they would soon participate in all those advantages arising from the Drama, which I have foretold to their fellow subjects.[106]

One can see the pressures and competition any francophone company had to confront during this period. Whereas the English-speaking players could rely upon a small but fairly predictable audience, literate and generally unprejudiced as to the morality of theatrical activity in itself, the former had to appeal to a very small élite. The journalist-historian-poet Michel Bibaud calculated that in 1825, for example, of the entire francophone population of the province (something over 400,000 people) only about 3.5 per cent could read.[107] Considering the classical, 'literary' nature of most plays presented in French, we know that it was to these literate few among the population that they were directed. Theatre, in French or in English, was not for the common man in this country at the time. Research by Baudoin Burger has shown that the average price of a ticket for the cheapest type of seat (the 'gods' or gallery) at an English play was equivalent in cost to a day's wage for an established teacher. The cheapest ticket for a French play was *generally double that amount*.[108] How many teachers, then or now, would be willing to sacrifice two full days' pay to see an amateur performance?

Perhaps the point should be repeated: all French-speaking troupes and actors were amateurs during this period, in contrast with their English-speaking counterparts, and were therefore subject to the fluctuations in quality of performance that one would expect. Worse still: female actors were almost unknown and were of the lowest skills and reputation in the rare cases where they did appear. Female roles were regularly played by men or boys, with concomitant sacrifice to verisimilitude. The Englishman John Lambert, travelling in Lower Canada in 1806-7, formed a low opinion even of the anglophone representations he had witnessed. Except for a couple of British officers he saw in an amateur performance, he found none who did not 'murder the best scenes of our dramatic poets.' He then went on to observe:

> It may be easily conceived how despicably low the [French-] Canadian theatricals must be, when boys are obliged to perform the female characters: the only actress being an old superannuated demirep, whose drunken Belvideras, Desdemonas, and Isabellas, have often *enraptured* a [French-] Canadian Audience. ... If they could procure a few females, and reduce Mrs. R., that *spirited* actress to a candle snuffer, their company might succeed tolerably well; although I much doubt whether the inhabitants are inclined to spend money enough in dramatic spectacles, to support a company for any length of time.[109]

In this parallel between the English and French stage in Lower Canada, during that period before 1825 when comparison is possible and useful, one must also mention the almost constant state of armed hostility between France and England before 1816, and the strict surveillance of any French-speaking immigration to this country for generations thereafter. Thus the most important catalyst for theatrical activity in English, the visits of touring American and British companies, was entirely lacking on the French-Canadian circuit until the visit of Scévola Victor's troupe in 1827. A longer view must also include the as yet invisible advantage that would redound to native dramaturgy in French, a generation later: as performances of English and American plays, especially the classics, interpreted by American or British actors, became the norm in English Canada, the urge or indeed the opportunity to create a Canadian repertoire was minimal. From their decided advantage with regard to theatrical activity in its most general sense, English-speaking Canadians, in a classic paradigm, through their reliance upon imported products, would long be unable to develop native talent. This is a topic to which I shall return later: it was not obvious in 1825, when the opening of John Molson's Theatre Royal seemed to herald a new age for English culture in Lower Canada.

The Beginnings of a Native Tradition
in Theatre

POLITICAL THEATRE AND PARATHEATRE IN
LOWER CANADA TO 1834

The opening of the Theatre Royal underlines the hegemony Montreal had
begun to enjoy by 1825 as a town which had become the centre of anglophone influence in Lower Canada and which, only seven years later,
would become incorporated as a city.[1] It was more probably due to the
pragmatism of the Theatre Royal's management than to its magnanimity
that their stage, it was soon made clear, was open to French productions
as well. Although local troupes were slow in responding, it was not long
before touring companies, committed to a turn in New York, Boston, and
perhaps Philadelphia (for French theatre remained quite popular in the
United States),[2] began occasionally to add Montreal to their circuit. Thus,
as we have seen, the troupe led by Scévola Victor made history, of a dubious sort, in its foray into Canada from New York in 1827. Ironically, his
absconding with the company's funds seems to have stirred up local theatrical activity, for there then was a round of benefit performances, by and
for his poor abandoned thespians!

Scévola Victor was the first of a series of transplanted Frenchmen who
exercised an important influence upon the development of francophone
theatre in Canada throughout the 1830s: people like Firmin Prud'homme,
Hyacinthe Leblanc de Marconnay, and Napoléon Aubin who, within a
year or two of their arrival, wound up in the forefront of literary, and
sometimes political, activity. We shall return to these influential immigrants shortly, but let us first focus on the French-Canadian actors, for it
is they upon whom any real and enduring success depended.

Towards the end of Monseigneur Plessis' twenty years as head of the Canadian Church, more and more overt intellectual dissatisfaction displayed itself among the French-Canadian élite.[3] This disenchantment was as much political as religious, for the attitudes which led to the Rebellion of 1837-8 were already forming. The educated and concerned Québécois had far more serious things on his mind than theatre or literature. The first of his concerns was politics, and that was the stage on which his energies would evolve, frequently in opposition to the wishes of Church or civil administration. To the extent that theatre might serve his political ends, as it had been used for so long by English-speaking Lower Canadians to serve theirs, it was a welcome tool. And it was a tool which had been fashioned over a long period already, by the time it came to its fullest flowering in the series of short plays that appeared in 1834, and which are generally referred to as the 'Status Quo' comedies.

A basic cause of the perennial difficulties encountered by theatre in French Canada until fairly recent times was the deep-seated ambivalence of that society's attitude towards it. On the one hand the Roman Catholic Church, the most influential institution in Quebec society, remained firmly opposed to any form of public theatricals, an opposition that was particularly consistent under the leadership of Bishop Plessis. Yet, on the other hand, to complete the dichotomy, every educated French Canadian had been exposed since his earliest catechism classes to paratheatrical pedagogic methods, to the extent that the dramatized dialogue/debate had become central to this educational system. This was particularly remarkable at higher levels. At the Jesuits' College in Quebec, as we have seen, plays were a legitimate part of the tradition. But just as importantly, the dramatization of the learning process was ingrained: topics of debate were set and pupils made to practise against each other on a daily basis. Once a week a prepared encounter took place, on Saturday morning (hence its name, 'la Sabbatine'); once a month, an even more formalized *disputatio* ('la Menstruale'), in which students were encouraged to impersonate the real or fictitious characters whose ideas they might be espousing and once a year, towards the end of term, came the only public session comprised of such dialogues, 'a sort of dialectical tournament, with all the dramatic interest of a wrestling-match,' as L.-P. Audet has characterized this tradition.[4] When the Jesuits' College was forced to close in 1768, its role was assumed by the Quebec Seminary, with the same pedagogic traditions. Theatre, in other words, remained suspect in that tradition, but the theatricality of intense debate was deliberately cultivated.

To repeat, this was in addition to the plays staged at various times during the academic year by various classes in the schools and *collèges*. Even during the long period of Plessis' ascendancy the performance, under strictly controlled conditions, of plays and extracts from plays seems to have continued to some extent. And as the system of *collèges classiques* took root and began to expand, this tradition of amateur theatricals expanded with them – all performances, it must be stressed, strictly supervised and not accessible to the public. There is no doubt that staff and students eagerly anticipated these presentations, in many ways making them the highlight of the academic year.

Thus the entire class of educated adults had developed a taste for dramatic forms, a taste that could not be entirely suppressed. The Church might make it difficult for amateur companies to enact plays, and impossible for those companies to last beyond a performance or two, but the natural or, more likely, the *ingrained* theatricality of the French Canadian had to express itself in some other fashion. Politics, with its innate drama, was a natural outlet for that theatrical training.

The tendency to dramatize discussion and debate was typical of the public press as well. Only two years after the Treaty of Paris the first newspaper appeared in Quebec City, and it and its successors exhibit, from their first editions, a strong leaning towards the dialogue form, particularly in cases where the topic is political, and thus potentially contentious, in nature. An obvious instance of this is a series of reports, English in one column, French in the other, purporting to be transcripts of the questions posed to Benjamin Franklin by a select committee of the British Parliament in 1766, on the subject of the infamous Stamp Act; with, of course, Franklin's responses to those questions. The dialogue appears on the front page of the *Quebec Gazette/Gazette de Québec* for Monday, 8 December 1766, and the sequels continue as first-page material for the next four issues (the *Gazette*, at this time, published once a week), terminating on 5 January 1767.[5]

The interrogation is interesting on intrinsically historical grounds, for the debate is presented in such a way as to ensure that readers' sympathies go to Franklin and the cause he represents. Obviously, one must be careful not to imply that a dialogue like this one is, in any real sense, 'theatre.' At best, this is paradramatic journalism. The format was doubtless chosen because it afforded a livelier, more effective, and perhaps more important, a far safer means of communicating the controversial views of the great American advocate than any series of articles or editorials.

A somewhat different rationale appears to underlie the next example of this form of presentation. It is entitled 'Liberty of the Press: Debate in Dialogue Form' and appeared a dozen years later in Montreal's first

French newspaper, *La Gazette du commerce et littéraire pour la ville et district de Montréal*. This dialogue too was topical to a greater degree than is first apparent, for debate on the subject of the press and its liberties was then under way in Canada, a debate exacerbated by the role of that medium in the current revolt of the American colonies. The subject, moreover, was of peculiar interest to the editor of that paper, Valentin Jautard, and its printer, Fleury Mesplet, since both had just experienced direct pressure (and were soon to experience a good deal more) from the British administration of the province.[6]

The two interlocutors in the text are the Admirer (*Admirateur*) and the Censor (*Censeur*), and they hew pretty closely to the arguments one would expect, given those titles. The Admirer is soon reduced to playing the part of 'straight man' in this discussion, for the Censor has most of the better lines and the last word. The conclusion reached is that the few 'dangerous' authors must be restrained, for the good of society: a surprisingly moderate one, given the editor and the time.[7]

Jautard had a decided preference for the dialogue form, and returned to it frequently during the brief life of this first newspaper in Montreal. Thus the issue for 11 November 1778 features a 'Dialogue between a Modern Rationalist and a Capuchin Novice,' in which the Rationalist (*Raisonneur*) interrogates the neophyte at length as to his reasons for entering a religious order at such an early age. Their exchange lasts almost two full pages (of the normal four in each edition), at the end of which the Novice appears to win out. It is, however, a Pyrrhic victory, in that many of the questions raised by the Rationalist have resonances going far beyond the answers the Novice can assemble. But one knows the strategy: had it not been perfected by Voltaire himself by this time?

Except to the extent (historically, a considerable one) that religion is politics in French Canada, this is not a 'political' dialogue, nor in general are the others appearing in Lower Canadian newspapers before the advent of the first paper established, owned, and directed by French Canadians, in 1806. For the intervening years, the next examples I shall cite were printed separately and circulated in pamphlet form, in the 1790s.

Two of them survive from 1792: a *Conversation on the Subject of the Charlesbourg Election*, written by Michel-Amable Berthelot d'Artigny, and an anonymous pamphlet entitled *Dialogue on a Current Topic, between Several Candidates and a Free and Independent Voter from the City of Quebec*.[8] The first of these is, of all the similar pieces we shall consider, the only one to provide its author's real name, and may have been a model for later publications of the sort. Its intention is blatantly political: the author, a French-Canadian lawyer who had been an unsuccessful candidate in the elections of spring 1792, ascribes his defeat, in this dramatized dialogue between two well-informed electors, to patent irregularities which had been allowed to take place, particularly at the poll in Charlesbourg, north of Quebec City. The text comprises ten pages and the number of copies printed is unknown. It is fair to say that the author displays no great literary gifts, but perhaps his persuasiveness is indicated by the fact that one of his successful rivals soon resigned, and Berthelot d'Artigny was then elected in his stead, by acclamation.

The second text from 1792 presents a conversation among six individuals, obviously chosen to represent the body politic: on the one hand a candidate in the imminent elections of the spring of 1792, and on the other a *seigneur*, a lawyer, a merchant, a mechanic, and a farmer. The views it espouses are stoutly patriotic, pro-British, and supportive of the new constitution. What is significant about the pamphlet, from our point of view, is neither its form nor its prosaic content, but rather the fact that, according to its title-page, it was originally intended to be *read aloud* at the regularly fortnightly meeting of the Constitutional Club, on Saturday, 19 May 1792, by one of that club's members. Other members arranged the printing of the three-page text, 'which an unforeseen accident prevented from being read' (*qu'un accident imprevue a empechéz d'être lû*), says the suspect French on the title-page.

If, in fact, the reading aloud (by one person, or by several, one wonders?) in dramatized fashion of these dialogues was a normal or even occasional occurrence, an entirely different light obviously is cast upon their 'theatrical' qualities. With that consideration in mind, let us examine, this time in more detail, a third example of a pamphlet from the 1790s, with a broader context than the two which precede.

We know a good deal more about the background and genesis of this third text, *The Canadian and His Wife*, which appeared in 1794.[9] Its publication was elicited by the political and military situation in that year: with England and France formally at war, relations between the British colonies and the United States were strained. A good deal of revolutionary propaganda of American origin had begun to circulate in Canada and the British administration there was understandably nervous. A new law governing formation of militia units had been passed at the end of May 1794, based on the concept of universal male draft, with actual manpower decided by the drawing of lots. But Lord Dorchester's agents encountered serious problems in their attempt to enforce this draft, and for a time the situation appeared precarious if any real threat were to emerge from the south.

It was at this juncture that *The Canadian and His Wife* was circulated, in some 500 copies. As John E. Hare has pointed out in the excellent introduction to his re-edition of the text, we cannot be sure who the author was, but there are good reasons for believing it may have been François Baby, principal French-Canadian adviser to Dorchester. If it was not Baby, it was someone in a position like his, for as Professor Hare points out, it seems certain that the pamphlet was written by someone in government, since the Governor's office paid for its printing.

The dialogue is between the French Canadian André and his wife, Brigitte, with their son, Joseph, appearing for one brief remark at the end. This time also the subject is highly political and specifically Canadian. André is a very well-informed citizen indeed, and is at no loss to explain, in condescending terms, how sensible and how essential the whole idea of a defensive militia is. Brigitte, on the other hand, has obviously been influenced by the anti-military propaganda emanating from the United States and circulating surreptitiously: all the objections and reservations she voices are based on rumours she has heard. Her husband replies fully and patiently to each point raised, expatiating particularly on the topic so much in the air on both continents, the question of liberty:

> Free, I assure you we are free – although we have established a Militia as they [the Americans] have done, we don't head off to attack others on their own territory. We marry when we wish; we work our soil as and when we please; we sell our lands, or barter them, along with the goods we produce, for as high a price as we can obtain. We have our grain sold abroad, and are not forced to accept in payment paper money as they [the Americans] are; and we attend the Church of our choice.

André, the simple *habitant*, is quite at home in even more abstract discourse on the nature of happiness and justice, and all of it in impeccable French. Brigitte, by the eighteenth page, is fully persuaded:

BRIGITTE
You are quite right, dear husband, and I feel our son Joseph should tell the Captain of Militia that he'll be ready to leave on short notice in four days' time.
ANDRÉ
Yes, that would be best, my dear wife. I say! – here's Joseph himself, let's see what he's got to say. Well, what do you think, son?
JOSEPH
I was listening to the two of you. I want to obey, and to serve my God, my King, and my Country. I shall do my duty just as you once did, father: you and a lot of others did it, and survived.

Thus ends *Le Canadien et sa femme*, with no attempt at humour or at breathing life and credibility into the personages who woodenly mouth their lines. Professor Hare wonders how effective such 'theatrical' propaganda could have been, since it is reliably estimated that about this time only some three per cent of the francophone population of Canada could read. May we not speculate, from the example of the second text from 1792 which was being printed only because an accident prevented its being read aloud to an assembled audience, that the form of this text and others like it is not gratuitous? That these texts, in other words, were intended to be read aloud, *dramatically*, by one or more of the favoured three per cent, for a group?

The third and last type of paradramatic literature which I shall identify, before returning to the Status Quo Comedies, was published, with minor exceptions, in the pages of the newspaper *Le Canadien*. Within a year after its establishment in 1806, this journal had adopted a strongly antagonistic tone, heightened with each passing election and leading inevitably to its suppression by civil authorities in 1810 for seven years. The first example we shall consider accompanies the issue of 29 August 1807 and is entitled *An Evening with the Candidate and His Girlfriend* (Veillée d'un candidat avec sa belle amie). With such a title, in a society whose public morals were as closely supervised as this one, one knows how the candidate in question will be treated!

Although not specifically identified, he appears to be Pierre-Amable de Bonne, the sitting member for the County of Quebec at the time, having previously represented the constituencies of York and Trois-Rivières. In these four pages his private morals and public principles are mercilessly portrayed, not without humour and skill. De Bonne, judge, member of the Executive Council, one of the chief spokesmen and 'pork-barrellers' for the Château Clique, founder of the rival newspaper, *Le Courier de Québec*, is made to paint his own character in his responses to the astute questions posed by his mistress. He is easily made to appear a thorough scoundrel, scornful of the credulity and ignorance of the Canadien electors whom he represents. The dialogue is direct and lively at times:

> – It'll all turn out all right, my dear: I have the French Canadians
> on my side: 'Les Canadiens sont des lurons, biribi,' ha!
> – What! the same Canadiens you've duped so often?
> – No offence, my dear: I know these Canadiens, I can count on them.
> – What! After all the tricks you tell me you've played against them,
> you think they won't be resentful?
> – You don't know French Canadians, my dear: you can dupe them
> as much as you want, then bring them back to heel when you

want. All you have to do is sing a few verses for them, tell them they're a great lot, 'des Lurons, biribi,' and other nonsense, and you're sure to have your way with them. A few bows their way to soften them up, a few words against the English to work them up. That's no problem for me![10]

Judge De Bonne quickly became the favourite target of *Le Canadien* and its four French-Canadian founders. Thus the issue of 14 May 1808 provides a similar dialogue, included this time in the regular columns of the newspapers, untitled and anonymous. Again the timing is important: just before the elections to be held in the summer of that year. In it De Bonne is again made to appear ridiculous and vain, proud of a speech he has just delivered at Beauport, for example, in which the keynote had been the comparison of his own political sufferings 'with those of Our Lord, and a few others like that.' And when he spoke at Charlesbourg, there were those who compared him with Saint Augustine! What worked in the countryside will surely be good enough for urban electors, for do they not all belong to the group he scorns? 'I guide my conduct by the number, and not the quality of the Electors. The vote of a knave is worth as much as that of a gentleman; it's the greater number that wins an election. And thank heavens, the numerical advantage does not lie on the side of decent folk!'[11] His nameless interlocutor (his secretary?) poses the same kind of leading questions as had his girlfriend in their dialogue the year before, but this time the text is totally devoid of humour, as a question comprising up to 350 words elicits a response just as tediously long. It is difficult to see how it could have been effective, whether read aloud or silently. De Bonne, in any case, continued to be re-elected with ease for the next few years. And it was because of libels of this nature that *Le Canadien* was suppressed and its printer and owners imprisoned some two years later.[12] Their campaign was too strident to have been successful.

Yet despite its apparent ineffectiveness, this is the type of political dialogue which served as direct ancestor to the first homegrown theatrical forms to appear in French Canada after cession. With the temporary suppression of *Le Canadien*, principal organ of the Canadien and Patriote causes before 1837 (the Patriotes were not organized until 1826), this vigorous form of journalistic paratheatre practically disappeared for a generation in Lower Canada. Apart from two highly tendentious dialogues apparently borrowed from foreign journals and dealing with the international situation,[13] one rare exception is a short piece in the renascent *Canadien* on 20 March 1822, dealing with the inextricable connections between religion, education, and politics in Lower Canada and entitled 'Dialogue between a *Curé* and a *Habitant*.'

The brief exchange is labelled a 'Communication,' and is remarkable for its directness and concision, as well as the fact that, for the first time in this sort of production in Canada, a realistic attempt is made to characterize the interlocutors by their level of speech. It begins:

CURÉ
Well, Pierre, any news?
HABITANT
No, I ain't got none, sir.
CURÉ
You didn't give any money for the Education Society?
HABITANT
No, sir. I ain't rich; and even if I was as rich as you, I wouldn't have given none![14]

The reason Pierre has not contributed to the campaign for establishing a comprehensive primary educational system (one of the goals of Bishop Plessis) is that he has learned that no school would be built in his own country parish, but only in the towns. Thus, he concludes, 'if we had given away our money, we would have been in a hell of a fix, we's got such a hard time scrapin' a livin' anyway.' So he will contribute nothing 'to eddycate the poor people that lives in town,' for he has enough problems of his own.

Here, in a quarter column, a politico-social problem is posed, two sides neatly identified, and a strategy proposed for the rural francophone majority. The piece is something of a minor masterpiece. By no coincidence, Bishop Plessis soon lost patience with Le Canadien (which, incidentally, he had himself helped to re-establish), and managed to have the paper suspended that same year. The contentious journal would not again become an important factor in French-Canadian politics until after its resuscitation in 1831 by a group led by Etienne Parent. And it was this group that found itself in the thick of the verbal fray represented by the Status Quo Comedies: themselves a natural culmination of long-smouldering animosities, as to their content; a natural evolution, as to their form, of the dramatized debates, pamphlets, and libels we have here encountered.

THE STATUS QUO COMEDIES (1834)

As the political divisions in Lower Canada became more pronounced in the years before the Patriote rebellion, journalistic warfare of the type evident in the De Bonne dialogue of 1808 again came to the fore, culminating in the sequence of Status Quo Comedies in 1834. The 'status quo' referred to is in itself explicable only in terms of the political situation which, on the Canadien side, focused more and more upon the person of Louis-Joseph Papineau; and on the other, Bureaucrate side, found its principal mouthpiece in the *Quebec Mercury* and (especially after the rupture between Papineau and its influential editor, John Neilson), the *Quebec Gazette/Gazette de Québec*. The Patriotes had by now become convinced of the innate injustice of the system under which the province was administered, at least as that system was interpreted by the Governor and Executive Council. The close circle of Papineau supporters (his 'clique,' later to be called his 'family') convened frequently during the winter of 1833-4 to summarize the various grievances they had been voicing for years, to formulate them for presentation to the legislature and, eventually, to the seat of British government in London. The resultant document became known as the '92 Resolutions,' and its supporters were soon labelled by the *Gazette*, 'Résolutionnaires.' Chief among its editors were Augustin-Norbert Morin, member for Bellechasse and co-founder of the influential paper *La Minerve* which, along with *Le Canadien*, served the Patriote cause; and the member for Montmorency, Elzéar Bédard, who presented the resolutions in the legislature on 17 February 1834.

Heated debate ensued, during which one of Papineau's supporters, Sabrevois de Bleury, excoriated the opposition for its firm attachment to the status quo. Neilson's *Gazette* leapt into the fray, supported by the shrill *Mercury*. The *Gazette*'s contributors accepted the collective pen-name, 'Friend of the Status Quo' (L'Ami du statu quo), and kept up a series of strongly-worded attacks on the 'Patriotes-Résolutionnaires' throughout March and April. *Le Canadien* and *La Minerve* under Ludger Duvernay responded in kind. The conflict escalated, in a sense, on 26 April, when the *Gazette* published a contribution in the form of a play wherein the principals identified with Papineau (but not, curiously, 'le chef' himself – perhaps because of Neilson's so recent and close collaboration with him) were taken to task. This is the first of the Status Quo Comedies, like all the rest never intended for performance, 'closet drama,' if one will, but decidedly couched in theatrical form.[15]

The scene is set in the library of the Legislative Assembly. Etienne Parent, who combined editorship of *Le Canadien* with the post of paid librarian, is trying frantically to compose a 'nice, sonorous editorial' on the theme of the 92 Resolutions, while a copy-boy stands impatiently by to hurry it off to press. Elzéar Bédard is the first to enter, and our pseudonymous author puts a revelatory salutation in his mouth: 'Well, good day, citizen editor,' he says, 'how are you today?' *Citoyen* could still evoke, in 1834, the spectre of the French Revolution and its worst excesses. The triple association Patriotes: Résolutionnaires: révolutionnaires is thus established, and would be developed throughout this and subsequent publications from the Status Quo side.

Then, with no great originality, the characters in the play enter in turn and reveal, in their own words, their motivations and machinations. Hector-Simon Huot, member for Portneuf and well known for his efforts to improve educational opportunities for francophones, reports on a campaign for signatures to a petition in favour of the Resolutions:

> Everything's going off marvelously! I've just had word from Pointe-aux-Trembles that our Resolutions passed through there with no problems. I've had news, too, from all the school-masters, whom I go round to visit every summer, as you know, and I can assure you that all is going well. It's amazing, the number of children's signatures we're going to get...[16]

This allegation about the use of minors' signatures had frequently appeared in the *Gazette*, in the communications signed 'A Friend of the Status Quo.' Whether the arrow was wide of the mark or not, its aim was clear.

Parent is then taken to task because his paper has been granted the printing concession for the Assembly, for which service he is still awaiting payment. On comes François-Xavier Garneau, back less than a year from his travels in England and France, and apparently still full of them. He is made to sound particularly radical, his speech brimming with revolutionary republicanism, seizing for example upon Huot's reference to a Member as 'The Honourable':

> 'Honourable'? – bah! If you had been to London and Paris as I have, *Messieurs* (excuse me, I meant to say *citoyens*), you would have seen what little fuss they make about 'honourables,' about marquesses, dukes, princes, or even kings! There, in those great cities, dustmen are treated with the utmost respect, for they belong to the people, they make up the proletariat.[17]

From what we know of Garneau's convictions, particularly those distilled over the next decade and a half into his great *Histoire du Canada*, this is good caricature, with a solid base to anchor the obvious distortion. But many of the personages so rudely lampooned in these comedies are now all but forgotten, with the result that one can no longer decide whether the author has seized upon some genuine characteristic and falsified it only by disproportion, or whether the individuals thus presented are the victims of unimaginative, one dimensional libel. Take, for instance, the case of Pierre Winter, lawyer and later judge: is the curious diction he is consistently assigned based on real speech habits of his? His interventions end with strange, rhyming phrases that resemble grammatical paradigms ('S'agirait-il donc de révolution, de guerre? Je le veux, nous le voulons. Je suis prêt, nous sommes prêts. Allons, à vos canons!').

To end the short, rather static play we have Etienne Parent finally finishing his sonorous editorial, sending the copy-boy off with it. Significantly, his last words are 'Alas! If some informer (*mouchard*) were to report the farce that's just taken place here, to the Friend of the Status Quo, we'd be in a fine fix!' And the author (who of course signs, 'A Friend of the Status Quo') adds: 'Admit it, Monsieur P., wouldn't you be tempted to believe, on reading the above, that there was indeed a *mouchard* among you?'[18]

The Résolutionnaires had indeed been concerned for some time about the possibility of paid informers in their midst, and this last sally was calculated to heighten that concern.[19] Five days later, on 30 April, the friend of the Status Quo struck again, and this time his text was distributed separately as well, as a pamphlet. It purports to be Act II of the first comedy, and its author begins with a prefatory shot directly at the opposition:

> Dear Mr. Editor,
> I hasten to send you the second act which I alluded to in my last communication. In so doing, I am keeping my word: something that the Patriotes don't always do!

Etienne Parent and H.-S. Huot are the only two characters to reappear from the first sketch, and the other two (L.-T. Besserer and J.-B. Grenier) have left little mark on history. The scene is again set in the library of the Assembly and again begins with a monologue by Parent. He is subsequently joined by the three others: Besserer, who is the first to arrive, even has the same salutation for Parent ('citoyen Editeur') as had Bédard in the first play. Moreover, an attempt has been made to lend consistency to the portrayal of Parent by having him frequently exclaim 'sac ... dié!' (*sacordié*, an attenuation of the ancient oath, 'by the holy body of God') as in the first play, no doubt a characteristic of his actual speech.

Despite this, it is difficult to believe that these two texts came from the same hand(s). The second comedy is much more confused than the first (a confusion heightened in Dionne's edition),[20] and much less direct. Symptomatic of its lack of direction is the central incident around which the play turns, an obscure affair involving an even more obscure personage, the twenty-three-year-old Dr J.-B. Grenier, cousin of Parent. Huot has brought the young man to Parent, so that the latter may compose a letter for him, 'in response to the allegation by that damned Friend of the Status Quo, who has the infamous audacity to ask him for an affidavit as to the meeting which took place at Château-Richer.'

Perhaps the incident was well known at the time. Young Grenier had apparently reported on a well-attended public assembly held at Notre-Dame de Château-Richer (near Montmorency, Bédard's riding) which, as so many such local meetings that spring, had come out strongly in favour of the 92 Resolutions. Our author believes that no such meeting had ever taken place ('No use denying it,' says Grenier, 'no such meeting ever took place there, any more than it did on the back of my hand'). But Parent and Huot are now depicted as abetting this falsehood, the former writing a letter in Grenier's name (in fact a letter signed 'J. Bte Grenier, Médecin' had appeared in *Le Canadien* on 11 April, protesting against such allegations), decrying the dastardly assault upon his veraciousness made by the Friend. There is not much else to this second text: Grenier is made to appear an ignoramus as well as a liar (he wants, for example, to append a '*post-rectum*' to the letter), Besserer is not much better, and both Parent and Huot are presented as petty schemers. The play ends artificially with the delivery of a message from Elzéar Bédard announcing a meeting to be held forthwith in his quarters, to discuss pressing business.

To this point Parent's newspaper had steadfastly refused to indulge in this sort of theatrical mud-slinging, although it had apparently continued to receive contributions of that nature from its readers. But the effect of this latest campaign by the anti-Patriotes was enough to change Parent's mind, although the first riposte of a 'dramatic' nature was muted in tone and much closer in format to the dialogues published since the 1770s than to the *Gazette*'s satiric sketches. It came on 5 May and purported to be a dialogue between two *habitants*, Olivier and Jean, on the current political situation in Lower Canada. Olivier here is the enlightened, informed observer, in the style of André in *Le Canadien et sa femme*, explaining calmly just how evil the existing régime is, and how the Governor-General (Lord Aylmer) has displayed particular bad faith in his treatment of the Canadiens and their leaders. Jean is grateful for the enlightenment furnished by Olivier, and the latter goes on, in long rhetorical sentences, to point out what Aylmer and his administration should do. Jean accepts the recipe without reservation:

JEAN
Yes indeed, I appreciate your point of view. But how do you expect His Excellency to speak in those terms? It's impossible, for he'd be speaking out against himself!

OLIVIER

He would have to do so, to be fair to everybody: for after all governments are only established for the good of the majority of the population![21]

There is not even a *nom de plume* appended to the work, and it seems to have elicited no reaction. But exactly a week later, on Monday, 12 May, *Le Canadien* included a playlet closer in form, content, and tone to the two which the *Gazette* had published. This play, whose existence has hitherto been ignored, I shall call the Third Status Quo Comedy.

The text covers 4½ close-set columns of the first page of the paper, making it only slightly shorter than the two plays published by the opposition. It is set in the office of Jean-François-Joseph ('Johnnie' Duval, suspected by the Patriotes of composing many of the Status Quo articles. There is only one other character in the sketch, Joseph-Thomas Amiot, a twenty-four-year-old lawyer accused of being the principal *mouchard* for the Bureaucrate forces. Despite its two interlocutors, the resulting conversation has evolved a long way from the dramatized dialogues of previous decades. Here we have a highly specific setting (just outside, then inside Duval's office in rue Saint-Louis, in Quebec City), easily identifiable participants in a dialogue that evolves, and some precise stage directions. The result is at least as good theatre as the first two comedies. Amiot, in the first scene, soliloquizes as he awaits entry to Duval's office, bewailing the hard lot of the paid informer:

No doubt about it, people like me are a wretched lot! ... What, is 'MOUCHARD' spelled out on my very face? Alas! to ply such a trade; and worse still, to do it for nothing! If there were even a job as Secretary, or Associate, or even First Clerk available in some attorney's office! But nobody wants me anywhere, not even the *Gazette* that I serve so well. There's not even the least little deal to be struck – a loan to arrange, a frock-coat to barter. Here I am reduced to spending the plentiful leisure my lack of clientele affords me, wandering around, snooping, spying, serving as stoolpigeon and errand-boy for the Friend of the Status Quo and his paper.[22]

So he skulks into Duval's office to beg him for a commission, however sordid. Duval is nervous, for he fears his complicity in the writings of the Status Quo party has been suspected. None the less, his desire to attack the Patriotes is even stronger than his fear:

> I shall have my revenge, I shall discharge the bile that Papineau
> has made me store up, and I'll vomit it out on our fine friends
> P[apineau], V[iger], H[uot], B[édard], P[arent], and B[esserer]. No
> need to be straightforward with people who won't listen to me!
> What does Truth matter, after all, if I can ruin the reputation of
> the clique in the minds of that lot of gallows-bait, the electors of
> the Upper City of Quebec![23]

Duval's noble end will be accomplished, we learn, by means of an article
he has just written for the next day's *Gazette*, and which he wants Amiot
to recopy in his own hand so that he and not Duval may be taken as its
author. As their conversation continues, the scheming dishonesty of their
whole party, as perceived by the Patriotes at least, is underlined. The publisher Neilson, the Attorney-General Hamel, the notary Glackmeyer, all
are portrayed as base conspirators against the name and good works of
Papineau, Viger, and (particularly) Parent. Duval then reads aloud the
communication he has prepared for the *Gazette*, impugning Parent's character and the way in which he has obtained his post as Librarian of the
Assembly. The letter is based on one that did in fact appear in Neilson's
paper on 1 May 1834, signed 'A Friend of the Status Quo,' and we learn
from a postscript to this dialogue between Amiot and Duval that the latter
had read that letter aloud, before its publication, 'last Monday [5 May],
between 9:30 and 10 a.m., in the office adjoining your study.'

> At which time you – yes, YOU, JOHN DUVAL, ESQUIRE, M.P.P., read
> out, in a loud and intelligible voice, the document which appeared
> the following Tuesday, addressed to 'The Editor of *Le Canadien*,
> Paid Librarian of the House of Assembly,' and signed 'A Friend of
> the Status Quo.' Don't trouble to deny it, for the text in question,
> read by YOU, JOHN DUVAL, ESQUIRE, M.P.P., was so clearly heard and
> so well understood that more than one person knew, on *Monday*,
> what was to appear *the next day*, in Tuesday's *Gazette*, [6 May],
> and they knew what the content of it would be.[24]

Le Canadien's first Comedy is signed 'Une Autre Fois' (Another Time).
    The initiative had now passed to the Patriote side, for this little con-
tribution sowed immediate confusion among the Bureaucrates. Johnnie
Duval complained bitterly, in the next issue of *Le Canadien*, about the
role imputed to him, protesting that it was all a mistake, and that furthermore it would cost him his seat in the forthcoming election. He demanded
to know the name of the author. A letter signed 'Une Autre Fois' re-

sponded in the following issue, justifying at length the claims made, mocking Duval from a distance, but refusing to identify its writer as long as the *Gazette* continued to print unsigned contributions. The 14 May issue of *Le Canadien* had printed a long communication, most of it in dialogue form, from 'C.D.' That dialogue purports to be a real conversation held between its author ('moi') and a rabid Status Quo supporter identified only as 'J...N' in which 'moi' wins, naturally, a clean victory. On 19 May another piece, which I shall call the Fourth Status Quo Comedy (and which again has been passed over until now) appeared in the same publication, and is entitled 'A Little Dialogue between two Friends of the Status Quo.'

The two 'Friends' are identified only as 'A' (Amiot) and 'H' (no doubt Attorney-General A.-R. Hamel, principal target of the Fifth Comedy, as we shall see). From the text we learn that the Bureaucrates are accusing Elzéar Bédard of being the one who overheard Duval reading the letter and who was thus responsible for the Third Comedy. H is appalled at this latest turn of events, fearing that their whole cause has been lost. When A asks why, he responds, exasperated:

> This, you dunce is why: Bédard is the last man you should have tried to throw the blame on. He was one of the ones we treated worst in our writings: how, then, would you ever expect him to keep the thing a secret? It's perfectly appropriate for him to have made use of his accidental discovery, and no reason for you to criticize him for it!
>
> A[MIOT]
>
> That's true. But what would you have us do? We had been caught out; we had to say *something*, and the only solution was to raise a cry about shame and dishonour. To bluff it, in other words.[25]

It is noteworthy that H is identified by A as 'notre Président' in this little sketch, which should remove any doubts as to whether the former is Attorney-General Hamel. This unfortunate man had been embroiled only three months previously in an incident explicable only through his lack of experience in his post. There had been rumours of irregularities during the previous election in Stanstead, and Hamel, asked for his advice by the administration, had declared the vote illegal and excluded the winning candidate, a Mr Child, although in doing so Hamel was acting contrary to accepted parliamentary procedure. One sees an allusion to this in H's closing remarks in this dialogue, for he threatens A: 'Just you wait until our committee meets again, you're going to be censured. And A responds:

'Take it easy, Monsieur: I'm not like ... you know who,' referring to the official censure Hamel had received in the Assembly.

But it seems unlikely that the author of this Fourth Comedy is the same as for the Third. In this one, there is no attempt to set the action precisely, very little humour, and no signature. Moreover, in the next play we shall consider, the Fifth Comedy, signed 'U.A.F.' (Une Autre Fois), although there is frequent reference to 'the play in *Le Canadien*' it is clear that the Third Comedy is the one concerned, with no reference to the Fourth. There seems no valid reason for the author(s) of the Third and Fifth Comedies to ignore or disclaim the Fourth, if it came from the same pen.

The Patriote side knew they now had their adversaries on the run, and this is the sense of the title of the Fifth and last play in the series, 'The Rout of the Status Quo' (Le Statu quo en déroute). The text was published separately, with the imprint 'Plattsburgh, N.Y.,' but almost certainly was a production of *Le Canadien*'s presses. One soon sees the reason for the false imprint, for this is the most direct of the Comédies du statu quo and its chief target was an important member of the Aylmer administration, Hamel. Indeed, the setting is Hamel's office in rue Sainte-Anne, Quebec City, and his discomfiture arising from the incident already mentioned provides much of the fun for the author(s). The play opens with a monologue by the Attorney-General: a fine portrayal, with overtones of Shakespearean parody, of the vainglorious officeholder:

> HAMEL (*pacing back and forth in his study*)
> Oh! what a lovely thing, to hold high honours! How glorious it is to be a Statesman, to see oneself, in the most demanding situations, act as Counsellor to him who governs! ... Am I then really the King's attorney-general? Alas! if all this were but a dream, how disappointed I should be! But no! it is not so: I feel full well that I'm a great, great man. Great thoughts, great plans, great *opinions* keep churning in my head!

But the word 'opinion' reminds him of the formal censure his opinion (*avis*) on the Stanstead election brought him, and his reflections turn bitter:

> Alas! cruel memory! That summons to the Bar of the House, the Censure, the Speaker's discourtesy: how heavy they weigh upon this heart of mine! ... The first time the Governor solicited my help, and I was so proud of it, had taken it as a point of honour, worked day and night on that damned *avis* that I wrote – and look how the whole thing turned out![26]

All of which is fair game, well within the rules established by the first two plays. Parent had been attacked personally, especially on the matter of his appointment as Royal Printer and Librarian, the Patriote group had been accused by name of fiddling petition rolls, falsifying reports of meetings, seeking to instil Jacobin-like revolution. In his continuing soliloquy Hamel, after considering resignation and withdrawal from a cruel, unappreciative world, decides to stay, and to counterattack: 'No, let's stay on. Let's seek vengeance. I must slander them, persecute them, these *Patriotes*! The Friends of the Status Quo will be meeting here this evening: I swear, I shall have my revenge!'[27]

Then, as in the first two plays, the others enter in succession, five of them, and hold the stage long enough to reveal their biases, their foibles, their bad faith. They have assembled in order to write an appropriate response to *Le Canadien*, and to deal with their collaborators Amiot and Duval. After a good deal of farcical squabbling, it is decided that Hamel will preside, and he does so with solemn, authoritative turgidity ('I hereby assume the Chair for the twenty-sixth time since the Closure of the last Session,' etc.). He then turns his attention to the two whose indiscretions have given *Le Canadien* the material for the Third Comedy and, in a good burlesque scene, he decides to issue a formal parliamentary censure against each of them. Here one knows that the author is fully enjoying himself, and the terminology used is meant to recall Hamel's own censure in the Assembly (the record of those proceedings had been printed in full in *Le Canadien* on 24 February):

> HAMEL
> Step forward, gentlemen, that I may impose an act of admonition upon you.
> JOHNNIE DUVAL (*his whole face contorted in a grimace*)
> Well, you should certainly know the style and the words for that...
> THOMAS AMIOT
> But there's no formal motion, to keep it within the rules!
> JOHNNIE DUVAL
> Let him get on with it; he's going to tell us something impressive, in French and in English.
> HAMEL (*in a solemn and imposing tone*)
> You, Johnnie Duval, barrister, Member of the Provincial Parliament, Friend of the Status Quo, editor of our writings; and you who peddle them for us, sire Thomas Amiot, barrister also and merchant:

WHEREAS on the 5th day of May inst., in the full light of day, although your orders were to act at night alone, and by stealth, you did compose, did read, and deliver a certain text addressed 'To the Salaried Librarian of the House of Assembly';

WHEREAS in so doing, you allowed yourselves to be caught red-handed, and did thus cause us all to be betrayed;

DUVAL

He's going to have a hard time finishing off this sentence!

HAMEL

...THEREFORE, I repeat, my duty obliges me to reprimand and to censure you. This occasion is all the more painful, because you were the ones we counted most upon...

DUVAL (aside)

Ah! he's talking like the Speaker!

HAMEL

...and who demonstrated the most zeal against the Patriotes. WHERE-FORE, to preserve our honour, and to make an example of you, I hereby censure and scold you; and you are herewith censured and scolded.[28]

After further similar antics, one of their number, Jacques Crémazie (brother of the poet Octave, and at the moment articling for admission to the Bar), is sent out to dig up whatever might be useful against the Patriotes. In his absence, the others begin divvying up future spoils, in what is an effective scene: Amiot will get Parent's post as Librarian; Edouard Glackmeyer, another lawyer associated with the Bureaucrates, will get the position of Clerk of the Court that he has been intriguing for; and Neilson, publisher of the Gazette, will get the printing concession: all this, if they agree to work for Duval's re-election in Quebec City.

But Crémazie returns to dissipate their elation with the news that Neilson has resolved to publish no more of their writings (this would explain, no doubt, why this is the last of the Status Quo Comedies), and that incriminating documents have been found on the desk of another of their number, David Roy (then a lawyer, later judge). To cap it off, Hamel's loud introductory soliloquy has been overheard (one sees the parallel with the two plays by the Bureaucrates). The gang breaks up in disorder and confusion, with Hamel urging a continued guerilla campaign in the press: 'Be prepared to write on, under a thousand different names! ... As for me, I shall continue my operations as well. We must seek revenge, revenge! ... Strike, strike hard, and especially against Papineau!' Which allows the clearer-minded Crémazie to mutter, ruefully, a verse from the then-popular refrain directed against the Bureaucrates: 'Ah! oui,' he says,

You've shamed the Bar, but who's to know?
Who's fault's it, then? Why, Papineau![29]

As to the authorship of these various texts, the name most often associated with the Patriote contributions is that of Elzéar Bédard, and the role we have seen allocated to him in the genesis of the Third Comedy (the essence of which he is purported to have overheard while waiting to speak with Duval on legal matters) corroborates that association. Contemporaries also saw the hand of François-Réal Angers in these texts, and this attribution to him has been strengthened recently by John Hare, in his introduction to the re-edition of Angers' 1837 work, *Révélations du crime; ou Cambray et ses complices* (Réédition-Québec 1969). Angers was then a twenty-two year-old law student articling in the office of H.-A. Huot, and his authorship (or at least his collaboration) does appear probable. It is curious, however, that the Bureaucrates, at least at the time, seem never to have suspected him. On their side, it seems certain that the two principal authors (there may well have been more) were David Roy and Georges-Barthélemy Faribault. Roy's participation was indeed suspected by the Résolutionnaires, who threw a rather wide net, hence his appearance in the last text. But no one seems to have been aware of the role played by Faribault, who later became an outstanding archivist and historian. I too can only speculate at this stage, for the authors of texts such as these would have had sound reason to ensure that their participation was known to as few as possible. And what was impossible for their contemporaries to establish with certainty, remains difficult today.

I have devoted so much time to these five plays because of their fundamental importance in the evolution of an indigenous tradition of dramaturgy in French Canada and because their role has generally been ignored in the past. It is essential to underline the fact that these are the first plays composed and published in French by natives of Lower Canada; that the primacy in that area which has hitherto been accorded to Pierre Petitclair's *Griphon* (see pp 116-21 below) cannot be justified; and that the five Status Quo Comedies are in fact much more representative of general literary activity in Quebec, much more central to the mainstream of social, political, and dramatic evolution at the time. Perhaps, indeed, if they were less deeply rooted in place and time, the genre which they represent would have prevailed. In the atmosphere of 1837-8, however, little time or energy was left for any type of drama except that being enacted at St-Charles and St-Eustache, and the dramatized dialogues, along with the plays to which they led, now remain lively testimony to the conflicting ideologies and personalities of a turning-point in Canadian history, rather than as signposts on the way to the evolution of native theatre.

Writing about the only three of these comedies he appears to have discovered (those identified here as the First, Second, and Fifth), the conservative N.-E. Dionne, seventy-five years later, gave his preference to the first two, from the Bureaucrate side, judging the last, *The Rout of the Status Quo*, to be decidedly inferior. Unfortunately, that opinion and in fact his very words have usually been echoed in subsequent references to these texts, which are not based on any detached attempt to read and evaluate them on their own merits.[30] I believe that such an attempt leads to quite a different conclusion: the productions from the Patriote side are every bit as witty and as well constructed, and on both counts *The Rout of the Status Quo* is superior. Moreover, the sequence of events suggests that they were more effective than the texts from the Status Quo supporters, and that is the real touchstone of this dramatic form.

These plays were constructed by men who had absorbed a certain knowledge of character depiction and dramatic action, a knowledge that must have come in large part from the educational system through which, considering their average age, they would recently have passed. But by 1834 there were other sources and the next sub-section will explore some of these. Political drama and 'paradrama' of the type described here reached an apogee of sorts, just before the Rebellion. The genre would continue to be practised and to evolve towards another such apogee, in the Confederation period, which forms the subject of a later chapter.

VISITORS FROM FRANCE: FIRMIN PRUD'HOMME

The opening of the Theatre Royal in Montreal led, by 1827, to the first visit of a touring company from France, that of Scévola Victor. The repertoire his troupe offered had been unsubstantial, consisting mainly of vaudeville and melodramas currently popular in Paris. In this respect Victor's was merely the first in a long line of touring French companies which, beginning in the late 1850s, would constantly misread, almost wilfully, the tastes of French-Canadian audiences while maintaining the hostility of the Church. In the interval between 1827 and 1859, however, those visits were rare and of little significance. Far more important in the evolution of native talent were the individual Frenchmen who began to show up in Montreal or Quebec after 1830. Three of them left an impact upon the history of theatre: Firmin Prud'homme, Hyacinthe Leblanc de Marconnay, and Napoléon Aubin.

The visit of Scévola Victor's troupe was a fiasco, as we have seen. The desperate straits to which members of his cast were reduced, and the fact that they had to resort to what was essentially public alms in order to find their passage back home, did little to raise the stature of the professional player in the public's eye. But their visit did lead to a degree of emulation by local amateurs, with another group calling itself 'Amateurs Canadiens' offering performances of traditional theatre hard on the heels of the professionals, in Montreal.[31] Until 1831 these amateurs dominated the scene, with a particularly impressive season in 1829, when two different rival companies, the Amateurs Canadiens and the Amateurs de Montréal, offered competing repertoires relying heavily on Molière.[32] Then came another 'bottoming out' of the cycle in 1830, when not a single French play is known to have been staged in Montreal.

But 1831 saw the arrival of a Frenchman who would exert considerable influence on the stage for the rest of the decade: Firmin Prud'homme from Paris, who claimed to have been a student of the great star of the French stage, Talma. How Prud'homme wound up living in Montreal is not known: he had first come to notice in December 1831, when he had performed a series of dramatic recitals, with scenes from Racine, Corneille – and from *Tartuffe*, the first known public rendition of any part of that play in Canada.[33] He was soon to be found working with the Amateurs Canadiens in their presentation of Molière's *George Dandin*, Ducis' French adaptation of *Hamlet* (apparently the first performance in Canada of any of these famous adaptations), and a short work he had arranged himself, to display his own histrionic talents, entitled *Napoleon on Saint Helena's Island* (Napoléon à Sainte-Hélène).

This one-act play (Prud'homme describes it merely as 'Historic Scenes') comprising sixteen pages may have exhibited a certain amount of courage on its author's part, for it is highly laudatory of the former Emperor at a time when, ten years after his death, his name still aroused great passion in the anglophone world, while a cult grew up around it for many francophones. The play has only two characters, Napoleon and his faithful aide, General Bertrand, both dressed in full regalia (there is also a cameo role, that of a British soldier, in Scene 4). One notes an intriguing romanticism, among the first manifestations of it in French Canada, in the setting:

> When the curtain rises, the scenery depicted is that of the Island of St Helena, with the sea in the background, an enormous rock on

the right, and on the left a colonial-style house. To the right, and a little in front of the rock, is a small settee in the grass, shaded by a tree.

Military music, evoking a mood of melancholy, is heard just before the curtain rises, and continues until Napoleon and Bertrand appear on stage.[34]

The first scene informs us of the petty indignities that the British warder has been imposing upon the unfortunate Emperor: spying upon his movements, intercepting his letters, quibbling over his household expenses. Bertrand soon has his master turn from these preoccupations to memories of his vanished splendour: his great victories, his generals, Masséna, Ney – Waterloo. The Emperor cannot bear the emotion welling up within him, and asks his friend to leave him alone a moment.

Scene 2 is a short, pathetic monologue, wherein the exiled emperor broods on his fate and that of France:

> I was not destined to die upon the throne ... They'll kill me here, but what matter: my memory will remain ... and France, free again one day, will shed a tear for me, perhaps. If St Helena belonged to France, I should love this wretched rock ... But France is as dead for me, I would cause it too much trouble ... all I ask of her is a recollection of me ... Alas! (*He sits, and opens one of his books*) Corneille! ... What a man was he – the greatest genius of the stage. If he had been alive in my time, I would have made him prince! ... (*Taking the other volume*) Racine! He reminds me of Talma ... how splendid he was! ... Were it not for my fear of ignorant prejudice, I would have decorated him. (*Opening the book*) *Andromache*! ... the very play for grieving fathers![35]

He reads some touching lines from Racine's *Andromache*, and they bring him to tears at the thought of his own son. Bertrand returns to interrupt this emotive scene, and as they start to wander off towards the sea they are intercepted by a British soldier who informs them of new orders: all troops on duty are to fire on anyone leaving the tiny compound to which Napoleon is henceforth restricted.

When General Bertrand protests heatedly against this newest indignity (Scene 5), his master reveals, with stoic calm, that it all matters little: he knows his last hour is drawing nigh. The Emperor then grasps the arm of his grief-stricken comrade and together the two mount the rock. At its summit, Napoleon turns towards the sea, doffs his three-cornered hat, and kneels to exclaim 'Adieu, France!,' as the curtain descends and the melancholy martial air sounds again.

It takes little analysis of this dramatic text to ascertain that there is nothing Canadian about it, and little that is original. Prud'homme uses colour, language, movement, and sound to create a mood of melancholy grandeur, but the whole effect is perilously close to the bathetic. His attempt reflects the wave of idealization of Bonaparte that was then evident in France and just nascent in Canada, the romantic rehabilitation of past imperial glories, the grieving at their loss. The only critic who has written about this text sees it as a sort of allegory, where the Emperor is to be 'perceived indirectly as the image of French Canada after 1760, cut off from all ties with the mother country.'[36] This may be stretching its symbolic intent: if the accepted time of Prud'homme's arrival in Canada (late 1830) is correct[37] and the date given for our text (1831) is not falsified, it is difficult to see how this French expatriate absorbed so quickly such an intriguing overview of the history and situation of Lower Canada. My suspicion about the originality of *Napoléon à Sainte-Hélène* stems from the word 'arranged' which Prud'homme inserts on his title-page, informing us also that the play was staged for the first time in Montreal on 28 December 1831. The word 'arrangé' was often used in the nineteenth century to cover everything from innocuous borrowing of themes from another author to shameless plagiarism: a prime example of the latter being some of the works of Louis Fréchette; of the former, the play *Valentine*, by the author we shall consider next.

On the whole, Firmin Prud'homme's contribution as author or 'arranger' of this text was less important than his role as organizer, director, and actor in other plays performed over the next few years in Montreal and Quebec. He, like Quesnel, was an important window upon a wider world: through him Lower Canada got to know Ducis' translations of *Hamlet* and *Othello* and was introduced to the theatre of Scribe. He also affected acting directly, in a way we shall never be able properly to assay: the year after his arrival he announced he was opening a school for literary appreciation and dramatic recital, apparently the first such enterprise in the history of Canada. Along with Napoléon Aubin, he was among the first to introduce into this country the Romanticism then sweeping France and which is so evident in *Napoléon à Sainte-Hélène*.

It is not known what success his school of acting enjoyed: probably not much, considering the reaction his traditional, stilted interpretation of certain plays evoked in the capital, by this time used to the stage manners of British stars.[38] The years 1832-4 were barren ones for public assembly in any case, due to the incredible ravages of the great cholera epidemic. Barren, that is, as concerns public performances of plays: 1834 was, after all, the year of the Status Quo Comedies.

ANOTHER VISITOR: LEBLANC DE MARCONNAY

It was in that year also that another Frenchman showed up in Montreal for an extended stay. Primarily a journalist, fascinated by politics, an influential Freemason, the mercurial Leblanc de Marconnay already had one published play to his credit on his arrival, *L'Hôtel des princes*, a one-act comic opera with lyrics by himself and De Ferrière, music by Eugène Prévost. This eminently forgettable production was of a type much in vogue in Paris, where it had had its première on 23 April 1831.[39] In the dozen years he spent in Canada, this enigmatic Parisian edited three different papers and produced at least two fiercely-worded political tracts directed against the Patriotes and their leader,[40] but more relevantly, two dramatic texts, *Valentine, ou la Nina canadienne* and *Le Soldat*.

In subtitling the first play 'la Nina canadienne,' Marconnay was acknowledging his debt to the well-known musical comedy, *Nina, ou la Folle par amour* (The Woman Driven Mad by Love), written by Marsollier des Vivetières, music by Dalayrac, first performed in Paris in 1786.[41] But in reality, only the most basic element of his plot, that of a young woman who has lost her reason because she thinks her lover is dead, is inspired directly by Marsollier's work. A careful comparison of both texts shows no direct borrowing by Marconnay, and he has developed the basic plot much more highly (but not necessarily better) than his immediate model[42] and transposed it to Canada. Such public acknowledgment of indebtedness was, unfortunately, uncommon in the nineteenth century (Fréchette, for example, would have retained a good deal more respect for his dramatic creations if he had not attempted to conceal his sources); and it is manifestly unfair, as well as inaccurate, to state (and it has been done) that Leblanc de Marconnay merely 'transposed' a successful play to a French-Canadian setting and signed his name to it.

Valentine has five major characters: Monsieur de Prainville, a retired ship's captain from France, now living in Canada; Valentine, his niece and legal ward, who is deeply in love with his nephew, Charles; Madame Derbois, a young Canadian widow; and the young Frenchman St-Léon, who loves Mme Derbois and is in pursuit of her hand in marriage. The action takes place 'in 1820, on the estate of M. de Prainville, on the banks of the St Lawrence,' and the focus is upon Valentine, who is suffering such deep psychological trauma from the tragic disappearance, some six years before (while serving on a British warship during the War of 1812-14), of her beloved fiancé, Charles, that she has since moved in a shadowy, unreal existence, barely recognizing the world about her.

The author's experience with play construction is obvious from the first scene which, although traditional in function, is none the less quite well done. Mme Derbois and St-Léon indulge in light, witty badinage, while at the same time providing the requisite information on Valentine, Charles's disappearance, and Prainville; and, of course, on their own relationship, for St-Léon has declared his love for her, but Mme Derbois is unyielding.

She does, however, persuade her suitor to co-operate with her in an attempt to dissuade Prainville (at whose house both are summer guests) from carrying out his plan to marry off his niece and ward, Valentine, to an old, rich, rheumatic sea captain, a friend of his. A neat blackmail of sorts is proposed by Mme Derbois:

ST-LÉON
Your wish is my command, Madame. But, just for encouragement: if I succeed in preventing that marriage, will you promise to marry me?

MME DERBOIS
I'll make a much more reasonable bargain: if Valentine marries Charles, I'll give you my hand in marriage – the same day!

ST-LÉON
That would be bringing back the dead, and I'm no Orpheus!

MME DERBOIS
Not a further word about it then: those are my conditions.

ST-LÉON
In that case, I'm condemned to eternal celibacy![43]

After the introductory scene, the other characters arrive in orderly fashion, and we are soon familiar with them all, and their interaction. There is the inevitable rural Québécois domestic, inevitably named Jean-Baptiste. In his few years in Lower Canada, Marconnay had obviously cocked a learned ear in the direction of Canadian speech and, apart from a few imprecisions, has managed to capture much its savour.[44] As with Colas, Jean-Baptiste's linguistic colour will provide – far more successfully than in Quesnel's play – much constant humour in Valentine. So will the language of Prainville, the retired salt whose nautical diction is, alas! sadly overdone by the time the first few scenes have passed (eg, his 700-word monologue on the charms and advantages of shipboard life, at the end of Scene 4).

Her arrival having been sufficiently prepared, the romantic heroine, our melancholy Valentine, appears, in a pathos-filled scene (5) where her love for Charles remains a constant obsession, where we learn of her parents' early death, and observe her own sweet disposition. When we have had ample time to realize just what an enormity would be her betrothal to Prainville's old friend, Gobineau, the news arrives: Charles is alive! He has returned: Jean-Baptiste has seen him!

The plot then takes another twist, for Captain de Prainville, man of honour that he is, has given his word to Gobineau (one assumes it had *not* been given to Charles originally?), and the dreaded marriage must go on. In a thoroughly unconvincing scene (8), Valentine and her long-lost Charles are reunited: a curiously distant reunion, with stilted, formal speech, and dominated by Charles's long account of his shipwreck on the west coast and his difficult return by land across the breadth of British North America. At length Valentine informs him of her betrothal and impending marriage, Charles and Prainville go off to discuss the situation, and Jean-Baptiste's comic monologue (Scene 10) intervenes, to cut the tension and permit transition to the next scene.

Which is a surprisingly effective one for, instead of alternating the comic and the poignant, both are simultaneously blended by the author. St-Léon is consternated by the news that Mme Derbois, despairing of changing Prainville's mind about the marriage, is preparing to leave forever. Meanwhile Jean-Baptiste, who has constantly vaunted St-Léon's unfailing joviality, keeps pressing him as to whether he will be coming to the homecoming celebration for Charles that evening:

ST-LÉON *(aside)*
Most likely she's afraid the marriage [to Charles] *will* take place, and that she'll be forced to keep her end of the bargain...
JEAN-BAPTISTE
Say, Monsieur St-Léon, you'se gonna come, ain't ya?
ST-LÉON *(aside)*
Was I, then, wrong to count upon her love?...
JEAN-BAPTISTE
You'll be dansin' wit' us all?
ST-LÉON *(aside)*
Women are so strange!
JEAN-BAPTISTE
I sure likes it when you takes part in somethin' – you's always so cheerful, you!

ST-LÉON (*aside*)
I don't know what I shall do...
JEAN-BAPTISTE
You'se always in good humour, never grumpy...
ST-LÉON (*aside*)
What distress I'm in!...
JEAN-BAPTISTE
You'se always laughin' ... But he's not even lookin' at me!
Monsieur St-Léon, Monsieur St-Léon!
ST-LÉON
Oh, clear out of here, would you!⁴⁵

But the resourceful St-Léon is not about to give up so easily. He decides to try a romantic ploy already well established in melodrama: a letter to Mme Derbois, announcing he is going to commit suicide. But as he is finishing the letter, and before he can sign it, Charles arrives, downcast because of Prainville's refusal to change his mind. Designedly, St-Léon takes him off to discuss their problems over target practice with pistols (from the first scene, St-Léon's predilection for this sport had been mentioned).

As the reader will have surmised, Valentine now comes along, reads (aloud) the unaddressed, unsigned, 'suicide' note, believes it has been written by Charles, and, on hearing the sound of a gunshot, swoons. Prainville and Mme Derbois come running. Prainville reads the letter, and announces that the handwriting is – St-Léon's. Whereupon Mme Derbois faints dead away. St-Léon arrives, in response to Prainville's shouts, just as his beloved, less stricken than Valentine, is regaining consciousness. So much for one loose end: now St-Léon persuades Prainville the only way his niece will ever regain her reason is if he writes another letter, consenting to her union with Charles. This, with great reluctance, Prainville consents to do. They leave the letter for Valentine to find, and all retire to watch.

The scene that follows (18) is another excellent example of blended genres: Valentine, delirious with grief, mumbles disconnected pathetic nonsense, while Jean-Baptiste, playing the rustic lout, takes her seriously. She is now the Indian chief at Hochelaga, waiting to greet Jacques Cartier:

Take this branch to him: It is a token of peace between my warriors and the French giants.
JEAN-BAPTISTE
Where you want me to take that there twig?
VALENTINE
To the French.

JEAN-BAPTISTE
Ain't been none o' *them* here for a long time!
VALENTINE
Is Fort Saint-Louis far away, then?
JEAN-BAPTISTE
We's English subjects now, we is.
VALENTINE
English? ... Alas![46]

Unfortunately, the scene goes on much too long in this vein, with Valentine switching to perfect nautical vocabulary, then singing a long song of forlorn love (to which Jean-Baptiste responds with the traditional Canadien folksong, 'Derrière chez nous y'a t'un étang') and, in general, raving expertly.

Finally she sits at St-Léon's writing desk, to pen a farewell note to all. There she spots Prainville's letter – and recovers perfect lucidity upon reading it. The dénouement is nigh: her wedding – and that of Mme Derbois and St-Léon – is set for the next day; in the distance, arriving voyageurs intone that epitome of French-Canadian folk-songs (via medieval France), 'A la claire fontaine' – and all ends in rejoicing.

Perhaps I have already suggested enough to enable an overview to the play to be drawn in a few lines. Its structure is that of traditional light theatre, with thematic developments placing it well within the current of Parisian theatre of the late 1820s. In that sense, and as Quesnel's *Colas et Colinette* had done two generations earlier, it represents a wholesome injection of modernity into the central vein of a traditionalist culture.

Quesnel's play, as we have seen, belonged to a genre peculiarly popular in France after 1750, a genre which, apart from its musical aspect, reflected theatrical values of the previous century, avoiding reference to contemporary problems. There is nothing specifically Canadian about *Colas et Colinette*. This is not true of *Valentine, ou la Nina canadienne*. Leblanc de Marconnay demonstrates a better ear for speech habits, both those of the privileged classes (the conversation, for example, between Mme Derbois and St-Léon which opens the play) and the working class (Jean-Baptiste).[47] The music is that of traditional French-Canadian folk-song (stemming, it is true, from a shared French heritage, more richly preserved in Canada). And there are Canadian politico-military references: the Battle of Chateauguay (26 October 1813), during the war of 1812; Jean-Baptiste's allusion to old Gobineau's setback, on Charles's reappearance, as being 'like the enemy, on Lake Champlain' (another reference to the same conflict); the evocation of the distant, glorious past of New France

(Jacques Cartier at Hochelaga). After only a couple of years in this country, Hyacinthe Leblanc de Marconnay seems to have acquired a strong
sense of the land and the people who dwelt in it.

Although he succeeds in portraying the mature relationship between St-
Léon and Mme Derbois in a convincing manner, the author seems utterly
at a loss to breathe credibility into the young and vibrant passion which
Valentine and Charles are purported to share, and this is a visible defect in
the play. It would, in fact, be generations before a dramatist writing in
French Canada could convincingly portray love scenes, and the attempt
was made infrequently; but perhaps one could have expected more from a
sophisticated Parisian. Yet for a popular audience, one feels that *Valentine,
ou la Nina canadienne* could be revived more successfully than anything
else written in Canada before 1860 (with the possible exception of Petitclair's *Une Partie de campagne*, as we shall see). With this one play,
Leblanc de Marconnay significantly updated the offerings of Lower Canadian theatre.

At the time *Valentine* was published (1836), Marconnay was editor of
the newspaper *L'Ami du peuple*, and had sought contributions from its
readers to aid in publishing the play. The edition was offered for sale on 6
February, at the performance of another brief dramatic work by the same
author, probably arranged in collaboration with Napoléon Aubin, and
entitled *The Soldier* (Le Soldat). (Actually, *Valentine* had been announced
as the play for that evening, but its performance had had to be cancelled
because of the illness of some of the cast.)

The Soldier also received the honour of publication that same year.[48]
The title-page describes it as an '*Intermède* [which could be translated
either as 'Interlude' or 'One-Act Opera'] in two Parts, with Singing, performed at the Theatre Royal, Montreal (Lower Canada) in 1835 and
1836,' which indicates one performance of the play on which we have no
information. The same title-page informs us that the work was 'arranged
[*arrangé*] by Mr. Leblanc de Marconnay,' and it has been assumed until
now that this reference constitutes the type of acknowledgment to a
French model that we have seen with regard to *Valentine*. But no one has
as yet identified a French original, and it seems much more likely that if
'arranged' means written in collaboration, or adaptation, then the co-
operation this time was with the Swiss francophone resident in Canada,
Napoléon Aubin, for we know that a short play ascribed to the latter was
performed on 23 October 1839, and that the work was entitled *Le Soldat
français*.[49] Nothing else is known about Aubin's work.

Marconnay's *Le Soldat* is a dramatized monologue with melodramatic
overtones. The French soldier presented is a hard-drinking, tough, jingois-

tic patriot. He is also brave, sincere, naïve, loyal, and very much in love with a serving maid, Rose. In the first tableau, he drinks and sings as he expounds his simple philosophy of life:

> No denying it, it's a great calling, to be a soldier: he who sheds his blood in defence of his country should be ranked right after the farmer, who slakes with the sweat of his brow the furrows that he tills! Back in my village I was a good-for-nothing – no taste for studies, no aptitude for the arts or sciences ... But I signed up for the Army, and now I can expect to make my mark in the world. And here I am: fed, clothed, laundered, all at government expense; an easy lot, for in exchange I have only to stand guard duty, go on maneuvers, learn how to charge in formation: 18 movements in 12 intervals – , learn how to take care of my rifle, and be killed at the first opportunity. I know that there are people who wouldn't particularly enjoy that prospect, but it's a fascinating life, and a marvelous education for young men![50]

As he concludes this encomium of the military life, cannon shots resound in the distance: a battle is about to take place. The soldier grabs his rifle and rushes towards the sound: 'Hold on, hold on a minute! Don't start the ball without me – I don't want to be the last one in the dance!'

The second part is set in a field hospital, where the soldier, his left arm amputated, is clinging bravely to life. His encounter with death has only strengthened his views and confirmed his courage:

> The medic who operated on me claims there's no hope, that I'm about to set out on the Last Trail ... Damned annoying, just the same, to have to leave this world when one would prefer to remain! But hell, you have to expect anything in this profession! The enemy has been beaten off, we won the battle, so it's not quite so hard to have to go.[51]

He has written a soulful, tear-wrenching letter for Rose, and he sings it for us at great length. He is sending her ten francs, which is what the doctors have offered him for his corpse. Would she please break the news to his mother – and his faithful dog? Then, with one last maudlin adieu to his chaste fiancée, our noble soldier collapses and dies on stage.

Again, the roots in melodrama are obvious: here is a 'tear-jerker' of the first order. But the signal difference from *Valentine* is the total lack of anything Canadian in *Le Soldat*. The hero is a Frenchman whose every chauvinistic thought is for the mothercountry. The play could well have been written by Marconnay before his departure from Paris, or with an eye to his return there.[52]

As was the case with Firmin Prud'homme, it was in another fashion that Marconnay contributed more significantly to the evolution of theatre in Canada. In 1835 he had helped found a grouping of expatriate Frenchmen, the Société française en Canada, which included Prud'homme and Napoléon Aubin. Marconnay soon became president and Aubin secretary of this semi-literary, semi-political society, and its members exerted a certain influence during the 1830s. The following year (1836) the author of *Valentine* was elected president of another group calling itself an Amateur Canadian Dramatic Society, and he contributed actively to the productions sponsored by that organization over the next few years, when political and military matters subsided enough to allow public performances. Aubin, then editor of the momentous one-man production, the newspaper *Le Fantasque*, in Quebec City, founded another theatrical group there in 1839, and this group took the curious name, Les Amateurs typographes, which soon included more than typesetters (*typographes*), and had a colourful career in the capital for many years.

A THIRD VISITOR: NAPOLÉON AUBIN

Aimé-Nicolas Aubin, referred to exclusively as 'Napoléon,' either because this was one of his baptismal names or because of his undying admiration for the great emperor,[53] had arrived in Canada in 1835 after a stay of six years in the United States. He had been born near Geneva in 1812, during that region's annexation to France, and thus preferred to identify himself as a Frenchman throughout his life. Like Leblanc de Marconnay, he had worked for a succession of newspapers in Montreal and Quebec City before founding first a short-lived, bilingual journal, *Le Télégraphe* (1837) and, later the same year, the memorable *Fantasque*, the tone of which kept him in constant difficulty with the authorities and even (January-February 1839) brought him imprisonment. But unlike Marconnay and Prud'homme, Aubin formed a strong commitment to his new country and spent the rest of a long and active life in Lower Canada.

The first program offered by his Amateurs Typographes took place on 10 June 1839 and included Voltaire's *Death of Julius Caesar*. That play had already been performed in Montreal in November 1815 by a 'Society of Young Canadians,' and had aroused strong reaction (see p 73 above), although 1815 was a far less sensitive year in Lower Canada than 1839. More curiously, one notes in passing that an adapted version of the work (along with other plays by the same author, such as *Zaïre* and *Mohammed, or Fanaticism*) was performed in the early 1830s at the newly-founded (1827) *collège classique* of Sainte-Anne-de-la-Pocatière, as part of the current rebirth of college theatre. It is purported that Voltaire's influence was surprisingly widespread in Lower Canada at this time, but even so, one does not expect to see an institution founded and operated by Catholic clergy accord so visible a role to the most pernicious assailant of the Church in eighteenth-century France![54]

But to return to 1839, and the performance of *The Death of Julius Caesar* at Montreal's Theatre Royal. Napoléon Aubin had been sent to prison on 2 January of that year, there to remain until 26 February, when Etienne Parent was suffering the same fate, both of them because of the 'revolutionary tone' of the newspapers they edited. Naturally, the authorities kept a close eye on Aubin even after his release. There were a few rumblings in the press after the first performance of *La Mort de Jules César* in June, but the nature of the play seems to have been unclear to those in civil authority. When the same work was announced for October of that year, however, a confrontation soon developed between Aubin's troupe on the one hand, and T.A. Young, Montreal's chief of police, on the other. The audience, mindful of the events of 1837-8 and of the trials, imprisonment, and exile of Patriotes still taking place, seems to have enjoyed the confrontation, and the performance of Voltaire's play (along with no less than three others) was interrupted so frequently by cheers and applause that the final curtain did not fall until two in the morning. The *Gazette* was indignant, decrying the blatant appeal to anarchy its correspondent perceived in the text,[55] and the civil authorities held an emergency session at which it was decided that, thenceforth, all public performances must finish by 11 PM. Frightened by the incident, the management of the Theatre Royal made it clear that Aubin and his troupe would no longer be welcome there. The Amateurs Typographes were thus checked for some time. But a full year later the owners of the Royal relented, the political climate having changed for the better, and the mettlesome company was back on the boards by January 1841.

The repertory chosen for this revival (Collé and Scribe) does not seem to have reawakened the public's enthusiasm and Aubin's group, after another year of desultory activity during which many of its principal members drifted away from Montreal (mainly to Kingston, Ontario, after its establishment as the capital of the province of Canada in 1841), went into a long cycle of wax and wane, very much like that of all the other theatrical companies whose fate we have so far followed. One of the troupe's later presentations should attract our attention, however: the enactment, in November 1842, of Pierre Petitclair's second play, *La Donation*, the first play by a native French Canadian to have been written, published, *and* performed in Lower Canada.

In looking back upon the theatrical activity inspired by these three foreign-born francophones, Prud'homme, Leblanc de Marconnay, and Aubin, one is struck, above all, by their enthusiasm and by the intense political awareness they manifest of the situation in Canada in these crucial years. Aubin seems to have come to the New World for economic reasons; the other two, probably because of the political situation in their homeland just before and after the Revolution of 1830. One suspects their activities in France may have led to their hasty emigration. Why did they choose Canada? It would be interesting to ascertain what exactly was the perception of this country by an educated Frenchman of the time.

PIERRE PETITCLAIR'S 'GRIPHON' (1837)

By striking contrast, and apart from the Status Quo Comedies, the only play published by a Canadian-born francophone during this troubled decade has very little to do with Lower Canada and nothing at all with politics. *Griphon; or a Valet's Revenge* (Griphon; ou la Vengeance d'un valet) is as resolutely unaware of the world outside its quaint eighteenth-century boundaries as was *Colas and Colinette* of the paroxysms shaking France at the time of its public performance.

Its author had been born in the little village of Saint-Augustin, near Quebec City, in 1813, had attended the Séminaire de Québec despite his humble origins (his parents were illiterate farmers), and then worked for a time as a legal copyist before forsaking the capital and moving to Labrador as tutor to the children of a prosperous tradesman. In explanation of the young author's apparent lack of political awareness in this play, one should mention that its date of composition is unknown, but must antedate, possibly by some years, its publication in 1837.[56]

Griphon, at the time of its publication, was an anachronism: an eighteenth-century situation comedy, grafted on the mainstock of a 'recipe'-farce. Jean-Claude Noël has pointed out aspects of the play borrowed from Regnard, Destouches, and especially Molière,[57] leaving little of the basic plot that is original. Characters, action, and situation are not really credible, and one must consent to suspend one's critical faculties for the duration of the three acts which compose the play. It is an amateur's production, and that too is hardly surprising: for Pierre Petitclair, as for every writer of imaginative literature in Quebec before the twentieth century, such activity had to remain an avocation only, something to which one

/

devoted time and energies left unspent in the pursuit of other, more acceptable, more remunerative occupations.

Griphon, the central character and victim of the less-and-less ingenious pranks of the two servants, Citron and Boucau, is an interesting portrayal. He is, according to his valet, nearly eighty, yet he pursues anything with a skirt and a pulse as vigorously as any villain in contemporary melodrama. Petitclair seems to have understood (perhaps insufficiently) that the old man has to be depicted with vices repulsive enough to exclude the reader-spectator's sympathy as he follows Griphon's successive misfortunes. Otherwise, as has been pointed out, the actions of Citron and Boucau move quickly from the realm of 'acceptable' farcical retaliation (the arranged meeting with 'Mademoiselle Emilie Dupuis,' who is really his own valet in disguise; the foisting of a laxative upon him, instead of wine) to an uncomfortable area approaching pure sadism.[58] This is where the modern reader observes a different level of interest, for one deduces that Petitclair, in his portrayal of Griphon, develops precisely the types of vices best calculated to repel a God-fearing Québécois of the time. It is worth re-examining the play from that point of view.

He is, first of all, a religious hypocrite, in a fashion directly reminiscent of the great Tartuffe himself. He seeks to countenance every vile intent with pious words, and one cannot help but recall Molière's paradigm. Let us observe how he tries to foist himself upon his young, naive serving maid, Florette (I, 5):

GRIPHON
Go see if the door is properly closed.
FLORETTE
The door? But I just closed it, me!
GRIPHON (*placing two chairs side by side*)
Come here and sit down, Florette.
FLORETTE
What do you want me to do that for?
GRIPHON
I have something to tell you.
FLORETTE
Yeah, I know – you always got somethin' like that to tell me!
GRIPHON
What? Listen, silly, isn't it for your own good, what I have in mind?
FLORETTE
Okay, okay, calm down! Here I am sitting down (*she moves her chair away, and sits*).

GRIPHON

Good! (*He sits down, bringing his chair up to hers; she again moves hers away.*) I want to explain to you the proper conduct for a decent girl to follow. I think of myself as your father, and you should consider yourself my daughter. Agreed?

FLORETTE

Well, gosh, I dunno – My father and mother are still alive ...

GRIPHON

I'm going to talk to you like a father. (*He moves his chair closer to hers; she moves hers away.*)

FLORETTE

I can hear you just as good from here.

GRIPHON

Listen to me! How sweet a thing virtue is, Florette! What joys, what delights it brings to those who love and practise it! What plea-sure there is in a clear conscience! Do you know what I mean?

FLORETTE

Well – sort of. You're talkin' like the *curé*, when he's preachin'.

Griphon manages to convince her to bring her chair closer. The lesson continues:

GRIPHON

Now, there's an obedient girl! You should know, Florette, that the first and main duty of a maid is to obey her master, just as a daughter's first duty is to obey her father. I hope I've just cured you of a serious defect in your character. Henceforth you must obey me, to the tiniest detail ... Let me see your eyes.

FLORETTE

What for?

GRIPHON

Don't you understand? You must obey!

FLORETTE

Well, all right. (*She stares at Griphon.*)

GRIPHON

Dear me! You're not well at all! Why didn't you say so?

FLORETTE

Who, me?

GRIPHON

Yes, you! (*He takes her pulse.*) Your pulse is terribly rapid!

FLORETTE
I ain't sick at all!
GRIPHON
Don't say that, Florette – you're very ill! (*He tries to kiss her.*)
FLORETTE
I don' want to! I don' want to!
GRIPHON
What! Another act of disobedience, Florette?[59]

But luckily for her, there is a knock at the door and Florette can retreat from his advances.

His *tartufferie* becomes more and more pronounced, as Griphon decides to respond to an invitation to an amorous rendez-vous with an unknown admirer. After primping and dressing in his best, where does he tell his serving maid he is going? 'I'm off to confession, Florette, that's why I'm wearing my new suit. While I'm gone, pray God that I make a good confession.' Even his multifold misadventures at the hands of the two valets do little to dampen his hypocrisy before the final, contrived resolution of the play. One suspects that his combination of sexual rapacity and hypocritical behaviour was intended specifically to shock the French-Canadian public for whom the work was intended.

But modern sensitivities find the valets too cruel and their 'revenge' exaggerated. After all, what real harm has the old man done to them? He had accused his own servant, Citron, of stealing a valuable ring from him, and the accusation is valid. Boucau, valet to a different master, is involved only for gratuitous amusement and gain. For both valets are dishonest, extracting money from Griphon on various pretexts, including funds intended for masses for the dead which they retain. Boucau's master, Monsieur Normand, who has been absent for most of the play (thus allowing the valets to find in his house a suitable forum for their plots against Griphon) returns unexpectedly to find the servants dressed in masters' clothing and carrying out the last of their elaborate deceptions. Does he punish the scoundrels, and at least apologize to his neighbour? Not in the least!

NORMAND
I understand what's going on, I understand! You, Monsieur Griphon, were out to seduce Citron. They did right, both of them, and in their stead I would have done even more! (*Griphon stares at Nor-*

mand.) Why look at me so astounded? Perhaps you don't know me – after all, I'm not one of the *belles* in the area! But as for me, I know Monsieur Griphon only too well. I know all about his nocturnal excursions, also! Disgraceful! Have you no better way of getting rid of your money? Look at all the poor people there are, and what a lot of prayers they would send to heaven in your name! Shame! A respectable [*sic*] old man like you![60]

So the perpetrators of all the indignities against old Griphon get off scot-free, and with praise. This is direct authorial intervention, as unconvincing as the ending of *Tartuffe*. It is obvious that Petitclair, by this time, has run out of resources, and the reader's interest too has flagged. (Perhaps the author realized this, for his other two surviving plays are limited to two acts.)

On the other hand, it is surprising to discover how much at home young Pierre Petitclair appears in his manipulation of scene and character, at least in the first two acts. In Act I in particular, his alternation of scenes is excellent, as we switch from the two valets to Griphon and back with the action rapidly advancing. One is impressed also with his frequently demonstrated flair for visual comedy: the scene between Griphon and Florette which I have reproduced in part, with the 'business' of their constantly moving chairs in attack and retreat (directly derivative, it is true, of Molière); another where the old man tries to kiss Citron (the latter disguised, of course, as a woman), in I, 12; Griphon's reaction as the laxative begins to work (I, 16) and when his chair is toppled and he is caned and made to crawl on hands and knees (I, 17). As we have seen, this penchant for the visual and farcical was characteristic of *Neglected Education* and other college plays from the preceding century. There are other aspects of *Griphon* cognate with that tradition also: the lack of significant female roles, the inclusion of an important role for a male in disguise, the awkward evolution of the plot, and the final moralizing. The author's formal education at the Seminary had ceased around 1829, by which time college drama was making a comeback from the Plessis era, as we shall soon see.

As with the Status Quo Comedies, the setting is Quebec City, although it is only the occasional reference which reveals this (Boucau, for example, in one of his disguises, challenges Griphon to a duel the following dawn on the Plains of Abraham); the plot could just as well have been situated in francophone Patagonia. Despite attempts to do so, it is difficult to establish any symbolic, social, or political struggle (such as class conflict) as a fundamental aspect of the play. Curiously, Boucau and the secondary characters, their friends the valet Champlure and the maid Fanchon, are made to speak just as correctly, just as 'standardly' as their masters. But at least Florette's accent and diction sound genuinely Canadien, no doubt recorded from faithful observation by Petitclair, as was the local French used by Leblanc de Marconnay. A farmer's son himself, Petitclair would have had ample opportunity to hear such colourful language, upon which he drew especially for his third play, *A Country Outing* (Une Partie de campagne).[61]

Griphon has long been recognized as the first play published by a French Canadian by birth, an honour that is legitimate, as we have seen, only if the authors of the Status Quo Comedies are ignored. Petitclair's play was never performed, and one must underline the fact that there is no recorded reaction whatever to its publication. The mere performance of a play by Voltaire, by Aubin's troupe two years later, evoked as much discussion in the press in a month as all of Petitclair's works combined were accorded until fairly recently. The historian recognizes, none the less, the importance of this first non-political play, obviously intended for performance and not necessarily 'armchair theatre' as the five Status Quo Comedies are. More than anything else, Petitclair seems to have chosen the wrong moment for the work: in 1837 French Canada had far more important things to occupy it. Even the author seems to have had more on his mind than dramaturgy: by the end of 1838 he had already left for the distant North Shore, there to remain, apart from occasional visits, for the rest of his life. When we return to his theatre, we shall find changes both in its format and its political awareness.

THE DURHAM REPORT AND ITS IMPLICATIONS FOR THEATRE

About the same time as he began to write, the very fabric of the society which had produced Pierre Petitclair was rent asunder by the 'Troubles' of 1837-8. It was decided that some reassessment of the situation was necessary. An alert, influential, biased, and controversial assessor was despatched to Canada by the imperial government in the person of John George Lambton, first Earl of Durham – a devotee, incidentally, of theatre in its many forms.

This is by no means the place to consider in detail the famous *Report on the Affairs of British North America* which resulted from his five-month stay in Lower Canada. But we must consider the evaluation he presented, in February 1839, of the state of the arts in French Canada. His remarks have often been reproduced and are still capable of kindling strong reaction today. But they have too often been reproduced out of context by partisans on both sides of the linguistic frontier in Canada.

The full text of Durham's assessment comes near the end of his Report, and purports to be a summary justifying the conclusion he draws on the following page: French Canada must be governed, and eventually assimilated by, English Canadians. Here, in its entirety, is his paragraph on the arts:

There can hardly be conceived a nationality more destitute of all that can invigorate and elevate a people, than that which is exhibited by the descendants of the French in Lower Canada, owing to their retaining their peculiar language and manners. They are a people with no history, and no literature. The literature of England is written in a language which is not theirs; and the only literature which their language renders familiar to them, is that of a nation from which they have been separated by eighty years of a foreign rule, and still more by those changes which the Revolution and its consequences have wrought in the whole political, moral and social state of France. Yet it is on a people whom recent history, manners and modes of thought, so entirely separate from them, that the French Canadians are wholly dependent for almost all the instruction and amusement derived from books: it is on this essentially foreign literature, which is conversant about events, opinions and habits of life, perfectly strange and unintelligible to them, that they are compelled to be dependent. Their newspapers are mostly written by natives of France, who have either come to try their fortunes in the Province, or been brought into it by the party leaders, in order to supply the dearth of literary talent available for the political press. In the same way their nationality operates to deprive them of the enjoyments and civilizing influence of the arts. *Though descended from the people in the world that most generally love, and have most successfully cultivated the drama – though living on a continent, in which almost every town, great or small, has an English theatre, the French population of Lower Canada, cut off from every people that speaks its own language, can support no national stage* [emphasis added].[62]

Durham's words are impressive, but as with most practitioners of the art of persuasion, he has here somewhat overstated his initial case. To affirm that Lower Canada, or at least its francophone majority, was in 1838 'more destitute of all that can invigorate and elevate a people' than just about any other nation on earth, is to indulge in obvious hyperbole; as is his second sentence quoted here, the best-known in the entire Report, qualifying them as a 'people with *no* history, and *no* literature' (by 'history' he means written history). Moreover, one soon realizes the speciousness of the argument he proffers concerning the impossibility for French Canadians, with their 'peculiar language and manners,' of understanding and appreciating the literature of France, since they are too far removed from it. Even if one acknowledges the much broader sense of the word 'literature' in Durham's day (so that it covers journalism, philosophy, essays in the broad area of social sciences, and the like), one perceives that his characterization of the products of French printing presses as 'essentially foreign literature' is inaccurate. Did Americans, then, find the literature of England just as impenetrable, 'conversant about events, opinions and habits of life, perfectly strange to them?'

But let us concentrate attention on his specific remarks on theatre. If one takes the year of his arrival and the one preceding it, his observations would seem justified. These were two of the most unproductive years for drama in Lower Canada – in French, at least. Professor Burger has pointed out that in Montreal and Quebec combined there were only four performances in French in those two years, compared with no less than ninety-four in English.[63] Certainly the political and military events of these years explain, to a degree, the relative paucity of francophone theatre: in effect, the French-Canadian majority were hostages to the minority. On the other hand, apart from the closing of the gallery of the Theatre Royal, from March to May 1838 (the period during which Sir John Colborne had suspended the Constitution of 1791), the anglophone population went about its business and its amusements little disturbed. As Burger puts it, 'the English-speaking minority never really felt its interests were threatened. Its cultural activities were little influenced by the social strife of the time.' Moreover, the French-speaking population was dependent upon its anglophone masters even for access to a stage:

> In Quebec City as in Montreal, the only theatre buildings in existence belonged to radical anglophones, and the entire furnishings of those buildings were those of the English stage: it was in these material conditions that French-Canadians had to operate if they wanted to stage a performance, unless they were willing to set up their own stage elsewhere, which they generally did not do.[64]

As far as the physical facilities for theatrical activity were concerned, in other words, there had been little evolution in French Canada over the preceding half century. The relative parity with English-language theatre had now disappeared, at least with regard to number and scale of performances. Insofar as it pertains to the *visible* aspects of theatre, then, Lord Durham's analysis seems correct. But that analysis ignores the changes already at work and those upon the horizon. Disguised under its apparent vigorous glow of health, English-speaking theatre in Canada was innately unhealthy, for all of its plays and most of its players were imports from Britain or the United States. As the historian of English-speaking theatre in eastern Canada, Murray D. Edwards, remarks:

> In most communities, the local citizens rose to the occasion and developed flourishing amateur theatres. Their popularity, however, was generally short-lived. A study of early records reveals a sudden move from amateur to professional theatre. The interesting and unfortunate point concerning this abrupt transition is that the professional theatre which supplanted the local efforts was invariably American or English. The native talent failed to mature and was apparently unable to compete with the attractions offered by the older cultures ... At the time local amateur groups should have been developing to professional status, encouraging playwrights, actors, and directors of their own, Canadians were sitting back and applauding the American or English stars, with the result that the growth of theatre in Canada was largely an artificial one.[65]

To a mind focused on imperial values, with all significant activity emanating from the nerve centre in London, the situation of the English-Canadian stage may not have seemed at all bad; for those conscious of a potentially new and different identity for English Canada, the outlook must have seemed disturbing. This is the main weakness of the Durham Report, a weakness which it would take the rest of the century to ameliorate. The situation would only improve quantitatively, not qualitatively, over the next several generations (Charles Heavysege's *Saul*, reasonably comparable with one of Quesnel's plays, would not appear for another twenty years, and even then as an exception: the first plays by Canadian-born authors writing in English would come a good deal later). By contrast, some of French Canada's perceived disadvantages implied the potential for qualitative growth. Its dependency on home-grown amateurs ensured the continuation of a nucleus of eager enthusiasts largely protected, as we have seen, from the often drastic economic results of a troupe's failure. It promoted the slow evolution of a local tradition, grafted gently (Leblanc de Marconnay's *Valentine*, for example) on to familiar stock, interpreted by troupes led occasionally by a foreigner (Firmin Prud'homme, Napoléon Aubin), but composed of local amateurs. More significantly, for the purposes of this book, there already existed by 1838 a basis for a native tradition in dramaturgy: Quesnel's *L'Anglomanie* and Leblanc de Marconnay's *Valentine* as hybrids, it is true, but more important for their potential, the Status Quo Comedies and the tradition they represent, and Pierre Petitclair's *Griphon*, unperceived by Durham as by most of his Canadian contemporaries, but an important step towards the evolution of native theatre, if only because it was the first step for an author whose own progress would continue.

In summary, francophone theatre in Canada in 1838 was not very healthy. It was, none the less, at least as vigorous as its anglophone counterpart, despite appearances; and its prognosis was better. Perhaps nothing better illustrates the danger in Durham's basic premise concerning theatre than its subsequent history: when the era of French touring companies came, in the second half of the nineteenth century, their success almost always was at the expense of local troupes – and local playwrights.

Towards the Development of a
French-Canadian Dramaturgy
1837-67

Petitclair's *Griphon* may have elicited no response, but that does not seem to have discouraged him immediately. In the fall of 1842 Napoléon Aubin's Amateurs Typographes offered two performances of a play written, it appears, expressly for that troupe by Petitclair and entitled *La Donation*. Audience response was favourable, and the play was published in the newspaper *L'Artisan*, in serial form, the next month (December 1842).[1] This represents an important milestone: the first play by a Canadian-born author to have been published *and* performed in this country.

La Donation (the word refers to a legal donation *inter vivos*) is, following to some extent the recipe for *Griphon*, another eighteenth-century comedy (of intrigue, not manners), grafted this time on to a nineteenth-century melodrama. The farcical element, particularly the visual one so prominent in his previous play, has here almost completely disappeared, and it is only the speech and mannerisms of the servant class, represented by the maid Susette and especially the manservant, Nicodème, which provide any trace of the comic. Again, the plot turns around a hypocrite, modelled closely on Molière's *Tartuffe*; but this time he is a younger, more threatening one, with none of the religious and sexual overtones of Griphon or of the seventeenth-century original. His name is Bellire, he is out for money, and he very nearly succeeds in swindling it from his intended victim, the rich Quebec merchant Delorval.

Delorval is sole guardian of his orphaned niece, Caroline. She is in love with Auguste, her uncle's trusted business subordinate, and he with her, although they have not yet admitted that love. But her uncle is totally under the influence of Bellire, investing his full faith in the intriguer's counsel. Delorval is now in his sixties, and despite his touchiness on the subject of his age, has been convinced by Bellire to prepare for any eventuality by bestowing his wealth on someone as a legal donation immediately. Naturally, Bellire hopes he himself will be the recipient of this endowment, but is chagrined to learn that Delorval has chosen Auguste instead, and that the young man will also wed his niece. Prepared for any such turn of events, Bellire has devised a clever scheme to alienate Auguste from his employer's favour. He first tries to discredit him by convincing Delorval that the young man is a wastrel, spending all his free time and money in a shady hostelry in town. When the merchant is reluctant to believe this of his long-term employee, Bellire springs a better-baited trap: he has an accomplice, Martel, forge convincing documents attesting that Auguste is already married and that he has abandoned his wife to seek Delorval's money through his niece, Caroline.

Delorval is persuaded (a little too easily, in fact). He decides to fire Auguste, to forbid him entry to his house and business or access to his niece. He also resolves that Bellire will be the only recipient of all his wealth as soon as the legal documents can be drawn up. But Bellire has not counted on the resourcefulness and devotion of the maid Susette: she arranges for her master to be present, hidden behind a screen, while Bellire and Martel gloat over their triumph, sneering at Delorval's gullibility as they outline their plans. But all this we do not know until the culminating scene (II, 21), where, with great dramatic effect, all are assembled while a legal act of donation is being read aloud. The *coup de théâtre* is effective: where Bellire (and perhaps the audience) expects his name to be read aloud as the recipient, Delorval intones, in a loud, clear voice: 'Auguste Richard and his wife, Caroline Delorval' Evil is crushed, justice and virtue triumph; and the short play ends with a rosy hue.

Structurally, the most striking difference from *Griphon* is its length: two fairly economical acts, compared with the former's lengthy and repetitive three. Petitclair seeks to establish a parallel development in the two acts, the first ending with a direct threat to the happiness of the young lovers and to the wealth they will inherit, that threat crystallized in a carefully prepared *coup de théâtre*; the second ending with an even more dramatic surprise (for we do not know that Bellire and Martel have been overheard by Delorval), and the full dissolution of that threat. But apart from those improvements in clarity and economy of plot, *La Donation*'s residual deficiencies in form are quite apparent, for they are those of the melodramatic genre. The chief of these is the abuse of soliloquy (twelve scenes are monologues) and asides. Unfortunately, this is joined by another baneful tradition of the *mélo*: gross oversimplification of character. Auguste is the noblest of youths, animated by his pure, unspoken love for Caroline. Delorval is an honest, generous, well-intentioned man led astray by a cunning scoundrel; and the latter is a two-faced, leering villain whose every entrance must have been accompanied by the hisses, boos, and jeers of the audience. A capital example of both defects comes in two consecutive scenes, in the second of which we meet Bellire for the first time:

Act I, Scene 10
DELORVAL (*consulting his watch*)
But what can be keeping Bellire this morning? He seems very late to me. I'm starting to feel a bit bored. A strange thing, that – I'm never in a good mood when he's not here! He's such a likeable person! ... Besides, he's so devoted to me, so sincere in his friendship, that I can't – well, let's say I just can't do without him! (*He exits.*)

Scene 11
BELLIRE
Oho! there's the fellow now, going into his office – He didn't see me. I wonder whether he's thought about the donation, the old fool! If I can get my hands on the money, I can do without his niece very nicely, especially since she doesn't seem particularly fond of me. She's even forbidden me to address a word to her, in fact! But what if he were to draw up the act of donation in favour of someone else – his assistant, Auguste Richard, for example? He thinks highly of him, and it's true that Auguste deserves it ... But here he comes – let's laugh a bit, to get him [Delorval] in a good mood![2]

It must also be conceded that there is little originality of plot in *La Donation*. Jean-Claude Noël, in his unpublished thesis on Petitclair and his works, has pointed out borrowings from Molière, Regnard, Beaumarchais, and Scribe, concluding that 'all told, there is practically nothing left that is original to Petitclair. The only recognition he deserves should be for his skill in reconciling these various borrowings.'[3] To these defects must be added the inconsistent level of speech used by the servants, the inadvertent Anglicisms,[4] the mistakes in plot preparation.[5]

Yet despite all this, one suspects that the work plays better than *Griphon* would have, a suspicion corroborated by the stage history of *La Donation*, performed some half dozen times before 1860. Its theatricality is unquestionable: for an audience that had not been trained to use esthetic criteria in assessing a play and willing to suspend disbelief long enough to be carried along by the rapidly evolving action, it was no doubt effective. Must one expect Petitclair's audience to be more sophisticated than he was?

This is not the only evolution one notices in the five-year period which separates the two plays. As with *Griphon*, the setting is Quebec City, but this time the reader/spectator is much more conscious of that fact. As to the central plot and sub-plot themselves, it is true that there is nothing therein that is strictly 'Canadian'; but there are ample references to contemporary Canadian concerns – fleeting ones, but all the more intriguing. The response of Bellire's accomplice, Martel, for example, when Bellire asks him what he would do if they were found out (II, 12). 'Well,' he says, 'I would go off and visit the Yankees' – a solution much practised during and after 1838. The intriguer himself is characterized by Suzette (II, 9) as a 'tyrant, a Sydenham': a surprisingly daring reference to Charles Poulett Thompson, Lord Sydenham, successor to Sir John Colborne in 1839, strongly detested for his role in effecting the Union of 1840, and dead only the year before (1841) in a riding accident in Kingston! This is the type of comment one might have expected to find in a play by Leblanc de Marconnay or one of the Patriotes, not in a work by the author of *Griphon*! It has been pointed out that Petitclair, for that first work, had entrusted his manuscript to the generally pro-Bureaucrate printer, William Cowan.[6] But what has escaped notice is that this second play was composed for, and interpreted by, that bane of the British administration, Napoléon Aubin. This suggests quite a personal evolution in the political orientation of our author. A final example from *La Donation* suffices: in II, 17 Nicodème, the loyal, rustic, simple Canadien, is asked by Delorval where Auguste is staying in Quebec City. In rue Champlain?

NICODÈME
Oh, no, sar! ... it's jus' in front o' that there square that stands fer Canada, 'cause they's chains all 'round it ... How's they call it? ... Ah, yes: the Place d'Armes.[7]

It would be another fourteen years before Petitclair would compose another play that has survived, and in discussing it we shall discover an evolution that is just as striking. But in the meantime his example had been followed by others, and it is their story which we should first trace.

THE REVIVAL OF THEATRE IN THE COLLÈGES CLASSIQUES:
ANTOINE GÉRIN-LAJOIE

Another factor at work which Durham had failed to observe was the slow
but definite rebirth of drama in the classical colleges of French Canada.
Soon after the death of the redoubtable Archbishop Plessis, one notices an
upturn in such activity, and as those institutions flourished under a
strongly recrudescent Church, theatrical productions flowered also. Some
had been severely pruned: many are the examples of a play by Molière,
Corneille, or even Racine from which anything resembling a love theme
had been excised, with minor and even major female characters erased or
transposed to male roles, with predictable results for the integrity of the
original.[8]
    This revival of college theatre seems to have begun as early as 1828,
under the watchful eye of that important renovator of Quebec's educational system, the abbé Jean Holmes, then Prefect of Studies at the
Séminaire de Québec.[9] By the early 1830s the practice had spread to several of the other newly founded secondary institutions of learning: the
Séminaire de Saint-Hyacinthe, founded in 1811 and formally chartered in
1833; the Séminaire de Sainte-Thérèse (1825); the Collège de Sainte-
Anne-de-la-Pocatière (1827); the Collège de L'Assomption near Montreal
(1832); the older (1803) Séminaire de Nicolet, on which latter institution
our attention will soon focus. The very fact of the foundation of all these
centres of secondary education in the period in question is ample evidence
of the Catholic revival which was building in Lower Canada as the
Church, strengthened by new blood from France, more confident of its
own role under British rule, and ultimately fortified in British-Canadian
eyes by the conservative policies it had espoused during the troubles of
1837-8, soon regained the primacy it expected for itself in French-Canadian society, and which the rise of the Patriotes had for a moment threatened.
    Some of the programs presented in the colleges were surprisingly rich
and diverse. At the Séminaire de Québec, for example, in conjunction
with the annual examination period, a whole series of plays or parts of
plays was presented on 12-14 August 1833. The students in first year presented a short moral play, Man Is Well Off Just as He Is (L'Homme est
bien comme il est); those in fifth, Natural Sorcery (Le Sortilège naturel);
in fourth, Molière's L'Avare, one of the least contentious of his plays; in
third, extracts from Corneille's Polyeucte (obviously those not involving
the major female role, Pulchérie), plus a dialogue in English, Alexander and
the Thracian Robber; the humanists offered a comic dialogue and a de-

bate, and the philosophers put on *The Trial of a Deaf-Mute Accused of a Crime* (Le Procès d'un sourd-muet accusé d'un crime).[10] A similar program was offered the same year at Saint-Hyacinthe. Sainte-Anne exhibited a puzzling predilection for that mocking spirit, Voltaire, as students there staged his *Death of Julius Caesar* and a scene from *Zaïre* in 1831, followed two years later by extracts from his play which had caused such a commotion in Dublin in 1754, *Mohammed, or Fanatism* (Mohammed, ou le fanatisme), all of them with no known adverse reaction.[11] With bowdlerized texts and young, inexperienced actors, these performances may have had little claim to artistic merit. But the essential point is that they encouraged the latent histrionic talents of a large segment of the educated élite of the province and, whether their instructors wished it or not, encouraged that élite to appreciate stage arts then and after their graduation.

This is precisely the milieu in which there arose the next young native writer, Antoine Gérin-Lajoie, and his case affords ample confirmation of the importance of college drama. Gérin-Lajoie was more fortunate than Pierre Petitclair, in that the new and ambitious impetus in education had already reached down to the primary system by the time he entered it. He entered the secondary system – in this case, the Collège de Nicolet – in the fateful year of 1837, and he and his classmates followed the evolution of the Rebellion with passionate interest. That interest lasted, and a few years later (1842) the eighteen-year-old Antoine was so moved by the fate of the forty-eight Patriotes deported to Australia that he composed the moving 'Un Canadien errant' (Once a Canadian Lad), one of the best-loved and most widely disseminated of Canadian folk-songs, to the music of an old French song.[12] Obviously, this young man was much aware of current social and political events; he was also, very rare in Canada at the time, a young man with a burning passion for verse. As he wrote of himself later, in his *Souvenirs du collège*: 'From the very first classes I attended, I felt within myself a burning passion for poetry. I began to read it at a very early age, and by the time I was fifteen, I had already rhymed a few scattered poems. I learned the rules of prosody all on my own.'[13]

About the same time he managed to obtain permission to establish a literary academy at the college (he was again most fortunate, in that the Director of Teaching was the abbé J.-B.-Antoine Ferland, who was to become an important literary critic and historian, later appointed to the chair of history at Laval University) at the same time, typically, as he was organizing the students of Nicolet into a regiment of cadets, of which he was then made 'General.' The poet and the patriot in him were to culminate two years later (1844) in his celebrated play, *Young Latour* (Le jeune Latour).

The text was actually written for the members of the literary academy he had founded, and it was they who prepared and presented it for the closing exercises of the college on 31 July 1844, with Gérin-Lajoie himself playing the title role. The source of this play is genuinely Canadian: Michel Bibaud's *Histoire du Canada sous la domination française*, first published in 1837. It is a seriously inaccurate source, in this case, as we shall see; but by the very fact of his choosing it the young author shows how quickly Bibaud's text had reached secondary students in Lower Canada (although they belonged to a 'race with no history') and how very seriously they took their patriotism in those years.

The plot is striking: the heroic tale of a military family, the de Latours, and their struggle for the little outpost of Cape Sable in Acadia in 1629-30.[14] In Bibaud's version the father, Claude de Latour, was a *vendu*, one of the first French-Canadian collaborators with the invading English – in this case, against the little garrison captained by his son, Charles (whose name Gérin-Lajoie changes, for some unknown reason, to 'Roger'). His attempts at persuading his son to yield to the English without a struggle having failed, the elder Latour leads an armed assault upon the outpost. But his son has rallied the defenders so resolutely that the English must withdraw and abandon the siege. The father, now caught between two camps, decides to throw his lot in with his son, who receives him with generous forgiveness. Patriotism, self-sacrifice, and will-power have saved the day.

Gérin-Lajoie's style is in perfect accord with this heroic setting. It is a frank emulation of that of Pierre Corneille, including the sonorous rhymed alexandrine couplets of the seventeenth-century master and the attempt at pithy, sententious aphorisms. His vocabulary, too, is that of Corneille and Racine, with a strong penchant towards preciosity.[15] Above all, it is the younger, more virile Corneille, intolerant of weakness, particularly any weakness towards the fair sex. The hero's character is fully sketched by his friend and confidant, Pamphyle (I, 4):

> He speaks his mind but once, and when he says 'I so will it,'
> Wait not on further words, for the earth, the sky,
> The very universe could crumble, could topple from their place,
> And yet he would repeat: 'Yea, so do I will it done.'[16]

There are, naturally, no female characters in the play, and the only woman referred to – the elder Latour's newly acquired, English spouse – is the principal cause of his disloyalty. That feminine element may be lacking outwardly, but it is curious to see its transposition to another scale. The author's apostrophes to his homeland are strangely equivocal in nature: in the song (written by Gérin-Lajoie, again to a traditional air) which precedes the opening of the first act, the speaker (a spokesman for his generation?) begins:

> I seek your glory only
> And your happiness, O my country:
> May the palm of Victory
> Crown the brows of thy sons!

Which is straightforward enough. But what is one to think of the next, extended metaphor?

> I am a young warrior whom love enkindles,
> But do you know the nature of this my love?
> *bis* { Ah! my soul, I love, thou know'st I love
>   This land where first I saw the light of day!
>
> Let another sing of his passion,
> Of the charms of his love, Iris;
> I shall sing of my country:
> For her alone I reserve my love,
> Her alone shall I pay court to,
> *bis* { For I love, my soul, thou know'st I love
>   This land where first I saw the light of day![17]

And lest one conclude, as some critics have done, that this play is as far removed from any reference to specific, contemporary reality as any 'sublime,' 'universal' production of French Classicism, one has only to read our poet's invocation to Champlain (p 43), or his praise of native courage:

> The Canadien is brave: his life he'll gladly give
> In order to stay true to his beloved land.
> Yea, the son of this soil is brimming o'er with valour:
> The blood of his brave fathers runs coursing through his heart.[18]

One has scarcely to read between the lines when Roger's former tutor (now an ally of his father) points out how much better Acadia will be under British rule:

> But if you love this land, will you not then rejoice
> To see it in the sway of a peace-loving monarch,

In the care of a kingdom and a nation
Whose Constitution you must needs admire?
You know full well indeed, the codes of English law
Attract admiring awe throughout this earthly globe:
The finest product shaped as yet by human mind,
And worthy of respect, as if a gift divine!

And when we see Roger's prompt reaction:

But if the Acadian were willing to surrender
Could he really expect to be governed as one nation,
While serving English masters?

Roger then touches upon a source of deepest concern for all informed
Canadiens after publication of the Durham Report, with its clear intent of
eradicating, in time, the French language:

My people love their tongue; to forbid us its use
Would reduce us to vilest slavery.
Indeed, this race was made to be dependent only
Upon the nation from which it sprang;
And were your King the most august of monarchs,
Were your government to promise us full justice,
To elevate Acadia to the rank of Albion,
Yet would I change no whit my present resolve (ii, 3).

Add to all this the wonderful tirade by Roger's friend Pamphyle against
that perennial target of French-Canadian scorn, the *vendus*, those willing
to sell their votes for personal advantage:

Who, ever prompt to bend before a master,
Prostitute for him their mercenary votes,
Sacrifice their liberties, their fellows and their rights,
Their country, for the vile lucre they can gain (i, 4).

and one sees that the young sympathizer with the *patriote* cause, the 'General' of his school's volunteer regiment, the composer of nationalistic
songs, remains faithful to his principles in *Le jeune Latour*.[19]
    The play has serious defects, of course, and critics have often dwelt on
them. The prosody itself is rigid and often defective. The author himself
was first to recognize this, acknowledging that 'the verse, especially in the

first two acts, shows evidence of the haste in which it was composed, and is sometimes slipshod and prosaic. I did not take time for proper revision of the text.'[20] It is also obvious that Gérin-Lajoie, in his emulation of the great Corneille, manages sometimes to produce only a caricature of his idol's style. As Séraphin Marion has put it, 'the pupil has imitated his model so well that he exaggerates the virtues and the defects of the master.'[21] And as the same critic points out, the characters are all too prone to indulge in long speeches and perorations which add nothing to advance the action of the play. Again, the young dramatist has little feeling for the exploitation of what little suspense there is in his plot. Thus in the curious scene (III, 8) where Pamphyle and Raymond (commander of Roger's troops, which he has declined to lead into the battle) await the outcome of the engagement, we have two soldiers appear, supporting Roger, who is wounded and whose sword is stained with blood. Whose? His father's? And what is the outcome of the battle?

But there is no cultivation of the dramatic potential here. Roger's first words merely inform us, very prosaically, of what has taken place. Let us not dwell too long upon these weaknesses: the author himself was pragmatic enough, a bit later, to see them, and to label this fruit of his twentieth year 'a college play, one that should never leave the college scene.'[22]

There has been an unfair tendency to criticize Gérin-Lajoie for the defects inherent in his acknowledged source. Historians now know that the two men who serve as focus for his play were in fact unprincipled rogues (and if the author had only known, Huguenots – French Protestants – in the bargain!) acting in collusion to sell off anything they could lay claim to, to the highest bidder. But the tale as told by Bibaud was generally accepted at the time – apparently even by Gérin-Lajoie's eminent tutor, the historian Ferland – and we must not expect a student, however gifted, to rise above his masters.

And despite its obvious defects and the resultant valid criticisms, this was a play almost perfectly attuned to the time and the public for which it was written. The first tragedy (although there is little that is innately tragic in the plot) to be written by a Canadian, it was composed at that very time and occasion for which it was best suited: the over-solemn, often pompous closing ceremonies of an academic year, in an institution dedicated to tenacious loyalty to the values of the past in the present. Even the grandiloquence, the overly sententious passages would have been welcomed by the relatively unsophisticated audience, since the literary criteria they had absorbed were, in the main, still those of seventeenth-century France. Gérin-Lajoie's play shows as much sensitivity to this time and this audience as his 'Un Canadien errant' had for another.

It is also indicative of another important change in the traditions of the *collège classique* that a broader audience seems to have been admitted for the première of this play, including representatives of two newspapers who received permission to publish the work in serial form six to eight weeks later. There seems to have been no objection to this on the part of the college authorities, nor to its eventual separate publication – despite *Le jeune Latour*'s insistence on the very Roman virtues invoked in the play, despite the suicide which Latour père is on the point of committing (II, 6), despite the fact that the only Judeo-Christian reference in the entire play is in the last act, when 'puissant Jehovah' is mentioned as favouring Roger's fortunes.

Antoine Gérin-Lajoie went on to play a role in the intellectual and literary awakening of his land, but never quite managed to fulfil the high promise he had shown. After admission to the Bar, he worked as translator (would young Latour have approved?) for the provincial Assembly, and eventually librarian to the Library of Parliament, in Confederation year, a post he retained until his retirement in 1880. His proximity to the hive of politics did not dampen his interest in that game: his *Catéchisme politique; ou Eléments du droit public et constitutionnel du Canada, mis à la portée du peuple* (Political Catechism; or, Elements of Canadian Public and Constitutional Law, Brought within the Scope of the General Public, Montreal 1851) is an earnest attempt to educate the population of his province to the central issues they faced in the years before Confederation; and his *Dix ans au Canada, de 1840 à 1850: Histoire de l'établissement du gouvernement responsable* (Ten Years in Canada, from 1840 to 1850: A History of the Establishment of Responsible Government), published in Quebec six years after his death in 1882, is a careful, impartial account of political evolution in that important decade. But it is for his contribution to French-Canadian prose fiction that he is best remembered today, since his two proselytizing novels, *Jean Rivard le défricheur* (1862) and *Jean Rivard économiste* (1864) with their fervent pleas to Québécois to remain on their ancestral territory and open up the land, helped to establish a theme which dominated Canadian prose for another long lifetime.

The institution (Gérin-Lajoie claimed it was his own idea) of a literary academy at Nicolet seems to have been one whose time had come for the educational establishments of Quebec, and most of the other colleges soon had their Académies. (There was a curious – was it coincidental? – parallel in public life as well, with the establishment of a Canadian Society of Literary and Scientific Studies and a renovated Société Saint-Jean-Baptiste in 1843, followed the next year by the famous Institut Canadien, to which we shall return shortly.) By 1850 most of these scholastic academies were operative and generally entrusted, as the one at Nicolet had been, with the preparation and presentation of dramatic texts.[23] Since all these colleges were operated by the Catholic Church, supervision of their choice of texts and performances was close, with permission refused on moral or political grounds for plays deemed capable of causing problems.[24] Nevertheless, despite these restrictions, theatre had returned and returned to stay this time, to the secondary educational system of the Province of Quebec. In time that fact would have visible effects on theatrical activity outside those institutions. For the moment, it was the clergy who, through these academic exercises, provided encouragement and continuity for the dramatic arts in French Canada.

THE CHURCH ENLISTS THE STAGE:
VERREAU'S 'STANISLAS DE KOSTKA'

These were heady years of growth and influence for the Church in French Canada. With the consent of British authorities a second diocese, Montreal, had been established in 1836, and others were soon to follow. A succession of strong bishops in the new diocese and the old ensured that growth did not lead to dislocation. Now the clergy could be strengthened by direct recruitment in France, and by mid-century the nucleus of those charitable and educational communities which would shape the social mould of Quebec for another century had arrived. More secure now of its own position, liberalized to some degree by the rising level of education of its native members and by the influx of new clergy from the mother country, the Church showed itself prepared to display a modest amount of tolerance for the theatrical activity of amateurs, as long as they fully understood within what bounds that activity was to be circumscribed. As Jean Laflamme and Rémi Tourangeau summed it up, in their seminal study: 'The Canadian Church, concerned with the consolidation of its own position after the Union Act of 1840, did not display open opposition [to theatre]. She did not accord it her blessing, but was none the less willing to leave it in relative peace.'[25]

But that tolerance would only be observed as long as theatrical activity remained Canadian, amateur, compliant, and highly moral in tone. As the same authors go on to remark, 'amateur theatre and college theatre, both of them subject to ecclesiastical supervision, remained confidently stable until about the end of the 1850s.' Theatre could survive, as far as the Church was concerned, but would never be allowed to progress out of its infancy. Confrontations were inevitable under these conditions, but they were surprisingly rare until French touring companies came to Canada in the late 1850s. In the meantime, details as to troupes and audiences are monotonously similar to those recorded above for the 1820s or, for that matter, for the 1790s: bouts of eager activity by enthusiastic amateurs interspersed with longer periods of inactivity as the energy and sparse capital assembled by the troupe ran out. There were few spectators, many debts, and constant awareness of the fragility of the tolerance extended to them by ecclesiastical – and sometimes civil – authority. The 1850s represent little change in the way theatrical activity was carried out in the cities of Lower Canada. No organic growth is discernible, but there is no weakening either: Petitclair's *A Country Outing* (Une partie de campagne) in 1856 is arguably better in its genre than anything produced before that date in French Canada; political 'paratheatre' of the type we have seen continued to appear in the newspapers, and in one witty satire, *Le Défricheur de langue*, in 1859; and for the first time, we have an example of college theatre written not by a student but by a priest teaching in one of the secondary institutions.

The play is called *Stanislas de Kostka*, was written by Father Hospice-Anselme Verreau for the students of the Séminaire de Sainte-Thérèse, and was performed by them in November 1855, for a restricted public. It deals with a crucial moment in the short life of Saint Stanislas Kostka of Poland (1550-68) when he decides, at the age of seventeen and against great pressure from family and friends, to enter the Jesuit order in Rome. The play is set in Vienna, where Stanislas and his older brother Paul have been sent by their father to complete their studies.

There are three acts (the author calls them 'Parties') and a total of fourteen scenes ('Dialogues'). In best classical tradition, the play begins *in medias res* and with a familiar and useful expository ploy, the arrival in Vienna of a friend, Auguste, who wants to see Stanislas because he has heard that his friend is ill. His conversation with Stanislas' servant provides all the background information we need. The next two scenes present Paul and his evil guardian, Bilinski, who have been using every means they could, including physical punishment, to dissuade Stanislas from squandering his money on the poor, the infirm, and the imprisoned. By the fourth scene, we are ready to meet the hero, who immediately informs his friend, 'Auguste, we're probably seeing each other for the last time.' Pressed to explain, he will reveal only that God has been calling him for some time, that he is about to make a momentous decision. To heighten suspense at the close of this first act, he announces that he is on his way to consult the Jesuit, Father Magius: when he returns, Auguste will know his decision.

The second act concentrates on the threat to Stanislas' ideals. It begins with a strategy session between his brother and Bilinski, who decide to summon Stanislas and make one last effort to convince him. This confrontation is an excellent didactic tool for the audience Verreau envisaged: they summon every argument against Stanislas' ascetic commitment, underlining his youth and relative inexperience of the joys and pleasures of life, insisting on his obligations to his famous lineage. Stanislas rebuffs them easily: honour, glory, wealth, pleasures are nothing in comparison with eternity. Moreover, a divine voice has been calling him:

PAUL
And where does it call you? (*After a few moments of silence.*)
You're finally revealing your hand: you want to forsake the world.
BILINSKI
And drag out your miserable existence in a cloister!
PAUL
You'll be a disgrace for Father!
BILINSKI
The shame of your family!
PAUL
So there we have your virtuous desires, your noble ambition: to become a laughing-stock for sensible people, an outcast from decent society!
STANISLAS
Brother, Heaven is what I desire![26]

In the end, Paul loses his temper and resorts to direct threats: he is planning a feast for that evening, and Stanislas will be there if they have to drag him there. The rest of the second act develops this threat in conversations between the hero and Auguste, and between him and Father Magius, who finally arrives. Act II ends with Magius refusing, on behalf of the Jesuits, to take in Stanislas because of the immediate political retaliations against the order which would ensue. So Stanislas decides to escape, to run away to Rome and join the Jesuits there.

At the beginning of Act III we learn that Stanislas has escaped from his guarded room and is being sought everywhere by Paul's men. They suspect his destination and all roads south from Vienna have been covered. While Bilinski, in the third dialogue (scene), threatens dire consequences for Magius because of his presumed collaboration, Auguste arrives to report that Stanislas has been discovered on the road to Augsburg and that Paul is about to catch up with him. The suspense is resolved in the fifth and last scene, when Paul returns to recount how, by miraculous divine intervention, he was prevented from intercepting his brother:

PAUL

I was about to reach him, when suddenly my horses stopped short. The coachman tried to drive them, with voice and whip, but it was no use: there seemed to be an impassible barrier in front of them, an invisible force nailing them to the ground.

AUGUSTE

Thank you, Lord!

PAUL

When I decided to return to Vienna, my horses recovered their strength and freedom of movement. So I understood that Heaven had taken my brother's side.[27]

Quickly, Paul decides to rid himself of Bilinski's evil influence, to amend his own ways, and to facilitate his brother's wishes. The play then ends with its longest speech, by Father Magius, drawing the obvious moral lessons from the incident.

From this brief description, it is clear that *Stanislas de Kostka* is the very epitome of college theatre. Its six male characters are irreproachable in their diction, good is painted in purest white and Bilinski in unrelieved black. Every scene has its edifying message, and virtue is rewarded in the end. Classical tradition is also obvious, in the economical use of plot, the total absence of visual, and consequent reliance upon reported, action, its respect of the unities of place, time and action. Father Verreau, twenty-seven years old at the time and Prefect of Studies at Sainte-Thérèse, knew his models well and extracted all possible dramatic effect from meagre data. This is the type of theatre he would have been exposed to himself, for he had attended both the Séminaire de Québec and Sainte-Thérèse when drama was an integral part of both institutions' curricula. And this is the type of theatre his superiors could approve of without reservation.

Unlike the case of Gérin-Lajoie's *Young Latour*, there are no newspaper accounts to inform us how the performance was received in 1855, but the fact that the prestigious *Revue de Montréal* decided to publish the play twenty-three years later, in a separate edition, suggests that it had had a lasting effect. For Verreau, who was soon to become Director of Jacques Cartier Normal School in Montreal, and later a respected professor of history at Laval's campus in the same city, this seems to have been his only experience in dramaturgy. The genre apparently did not interest him, except as a didactic tool: as a means, not an end. The criteria he used for *Stanislas de Kostka* would have been just as valid in 1655, as in 1855, in France as in Canada.

THE CHURCH VS FRENCH PROFESSIONALS:
'LES SOIRÉES DU VILLAGE' (1860)

H.-A. Verreau's only play is an innocuous example also of the Catholic Church's progressive appropriation of certain theatrical forms for purposes of edification or propaganda. In the second half of the century, that tendency would accelerate, and sometimes take less innocuous and far less theatrical form, as we shall see in the case of the *Soirées du village*.

The Church's hegemony in French-Canadian society suffered no serious challenge during the 1840s. But the potential for challenge was already there in some of the intellectual organizations which were a product of that decade and in some of the newspapers appearing on the scene. I have already mentioned some of the literary and cultural associations which began to spring up in the *collèges classiques* and in Quebec society in general, about the time of Gérin-Lajoie's *Young Latour*. One of the most vigorous of these for a time, and the most influential, was the Institut Canadien, founded in Montreal in 1844, with branches soon following in Quebec (1847) and Ottawa (1852). The Institut in Quebec City had a long and fairly untroubled existence, concentrating on the acquisition of books for the establishment of a good library, on lectures, conferences, and public debates. But as time went on the parent group in Montreal attracted political reformists and republicans unwilling to accept the Church's conservative social views. Confrontation was inevitable. One of its first members had been Antoine Gérin-Lajoie, elected President of the Institut in 1845, at the age of twenty-one, and Secretary of the Saint-Jean-Baptiste Society the same year. Young Wilfrid Laurier was also an active participant in the group's activities until its more and more serious encounters with the Bishop of Montreal, the formidable Ignace Bourget, made membership a social and political liability.

The famous *affaire Guibord* (1869-71), following upon the heels of repeated assaults by Bourget and a formal condemnation of the Institut by Rome, took away the membership and much of the force of this remarkable organization. A great deal of ink and venom had been spilled on both sides by then, and the contest had some unwelcome side-effects for theatre, as the threat of foreign players combined with the threat of native free-thinkers to arouse the Church's ire. That conjunction occurred in 1859-60, when an experienced French professional company arrived to offer in Montreal and Quebec a wide variety of fare in more than fifty performances: by far the most significant theatrical activity to that date.

The most striking aspect of their extended tour was the drastic modernization they introduced into the repertoire hitherto available to theatregoers in the province. As Professor Hare has observed:

> These actors brought with them a selection of contemporary plays, by Bouilly, Dennery, Labiche, etc.; following the tradition of Parisian *théâtre de boulevard*, they changed programmes every second or third night, offering vaudeville, melodramas and comic-opera. In this way light, so-called 'commercial' theatre shaped the tastes and the repertoire offered thereafter by amateur groups.[28]

This was 'commercial' theatre because, unlike the amateurs who played for charity or for personal satisfaction, the visiting troupes had to make money at the box-office, and had thus to offer what was 'selling' in other dramatic centres and which they calculated would sell in Canada. Their instincts, and frequently their taste, were consistently questionable, it is true, as they seem to have completely misunderstood the nature of their French-Canadian audiences. But on that point they have been sufficiently belaboured (particularly by the impassioned Léopold Houlé, in his *Histoire du théâtre au Canada*). This repertoire, from the 1870s on, would begin to influence native players and native playwrights, as Professor Hare has suggested; and the influence would not, in general, be healthy, whence many of the hastily botched adaptations, the acknowledged and unacknowledged plagiarisms, and much of the eminently forgettable theatre which would, in part, characterize the last and more 'productive' third of the nineteenth century in Quebec. But there is no known emulation by local dramatists of these French productions in 1859-60. Their interest for us lies in the response they elicited from the Church, which had not forgotten the lessons of the French Revolution and which had followed in dismay the evolution of French culture and politics in the first half of the century.

Soon after they announced their program for the summer of 1859, Bishop Bourget, ever vigilant, decided that the time had come for a public condemnation, since their offerings included works by the 'immoral' Alexandre Dumas *fils*.[29] Bourget sent off a circular to all clergy in his diocese: 'On reception of the present letter, you will please issue strict instructions, in your sermons, against attending Opera, the Theatre, the Circus, and other profane amusements which now constitute a real source of scandal for our towns and countryside.' The Bishop knew how to persuade the rural majority of his flock, for he then goes on to comment:

> These disorderly amusements are all the more regrettable, in that they could very well bring upon us the frightful punishment of a

poor harvest, and thus frustrate the hopes of a fine crop aroused in us now by the sight of our flourishing fields. For the Lord God may search through the stores of His wrath and find a scourge for us, if we exhaust His long-suffering patience. How right it is, then, that we should direct our indignation and our ire against these vagabond strangers who come amongst us and expose us to the just wrath of Heaven, by poisoning our land with their dangerous spectacles. Alas! they drain considerable wealth, which we sacrifice to our pleasures, whilst refusing it to Charity![30]

Bourget, as his letter implies, had more than one reason for reacting as he did.[31] He had other targets in view. His conflict with the Institut Canadien had come to a head about this time. The Bishop in fact had had his eye on that organization for some time, since he had first examined the catalogue of its library for 1852 and found therein a whole host of works the reading of which was prohibited to Catholics by the Church's *Index*. Even then, if the Institute had restricted itself to the realm of literature, Bourget no doubt would have been less vigorous in his reaction. But as the historian Mason Wade points out:

The Institut was not only a literary society; its leaders were also the leaders of the *Rouge* party, and they revolted against Bishop Bourget's authority in part because of the open alliance of the hierarchy with the Conservative Party. Since the *Rouges* believed in the new republican ideas which in Europe had endangered the position of the Church, the French-Canadian hierarchy was naturally inclined to ally itself with their political opponents. The new democracy of the nineteenth century had no appeal for the clergy, who were alarmed by the increase of official corruption and election disorders at home and by civil strife in Europe. Democracy was also tainted for them by its derivation from the suspect intellectual fathers of the French Revolution, and by the fact that its disciples went to still greater extremes than the leaders of the unsuccessful Rebellion of 1837-8, which had endangered the survival of French-Canadian nationality. The *Rouges* openly advanced the doctrine of the separation of Church and State – a doctrine repugnant to the Catholic tradition, which holds that such separation may be tolerated but not approved – and they gloated over the republican successes in Europe, which deeply distressed the innately conservative and monarchist French-Canadian clergy, who at this period identified themselves more closely with Rome than at any time since the days of Bishop Laval. The *Rouges* also were sympathetic to American ideas, ever distrusted by the clergy, and inclined to annexationism, which the clergy thought would doom French-Canadian Catholicism.[32]

It is in this light that we should appreciate the pastoral letters which Monseigneur Bourget issued in 1858, strongly condemnatory of the Institut Canadien in his diocese, of its policies, its members, and its library. In this light also we should see his attack upon theatre the following year, for that theatre had been supported strongly by a third target of the Bishop's fire: the anti-papal newspaper *Le Pays*, the voice of the *Rouge* party controlled by Louis-Antoine Dessaulles, an influential member of Montreal's Institut. Bourget intensified his attack the following spring, with another pastoral letter directed explicitly against *Le pays*, listing prominently among his charges against it the fact that the newspaper praised actors and urged its readers to attend the theatre.[33] Of the three targets, one suspects that theatre was by far the least central in Bourget's plan, but it was a convenient means of isolating Dessaulles, and through him, the Institut.

The more or less official organ of the diocese of Montreal, *L'Echo du cabinet de lecture paroissial*, now began an intensive campaign against the stage, regurgitating the now-familiar objections of Greek philosophers, Church fathers old and new, of Nicole, Bossuet, and (perhaps surprisingly) Jean-Jacques Rousseau. Other Catholic publications soon followed, and the opening years of the 1860s seemed all too similar to the atmosphere in New France under Monseigneur de Saint-Vallier. At the same time there appeared another form of theatre, or rather paratheatre, best represented by a two-part series entitled *Les Soirées du village, ou entretiens sur le protestantisme* (Village Evenings, or Conversations on Protestantism).

The first part, published in Montreal some time before 1860, is subtitled *Les Saints protestants: Saint Luther*; the second part bears the imprint, 'Montréal, 1860,' and is devoted to another 'Protestant Saint,' Jean Calvin.[34] There may have been other subsequent texts in the series, but I have not yet identified them.

Interlocutors in the first text are Monsieur Dupuy, 'an excellent schoolmaster, very well educated'; Monsieur Constant, 'skilful physician and good Christian'; Pradier, 'Churchwarden of the Parish, very diligent in attendance at Church services'; Morin, 'a retail merchant and the soul of integrity'; Teissier, 'an old man venerable for his common sense and his patriarchal manner'; and Boirude (the name translates as 'Hard-drinker'), 'a *habitant* who has not always been temperate in his habits.' The work is anonymous, but its author was no doubt one of the clergy, as we shall see.

From this title and list of characters, one already deduces what type of text we are dealing with. In French Canada the wheel had now come full circle since 1694 and the Church had decided to espouse a form of drama for its own proselytizing ends, shaping it instead of combatting (or at least resisting) it. The School-master opens the 'Conversation' with a question that displays the concerns of the Catholic clergy about this time, on the question of the many itinerant preachers in the province:

> Tell me, Doctor Constant: who is this stranger whom I saw circulating in the village yesterday?
> THE DOCTOR
> He's a preacher, a bible-seller.
> THE SCHOOL-MASTER
> Indeed! Do you know if he sold many?
> THE DOCTOR
> Some, but not a great many.
> THE SCHOOL-MASTER
> And he did some preaching, no doubt?
> THE DOCTOR
> Yes, but I didn't go to his sermon. The others here did, and can tell you about it.
> BOIRUDE
> Yes, I went, and I listened carefully – a lot more carefully than I ever listen to our Curé's Sunday sermons![35]

The School-master then elicits information from Boirude as to what the preacher said, and the list is a predictable one: Priests are mercenary. Masses for the dead are ludicrous for Purgatory does not exist. Indulgences are stupid. The Pope is the Beast of the Apocalypse. ('Here,' says Boirude, 'he spoke to us of a famous German named Luther who, according to him, proved beyond doubt all the things I've just mentioned.') It is nonsense to adore the Virgin Mary. Confession is useless, invented by priests to control the populace. We must all return to a more personal reading of the Bible, despite the clergy's opposition. And so on. The itinerant preacher's message certainly affected Boirude, who concludes: 'Seems to me we'd all live a lot more easily, and peacefully. All we'd have to do would be to read the Bible, or have it read to us. That's a good deal easier than what our priests now demand of us!'

From this point on, the School-master takes over the conversation, as he sets out to demonstrate the pernicious heresy of the doctrines preached to them the day before, 'and which are nothing other than Protestantism, once embellished with the false title of "Reformation".' He undertakes a long biography of Martin Luther (it accounts for most of the rest of the text, with only occasional interventions and questions from his audience), quoting verbatim long passages from primary sources, even providing footnotes for each reference he cites. As one would expect, the indictment is expert, and the prosecution thoroughly convincing for his listeners in the piece.

The concern demonstrated here was real, and the Roman Catholic Church in Quebec was not merely starting at shadows. In recent years there had been more and more incursions by zealous evangelists into the countryside, some of them francophone Swiss Calvinists (whence the general appellation, 'Suisses,' for these preachers); there had also been a small but disturbing number of notable defections from clerical ranks, the most memorable of them being that of Charles-Pascal-Télesphore Chiniquy. He was a Québécois born and bred, ordained a priest, and he soon attained national celebrity with a vast popular crusade against alcohol in the 1840s. But the temptations of the flesh (even without Demon Rum) proved too strong for Chiniquy, and after a series of scandals he had been defrocked by Bishop Bourget in 1851, then excommunicated in 1856. He then became a Presbyterian minister and was soon back in Quebec, leading another vigorous campaign, this time an anti-Catholic one. The Church had cause for alarm, and publications like *Les Soirées du village* are visible earnest of its concern. They were, in a real sense, retaliation in kind, for Chiniquy and his like were themselves skilled pamphleteers who often wrote in dialogue form. Some of the apostate's writings were disseminated far and wide, well into the twentieth century, particularly his persuasive tract against celibacy, *The Priest, the Woman, and the Confessional* (Montreal 1875). One suspects this is what underlies remarks like that of old Teissier, after the School-master's long explication is complete: 'But according to what I've been told, right here in Canada we have a few misguided priests who have been converted to Protestantism and taken wives. Because of which they have been welcomed and treated with great respect by the descendants of the monk Luther and the nun Bora [Katherine von Bora, who had defected from a convent and whom Luther married in 1525]' (p 42).

Which intervention leads to one of the few remarks by the merchant, Morin – the only speech in the entire text with something resembling humour: 'Oho! Now I understand why a certain Protestant gentleman came to see me the other day, to rail against the celibacy of the clergy. No doubt he wanted to see us all become offspring of priests [Fathers] and

Sisters. Then it wouldn't be long before we became *brothers* through and through! (p 42)

Let us not linger too long over the second text, for we have already seen the tone and format. It is devoted to a similar exposition and indictment of the life and teachings of Calvin, which teachings had been made current by the Suisses and preachers like Chiniquy.[36] The personages convened are the same as before (Dupuy, the School-master, has had his name slightly altered to 'Dupuis,' and the Doctor has become a Notary, although he retains the same name, Constant), and the author assumes his readers are familiar with the first text, in his opening remarks. Again, it is the School-master who is entrusted with the task of exposing Calvin's evil ways and aberrant doctrines, but this time he receives assistance from the Notary, Constant. Calvin's inconsistencies, his persecutions of dissenting colleagues, his belief in predestination are systematically detailed, then assailed. On page 78 the School-master mercifully sums it all up again: 'Such was the Father of the Church of Geneva; such were the results of his so-called Reformation. And if the preachers now circulating everywhere here in Canada whom we call 'Swiss,' are really Swiss in origin, it's very probable that their source can be traced back to Calvin, and that they are his spiritual descendants.' The others agree. The Notary suggests it is time for all to retire (here the reader agrees wholeheartedly!), and Boirude, on the eightieth page of this laboriously annotated text, has the last word: 'In my sleep, I expect I'll see poor Servet [condemned to death by Calvin for his heresy] and his executioner, the Pope of Geneva.'

Les Soirées du village cannot really be examined with the criteria we have used for other texts thus far. It is only marginally Canadian, marginally dramatic in form. The obvious similarities are with the political dialogues we have examined (in particular, the anonymous text from 1794, *Le Canadien et sa femme*), which seem to have been a form perennially favoured in French Canada. But the same important question must then be posed again: were texts such as *Les Soirées du village* meant to be read or 'interpreted' aloud, as was the case with at least one similar dialogue from the 1790s, and perhaps with all of them? If so, of course, their relationship to more usual dramatic forms is closer than appears at first sight.

There is little doubt that a Catholic priest was the author of this text. The very thoroughness of the case constructed against Luther and Calvin indicates the product of a mind immersed in theological and apologetic literature. On the other hand, no dramaturgical talent is evident, unlike the case of *Stanislas de Kostka*. There is no attempt at creating suspense, no characterization: apart from a certain healthy frankness in the early remarks of Boirude, the interlocutors are interchangeable in their diction,

and that diction is 'textbook French.' How could one possibly retain verisimilitude when a character (the School-master) quotes – with footnotes –
extracts amounting to hundreds of words at a time, from various texts? In
form and in content, *Les Soirées du village* are an extreme case of the
Church's appropriation of drama for purposes of propaganda. The rest of
the century would see examples that are far more traditional in form, far
less homilectic in content: melodramatic attacks upon social abuses such as
alcoholism (*Valiquet's Guest, or The Sinister Stew*, published in 1869 by
Father Jean-Baptiste Proulx); well-written exhortations in favour of colonization and social action (*The Pioneers of Lac Nominingue, or The Advantages of Colonization* [*Les Pionniers du lac Nominingue, ou les Avantages de
la colonisation*] by the same Father Proulx, in 1882; *Exile and Fatherland*
[Exil et Patrie], by Father Edouard Hamon, performed at Montreal's
Collège Sainte-Marie in 1870); plays drawn from Canadian history, infused with a strong patriotism in the spirit of Gérin-Lajoie's *Jeune Latour*:
Chomedey de Maisonneuve, by Monsignor Sylvio Corbeil (1899) or *The
Discovery of Canada*, by Brother Alphonse-Stanislas Roberge (1899). One
priest, Alphonse Villeneuve, continued in the tradition of *Les Soirées du
village* in that his 'plays' are composed of personal attacks and are unplay-
able: his lurid *Infernal Comedy, or Liberal Conspiracy in Hell* (1871-2) in
533 pages, directed primarily against the Sulpician Order in Montreal, then
at odds with Bishop Bourget; his *Antidote, or Falsehoods, Errors, Deceits,
and Blasphemies of the Apostate Chiniquy*, in two separate printed dialogues
(1875), the latter of which, in particular, bears remarkably close resem-
blance to our model.[37] These texts obviously parallel the paradramatic
activity manifested in French Canada's newspapers at the time, on political topics.

'ARCHIBALD CAMERON OF LOCHEILL, OR LES ANCIENS CANADIENS' (1865)

But only one more dramatic text composed by clergy survives from the
period which concerns us, *Archibald Cameron of Locheill*, performed at the
Collège de l'Assomption in 1865, repeated dozens of times thereafter on
college stages in Quebec.

The text is an adaptation of part of the novel by Philippe Aubert de
Gaspé, *The Canadians of Old* (Les Anciens Canadiens), first published in
Quebec City two years previously and generally considered the most
important novel of nineteenth-century Quebec. The adaptation is by two
priests, twenty four-year-old Joseph-Camille Caisse and thirty-two-year-old
Pierre-Arcade Laporte, both of them graduates of the Collège de l'Assomp-

tion, both instructors there in 1865. The title of their original text, which survives only in manuscript form, was *Archibald Cameron of Locheill*, the full name of one of the protagonists in Aubert de Gaspé's original. A Scot by birth, he has been befriended by a noble French-Canadian family and educated along with their scion, Jules d'Haberville. Although the two became the closest of friends, they are now separated by the bitter war for the conquest of Canada, Archibald ('Arché') as a lieutenant on the British side, Jules as an officer on the other. Caisse and Laporte have chosen the most dramatic twenty-four-hour period in the original story, beginning with the night before the battle on the Plains of Abraham. With largely insignificant modification, the play as they composed it was published by G.W. McGown in 1894, and this is the edition which, being easily accessible, we shall work from.[38]

The play is in three acts, very well designed to heighten suspense and to present all facets of the central conflict between Arché and Jules. The adaptors have certainly improved upon the structure of Aubert de Gaspé's novel, which tends to be far too discursive for modern tastes: the first scene of Act I has Jules and a fellow officer, De Saint-Luc, in conversation, and we quickly learn of the pending battle and the rumour that Arché is one of the leaders of the enemy's troops. Jules is indignant: 'What! Arché bearing arms against Canada, the country that sheltered him in his misfortunes! ... Arché, betraying my father, betraying me, his friend and brother? ... If that were so, I would despise the wretch just as strongly as once I loved him!' (p 5) The atmosphere of 1760 is recreated in this first act by traditional songs such as 'O, Carillon,' by habitant legends and ghost stories exchanged by the francophone troups as they sit around their campfires, awaiting the battle they know will come on the morrow. The common soldiers (Dubé, Fontaine, José) are made to speak in a colourful, archaic, rural French, while their superiors, as again in Aubert de Gaspé's original, speak 'society French.' Act I ends with confirmation that Archibald Cameron of Locheill is indeed a leader of the opposing troops that have been burning *habitant* homes and barns, and that they will meet him in battle the next day.

Act II, logically, switches to Arché, and opens with his melancholy monologue, which is interrupted by a party of Indian raiders, allies of the French, who take him prisoner. II, 2 allows the adaptors' flair for the dramatic to come to the fore: we have Arché lying bound, front and centre stage, while the Indians decide how best to torture and despatch him. But the French Canadian, Dumais, arrives, whose life Arché had once saved, and he manages eventually to free Arché from their clutches. He returns to his own camp, where Major Montgomery, his sworn enemy, orders him to proceed towards the Plains of Abraham, burning everything in his path. The Major, we also learn, is a thorough scoundrel and has prepared a mortal trap for Arché on the battlefield that day.

Act III is preceded, the stage directions tell us, by a *tableau vivant* depicting the battle. 'This *tableau*,' we are told, 'has the double function of arousing the audience's interest and preparing it for a proper understanding of the Third Act.' We rejoin the action towards the end of the battle: Arché, we learn, has survived the trap Montgomery had prepared for him. There is a rapid juxtaposition of scenes on both sides of the conflict, as the action sways back and forth until the crucial scene (Scene 6) where Jules and Arché finally meet by chance on the sidelines. The confrontation has been well prepared, and Caisse and Laporte play skilfully upon the reader/spectator's emotions as Jules refuses to accept his adversary's poignant attempts to explain and excuse his behaviour. Arché sinks to his knees, beseeching Jules:

> Must I beg you? ... Here I am, on my knees. I implore you, tell me you forgive me...
> JULES (*visibly moved*)
> Stand up, Archibald of Locheill!
> Scene 8: JULES, ARCHÉ, joined by MONTGOMERY
> MONTGOMERY
> What is this I see! What, Archibald Cameron of Locheill, one of His Britannic Majesty's officers, on his knees in front of the despicable foe!
> JULES (*drawing his sword*)
> Who gave you permission, Major Montgomery, to come and insult me thus? Unless you are as cowardly as you are insolent, prepare to defend yourself!
> ARCHÉ
> What are you doing here, Montgomery, you base spy?

When Montgomery then threatens Arché with recourse to General Murray, Arché produces a letter from the General, praising his conduct in the battle, branding Montgomery a coward and traitor, and offering Arché promotion to the rank of Major in his stead. But we learn that Arché has refused the promotion and wishes to retire his commission so that he will never again be forced to fight against the nation he loves so well. Jules is still not prepared to forgive him, although he continues to struggle with his emotions. Arché bids him adieu, sadly, and is about to depart.

JULES

Halt, Arché. (*Aside:*) No, he cannot be as guilty as it appears, since he so readily sacrifices his most brilliant and most legitimate future prospects in favour of gratitude and friendship. (*Holding out his arms:*) Arché, my friend, I forgive you! (*Arché rushes into his friend's arms, shouting:* 'Brother!') (pp 46-9).[39]

And the play ends with the two swearing eternal friendship once more, all conflicts now resolved.

I shall not dwell on the obvious symbolism, at the national level, of this idealized conflict between the two protagonists: it has already attracted reams of comment on Aubert de Gaspé's novel, for the play is very faithful, in that respect, to its source.[40] Its première, on 19 January 1865, was an enormous success according to contemporary reports,[41] but must have been less impressive than the performance on 11 July of the same year, for the elderly novelist, now approaching his eightieth year, was present, arriving with great pomp in a steamboat from Montreal and to a rousing welcome from staff and students. He expressed his delight at the three-hour performance, which apparently had a strong emotive effect upon the audience.[42] A medal was even struck to commemorate the occasion, a theatrical summit and indeed one of the intellectual highlights of the decade. The newspaper *La Minerve* was warm in its praise: 'On behalf of the nation, we congratulate the College for the patriotic ideal which has inspired it on this occasion. An inexpressible emotion invades one's heart and mind at the performance of this national drama: we seem to see the Canadiens of that former age come to life before our eyes, in all their sublime simplicity and their heroic charm.'

A 'national drama' was indeed what the play seemed to represent, and that is part of its success. Fathers Caisse and Laporte have taken the best of the novel, powerful in its own right, and improved upon it by their economy of action and dialogue. The music, the *tableau vivant*, the flickering campfires, the frequent salutes and presentation of arms in military drill, all heighten the dramatic conflict. To quote from *La Minerve* again:

At times we have the accent and diction of the *habitant*; at times we have a whole tribe of Indians arriving with their whoops and cries, and we see them in their war-paint, tatooed, crowned with feathers, slipping through the brush with their burning eyes, leaping upon their victim with the agility of a snake, and with their fearful cries, their dances, their death-songs. We learn more in these few hours of the performance than we would in several years of reading about it.[43]

Yet these visual and audible embellishments do not detract from the central dramatic conflict, which remains psychological, exploited with considerable skill. It is a pity that neither author seems to have written again for the stage and that they probably considered their text a mere transposition of the original material, all credit going to the novelist. If so, let us temper their modesty: they have achieved far more than that, and succeeded in reviving, if only for that one performance, the very best aspects of seventeenth-century *réceptions* in French Canada, adapted to their own time.

Archibald Cameron of Locheill joins the energies of Church and *collège* in much the same way as Verreau had done in his *Stanislas de Kostka*. But its real predecessor is not that play, but rather Gérin-Lajoie's *Jeune Latour*, in its adaptation of a recent work (Bibaud's *History*), its insistence on nationalistic patriotism, its multiplicity of exclusively male characters (more than a dozen in the 1865 work, and with the love story that had been central to Aubert de Gaspé's novel completely excised); and most curiously, in the relatively small role accorded to religious belief in both plays. They are both a whole world away from *Les Soirées du village*, for the Church's role in this final play is positive, helping to shape a healthy, home-grown dramatic tradition.

POLITICAL THEATRE AND PARATHEATRE 1837-67[44]

Rouges, Bleus, and the Struggle for Responsible Government (1848)

The minor dramatic genre which reached an apogee with the Fifth Status Quo Comedy, *The Rout of the Status Quo*, in June 1834, practically disappeared from the newspapers of Lower Canada for the next few years, as the Bureaucrate side licked its wounds. It was not until real political debate in the Canadas intensified again in the late 1840s that the peak of another cycle would be reached, predictably, with political dialogues in partisan newspapers. Not that the format had disappeared in the interval: in the fall of 1837, for example, the genre was revived briefly in the newly established Montreal newspaper *Le Populaire*, edited by the ubiquitous Hyacinthe Leblanc de Marconnay. Most of the first page, and part of the second, of the issue for Friday, 27 October, is taken up by a 'Conversation between Two Canadian *Habitants*,' on the subject of the current political situation. The dialogue purports to have been sent to the editor from someone now resident in Philadelphia whose pen-name is 'One Who Has Visited Canada.'

Papineau is the main target of the piece, and the timing is important: just after the noisy meeting of Patriote leaders at Saint-Charles on 23 October 1837, and just before the confrontation between the Patriote Sons of Liberty and members of the Doric Club in Montreal on 6 November. At a time, in other words, when hostilities were in the air, but almost a month before the first serious conflict at Saint-Denis. The interlocutors are Jean and Pierre, and the dialogue begins:

> JEAN
> I say, neighbour, I've just heard a bit of news that I find quite astonishing.
> PIERRE
> What's that, then?
> JEAN
> They say Mr Papineau has turned his coat; that is, he's given up the honourable post he occupied and has turned to the lowest of trades –
> PIERRE
> Bah! What slander! Would you ever doubt the honour and probity of Mr Papineau?[45]

What Jean has heard is that *le chef* has taken to brigandage and smuggling, an obvious reference to the efforts then under way by some Patriote organizers to procure money and arms from the United States. Despite the similarity with so many such journalistic dialogues, it is interesting to note that the dynamics of this one moves in an opposite direction: from initial defence of Papineau, Pierre turns to indignant hostility towards him as Jean builds up his case. Pierre decides that the Patriote leader is money- and power-hungry: apparently he will betray all of Canada to the Americans in exchange for a well-paid post in the resulting republican government. And in much the same way as André had done in *Le Canadien et sa femme* (1794), Jean excoriates the Americans for their intolerance and duplicity:

> Don't you know the Americans detest our religion, our laws and customs? After burning down the convent in Boston, what didn't they do to besmirch the morals and character of our priests and the worthy nuns of Montreal! Didn't we see a bill brought before Congress five or six months ago, proposing a law which would prohibit entry to American territory to anyone who didn't renounce the Catholic faith? And that's what Papineau holds up to us as a model of liberal ideas![46]

There is occasional wry humour in the text, but its general tone is too serious and most of the speeches far too long. The author (was it perhaps Leblanc de Marconnay himself?) has not improved upon the Status Quo dialogues nor even upon the first De Bonne dialogue of 1807, *Veillée d'un candidat avec sa belle amie*. Moreover, the piece seems to have elicited no response in kind from Papineau's supporters: the history of events in November 1837, no doubt explains that absence.

Three different types of dialogues characterize the 1840s, but only the third type has any close connection with the forms we have already examined. I shall not dwell long upon the first, for it is merely the adaptation of a dialogue written by a minor French author, Louis-Marie de Lahaye, vicomte de Cormenin (1788-1868), briefly popular in France and Canada, and probably one of the models for works such as *Les Soirées du village*, examined in the preceding chapter. This dialogue is entitled a 'Conversation between two Canadian Farmers' and it appeared in the ultraconservative *Echo des campagnes*, published in Berthier on 7 November 1846. In it the two farmers, François and Pierre, discuss the role of religion in country life. In the course of their wooden dialogue they come out firmly on the side of the Church, its ministers, and its policies, while affirming a theme destined for a hardy future in French Canada, the superiority of rural over urban values: 'For most urban workers, life is defined by the work-place and the tavern, and swept along like a whirlwind. But for country-dwellers, the parish is their little *patrie*, their second *patrie*, their true *patrie*, almost. Now who represents the parish? Is it the school, or the Mayor's office? No, it's the Church!'

An editor's note at the end informs us that the piece, which occupies most of the first page of the paper, was taken from Cormenin's work entitled *Entretiens de village* (Village Conversations), with some of the diction obviously modified in order to provide local colour (of which there is very little); but that the original author's ideas have been 'religiously' preserved. There were several such extracts from Cormenin's text circulating in Canada at the time, some of them printed under separate cover.[47]

The other examples come from a journal at the other end of the political spectrum, the Montreal newspaper *L'Avenir*, founded in 1847 by members of the nascent Rouge party and operated by a committee of collaborators (the so-called 'Group of Thirteen') under the general leadership of J.-B.-Eric Dorion, then only twenty years old. The first sort of dramatized dialogue it turned to is in verse, the only examples of that format in French Canada to that time, apart from the short satirical poem, 'Bonaparte & son Mamluck,' published in 1814, almost certainly borrowed from a European source (see ch. 3 n13 above). There are two in the series, the first appearing on 18 December 1847 under the heading, 'poésie canadienne,' and entitled 'The Dissolution [of Parliament]: The Governor in Council.' It is described as a 'Canto with Six Voices,' the six being Governor-General Elgin; 'Papineau' (in this case Denis-Benjamin, brother of the Patriote leader and the only French Canadian in the outgoing Tory administration of Henry Sherwood); Dominick Daly, minister in the same cabinet; William Badgley, Attorney-General East under Sherwood; and a sort of chorus, 'An Unknown Voice.' Each speaks in turn, in octosyllabic verse:

THE GOVERNOR OPENS THE SESSION
I, Lord Elgin of Kincardine,
Friend of the brave Canadien,
Wish only the greatest good
For the people, who are being plundered.
PAPINEAU
Heavens! That's the end of this ministry, then!
DALY
Who is this demon disturbing my repose?
BADGLEY
Good Lord! What a nasty bit of news!
UNKNOWN VOICE
Aha! Tremble now, you fools!

For six such stanzas, the Governor upbraids them for their incompetence, ignorance, and venality. He dismisses their cabinet, rejoicing:

Now, thank heaven, I am free!
I've chased off these ninnies, thank the Lord.
Ministers of that calibre
Are useful only in gaming-houses!
PAPINEAU
Counting them up, I've four thousand pounds.
DALY
I've got almost twice that much.
BADGLEY
I've hardly enough to live on for a year.
THE VOICE
Go live like a penitent, you numbskull!

The seventh and last stanza is the Governor's proclamation of the upcoming election, issued by Lord Elgin on 6 December 1847. He urges all French Canadians to participate, for:

Those who oppressed you in the past
Are now powerless today.
Come, let your own popular leaders,
Once elected, aid me in my task.[48]

Only the author's initials appear, those of Louis-Thomas Groulx (1819-71), a Montreal lawyer and minor poet best known for his collection, *Rêveries d'un bon chrétien* (Joliette 1868), an occasional contributor to *L'Avenir*. But as that paper's political orientation became more clearly defined over the next few months (against the Union, in favour of the recently returned rebel, Papineau, and his policy of annexation to the United States), Groulx withdrew his support from *L'Avenir* and contributed instead to its opponent, *La Minerve*. Meanwhile, another dialogue of his in verse form appeared a month after the first (15 January 1848), and was this time given prominence on the front page.

The rubric is again 'Poésie canadienne,' the title, 'The Return of the Ministers.' The same characters reappear, minus Papineau (he had resigned on 29 July 1847, retiring permanently from politics) and the 'Unknown Voice,' for in the interval the elections had been held, with Daly and Badgley returning to office. The poem is again composed of seven stanzas of eight lines, eight syllables to a line, and begins:

THE GOVERNOR
What! You're back again?
Who the hell managed to elect you?
This is an unpleasant trick, gentlemen:
What! Have the people gone mad?[49]

Daly and Badgley then explain the underhand tactics they have used to win, and the piece ends with the Governor's announced intention to get rid of them soon – a promise kept two months later, making way for the first 'responsible' ministry of Baldwin and La Fontaine.

These two examples of paratheatre in verse are interesting only for their form and the relative moderation of their tone. They offer sharp contrast with the other examples of the genre we shall see in *L'Avenir* from then on, examples that are much closer to the paradigm of the Status Quo Comedies of 1834. Two political playlets appeared in August 1848, and they soon led to unexpected drama, in a real sense. In that crucial year of the struggle for responsible government in Canada, feelings ran high. Opposition to *L'Avenir*'s policies was concentrated in three Montreal newspapers: *La Minerve*, under the aging but still formidable Ludger Duvernay; *Les Mélanges religieux*, semi-official organ of the Diocese of Montreal and of the journal's founder, Bishop Ignace Bourget; and *La Revue canadienne*, founded three years previously and destined to cease publication a few months after the period which, in the late summer of 1848, shall concern us. It is important to identify these three newspapers for they, through their editors, are principals in the two political plays in question.

The first of these is entitled 'An Inside Scene' (Une Scène d'intérieur), and it occupies the first one and half pages (about 4000 words) of the issue for 2 August 1848. It opens with four characters assembled, identified only by their Christian names: Ludger, Octave, Hector, and Georges, joined almost immediately by 'a Famous Warrior Doctor.' This is where the background of the conflict is important, for 'Ludger' is Duvernay of *La Minerve*, 'Octave' is Louis-Octave LeTourneux, editor of *La Revue canadienne*, 'Hector' is twenty-two-year-old Hector-Louis Langevin of *Les Mélanges religieux*, 'Georges' is George-Etienne Cartier, a future Father of Confederation, like Langevin. And the 'Warrior Doctor' is none other than Dr Wolfred Nelson, leader of the Patriote victors at the battle of Saint-Denis in 1837, recently returned from enforced exile in Bermuda and already back in the thick of things.

It was in fact Wolfred Nelson who had precipitated events that summer with his strident attacks in the public press against the reputation and policies of his erstwhile ally, Louis-Joseph Papineau. In a long letter in *La Minerve* on 10 July, for example, he had accused Papineau of cowardice in leaving Saint-Denis before the battle, and had in fact repudiated his entire conduct during the uprisings of 1837-8. Our play is a response to that provocation, and its dramatic pretext, reminiscent of 1834, is made clear in its subtitle, 'An Account of a Meeting of the Committee Entrusted with Supervising the Edition of the Letters of a Famous Warrior Doctor.' The play begins with mutual accusations of incompetence in the group's handling of their campaign against *L'Avenir*, Papineau, and their supporters. Georges wants them to concentrate on overall strategy, and intervenes:

> Come now, that's not the way to do things! You have to understand, Octave, that to wage a battle one has a vanguard and the main body of troops. You are our vanguard. *La Minerve* is the bulk

of the army. Now if you blunder into engagements at times, you don't expect us to risk the whole army to support you, do you?...
OCTAVE
Yes, but I'm made to look like an imbecile in the whole affair!
GEORGES
Well, you certainly try to make Papineau look like a fool, a madman, a maniac!
HECTOR
That's just a polemical ploy. And besides, how are you going to reproach him for that? It's your orders he's following!

Georges manages to placate Octave with the promise of a fat job to come, in payment for his present services. Then they all set about devising a plan of attack against the credibility of Papineau, in a scene whose main intent is in fact to destroy Nelson's. The latter is portrayed as slow-witted, condescending (he constantly treats them all as 'little,' as they must all have appeared, by comparison with his height of 6'4"), constantly boring everyone with his references to his own bravery at Saint-Denis. He is ready to fabricate proofs for the wild statements he has made in the press:

THE DOCTOR
Come on, little Octave, find me some way to do it, for although I know how to conduct myself in battle –
OCTAVE
Invite Mr Papineau to come and see the written proof at your own house. He won't go, because he knows there is no such proof. And ninety per cent of *La Minerve*'s readers will be satisfied!
LUDGER (*clapping his hands*)
Bravo! Bravo! Octave! You're a fine fellow: I move that we have a dinner for you!
HECTOR
Hurrah for Octave! He's a sharp one, he is!
THE DOCTOR
It's a good ploy. Where should I write that sentence?
OCTAVE
Here, damn it! (*showing him the manuscript*)
THE DOCTOR
All right. Any other changes to be made?
GEORGES
My word, yes: let's correct the mistakes in French.

OCTAVE
Are you serious? What a dumb thing that would be: we should
multiply them, rather than making them fewer!
LUDGER
Why?
OCTAVE
Quite simple: How do you expect people to believe that it's our
brave Doctor writing, if there are no mistakes in French?[50]

They finally finish composing the famous letter and the Doctor leaves.
Georges has the last word on their pugnacious colleague: 'Now go ahead
and try to make legislators out of material of that sort!' And thus the play
ends, with the signature, 'Tuque Bleue,' a double allusion to the distinctive head-dress of the *habitant* and to the colour of the political party to
which all five characters adhere.

This little dialogue had an immediate effect, especially upon George-
Etienne Cartier, then at the beginning of his distinguished political career
(he had been elected member for Verchères in a bye-election in April
1848, but did not actually take his seat until the following year). Cartier
marched to the offices of *L'Avenir* within a few hours of its publication of
the satire and hotly demanded satisfaction for the aspersions upon his
character and conduct that he perceived in it. I shall let him tell his own
story, translated from the second page of *La Minerve* the following day (3
August 1848):

> *L'Avenir* of the 2nd inst. contained a communication in the form of
> a dialogue signed 'Tuque Bleue,' in which the interlocutors are
> identified only by their first names. Yesterday morning I met a
> friend of mine who told me that someone connected with *L'Avenir*
> had hinted to him that I was the person alluded to in this dialogue,
> under the name 'Georges' ... Since this communication, if it was in
> fact referring to myself, represented nothing but a tissue of false
> and misleading insinuations and allegations, I felt justified in trying
> to extract a formal statement from the editors and collaborators
> who compose and publish this newspaper ... I was also entitled to
> obtain the name of the cowardly and anonymous correspondent, in
> order to find out from him if he had intended any allusion to me,
> and in the case of an affirmative reply, to demand satisfaction from
> him for the publication of such falsehoods. Yesterday morning
> about eleven, accompanied by a friend, Mr [Richard] Hubert, a

lawyer of this town, I went to the office of *L'Avenir*, where I met
Mr J.-B.-E. Dorion, who sports the grandiose title of 'Managing
Director of *L'Avenir*.'

Cartier then goes on to describe how he had made his demands for information to Eric Dorion, one of three brothers involved in the pro-Papineau,
anti-Union campaign of the Rouges, and nicknamed 'l'Enfant Terrible' because of his youth (he was then twenty-two), his fiery temperament, and
his diminutive stature. 'At first sight,' says Cartier, 'I was overcome with
the type of pity and commiseration one normally feels upon encountering
an adolescent.' But Dorion stood his ground. He indicated his willingness to
fight a duel, if that was what Cartier wanted, but refused to accept responsi-
bility for his correspondents' opinions or to reveal who 'Tuque Bleue' was,
unless certain conditions were met. This we learn from his own version of
the incident, for *L'Avenir*, on the third page of its issue of 5 August (at this
stage, the paper published only twice a week), described the visit in two
separate articles, accompanied by letters from an eyewitness.

The first article is entitled 'Georges,' and describes the conversation
with Cartier in dialogue form. The latter had obviously come to provoke a
duel, in the fashion of the time, and was exasperated at not finding an
appropriate opponent. Young Dorion had the presence of mind to summon a colleague, Louis Plamondon, whose letters certify the accuracy
of Dorion's account. Cartier, frustrated, finally stormed out. His long
account in *La Minerve* ends:

> Wanting to make an end of the matter with Mr Dorion, I asked
> him peremptorily, and for the last time, whether or not he was
> willing to provide me with the correspondent's name. He declined
> to do so. Thereupon I stated to him that both he and his correspon-
> dent were cowards, and that his whole newspaper was constructed
> on a foundation of irresponsible cowardice. I then withdrew along
> with Mr Hubert, rather indignant, for there was in fact matter to
> arouse indignation in such treatment. There is no need for com-
> ment on the facts I have here reported. Now the public is in a sit-
> uation to judge the value of *L'Avenir*'s insults.
>
> Your obedient servant,
> GEO. ET. CARTIER.

Montreal, 3 August 1848.

> I affirm as true the statements made hereinabove, which can also
> be attested by Mr Lewis Harkin, a merchant of this city, who hap-
> pened to be there present with me.
>
> R.A.R. HUBERT.[51]

Such heavy-handed response was obviously not called for, and troubles
were just beginning for Cartier and his friends. *L'Avenir* set out to counterattack the statements by Nelson impugning Papineau's courage, and
this campaign was highlighted, on the Rouge side, by a lengthy letter
signed by a relative by marriage of Cartier's, one Henri Lapparre, on the
front page of its issue of 9 August 1848. The first half of this letter is
dedicated to excusing Papineau's conduct at Saint-Denis, where both Cartier and Lapparre had fought. That done, Lapparre turns to Cartier:

> The second statement I seek to rectify is the one that purports to
> prove that little George E.C. was courageous at the battle of Saint-
> Denis. Here are the real facts with regard to the latter, the facts
> such as the Doctor [Nelson] knows them, and as little George
> knows them, better than anyone else. Just imagine, Mr Editor, our
> little George decked out in an old homespun jacket made to fit a
> real man, and wearing an immense *TUQUE BLEUE* [in italics in
> the original] that hung down the middle of his back, as wide as it
> was long, so that it could probably have covered all of him, if nec-
> essary, as big as he was at that time![52]

So 'little George,' according to Lapparre, had spent the whole day trem-
bling and whimpering in a corner, finally seizing upon a pretext for leaving the scene of battle and seeking munitions for the patriote troops. One
now sees the sting in the 'Tuque Bleue' title of the first play, and under-
stands Cartier's ire.

On 26 August *L'Avenir* struck again with another playlet whose title I
shall translate as 'The Devil by the Horns: Concerning a *Tuque Bleue*'
(the French is more suggestive, 'Le Diable à quatre' referring at the same
time to the four protagonists in the piece). This time it appeared under
the rubric, 'Tribune du peuple. Liberté de penser' (The People's Tribunal.
Freedom of Thought), thenceforth reserved for contributions from 'correspondents,' whereas the first text had no such protective cover. The
dramatis personae are already known to us, and the play begins:

> OCTAVE (*running in breathlessly, a paper in hand*)
> Georges! Georges!
> GEORGES (*turning around*)
> What's going on then, for heaven's sake? You seem so distressed –
> is your office on fire?
> OCTAVE
> No, but there's enough to make one run, even so. Look at this!

(he shows him L'Avenir)...
GEORGES
Hmm – it's signed 'Tuque Bleue' – must be rather dumb.
OCTAVE
More lying than dumb. But just the same, everything in it isn't
false. Someone must have talked. Sounds as though this fellow has
heard the whole thing!

The strategy is thus remarkably similar to that of the Status Quo Comedies, implying that a *mouchard* has once again been active and thereby
sowing suspicion in the ranks of the Bleus. Octave develops this theme in
a long monologue, listing the partisans he knows and assessing the loyalty
of each. His thoughts are interrupted: 'Ludger and Hector enter, making
everything around them tremble. Octave finishes his interesting monologue, and from the mouths of all three comes, at the same time, the distressed exclamation, "Well, did you read it?"'
    They too are dismayed at the precision of the details supplied by 'Tuque
Bleue.' Georges, they think, has not been treated too badly, but Octave
and the Doctor will have trouble surviving the assault. So they advise
Louis-Octave LeTourneux of *La Revue canadienne* to respond in kind, and
the other two editors will follow. Georges, meanwhile, has been reading
the original 'Tuque Bleue' dialogue, and finishes it just as Nelson enters.

THE DOCTOR
Good day, my dear Georges. What's going on, you seem upset? [In
English:] What's the matter?
GEORGES
Here, read this d....d paper: It concerns you, they're talking about
you, too. Bunch of little scoundrels! All they have on their side is
their impudence! A newspaper in diapers! And contributors that
should be! A Managing Director three feet tall who dares attack
you and me! I can't understand it: everything's gone amiss!

Nelson is apparently too thick to understand the implications of the incident, but Georges is beside himself. He sends Hector off to seek his
friend Richard Hubert, obviously to serve as his second. Ludger asks what
his intentions are.

GEORGES
I'm going to slap their faces, one after the other!

LUDGER
That's a damned big job you're taking on. You be careful: slapping someone weaker than you is cowardly; someone stronger, and you get two in return. If you were to attack P.[apineau?], for example, you'd scarcely reach his chin!

'Richard' arrives, and he and the others try to reason with Georges. But all the latter wants is his friend's service as second in a duel, as soon as he finds someone to fight. But who is Tuque Bleue? By this time, the Doctor has finished reading the playlet as well. His solution: he will write another letter against Papineau, in English this time perhaps, since Papineau must be at the root of all their problems. Georges holds out for a direct attack and the others cannot dissuade him. He and Richard finally leave for L'Avenir's offices. Half an hour later he is described coming back up the street, furious, gesticulating wildly. Here the author uses some of the vocabulary Cartier had used in his letter to La Minerve, calling Dorion and his friends 'a bunch of d...d cowards,' 'poltroons,' 'marmosets.' Then, in a transparent tactic, Georges explains Dorion's reasons for refusing his request and Duvernay leaps in to side with the editors of L'Avenir. 'I will overwhelm them with reproaches in La Minerve,' he says, 'but just between you and me, I must say they were right, and I would have done the same!'

To end the play, which is some 6000 words in length, Georges agrees ruefully with Ludger:

You're probably right, after all. I shall be more careful next time.
LUDGER
Have you ever gone hunting ducks?
GEORGES
What's the meaning of that question?
LUDGER
Answer anyway.
GEORGES
No, I haven't.
LUDGER
Well, my friend, once you've missed your duck [a play on the word 'canard'], it doesn't come back!...[53]

If a primary intention of this second play was that of exasperating George-Etienne Cartier, the author succeeded admirably. Cartier demanded to know who was responsible. First to accept his challenge again was the diminutive Eric Dorion, enfant terrible of the editorial crew. Cartier refused to fight with a 'three-foot tall marmoset,' and twenty-three-year-old Joseph Doutre then volunteered and was accepted. The duel was arranged for dawn the following day, on Mount Royal. As Aegidius Fauteux recounts, the two combatants and their seconds met as arranged, preparations were completed, and the test was about to begin when Cartier's elder brother, Damien, arrived with several Montreal policemen to interrupt it. Doutre and Cartier had to appear in magistrate's court, where they were let go with a stern warning.[54]

All might have ended there, had not the editors of *L'Avenir* suggested, a few days later, that Damien's intervention had been arranged in advance, with the full knowledge of George-Etienne. This time the latter's rage knew no bounds, and a second duel was forthwith arranged, on the other side of the St Lawrence near Chambly, where no police could intervene. Then, in a scene parlously close to the sham fight we shall see in Raphaël-Ernest Fontaine's *Un Duel à poudre* (1867), the two marched off their ten paces, turned, aimed, and fired. Both missed, cleanly. Newly-loaded pistols were brought and they tried again, both apparently aiming as close as they could, in the custom of the day, without seeking to inflict a mortal wound. This time a bullet from Cartier's pistol pierced Doutre's hat, honour was thus considered redeemed, and the two duellists left the field of honour.

In epilogue, their enmity continued for the next dozen years or so, but had sufficiently abated some twenty-five years later that Joseph Doutre pronounced Cartier's funeral elegy and helped bear his old foe's coffin to its final resting place. Was Doutre really the author of these two satirical plays? It was young Charles Daoust, another member of the Committee of Thirteen, whom Cartier first suspected, because of his previous articles in *L'Avenir*. Another name suggested was that of Louis-Antoine Dessaulles, president of the Montreal branch of L'Institut canadien, future editor of *Le Pays* and author also of several long anti-unionist articles in *L'Avenir*, signed 'Campagnard.' Certainly we know Dessaulles was then putting the finishing touches to his book, *Papineau et Nelson: blanc et noir*, in which he sought to defend his uncle, Papineau, against the serious accusations of his adversary. But all told, it is Doutre that I suspect, if only because it was he who accepted Cartier's challenge and fought the duel. How could Daoust or Dessaulles, with the fiery temperament that was the trademark of each, allow someone else, someone innocent, to take up arms in their stead?

Perhaps it should also be pointed out that the very length of these plays is only too consistent with Doutre's style as we know it: his pioneering novel, *Les Fiancés de 1812* (1844) comprises some 500 pages of loosely-written text. Doutre had been only nine years old when the Status Quo Comedies appeared and it is thus most unlikely that his two playlets were directly influenced by them. Yet one cannot help but remark a striking similarity in format, tone, intent, and even tactics. The texts from 1848 are more verbose, less varied, and less witty, but they none the less display a certain talent for character depiction (particularly of Wolfred Nelson), and a sure sense of satire. It is significant that in this year, the most crucial in Canada's history since the Rebellion, the deep conflicts at work should find expression again in dramatized dialogue. One feels that the fact of Doutre's recent graduation from the Collège de Montréal, another of the many institutions of secondary learning where dramatized debate was an integral part of pedagogic method and where college theatre had long been performed, was not coincidental to his decision to express his opposition in dramatized form.

Macdonald, Taché, and the Ministerial Crisis of 1856

It was another eight years before political paratheatre returned, following its predictable cycle, again in *L'Avenir*. Again, it was a moment of high drama in Canadian politics which gave birth to the longest political play to date, *La Dégringolade* (The Tumble, ie, the collapse of a ministry), comprising twelve characters and more than 17,000 words. Its three acts are spread out over four issues of the paper, between 1 February and 22 February 1856.

The only character to reappear from the plays of 1848 is G.-E. Cartier, now Provincial Secretary for Canada East in the cabinet of Sir Allan MacNab. Most of the other names represent the most prominent men in Canadian politics at the time, nine of them members of the same cabinet: the old, gruff, gouty MacNab himself; Etienne-Pascal Taché, Receiver-General; John A. Macdonald, Attorney-General for Canada West; Lewis Thomas Drummond, Attorney-General for Canada East; William Cayley, Inspector-General; Joseph Cauchon, Commissioner of Lands; Robert Spence, Postmaster-General; John Ross, the Speaker; and François-Xavier Lemieux, Commissioner of Public Works. There are, in addition, two anonymous 'lackeys,' which I have identified: Joseph-Charles Taché, nephew of Etienne-Pascal and future editor of the journal, *Le Courrier du Canada*, and Thomas-Jean-Jacques Loranger, member for Laprairie.[55]

The play is set in Government House, Toronto and is dedicated, with tongue in cheek, to the Governor, Sir Edmund Walker Head. The dramatic pretext, once again, is a meeting of the group to be satirized, in this case an emergency cabinet meeting called by MacNab in order to decide upon the strategy they will follow in the forthcoming parliamentary session. And the main target of the writer's sarcasm is E.-P. Taché, presented here as a shameless profiteer and a flunkey to the anglophones in Mac-Nab's ministry. Taché, of course, is the author of the famous remark that 'the last cannon shot fired in America in defence of British rule, will be fired by a French Canadian,'[56] an affirmation he is made to repeat often in the play. His nephew is depicted as shallow, self-interested, and devious. MacNab arrives and directs the group to calculate his government's chances for survival. There are none, according to the comical mathematics they bring to bear on the problem: the Tory majority in Canada West is fading fast, and they will be unable to count on more than twenty-five votes. Whereupon the Prime Minister loses his temper: all this is the fault of Macdonald: 'Don't you see? Johnny is preparing to play the same role against me as Brutus did against Caesar! Johnny is my pupil, it's to me that he owes all his political influence, and yet today it's obvious that he's plotting against me...'

To dispel their mutual animosity, the group decides to pause for a drink before resuming their grave deliberations. As they open their flagons, the first act ends with a lively round of political songs sung by MacNab, Macdonald, Cayley, Spence, and Ross, in which each reveals, in a stratagem that is a distinct improvement upon the monologues of 1834 and 1848, the meanness of his own political motivation.[57] Act II finds them refreshed, ready to face the alarming state their party is in. MacNab now reveals his simple plan: 'First of all, I want to count your votes for the next session. *Après moi le déluge*: I don't give a fig how you manage after that!' He will leave them alone to find the right solution. The instant he leaves, Macdonald takes over, consulting first his close supporters, Lemieux and Cauchon. Lemieux's response is unambiguous:

In a word, here's what I think: in Upper Canada, we'd have to get rid of MacNab, Ross, Cayley, and another whom I shan't name. In Lower Canada, we'd have to rid ourselves of Taché, Cartier, Cauchon, and Drummond. Taché, because he's responsible to no one, laughing at everybody as he stuffs his own pockets, because he's detested for his 'last cannon shot,' and finally because he's shamed himself by declaring that he's proud to be a colonial. Cartier, because he brings nothing but dislike and ridicule upon the government, because he's turned his coat too often, not to mention his *tuque bleue...*

The solution he proposes is radical in political terms: 'MacNab, Cayley, and Ross, as well as Cartier, Cauchon, and Taché are prepared to go to any extremes of Toryism. For our part, we have to bring about a crisis from which you and I shall emerge as representatives of enlightened Liberalism.' The 'Tumble' is about to begin. To close the act, Joseph Cauchon, editor of the right-thinking *Journal de Québec*, quotes the Bible to encourage all hands to have another drink or two. And, in what is a trademark of *La Dégringolade*, the French Canadians in the group launch another lusty political song.[58]

The third and last act is by far the longest, extending over two issues of *L'Avenir*. MacNab returns to see how his cabinet's deliberations are going, only to find it in mounting disarray, mainly because of the drink its members have by now consumed. The act's structure reflects their mental confusion, as they leap from topic to topic, expending much wrath upon the francophone press, which has too often been lukewarm in its support. MacNab admonishes them, insisting that they come up with a viable plan for survival at once, and leaves them for a second time. Once again it is John A. who takes control of the unruly session:

> The meeting which is about to end has brought two important facts to my attention: first, that Parliament is falling apart, and doesn't support us; second, that public opinion outside Parliament is abandoning us because the press that supports us is of no account, when not directly harmful to our cause. The result of this double fact, you know it as well as I do, is to be the tumble [*dégringolade*] of all of us!

Stoically, Macdonald proposes a toast to 'our approaching common collapse.' And the melodious Cartier intones another satiric song at his and their expense, this time to the tune of the *Marseillaise*.[59] Thus the fictive *Tumble* ends.

The real one was not long in following. The anonymous author (he signs, 'An Unwilling Subject' (Sujet malgré lui) was well informed, for this was indeed Allan MacNab's last ministry, replaced three months later by that of Macdonald and Taché. My own research has not succeeded in establishing the author's identity. If it was again Doutre (and there are many similarities with *Tuque Bleue*, including a direct allusion to the title), his talents had certainly matured in the interval, for *La Dégringolade* is better constructed, better written, and above all more humorous. Perhaps most significant among its innovations is the widespread use of political songs, reminiscent in their way of the savage satirical *vaudevilles* in Quesnel's *Républicains français*, but distinctly Canadian this time, in a tradition that leads directly to Elzéar Labelle's *Conversion of a Fisherman*.[60] In the following decade, as we shall see, music and politics came to be inextricably intertwined, and in conjunction with an apposite theatrical form, would lead to the establishment of a new and enduring genre in French Canada.

This was not quite the end of *L'Avenir*'s dramatized campaign against Taché, Macdonald, and their allies in 1856. Another, much shorter, play appeared in the issues of 30 May and 5 June, with the title, 'The Crisis: A Little Comedy in One Act.' The first scene is a dialogue between Macdonald and Spence, worried about the motion of confidence that Cartier's intransigence has brought upon them:

M. SPENCE
I wouldn't care about the motion at all, it there were some way of staying in power with a Lower Canadian majority. But if we try to do so, you're going to see all our friends go tumbling over [*dégringoler*] to the Opposition side, in less than a week.
M. MACDONALD
Don't I bloody well know it!
M. SPENCE
Then what can we do? What irks me, is not being able to apply one good kick to that most intelligent area of Cartier's body!...[61]

They review their chances for surviving the crisis, denigrating most of their supporters from Lower Canada as they go. The next five scenes are all short, and they appeared on 5 June, four days after the vote on the motion of non-confidence had actually been held, and which the government had won by a mere four votes. There is a distinct air of bitterness about the text this time. First, Macdonald and Cartier appear, wondering what their next move should be. Hearing Spence and Taché in conversation, they hide behind a curtain while the second pair tear Cartier's reputation to shreds, revealing their own cupidity in the process:

M. TACHÉ
If it didn't pay so well, I'd throw this whole thing over!
M. SPENCE
Yes, but £1800, that's not hay!
M. TACHÉ
You're right. As for me, I can't make up my mind to leave it behind![62]

Spence then goes off to vote, while the others quarrel as to tactics. The result of the motion's defeat is then announced, but Taché is against surrender: half a vote would justify clinging to office (and salary), as far as he is concerned. Cartier is given the last word, 'The ministry is dying, but it won't surrender. It's a bulldog ministry!'

It would certainly appear that *La Crise* came from the same pen as had *La Dégringolade*, but the second play lacks depth and density. It is also lacking in the musical satire that had so helped to enliven the first. It should also be pointed out that, at least by comparison with the political plays from 1834, these two are demonstrably less effective: they did nothing to block the political careers of Macdonald, Cartier, Taché, and Drummond; and the new coalition *L'Avenir* opposed so strenuously long continued to dominate in Canadian politics.

Political Theatre in Quebec City: 'Le Fantasque' (1857)

Montreal's newspapers were not the only ones enlivening political topics with paratheatrical forms in the 1850s, witness the two examples I shall take from Quebec's re-established *Le Fantasque* in 1857. The subject of the first one is another pan-Canadian concern at the time, the location of the new and permanent capital of the Canadas. The paper in question no longer had any connection with Napoléon Aubin, but the editors of this second attempt at reviving his original journal (this one is generally referred to as *Fantasque III*) tried, with occasional success, to emulate the wit and mocking tone Aubin had infused into the first series. From its second issue, on 26 November 1857, this 'Critical Review of Men and Things,' as it styled itself, showed a marked preference for dramatized dialogues on political subjects. The first one examined here has the involved title, 'The Future Site of Government; or The Quarrel among Five Towns: A Slightly Fantastic Account of a Very Real Dream,' and occupies the first six and a half pages of the issue.

This was the period, let us recall, when the government of the United Canadas rotated among Kingston, Toronto, and Quebec, just before the British Parliament decided on Ottawa as the permanent site for federal authority. Our dialogue has representatives of five Canadian towns competing for the honour: Toronto, Kingston, Ottawa, Montreal, and Quebec, introduced to us in personified form at the beginning. After their introduction, the five towns speak in turn, putting forward their case for recognition. The tone is humorous and an attempt is made to characterize each speaker in a general way. Thus Toronto's representative lards his presentation with English phrases, and is haughtiest in his demands:

There is only one town worthy of that distinction, and it's Toronto!
Do you know why? First, because Upper Canada should win out
over Lower. That is written on high, and is in the nature of things.
Upper Canada is English, hang it! and proud to be so! That's not
all: the English must rule other races, or in other words Upper
Canada, being British, must have control over Lower Canada,
which is French. That's why we are the 'superior' race here,
whereas down there (pointing to Lower Canada) is *not* the place
where you'll find – you know – 'superior' people![63]

Kingston states its case, Ottawa and Montreal theirs. Quebec, last in line,
wishes to avoid controversy and thus calls in the neutral observer, Trifluvianus (ie, the native of Trois-Rivières) to speak in its stead. Trois-
Rivières then gives the longest and sharpest speech of all, ridiculing the
pretensions of Toronto in particular and the campaign led by George
Brown of the *Globe*, pointing out the military weaknesses of Kingston and
Montreal and the isolation of Bytown. Only Quebec City makes any sense
as capital (hardly a surprising conclusion, for a newspaper published in
that city); and that, Trifluvianus predicts, is what the British Parliament
will decide as well. At that stage the discussion breaks down, 'the interlocutors leave the room, looking askance at each other,' and the text ends
with the promise of a second act to follow soon, a promise that, for reasons easy to deduce, the author was unable to keep.

In its abstractness and its quaint use of personification, this text is a
unique example, to that point, among political dialogues in French Canada. A second dialogue from the same paper in the same year is shorter,
livelier, and closer to the native traditions of the genre. It appears in the
issue of 3 December 1857, is entitled 'The Ministry Judged,' and is signed
'Martin-Pêcheur' (Kingfisher). It is addressed to 'The Contributors to *Le
Fantasque*,' and begins:

Gentlemen:
    Day before yesterday, as I was making my way up the Côte
Lamontagne as best I could, walking-stick in hand, struggling along
with short steps, there were two men in front of me, proceeding
towards the Upper Town as I was. One of them was Maxime, the
sweeper, the other Benjamin, an oyster-seller of my acquaintance.
The following dialogue took place between our two friends, here
reported almost word for word.

The subject of their discussion is the apparent injustice in the distribu-
tion of cabinet posts: Montreal has four, Quebec City only two. Both men

speak a deliciously genuine Québécois French, perhaps the best example to date. What alarms Benjamin, the oyster-seller, is the implication for his trade:

> All I can say is, if they ain't no ministers from Quebec, it ain't good for business, 'cause when they's lots of 'em, it brings the price of oysters up. They eats so many oysters, those guys!
> MAXIME
> They eats, and they pays for sweepin', too. I was just thinkin' about one of them gentlemen who used to pay me two twenty-five cent pieces a day, not a word o' lie, to sweep his hall and doorstep!
> BENJAMIN
> How's that, then?
> MAXIME
> I'll tell you now. First I used to sweep in the mornin', then again at noon, 'cause a lot o' folks would come to ask for jobs 'n stuff, an' the floor took a lot o' scrapin'. Then I had to do the same thing in the evenin', without fail!
> BENJAMIN
> An' you got four bits for all that? Ain't too much, for sure!

So the two decide to vote for a current candidate from Quebec City, Alleyn, and 'Kingfisher' asks his readers, shouldn't they do the same? To which the editor responds, somewhat enigmatically: 'Since "Kingfisher" wants to know what we think, we state that the decision he has taken to support M. Alleyn seems like a good one to us, and that after all, one only has to remember the proverb, "A sparrow in hand is better than a flying goose".'[64]

By comparison with all preceding paratheatre in French Canada since the innocuous dialogues of the eighteenth century, these two examples from *Le Fantasque* stand out for their moderation of tone and, especially with this second text, for their good humour. It is true, of course, that the political issues on which they focus were not divisive of francophones as the others had been. When such a divisive topic as Confederation came to the fore, a return to the adversarial form was also predictable.

'Literary'-Political Theatre: 'Le Défricheur de Langue'

The next example merits closer scrutiny, for it represents obvious evolution within the genre and its authorship and intention are more than usually complicated. *Le Défricheur de langue* (The Pioneer in the Field of Language) was published in 1859 under the humorous pseudonym of 'Isidore de Méplats,' and described as a 'tragédie-bouffe.'[65] This hybrid parody was actually composed in largest part by Hubert LaRue, recently appointed Professor of Medicine at Laval University (he was a graduate of the Séminaire de Québec, parent institution of the university, officially founded in 1852), and who would help establish the following year (1860) the influential literary periodical, *Les Soirées canadiennes*. LaRue was aided and abetted by the physician Joseph-Charles Taché, politician and historian, the first Canadian to be awarded the decoration of Chevalier de la Légion d'Honneur on the occasion of his representing this country at the Paris World's Fair of 1855. He too, participated in founding *Les Soirées canadiennes*, along with the critic-historian Father H.-R. Casgrain and two others we have already met, Antoine Gérin-Lajoie and his mentor at Nicolet, Father F.-B. Ferland. A third member of the medical profession (before the advent of golf or curling, doctors apparently had more time for literary dabbling), one Dr Wells, contributed a line or two to our play.

The target of their satire is also compound: separate articles which had appeared in the first periodical in French Canada devoted primarily to literature, *La Ruche littéraire et artistique*, by the then editor of that journal, the Frenchman Henri-Emile Chevalier, and a compatriot in Canadian exile, the obscure Félix Vogeli. Chevalier, induced to leave France because of journalistic articles of a political nature he had published there, had been established in Montreal since 1853, and had become proprietor and editor-in-chief of *La Ruche littéraire* shortly afterward. His offending article was entitled 'The French Language and Canadian Nationality' (La Langue française et la nationalité canadienne), and is a good example of the ill-digested extravagance that would often pass as linguistics before that discipline established a more secure basis for itself. Chevalier declares, 'Language and Nationality, the two terms are not *homonyms* [*sic*], but synonyms.' Furthermore, (tacking closer to logic), 'it was Language that gave birth to Nationality; who nursed it, who fosters it, and who will guide it to prosperity in the course of time.' His thesis continues: the innate impulse of language is towards fragmentation, as with Classical Greek:

Athens has its accent; Thebes, its euphony; Lacedaemon its particular turn of phrase. Thus also the other cities. Homogeneity is destroyed, as much through the disparity of dialects, as through their autonomy: internal Harmony is lacking. Greek nationality belongs to the neuter gender. It has no sex. The language disintegrates, piece by piece. Thus the Greeks, strong in their ability to defend themselves, are weak when it comes to aggression. They are

not an innovative people. They do not carry the torch of civiliza-
tion, but allow it to be wrested away from them. Why, then? Because their own language, ie, their nationality, was interred beneath
the Tomb of Homer, wrapped in the Shroud of Hesiod.[66]

Along with the facile anthropology, one sees the pretentious style that 'Isidore de Méplats' will parody. But we must not leave Chevalier's long article before hearing what he has to say about the evolution of language in
America:

> *Realism*, it must be acknowledged, is the direction in which public
> consciousness is now headed. Thus the American language – a
> spoken language, primarily, and one that is not by any means the
> English language – the American language, impatient of Grammar
> and scorned by artists, possesses boundless affection for machinists,
> industrialists, manufacturers of all types ... Thus the United States,
> which probably has as many or more newspapers than the whole of
> Europe, has practically no literary authors. For the Americans,
> thought is incorporated into words: it is not tipped off into the
> mould of the abstract language of Reason.

Thus the American's 'need to create, and to create quickly' has made him
produce a language not so ornate, so rich in abstract expression as that of
Greece or Rome; but 'when the American puts down his pioneer's stave,
he will speak a finer, more careful language, smoother-flowing, nobler,
and richer than English.'
   For this reason the American 'needs nouns'; and 'when America is pio-
neered [défrichée] and settled, his language too will be *défrichée*.' He
sums up: 'Despite what the purists may say, we are not afraid to affirm
that the vernacular idiom in Canada, even though it may appear dis-
jointed, has a decided advantage over virgin languages: it expresses itself
more economically, and more precisely.' To his rambling grandiloquence,
Chevalier adds several syntactic and logical errors, thus providing easy
game for his attackers. As to Vogeli's role, he had contributed a pompous
article to *La Ruche littéraire*, entitled 'The Story of a Good Poem' (Histoire d'une bonne poésie) – the poem in question, it turns out, being one
he composed himself, in poor French and abysmal prosody. But he is a
minor target here: his French nationality (he was a veterinarian, only recently arrived in Canada) and his fawning letter to Chevalier which had
accompanied his poem, were sufficient cause for his inclusion in the bar-
rage of satire from the Doctors. Before examining their text, here is one

final, significant piece of information about Henri-Emile Chevalier: he was an active and influential member of the Institut Canadien in Montreal and therefore a target of the campaign by Bishop Bourget to which I have alluded earlier. Indeed, this offensive led by LaRue must be placed clearly in the context of the Church's reaction against nefarious 'foreign' influences in the 1850s. LaRue and his friends, products of an educational system controlled by the Church and indeed, in the former's case, employed by it, have taken up cudgels on its behalf.

Their play itself is in three acts, and is composed mainly of rhymed alexandrine couplets, the exceptions being the short Act II, which is a prose summary (written, LaRue informs us, by Taché)[67] of what is supposed to be a pantomime, and the even briefer intermezzo in Act III, where the Chorus intervenes in quatrains of seven and eight syllables. Act I is highlighted by a daft dialogue between Messrs Chevalier and Vogeli, in which each spouts the fustian phrases which, extrapolated now from their original context, sound even more ludicrous than they did then. As their lofty conversation progresses, along comes The Greek Language to interrupt them:

> Sire, please pardon me, for I am the Greek Tongue
> And have just now arrived, via the Port of Quebec.
> My friends have told me of the dolorific fate
> *La Ruche* has imposed upon me ... better, a hundred times better, death
> (*Indignantly*) Make me *neuter*? ... never! never!
> CHEVALIER
> What can one do?
> THE GREEK LANGUAGE
> The Shroud of Hesiod, in Homer's great Tomb,
> Before the sun sinks on the horizon,
> Will inter my remains under the moist sod!
> I shone so long with my *Harmony*,
> With my *Disparity*, my *Autonomy*
> That, in recompense, you're stripping me of my *Sex*!
> O too cruel fate! (*Invoking Greece's glorious past*)
> Help me, Demosthenes! ... Arise, noble archipelago!

Thereupon The Greek Language faints, and Monsieur Vogeli wipes her brow with his handkerchief as he has her sniff powdered stag's-horn. But of course her fate has already been sealed, and Chevalier soon proclaims her dead. Was it not inevitable?

Nationality!
Thou it is who pursuest all, in thy fateful fashion
Ever since thou steerest the chariot of *homonym*
And since appeareth on thy lap brilliant *synonym*!

Act II is a baroque pantomime, as I have mentioned, in which The
Greek Language is interred with solemn ceremony in Hesiod's shroud,
while the great figures of Grecian antiquity, from Diogenes (complete
with lantern) to Praxiteles, join in the funeral procession. Act III brings us
back to Vogeli and Chevalier, soon informed by a servant that Grammar
wishes to enter. She may not: she is to be banned forever from these
quarters. Then the servant returns to announce that an American seeks
admission.

THE AMERICAN (*entering in businesslike fashion*)
The great need of creating, and creating quickly
Wears out my arm, and quickens my heartbeat.
From morn to eve, for a whole century
I've been brandishing my stave, like a glorious pioneer!
Material progress certainly has its attraction,
But with it alone, a nation is quite rustic.
So I want to *pioneer* my impatient Tongue,
And am therefore pursuing the Noun...

The American's speech is interrupted by the bizarre Intermezzo-Chorus,
recited by The Iroquois, The Pirate, The Huron Woman, Oroboa, the
Heroine of Chateauguay, and The Trapper, all being titles or characters
from Chevalier's loosely-written works of fiction, many of them having
appeared in *La Ruche littéraire*. Then the American resumes, in the same
parodic vein: he has been sent to seek Chevalier, the 'abyss of knowledge,' to find out what will be the fate of his nation. This is the opportunity for poor Monsieur Chevalier, butt of all this savage sarcasm, to speak
his prophetic words:

When thou glimpsest the spuds growing in thy field
Then shalt thou see thy disparate Tongue improve;
When the thistle's buds give birth to the rose
Then shall thy mouth take over from thy nose [a reference, appa-
rently, to the 'nasal' qualities of North American speech?]
Return, friend of mine, to thy native shore:
There shalt thou find the Noun, after all thy pioneering [dé-
frichage].

The few critics who have bothered to deal with *Le Défricheur de langue* have been inclined to treat it in isolation as a curious anomaly in the development of French-Canadian literature. I hope the present reader will consent to see it, rather, as a natural step in the evolution of a native tradition in dramaturgy, in a genre with roots as ancient as polemical literature in Canada. It is not by accident that this dramatic form (the words are meant precisely, implying setting, stage directions, evolving characters, and divisions into acts and scenes) was chosen by three graduates of the educational system of Lower Canada: lampooning in dramatized form is at least as old as the first newspapers and the manuscript plays from the 1780s that we have examined. It was used by each successive generation thereafter, and in fact has never disappeared in French Canada, for it is the most ingrained of literary forms. Whatever the target – Americans, Bureaucrates, Patriotes, individuals, Protestantism, a ministry, a policy, a newspaper, or an institution – the natural tendency of the educated French Canadian has been towards the dramatized political dialogue. LaRue's text is closely related in its genealogy to the Comédies du Statu Quo. It is just as direct as the best of them, it is wittier and more sophisticated, and if only from that point of view, mirrors the more firmly established society of its time.

LaRue's *Défricheur de langue* lacks one important element, however: it is obviously 'armchair' theatre like its predecessors, never intended for performance. That final missing ingredient would be added eight years later, in a work that is undeniably theatre, undeniably political, undeniably a culmination of the long development I have attempted to trace here: Elzéar Labelle's delightful satire on Confederation, *The Conversion of a Nova Scotia Fisherman* (La Conversion d'un pêcheur de la Nouvelle-Ecosse).

Theatre and the Politics of Confederation

Predictably, the 1860s saw an intensification of political debate, reflected in dramatized dialogues, some adopting new forms. The whole topic of Confederation was a fertile testing ground for new and old tactics in the genre, and I shall give three examples of the directions such tactics could take. The first is the shortest and most traditional. It is entitled 'Confederation and John Bull' and it appeared in Quebec City's *L'Electeur* (which described itself as a newspaper of 'Politics, Caricature, and Criticism') on 25 May 1866. The text is accompanied by an illustration depicting that personification of all things British, John Bull, in top hat, waistcoat, and frock, confronting three stock characters from the traditional *commedia dell'arte*, whose presence is explained in the opening description:

> The footlights go up, the curtain rises, the comedy begins. Harlequin embraces Columbine while Pantaloon goes through his pirouettes. As the audience in the pit laughs at this slapstick, let us go behind the scenes. It is backstage in the shadows that nations' destinies are moulded, in the crucible of burning cupidity, of greedy ambition. That is where plans are shaped, where they prepare those colossal gymnastic stunts which will be performed before the astonished eye of Public Opinion. John Bull and Confederation are conversing. Let us listen in.
>
> JOHN BULL
> What is this vampire?
>
> CONFEDERATION
> I am the chrysalis, the pupa out of which will come an English monarchy, implanted in the New World. Just a larva at the moment, I shall later become a Gorgon, prolific in evil. I am not, as was first thought, a democratic conception. No, infamy gave birth to me. I implement the same system you observe in politics, John Bull: I absorb other countries and nationalities, sacrificing all that is deemed sacred upon the altar of self-interest. In short, I am a great prostitute.[68]

Their dialogue continues for a few more exchanges, which merely develop Confederation's description of British intentions. The message is unrelievedly hostile to the federal scheme and hints at conflict to come. Confederation summarizes:

> There will probably be blood spilled. We haven't heard the last of civil war, especially in [Upper and Lower] Canada. Ask what the oppressed nations of Europe are told. Ask Poland, Hungary, Ireland: the gallows have been made ready!
>
> JOHN BULL
> Come! I see you understand these things very well, daughter!
> (*John Bull and Confederation withdraw.*)[69]

I shall not spend much time on the second example, for it more properly belongs to the history of music in Canada than to theatre. It is a cantata, or lyric oratorio, entitled *Confederation*, and although it appears to have been completed by the summer of 1867, it was first performed publicly the following January at Montreal's Hôtel de Ville.[70] Its music was composed by the prominent musician Jean-Baptiste Labelle, whose name figures in the next work as well, and the words were by the much-travelled Auguste Achintre, born in France in 1834, a cavalry officer whose chequered career to date had included a period as journalist and editor in Haiti (where his political views brought him a death sentence which he managed to evade), a brief stint as that country's ambassador to the United States and a brief experience as a professional actor in one of the francophone troupes from New Orleans which visited Montreal in the early 1860s, a first example of the direct influence of those tours upon dramatic literature in Canada. Achintre had been living in Canada only a couple of years when his cantata was published.

In direct opposition to the preceding text, this one is a resounding paean to the new order of things in Canada. It opens with a choral Prayer to the Eternal Being:

> French and English, children of the same father,
> Let us all together, on this solemn day,
> Ask the Lord on high to bless our Land...

Then follows a stirring recitative, 'A Glance at the History of the Colony,' recalling the exploits of Columbus, Cartier, and Champlain, interspersed with lyric choruses. Special prominence is given to the patriotic song composed by George-Etienne Cartier (to whom Achintre's cantata is dedicated), 'O Canada, mon pays, mes amours!', after which the Canadian provinces speak in turn, led by Lower Canada, represented by farmers; Upper Canada, by pioneers, Acadia, by a woman who laments:

> Lost and wandering in the barren wilderness
> I weep, alas! and sorrow at my fate!...
> But cease now, tears! for sweet Evangéline
> Has told the sorrow of our Acadie.
> The past expires 'neath the weight of time,
> My future offers peace and happiness.

Nova Scotia is represented by fishermen and sailors, whose songs include the Acadian classic, 'Partons, la mer est belle!' New Brunswick's workers sing to the beat of their hammers and anvils, and finally the four provinces join in a quartet:

On our own honour, on our fathers' faith,
Each one here swears, before us all assembled,
To aid and to defend against all comers
Canada and her four flourishing provinces.[71]

Auguste Achintre's heady intoxication with Confederation seems not to
have lasted, judging from the direction some of his later journalistic activity would take in this country, and even in 1867 its intensity was uncommon in French Canada. The third and last piece we shall examine strikes a
middle ground, between the total opposition of 'Annibal Chamouillard'
and the uncritical praise of the second. It is a lively, good-humoured work
representing the culmination of the dramatic genre whose fitful evolution
we have been following to the Confederation period.

ELZÉAR LABELLE'S 'CONVERSION OF A
NOVA SCOTIA FISHERMAN' (1867)

The hybrid nature of this last 'political' play displays the mixed genealogy
I have tried to trace: it is a dialogue, in the strict meaning of the term,
involving only two characters, the Nova Scotia fisherman, Morufort
('Strong-Cod'), and the Québécois farmer, Pierrichon; the musical element is important (the author describes it as an operetta in one act),
although less so than for Achintre's cantata; and it is theatre, theatre to be
performed, unlike most of the other works in this category in French
Canada. Its focus is politics, the politics of Confederation.

The scene is set in Montreal just opposite the central point of commercial
activity, the Marché Bonsecours. Morufort is the first to enter, carrying a
codfish, walking-stick, and valise. The format follows the same tradition as
Quesnel's *Colas and Colinette*, songs alternating with long prose passages.
From the Nova Scotian's first aria and monologue we learn he has walked
all the way to Montreal to get to the bottom of things. Why have the fish
left the shores and rivers of his province? Why is the whole economy in
such a sorry state? 'Since even our cows won't give no milk, 'cause of their
danged Confederation – You can't tell me it ain't because o' their change in
the Constitution.' Pierrichon enters, carrying trade goods and a purse full of
money. Unlike Morufort, his step is lively and his expression joyful: 'My
goodness, how good business is! I come here t'day t'the cattle market, with
three bulls, six sheep, a cow, two turkeys, my wife an' me. By gosh, believe
me or not, by my honest mug, but the whole shebang went so fast, I'm still
lookin' fer me wife, she disappeared with the lot!'[72]

The Quebecer's monologue and song are high in praise of the new
political system which has done so much for his business. After much circumspection, he and Morufort introduce themselves in a lively duet, with
much mimed action: 'While they sing this duet, they both move back-
wards, one with his face turned towards the audience's right, the other
towards the left, until the point when, as they meet, they run solidly into
each other. After a few seconds' astonished pause, they begin to sing.'
Eventually they undertake a conversation. Morufort recounts his genealogy, and the present tribulations of Acadia:

> She was all goin' along jus' fine, an' there I be, livin' happy among
> me codfish, me wife an' kids – seventeen o' them I has already,
> then damn politics comes along an' shakes up our province. Even
> the water in the gulf got affected, an' all the fish, instead o' bitin'
> at lines, took the bit in their teeth an' headed out o' the country!

Before expounding his own political opinions, Pierrichon decides it
would be wise to soften up the newcomer, offering him a drink from his
bottle. A delightful drinking song follows, with Morufort adding his bit:

> To old man Howe I'd drink
> Spiritedly, from morn till eve;
> He's the one to fight the problems
> Caused by your government here.
> PIERRICHON
> To the health of George-Etienne
> I eagerly drain this glass!
> The greatest defender of all
> Of this Canadien race!

Finally they get around to discussing the political situation, the Quebecer
defending Confederation, the Nova Scotian decrying it, their differences
crystallized in another duet to 'The New System,' the longest lyric portion
of the play, where one verse contradicts the other (Pierrichon sings, referring to Cartier, 'He merits, indeed, the title/Protector of Canada,' and
Morufort responds, 'He merits, indeed, the title/Destroyer of Canada').
Each ends up with more respect for the other's opinions, and Pierrichon is
ready to attempt the 'conversion' of the fisherman. Why doesn't he follow
Joseph Howe's example, exchanging his principles for a secure, well-pay-
ing position? Pierrichon explains:

I was jus' talkin' to our Member about findin' a spot fer me godson in gov'ment work, an' he tol' me yestaday that the job was a sure thing, even if they's no need fer the job. You see, them folks like to encourage business, eh? So lookit, me godson can wait fer another chance, an' you'll take his spot.

MORUFORT

What! A job fer me! ... But that's impossible, Monsieur Pierrichon, me that said so much stupid stuff agin' yer gov'ment!

PIERRICHON

You weren't stupid enough to go and say it to them, at least!

MORUFORT

That's true, it was jus' between you an' me, an' 'twas the heat o' the moment made me say things – well, you knows what I mean? – You gets all worked up – excited – an' you winds up bein' unjust![73]

Obviously, the fisherman is ready for conversion now, if he can become Inspector of Cod Livers, at 400 piastres a year. And the operetta ends with another long duet in which they salute the political system, launching their new-found friendship with more swigs from Pierrichon's bottle.

Elzéar Labelle's text is as devastating for one side of the political question as the other and in fact is a clever assault on the well-known, long-ingrained traditions of graft and corruption in Canada. That stance is consonant with the general political activity of Labelle and his brother Ludger, involved since their youth with every election campaign in sight. His brother-in-law, A.-N. Montpetit, in the biography of Elzéar which accompanies the posthumous edition of his works, reports how he sniped at politicians for fifteen years: 'On the eve of every election the most important men flocked to his doorstep, looking either for his support, or, if that were not available, his neutrality ... To what political party did he belong? To all of them, and to none.'[74]

Labelle is one of those short-lived lights on the horizon of literary activity in Quebec: dead of consumption in 1875 at the age of thirty-two (his mother had died of the same disease in his youth, and his brother as well, at thirty-five), leaving behind a reputation for unconventionality and verbal brilliance to which the clever, varied (and generally untranslatable) puns in *La Conversion d'un pêcheur* attest.[75] It is not known when the première of his operetta took place, but certainly by 1869 it had become part of the regular musical repertoire in Montreal, performed by two actors who soon acquired a reputation for their interpretation of it, and accompanied by Elzéar's cousin Jean-Baptiste Labelle, who had arranged the music for this

work, and for Auguste Achintre's cantata to Confederation.[76] Edmond
Lareau, writing in 1874, assures us that 'every time this hilarious piece is
included on the program for a concert, its organizers can rightfully expect
a large attendance and healthy receipts at the box-office.'[77] Its last known
public performance was in 1899,[78] so this is by far the most enduring as
well as the most ingenious example of political theatre, the culmination of
a genre whose evolution goes back to the very roots of French Canada.

'SOCIAL' THEATRE TO CONFEDERATION

Having followed two of the sometimes merging sideroads of drama, the
pedagogic and the polemic, to the period of Confederation, let us now
turn our attention to what in other occidental societies would be the main
avenue of modern theatre. There are only three milestones left: Petitclair's last surviving play, *Une Partie de campagne* (A Country Outing) in
1856; L.-H. Fréchette's *Félix Poutré* (1862); and R.-E. Fontaine's *Un Duel
à poudre* (A Gunpowder Duel), in 1866.

Petitclair's 'Une Partie de campagne'

Pierre Petitclair's third play (we know the titles of two more comedies,
but neither has survived)[79] was completed by 1856 and performed publicly
in Quebec the following year by a troupe calling itself 'Les Amateurs canadiens-français,' an appellation dating back to the 1790s. It was published
after the author's death (in Labrador, in 1860) by a relative of his, the
printer and amateur impresario Joseph Savard, in 1865.[80] *A Country Outing*
has obvious similarities with *La Donation*, and reminiscences of *Griphon*,
but has most in common, thematically at least, with a play the author may
not have known, since it remained unpublished until the twentieth century (although there was a manuscript copy of it available at the Séminaire
de Québec, which Petitclair attended): Joseph Quesnel's *Anglomanie*. In
both texts, the central theme is the danger of aping British ways, demonstrated in both cases by the ridicule which results for one who has done so
to extremes. Both plays, needless to say, are specifically Canadian in focus
and of enduring interest.

    William, the 'Anglomaniac' in Petitclair's play (his name had been
'Guillaume' until recently)[81] is a more antipathetic figure even than Colonel Beauchamp in Quesnel's work, for the colonel at least knew when he
was defeated. After only a year's study and contact with anglophones in
the city, William has been brought back to his native village (which
appears to be Saint-Augustin de Portneuf, Petitclair's own birthplace) by

his father, Louis, for a visit. They have brought with them an English friend, Brown, and Brown's sister, Malvina, who is the object of William's interest and hopes. They are all staying at the home of Louis' brother, Joseph, who has a daughter, Flore.

We learn that William, before leaving the village, had won the love of Eugénie, one of Flore's friends. Despite having sworn her eternal loyalty (in a letter she has usefully retained), William is now so dazzled by Brown's sister, who has just returned from an extended stay in France, that he will not even acknowledge Eugénie's existence. Nor will he recognize any of his former friends and neighbours in the village, for he can no longer bear their rustic, Canadien ways. Even his father has begun to despair of him: 'His arrogance, his vanity, his Anglomania,' he confesses, 'are defects of his that I've long tried to cure, with no success so far' (I, 1). Petitclair spends all of the first act grooming William/Guillaume for a fall; that fall, in Act II, will be a spectacular one.

The 'Anglais,' Brown, on the other hand, turns out, like his sister, to be an unexpected enthusiast for French-Canadian customs and speech and wants to remain in the countryside forever. He insists on speaking only French, despite his hilarious massacring of it and despite William's desire to speak only English with him. A careful counterpoise has thus been introduced by Petitclair, an indication that he has grasped the complexity of the issue and a sign of his maturing since the black and white simplifications of La Donation. The balance, it must be admitted, is by apposition only: taken as individuals, William, Brown, and the others have no more depth or credibility than Boucau, Citron, Auguste, or Bellire. But I shall come back to that.

Among the former friends William has managed to alienate is his cousin Flore's fiancé, Baptiste, to whom he even owes his life after a boyhood accident. It is Baptiste who enjoys the first, delicious revenge in Act II, as he arranges for our Anglophile to receive a thorough ducking while out boating on a pond. With Brown's collusion William is soon decked out in the archetypical habitant costume he despises, including the homespun breeches and red bonnet made famous by the Patriotes, since his own clothing is too wet to wear. And he must meet Malvina while so attired, thanks to the stage-managing of the ingenious Brown; then after her, all the villagers he scorns, as they assemble for music and dancing (II, 14). William, unable to bear the humiliation any longer, escapes and immediately runs into Malvina again, who has discovered his infidelity to Eugénie by reading her letter. At this point Brown and Eugénie appear and happily announce their forthcoming wedding. William's discomfiture is now complete when he learns that Malvina is already married (her brother had insisted she keep it a secret, the better to dupe his 'friend'!), and he is left out in the cold, loveless and friendless.

Petitclair's message is clear, the same one proclaimed by Quesnel and which would be repeated so often to our own day: one must remain faithful to one's own past, to one's cultural, societal, linguistic, and personal roots. What is curious is the author's method of fortifying that message through the anglophones in the play: Brown, as we have seen, but also his sister. In her first appearance (I, 11), William greets her, in English:

> I hope you had a pleasant morning walk.
> MALVINA
> Extremely pleasant, Sir. The country looks so beautiful! But why don't you speak French, Mr William? [The rest of the passage which follows is in French in the text.] Why don't you speak French to me? You know I'm terribly fond of that language.
> BROWN [in his execrable French]
> (imitating his sister) 'You know I'm terribly fond –' My sister he is talk gooder French dan me, I tink – But me will learn soon – 'You know I'm terribly fond,' eh?
> MALVINA (to Flore)
> I think your cousin would prefer to forget his own language, mademoiselle.
> FLORE
> There are a lot of other things he'd like to forget as well, and indeed he has managed to forget quite a few of them.
> WILLIAM (to Malvina)
> In your presence, mademoiselle, I forget everything, and am reduced to admiration of you, angel that you are – In any case, as you know, English is more fashionable.
> MALVINA (laughing)
> Ha! ha! ha! – 'Fashionable' to scorn one's own language! And here I thought it was only certain members of the Legislative Assembly who had that privilege!
> WILLIAM
> You're just as sharp-tongued as ever.
> FLORE
> It is also 'fashionable' to have no human sentiments. (William stares at her sternly.)[82]

This is the only direct political barb launched in the play: one does not expect it to be launched by an anglophone. Critics have referred to Petitclair's 'timidity,' perhaps this is an example of it.[83] But perhaps also, if the ideal is tolerance and understanding of others' culture, along with fidelity to one's own, such criticism of francophone *vendus* is more effective from the mouth of an 'Anglaise.'

The weakest point in this play, as already suggested, is the depiction of character. Brown is prone to the same gratuitous and cruel practical joking that characterized Citron and Boucau in *Griphon*; William's sudden infatuation with all things English is too extreme to be credible; Eugénie is all passive, pathetic charm; Malvina's cruel teasing of William is never justified. As the leading specialist on Petitclair's work, Jean-Claude Noël, points out, the result is that instead of a play concerned with a serious social problem, we have an exaggerated example of its effects on exaggerated characters.[84] The author has trivialized the central threat to the survival of his own culture.

A Country Outing, on the other hand, represents considerable progress in the development of Petitclair's skill as a playwright. Even his weakness in exploiting the central theme should not obscure that theme's relevance, particularly in contrast to the distant focus of his first two plays. This third work is much better structured as well, with near-perfect balance between the two acts, the first winding tight the springs of the action, the second releasing their tension. The dialogue, by and large, is also much more natural, with far fewer asides and monologues, the bane of *La Donation*. And Petitclair has developed the ear for language evident in *Griphon*, showing particular skill in his depiction of social class and region through diction. There are four distinguishable differences of level here: the 'correct,' standard French used by Louis, William, the convent-educated Eugénie and Flore and, perhaps surprisingly, Malvina; then there is the subtle difference recognizable in the speech of Louis' brother Joseph, who has remained in the countryside: a grammatically correct French, seasoned with colourful appropriate Canadianisms that are characteristic of the educated country-dweller.[85] Third, there is the colourful, here sometimes exaggerated, speech of rural, illiterate Quebec used by Baptiste and the other villagers who appear in II, 14. And finally, of course, the fractured variant so good-naturedly employed by Brown. Moreover, as J.-C. Noël has pointed out, Petitclair seems to have taken for himself one of the principal lessons of *Une Partie de campagne*, in that the Anglicisms he had inadvertently used in the first two plays have virtually vanished in this one.[86]

In its first performance the play, according to the report in Quebec City's *Le Canadien*, 'kept the audience in paroxysms of laughter,'[87] and the report rings true. Certainly the earthy language of Baptiste and some of his friends, the physical pranks, and the imaginative assault upon

French vocabulary, syntax, and gender led by Brown, the music (reels and traditional country tunes) and song (the play ends, as did Leblanc de Marconnay's *Valentine*, with a rousing chorus of 'A la claire Fontaine'), the effect of William's sartorial metamorphosis and his discomfiture, should have kept an appreciative audience entertained at some length. When the same group of amateurs, under the leadership of the printer Joseph Savard, were searching for an appropriate work for a program sponsored by the patriotic Saint-Jean-Baptiste Society, which was to attract funds for the erection of a monument to celebrate the 100th anniversary of the Battle of Sainte-Foy in 1760, they quite naturally hit upon *A Country Outing*. Again, along with a stirring speech by the Society's president and to the accompaniment of its marching band, the performance was a great success.[88] The last known performance of this play was in January 1866, and again it seems to have been well received.[89] It deserved to be, for it is Petitclair's best work.

Before leaving the theatre of this amateur playwright, writing for amateur performers, let me underline the fact that the progress we observe in his skills is probably due entirely to his own efforts. The second half of his life had been spent in near-total isolation, on the North Shore or in Labrador, where there was little opportunity to benefit from the advice of others. More significantly, the newspaper accounts of performances of his plays never offer constructive criticism, confining themselves to the most general of comments. The only comment, for example, in *Le Journal de Québec*, which had advertised the upcoming performance of *A Country Outing* on 21 April 1857, reports on that performance in its issue of 25 April: 'Theatre: The Amateurs Canadiens successfully performed, on Wednesday evening, three nice plays entitled: *La Partie de campagne*, *Le Sourd*, and *La Soeur de Jocrisse*.' And adds not another word on the subject. Nor is his an anomalous case: after construction of the Theatre Royal there is little critical comment, in English or French, on the quality of francophone performances, particularly of 'social' theatre. Without competent dramatic criticism, an author had to be his own guide.

Fréchette's 'Félix Poutré' (1862)

With Petitclair's third play as the only surviving example from the 1850s, that decade was obviously not a promising one for the composition of non-pedagogic, non-polemical theatre in French Canada. But public theatrical activity picked up perceptibly in the spring and summer of 1859 with the advent of the French touring companies whose regular arrival thereafter characterized the rest of the century. At this stage, the role of newspapers was confined to accepting advertising for these performances, with only occasional comment and rare attempts at evaluating them. Apparently editors, after observing how Monseigneur Bourget was prone to react, in the case of *Le Pays*, against any visible support of those troupes and their repertoire, judged it wiser to accept their windfall income without jeopardizing their standing in the Church's eyes. Nevertheless, these tours could not help but evoke interest in theatre in the two cities where that activity took place.

Five years after the successful enactment at Quebec City's Salle de Musique of *A Country Outing*, an even more important première took place at the same theatre, on 22 November 1862.[90] An advertising campaign had begun in early November, with impressive announcements in Quebec newspapers. It was to be a 'Grande Soirée,' with full orchestra and comic songs to enliven any pauses, the young author's name was featured prominently, and an extensive summary was provided of the prologue and three acts which composed the play. But the boldest print of all was reserved for the title of the play: *FELIX POUTRE, or Escaped from the Gallows: Episode of the Canadian Revolution, 1838.*[91] This was astute advertising, for that name, in the late autumn of 1862, had come to special prominence. In the spring that year there had been published in Montreal a slim volume, *Escaped from the Gallows: Souvenirs of a Canadian State Prisoner in 1838*, by Félix Poutré, ghost-written for the illiterate author by his friend Médéric Lanctot.[92] Poutré's work had aroused much interest, reinforced by a few public lectures the author gave that summer and autumn.

The first edition of the play was not published until 1871, and it appeared without Fréchette's name, for reasons examined below. Instead of the three acts and prologue of the 1862 version, of which no trace survives except the summary in newspaper advertisements, the published text has four acts, the prologue having been expanded to form Act I. Judging, again, from the summary, there were no other changes from the original stage-play.

The première was a brilliant triumph for the almost unknown author: Poutré himself had been invited to the performance, and both he and Fréchette received a warm ovation from the audience. Two months later the play was revived and soon after became a classic of the amateur stage in French Canada, with countless performances extending well into the twentieth century. Fréchette had touched a responsive chord, twenty-four years after the Patriote Rebellion, in this first attempt to portray that conflict on the Canadian stage. In 1862, as mentioned, he was little known, with a couple of poems and an article or two in newspapers as his only publications. The career which would make him the best-known writer in Canada in his day, the 'poet laureate' of Quebec, had hardly begun: at the moment, he was twenty-three years old, a recent graduate of the Collège de Nicolet, which had already produced Antoine Gérin-Lajoie (Fréchette's chequered educational career had previously taken him to the Séminaire de Québec and the college of Sainte-Anne-de-la-Pocatière, both of which, like Nicolet, featured theatre prominently in their curricula), enrolled as a law student at Laval. Much taken with Poutré's memoirs, which he had read that spring and probably heard discussed by the group of French-Canadian intellectuals which gathered sporadically at the Crémazie brothers' bookstore, and which comprise the literary generation of 1860 (sometimes referred to as the 'Quebec School'), he had decided to 'dramatize' those memoirs. With his proverbial facility, he had done so in the space of a few weeks.

Both the original advertisements and the title-page of 1871 describe the play as a 'Drame historique,' the word 'drame' signifying, in such a context, a play combining tragic and comic elements and dealing with modern ideas and concerns. The genre is eminently characteristic of nineteenth-century European theatre, and the description is appropriate for *Félix Poutré*. The synopsis of the plot is simple: twenty-one-year-old Félix, committed Patriote, recruiter of troops and armament for the Rebellion, is betrayed by a spy, Camel. Imprisoned and awaiting execution, he decides to feign madness in order to escape the gallows. Successful, he is released; and Camel, at the end, is arrested for forgery. The first act is the one which best displays Fréchette's skill in dramatizing the original material, and I shall concentrate upon it. The play begins with a scene involving the traitor Camel and a policeman:

> CAMEL (*wrapped in a large coat*)
> Do you see that door over there?
> POLICEMAN
> Yes.
> CAMEL
> That's the one. You are to arrive at midnight, do you understand? That's about the time all the Patriotes will have gathered inside.
> POLICEMAN
> Are there many of them?
> CAMEL
> That depends. In any case, come in strength, for those bandits are armed and may try to put up a fight. Be careful to protect me, if they try to lay a hand on me –

POLICEMAN
Don't worry! In what part of the building are they to meet?
CAMEL
You will be led to it. Since they've strictly forbidden the use of any
type of light in the corridors, they won't see your uniforms until
they've let you into the meeting room. The password is 'Vengeance
and Liberty.' When they say, 'Who goes there?' you answer, 'Bru-
tus!'
POLICEMAN
Very well.
CAMEL
That's settled, then. See you at midnight.
POLICEMAN
At midnight! (*He exits.*)

There then follows a melodramatic monologue by Camel, just in case
his treachery had not been rendered obvious in that brief first scene. After
gloating over his scheme to trap the Patriotes he exclaims, in words curiously reminiscent of those of Attorney-General Hamel in the first scene
of *Le Statu quo en déroute*:

Camel, Camel, you're a great man! You're destined to become
Prime Minister, at the very least! – It must be ten o'clock now:
they must all be there. Let's go in! (*He gives three measured knocks
on the door at rear.*)
VOICE (*inside*)
Who goes there?
CAMEL
Brutus!
VOICE (*inside*)
The Password?
CAMEL
Vengeance and Liberty! (*The door opens and Camel enters.*)
(*The scene changes to represent an underground room. Several conspi-
rators are grouped around a table. One is near the entrance. Weapons
of all sorts hang on the walls.*)[93]

Apart from the monologue, these opening scenes would probably be effective in a modern television 'thriller.'[94] Scene 3 as well, which continues
the tone: Cardinal, one of the historic Patriote leaders who would be exe-
cuted, receives reports from agents, identified only by number, who are

operating all over Lower Canada and the adjacent American states ('No. 36 has gone to Washington to negotiate with authorities there. No. 17 writes from Burlington that a large shipment of arms is to be sent us from Albany ...'). Duquette, another real participant in the Rebellion put to death by the British, arrives to give his report. He is the first to allude to the hero of the play, describing him in glowing terms ('21 years old, athlete's build, a wrist of steel and stout of heart –'). Felix's entry is thus prepared and he immediately impresses all present with his courage and resolution when he enters. The young man is trusted with recruiting arms and men and made to swear solemnly on the Bible to devote all his energies thenceforth 'to chase *les Anglais* from Canadian soil, and not to cease while a single one of them remains within its confines.'

> FELIX
> I promise, on my own head and my honour! (*a knock is heard*)
> THIRD CONSPIRATOR
> Who goes there?
> VOICE (*offstage*)
> Brutus!
> THIRD CONSPIRATOR
> The password?
> VOICE (*offstage*)
> Vengeance and Liberty!
> THIRD CONSPIRATOR
> Enter! (*He opens the door. Ten policemen enter.*)
> Scene 6 (*the preceding, plus the policemen*)
> CONSPIRATORS
> We are betrayed!
> CAMEL (*aside*)
> Already! They weren't supposed to be here until midnight!

Camel shows his own papers and orders the policemen to arrest the conspirators. Then comes the *coup de théâtre* to end the expository act: these 'policemen' are in fact Patriotes, 'planted' by Cardinal in order to trap the spy he knew was among them. So they drag Camel off for safekeeping and with triumphant cries of 'God save Canada,' send Félix off on his mission, as he muses, 'In six months Canada will be free! – But what about me? – In six months, Félix Poutré will be dead, or a great man!'

These excerpts should suffice to give the cloak-and-dagger flavour of the fast-moving first act, the most effective and most original in the play. The Leméac edition (Montreal 1974, in the Collection Théâtre canadien series), with its excellent introduction by Pierre Filion, reproduces in an appendix large portions of the original text of Poutré's memoirs, to show how close Fréchette's version is. Page after page of the dramatized text reproduces, word for word, that original, but only one scene (5) in the first act draws heavily upon it. Without doing any violence to the original, Fréchette has provided more dramatic suspense than in Poutré's entire volume; and he has introduced an essential motif, the treachery of the spy Camel who, for reasons the reader never learns, has sworn to destroy the titular hero. Camel is, in fact, as Pierre Filion points out, the only character whom Fréchette has added to the cast in the memoirs and his function, although tenuously credible at times, is thoroughly justified.

Act II follows Poutré's activity in the countryside near Napierville, and ends with another *coup de théâtre* almost as effective as in I: Camel, who has somehow escaped custody, has tracked down the hero, and is about to arrest his father because he will not reveal his son's whereabouts:

CAMEL
Père Poutré, I am summoning you one last time, in the name of the law, to reveal the whereabouts of your son, Félix Poutré.
Scene 11 (*the preceding, plus Félix*)
FÉLIX (*entering*)
He's right here!
POUTRÉ SENIOR
My God!
CAMEL
Soldiers, leave that man alone, and arrest this one. Félix Poutré, you are hereby made prisoner, in the name of the Crown of England!

Acts III and IV, in a reasonable attempt at balance in structure, concern Félix Poutré's imprisonment. Cardinal and Duquette reappear as prisoners, to die nobly within our hearing. In these three acts, Fréchette strays very little from the spirit and the word of his source and signs of constraint are apparent. As was the case with Pierre Petitclair, he seems almost constantly to have misjudged the intelligence of his audience, leaving nothing to subtlety. Consequently the monologues and the asides multiply, as Félix explains over and over again that his insanity is feigned, that his words and actions are designed towards that end, that he is still the great-hearted hero. We know that the 'mad' scenes were the ones most appreciated by certain audiences (or at least by certain amateur actors), since they allow free play for exuberant overacting and account to a large degree for the incredible popularity of the play with college and amateur groups. Pierre Gobin has offered illuminating insight into the ambivalence of that 'madness' itself;[95] and Jean Béraud describes how a former journalistic colleague of his, Aimé Blanchard, had made a personal speciality of the title-role in an impressive number of performances over a span of forty years, despite the strenuous physical demands of the part.[96] There are wonderful pretexts for retaliation against the *maudits Anglais* too, as in IV, 8, when Félix takes on the English doctor whose spoken French is parlously close to that of Brown in *Une Partie de campagne*:

DOCTOR (*To Béchard*)
Is he have take medicine I him give yesterday night?
BÉCHARD
Yes, I gave it to him myself.
DOCTOR
...He is worst dan horse! Bien, bien, good, very well: me give more good one bye and bye. (*He tries to take Félix's pulse, but Félix seizes his hand so hard the bones crack.*)
FÉLIX
How are we now, monsieur l'Anglais?
DOCTOR (*trying to free his hand*)
Ouch! Ow! Ow! ... Oh! Oh! by God! – let me go – you is hurt me – Ow! Ow! you damned fool!
FÉLIX
Me, a fool? Aha! you say I'm a fool! Just hold on a bit, you old rascal! I'll show you what a fool I am! (*He floors the doctor and tries to strangle him.*)
DOCTOR (*in English*)
Oh! help! help! – murder! – for God's sake, take me away!

Despite the overdone histrionics, there is no doubt it is great fun – to the utter obscurity, much of the time, of the potentially tragic element inherent in the plot. Nor has Fréchette exaggerated his source, for Poutré's original had also placed much emphasis on the action-filled madness scenes, milking them to their limit. The minor brush-strokes that our dramatist has added are astute: in II, 8, for example, where the memoirs give Félix twenty minutes to escape before Camel's arrival at his father's house, and which Fréchette reduces to ten; in IV, 11, when Félix has just been freed and is leaving the prison yard, while the *habitant* Toinon watches through the wicket-gate, in what has to be an intentionally suggestive scene:

BÉCHARD
What's going on?
TOINON (*laughing*)
Oh, he's crazy, he's crazy!
BÉCHARD
What's he doing?
TOINON (*laughing*)
He's taking them off – he's taking them off – he's taken them off – He's crazy, he's crazy!
BÉCHARD
What's he taking off, you imbecile?
TOINON (*holding his sides with laughter*)
He took 'em off, an' then he put 'em on his back! –
BÉCHARD
What?
TOINON
His boots! – and then he took off in the snow, in his bare feet!

For a hundred years, critics of French-Canadian literature have tended to dismiss Fréchette's *Félix Poutré* for two reasons: first, because historians have demonstrated beyond doubt that its real-life protagonist was in fact no Patriote hero but a traitor, in the pay of the British;[97] second, because this work, like all Fréchette's surviving plays save one (*Papineau*, in 1880), was 'borrowed' from another source. My only comment on the first point is analogous to what must be said about Gérin-Lajoie's *Jeune Latour*: nearly everyone else, in 1862, seems to have been duped by Félix Poutré's self-serving memoirs as well. Within a few years, Fréchette had begun to entertain doubts, whence the nameless edition of the play in 1871; whence, also, the fact that he expressly disowned the work in later years, forbidding its republication (in fact, no edition of *Félix Poutré* with Fréchette's name on it ever appeared in his lifetime). The second criticism is more relevant, and the story of his plagiarisms from other authors is not edifying: in drama his *Retour de l'exilé* (The Exile's Return), performed and published in 1880, borrowed without credit from the novel *La Bastide rouge* by the French author Elie Berthet; *Véronica*, performed in 1903 and published in 1908, written in large part by his acquaintance, the French-man Maurice de Pradel. Paul Wyczynski has fully documented the whole shabby tale of those borrowings, and I have nothing to add.[98] But whereas *Le Retour de l'exilé* was written without the knowledge or consent of its original author, and whereas Pradel colluded, at least to some extent, with Fréchette on *Véronica*, the young author had made no attempt to conceal his source in the case of the first play. Indeed, had he not invited Poutré himself to the première and shared its success with him? Before the introduction of copyright law in Canada, this was rather handsome recognition.

Both criticisms, to the extent they are valid, do not bear upon the merit of the play itself, in the light of its enthusiastic acceptance and its role in the evolution of drama in French Canada. Fréchette demonstrates himself to be a more skilled adaptor than even Fathers Caisse and Laporte, and far superior, in his ability to construct a play, to Gérin-Lajoie and Pierre Petitclair. He was also the first Canadian playwright to take contemporary history as his theme and treat it in evocative nationalistic fashion, a procedure that, as Etienne-F. Duval has pointed out in his unpublished doctoral thesis, 'Le Sentiment national dans le théâtre canadien-français de 1760 à 1930,' and its resultant *Anthologie thématique du théâtre québécois au XIXe siècle* (Leméac 1978),[99] soon became basic to nineteenth-century theatre in French Canada. With its political dimension, with its past (and in this case, future) in college theatre (most evident again in its multiplicity of characters, all male, and the total absence of a love theme), *Félix Poutré* joined the strongest currents at work in the backwaters of dramatic literature and directed them towards a more public watershed. This point must be stressed, for only the public stage could deal sympathetically with a topic such as the Rebellion of 1837-8. Before the 1860s, and indeed for some time after, no college stage, while under the supervision of the clergy, could take such a provocative stand in portraying that bitter conflict.[100]

R.-E. Fontaine's 'Un Duel à poudre' (1866)

The effects of Louis-Honoré Fréchette's play were not immediately obvious, however, and the early 1860s saw no other young dramatist arise. Newspapers continued to take little interest in the stage, except for outstanding occasions such as the performance of *Archibald Cameron of Locheill* in 1865, although they continued to publicize the offerings of French troupes on tour. English Canada, with its professional companies now long established and continually reinforced by touring professionals from Britain and the United States, seemed little concerned about the almost total absence of native playwrights and indeed, after passing recognition of British-born-and-educated Charles Heavysege's *Saul* in 1857, paid little attention to such efforts thereafter. And the quaint, amateur theatrical activity of French Canada continued, much as it had done in the 1840s and 1850s. Apart from an intriguing allusion to a short play in the form of a *proverbe* entitled *A quelque chose malheur est bon* (Misfortune Has its Good

Effects), written by one J.-F. Gingras and reportedly staged at the Salle de Musique in Quebec in 1863,[101] there is no mention of the publication or performance of a Canadian play, apart from the college stage, before 1866.

Fréchette's play had dealt with national conflict, a real and serious one. Raphaël-Ernest Fontaine's work, *A Gunpowder Duel*, deals with a sham conflict, based on a trivial and local incident. It was first performed by amateurs in Saint-Hyacinthe, the first known example of drama staged there outside the Collège de Saint-Hyacinthe (which had included theatre in its curriculum since the 1830s, to the occasional discomfort of Monseigneur Bourget),[102] on 30 October 1866, and was published there two years later.[103] It had been written by a twenty-six-year-old graduate of the local *collège*, who combined the professions of law and journalism before becoming Mayor of Saint-Hyacinthe and later a judge of the Court of Appeal in Quebec.

Un Duel à poudre is a short comedy in three acts whose protagonist is an unfortunate, one-eyed gentleman much impressed with his own – questionable – noble birth, but without a penny to his name. Cruelly rebuffed by women of his own class because of his ugliness and poverty, he proposes marriage to a kitchen maid, Josephte, who readily accepts. But her parents, once they have met the hero, Jacob Pelo de Patauville, smell a rat and ask for proof of his supposed wealth and standing. He gingerly retreats from the engagement, only to receive a summons demanding a large sum of money for his breach of promise. At which point 'friends' of his decide to teach him a lesson, provoke a duel between himself and the lawyer for Josephte's family, a duel that will be fought, unbeknown to Jacob, with pistols loaded with gunpowder only, and no bullets. Convinced that he has murdered his opponent, Jacob Pelo de Patauville flees the region forever, to the vast amusement of the others in the piece.

Structurally, the play has few defects, rushing neatly to its conclusion. Act I deals with Jacob's courting of Josephte and ends with the promise of marriage. Act II is mainly reported action, as Jacob recounts his misadventure at her parents' house and ends with the arrangement of the duel. Act III deals skilfully with the duel itself, and the hero's humiliating departure. Fine use is made of rustic diction, especially in the case of Josephte, contrasted with the pretentious language of Patauville. That verbal atmosphere is enriched in II and III with the Anglicized French of the merchant, John Fletcher, and the more butchered version (often reminiscent of that of Brown in Petitclair's *A Country Outing*) used by another 'Anglais,' the salesman Tom Sweeney. Each act has a different setting (the kitchen of an inn where the heroine is employed; a hotel lobby; a clearing in the woods where the duel will take place), and Fontaine takes great pains to establish the atmosphere, as the opening description attests:

The stage represents the kitchen of an inn: a stove at rear, and at centre a table laden with trays, dishes, and utensils. A large tin bowl full of potatoes. Josephte is seated at the table, plucking a chicken, dressed in a housecoat with sleeves rolled up and no crinoline. Jacob lounges on a chair next to her, in a white hat, bamboo walking-stick, yellow trousers, and wearing a pince-nez.

As she plucks her chicken, Jacob tries to declare his love, in the exaggerated diction of preciosity, on his knees and in tears:

JOSEPHTE
Don't bawl, m'sieu, that'd be awful. Take it easy: I believe you, I believe you. Just the same, the whole thing seems kinda queer to me. I guess you really loves me, eh? Well, prove it to me, and then we'll see.
JACOB (*rising and gesturing violently*)
Prove it to thee, o wonderful nymph? O my Sylph! Lady of my dreams! O yes, my soul's ideal, I shall, I swear that I shall prove it to thee! Shall I go seek Napoleon-like glory on the field of battle? Must I deliver my country from the clutches of that vulture, Albion? Shall I exterminate the Fenians? I am a captain in Her Majesty's Forces, and shall spill rivers of human blood ... My genius, inspired by thy love, will produce wonders in the arts and sciences. I shall grope –
JOSEPHTE (*astonished*)
Grope for what?
JACOB (*continuing*)
Grope the bowels of the earth and bring forth the shining treasure it hides in its bosom. (*out of breath:*) Shall I? Shall I?
JOSEPHTE
No, no, M'sieu! Jus' you go an' fetch a pail o' water fer me!
JACOB (*continuing*)
Shall I annihilate thy enemies? Place thee in a palace? Bedeck thee in silks, in gold and precious stones? Say but the word, I am thy slave, thy lap-dog. Dictate, choose, ordain!
JOSEPHTE
All right, then, m'sieu, I ordain you to go an' fetch me a pail o' water, an' an armload o' firewood.
JACOB (*running off*)
I'm on my way, I hasten! What would I not do to please thee?
(*He returns carrying a bucket of water with his two hands, brings it to Josephte, and clumsily spills some of it.*) [104]

Despite his looks and his awkwardness, Josephte is impressed by the offer and decides to accept it. Then, for the first time in the history of French-Canadian stage, we have a hug and kiss to end the scene. Unfortunately for the couple, her employer arrives at that instant, fires her, and chases off poor Jacob. Act II introduces us to four new characters, all of them, like the first two, apparently modelled on participants in the real-life incident. There is the doctor, Toubeau, a direct descendant of Molière's physicians, with his ludicrous prognoses couched in Latinized nonsense, the merchant Fletcher, and the two lawyers, Francœur and Le Bourdon, who will play a central role in arranging the mock confrontation, all of them overjoyed at the opportunity to laugh at Jacob's misfortune and arrange further ones for him. He is so gullible that this presents no difficulty, and his sense of *noblesse oblige* is strong enough to impel him to fight for his honour when provoked by Le Bourdon. The duel having properly been prepared, Act II ends with a mournful monologue by Jacob, as he prepares a letter of farewell for his father:

Dear Father,

By the time you receive this letter, your son's life will have ended. A Patauville who has been insulted must kill the person who insults him, or die avenging his honour, weapon in hand. Farewell.

Your unfortunate son,
Jacob Pelo de Patauville.[105]

The third act is shortest, comprising only four pages. From its outset, we are informed that the pistols are loaded with blank charges, so that Jacob is the only one unaware of that fact. Two new, minor characters are introduced, Sweeney and Pinard, and they do their best to destroy Jacob's resolution:

FLETCHER

Let's get to it, then! Mr Picard and Mr Francœur, seconds for Mr Le Bourdon, come with me to load the pistols, and you two, Messrs Jacob and Le Bourdon, kindly withdraw. (*Le Bourdon and Jacob move aside, and the four seconds and witnesses come together. Fletcher opens the gun-case, and they begin to load the pistols.*)
SWEENEY

Is we gonna use round bullets or pointy ones?
TOUBEAU

Pointed ones would be better, since they kill more effectively.
PINARD

That's right, let's use those, since it's a duel to the death!

JACOB (*aside, mournfully*)
To the death! O Lord, I'm choking!
LE BOURDON (*aside*)
Those idiots are liable to put real bullets in! (*Francœur gives him a nod.*)
PINARD
Come on, Fletcher, let's put a second bullet in each. These gentlemen have to kill themselves properly.
JACOB (*aside*)
They want to make a sieve out of me! Jesus, I'm not going to survive this one!
FLETCHER
At ten paces, right?
FRANCŒUR
Right!
PINARD
Five would be better.
JACOB (*aside*)
Aargh! That chap's out of his mind!

For maximum dramatic effect, the first volley has no visible effect, although Jacob is sure his adversary's shot pierced his clothing. On the second, Le Bourdon falls and feigns death.

JACOB
My God! I've killed him! (*All surround Le Bourdon, except Jacob.*)
FLETCHER & TOUBEAU (*to Jacob*) [*in English*]
Run! Patauville! run!
PINARD & FRANCŒUR (*to Jacob*)
Sauvez-vous, Patauville! Sauvez-vous! (*Jacob does not move.*)
TOUBEAU (*bending over Le Bourdon, examining him, and taking his pulse*)
He's done for: the bullets have fractured his cranium, transpierced his temporal bones, and lacerated his occiput!
PINARD (*to Jacob*)
Run! Run away!
SWEENEY (*seizing Jacob and dragging him off*)
Come with! You is follow me! Run! (*Jacob and Sweeney run off.*)[106]

Le Bourdon and the others then roar with laughter, and Jacob is last seen disappearing with his faithful dog, intent on leaving the country forever.

Doctor Francœur proposes: 'Let's go and have lunch, my stomach's crying for food! Poor Pelo! Well, that's how a Gunpowder Duel ends!' And all exit laughing, as the curtain falls.

In general, the economy of action in this play is admirable. There has been considerable digression in the plot between Acts I and III, but the pace is so brisk that that may pass unnoticed in performance. Monologues are not abused and in fact help to advance the action. Careful attention has been paid, as we have seen, to characterize individuals by vocabulary and accent, and this is heightened by explicit physical settings. The main defect in the play is its unsatisfactory emotional economy. Even more so than in the case of the old man Griphon, the protagonist in *Un Duel à poudre* does not appear to deserve the constant punishment he is accorded. He is fatuous, gullible, physically unattractive, and prone to magnify his noble lineage, but there is no clear suggestion in the play that his designs on Josephte are less than honourable, he is courageous enough to face death when forced to, he displays loyal filial affection and even a degree of generosity towards the 'friends' who seek to destroy him (the will which he draws up at the end of II, 13 bequeaths them his only possessions). The reception he had received from Josephte's parents when both joined her in whipping and pummelling him at their house should have been more than enough to settle that score. The further emotional suffering imposed on the poor wretch before, during, and after the duel seems to amount to pure sadism.

But there is a factor which may serve to compensate for that major weakness in Fontaine's play, and which does not serve for *Griphon*: the incident it portrays is based closely, as I have said, on a real occurrence in his home town some years before. Charles-Philippe Choquette, in his *Histoire de la ville de Saint-Hyacinthe*, reports that Jacob Pelo de Patauville represents an individual who had in fact offended certain young citizens of the town and that a duel quite similar to the one Fontaine portrays had been contrived. A lawyer by the name of Bernier agreed to play the victim, smearing himself at the crucial moment with animal blood he had concealed on his person. And the original 'P.' disappeared from the area, not to return to Saint-Hyacinthe until some forty years later, at which time he was given a copy of Fontaine's play and discovered the cruel hoax that had been played on him.[107] Since *A Gunpowder Duel*'s only known performance was before locals who could be expected to know the background details and the originals of the characters depicted, the imperfect delineation of those characters, as viewed from a less privileged position, would have had much less impact. Perhaps the original of Jacob de Patauville was in fact an utter swine, deserving the punishment meted out to him.

Perhaps Fletcher, Dr Toubeau, and the two lawyers had sound reason for their spite. Posterity is left with their incomplete, unsatisfactory dimensions.

Aegidius Fauteux suggests that the real purpose of Fontaine's play was to ridicule a political adversary.[108] Although he offers no proof of that statement, such an objective would have been entirely consistent with what is known of Fontaine's political activity before his appointment to a judgeship (in itself, then and now, often a reward for such activity). His only other venture into theatre underlines that point, three years after *Un Duel à poudre*: the short, satirical piece entitled 'A Taffy-Pulling Party: A Political Stew in the Honour of Pierre-Samuel Gendron, M.P. for the Riding of Bagot,' directed principally against George-Etienne Cartier and his local supporters.[109] This latter play, apparently never performed or indeed intended for performance, emphasizes how tenuous the distance can be between the theatre I have here categorized as 'political' and the other two which are not.

Conclusion

The formative period for native dramaturgy in Quebec does not end in 1867. Indeed, many have argued that it ends only after 1937, with the advent of Emile Legault and his Compagnons de Saint-Laurent. But by 1867 a tradition of theatrical activity, including that of composition, had been established in French Canada. Three main streams contributing to that tradition have been delineated here from their wellsprings in this country: the religious-pedagogic, the political, and the 'social,' whose currents often meet and at other times take widely divergent channels. It is this third category, theatre written primarily for entertainment, which clung most precariously to existence in the period concerned and which continued to do so for another generation. But by mid-century the shaping factors had all become apparent.

The principal reason for the insecure status of social theatre is obvious: it is the dramatic vein most dependent upon the existence of a cultured, cohesive, predictable public. Unlike college theatre, with its captive audience and players; unlike political theatre, which survives without performance, social theatre is by definition a collective and therefore an urban phenomenon, dependent upon the existence of a social, economic, and cultural élite sufficiently numerous to provide continuity. In the 1860s those fundamental requirements began to establish themselves in the two urban centres of French Canada, Montreal and Quebec City. The francophone population of Montreal grew from 48 per cent of the total of 90,000 in 1861 to 56 per cent in 1881; in Quebec, from 56 per cent of 51,000 inhabitants in 1861 to 82.8 per cent in the same period.[1] And literacy, that other decisive factor, rose from barely half of francophone adults in Lower Canada at the time of Confederation to half as many again fifteen years later. Within a generation and a half, 'social' theatre had a clientele large and reliable enough to warrant the appearance of the first professional, local troupes, along with the facilities necessary to accommodate them.[2] As public support became predictable, it became a potent factor stimulating dramaturgical activity as well.

But even in 1867, the finishing-point of this book, public dramatic activity remained amateur, cyclical, and unpredictable. So did the writing of plays for the public stage. And in the absence of a cultural élite of adequate size and cohesion, it was the Roman Catholic Church which remained the most pervasive factor shaping cycles of theatrical activity in Quebec, for it was the Church which exerted the most powerful and the most direct influence upon the individual Québécois. We must be careful to avoid oversimplification in assessing that institution's impact upon the public stage and hence upon 'public' dramaturgy: its role is complex and certainly not exclusively negative, in those 227 years from 1640 to 1867 (ie, considering *Le Théâtre de Neptune* as an isolated anomaly). As Jean Laflamme and Rémi Tourangeau have conclusively established, there never was any all-out war between Church and Stage in French Canada. If there had been, there would have been only one possible victor in those days, and even the most superficial study of the period shows which it would have been.

The Church's effect upon theatrical activity in French Canada was exercised principally in two different – and only apparently contradictory – ways: the first, a negative one; the second, decidedly positive. Over the centuries, the hierarchy of the Church in Quebec was fairly consistent in its stance towards the stage: In theory, it found public performances potentially dangerous from a moral (and occasionally doctrinal) point of view. It therefore disapproved, but that disapproval manifested itself in a variety of shadings and hues, from the implicit censure of a Father Jérôme Lalemant in 1646 to the explicit, threatening tone of a Bishop Ignace Bourget, more than 200 years later; but with its most overt example occurring in the *affaire Tartuffe* of 1694. These are differences only in degree of reaction, explicable by the nature and quality of the public performances in question. It thus became a matter of situational tactics: the overall strategy remained consistent, throughout the Old and the New régimes in Canada. There was a brief period (early 1760s to late 1780s) when the Church, diffident about its own authority under British rule, appeared unable to react. There was another, even briefer, in the 1820s and 1830s, when public attention and the momentum of history seemed fixed in the orbit of political, not religious, attraction. But by 1789-90, as I have shown, the Church had found tactics appropriate to the time, in the interaction between Quesnel's troupe and the Montreal clergy. By 1840 also, the centripetal forces of Lower Canada's quintessentially conservative society had sought their natural channel, under their natural leaders: the clergy. Between 1694 and 1859, apart from these two short interregna, *there were no overt confrontations between stage and pulpit*. And when the Church felt the time had come to attack, in the latter year, the object of its suspicion and hostility was the system of values reflected in imported French theatre, ostensibly identifiable with continental liberalism, inimical to the Roman Church. The ancestral mother country by now appeared as a godless, immoral, denatured stepmother, all the more dangerous because her blandishments were conveyed in fondly remembered accents in that period following the resumption of diplomatic and cultural relations with France, symbolized by the arrival in 1855 of an official French vessel, *La Capricieuse*. The Church and the journals sympathetic to it knew danger when they smelled it. As a contributor to Montreal's *Le nouveau Monde* wrote in 1868, when a French company had arrived in town to present two works of questionable moral tone:

> For six months, Paris was entertained by these performances. But the Paris which went to applaud the ridiculing of honest husbands, the deifying of prostitutes, the debasement of filial respect, was not the Paris of decent people, in the true meaning of those words, one can be sure. For a long time now, Parisians have only found entertainment in scenes of prostitution and adultery; and in order for *La Duchesse de Gérolstein* and *La belle Hélène* to have achieved so much success, they needed a much stronger dose of immorality and vice than is average.[3]

This loose reputation and shady repertoire of French touring companies elicited a fairly consistent reaction from the Canadian hierarchy to the end of the century, when the original single diocese in 1836 had become ten, and the francophone population, despite massive emigration, had trebled in the province in the same period. The number and length of professionals' visits increased accordingly. Thus we have Monseigneur Louis-François Laflèche, Bishop of Trois-Rivières, warning his flock in 1880 about the attractions of such dangerous foreigners, without, however, explicitly condemning theatrical activity in itself: 'When troupes of actors, and particularly French actors, appear amongst you, you must take care not to attend their performances unless you are assured, upon good authority, that they do not offend against morality. It is, unfortunately, only too true that most of them are atheists, freethinkers, or debauchées: be very careful not to encourage them.'[4]

Faced with the necessity of decrying imported theatre by imported professionals, church authorities quite naturally demonstrate what may at first appear to be a surprising severity towards local, amateur productions. But again, this is not so much an inconsistency as a pragmatic adjustment to local conditions, some of which could on occasion prove embarrassing. Such as the incident in Acton, in the new (1852) diocese of Trois-Rivières, when the *curé*, a certain Father Ricard, had stepped in and prohibited performances by a vigorous group of local amateurs. Father Ricard reported to his superior:

> Then they all professed to be shocked and scandalized. The notary, Migneau, taking upon himself the role of highwayman, came by at midnight and fired three pistol-shots in front of my presbytery. On the same occasion he pinned a notice to my door: 'If you are going to speak out again against dances and balls, we shall do our best, through our bishop, to have you run out of Acton.'
>
> This is what they are trying to do today. Our *amateurs* of theatre and dancing, our destroyers of Sunday decorum, wanting more liberty, are uniting in order to lie to their bishop, and to ask for my recall.[5]

The Church, to reiterate, was quite consistent in its overall attitude towards public, social theatre, in the period which concerns us. But it is easy to exaggerate the importance and effectiveness of its opposition. Considering the enormous strength that formidable institution is purported to have exerted after mid-century, why were there *so many* letters, circulars, and mandamuses issued in the second half of the nineteenth century? Does that very fact not indicate problems with obedience, in a rapidly urbanizing, more educated society? Father J.-C.-K. Laflamme, at the time an instructor at the Séminaire de Québec, lets us read between the lines when he writes of the tactics employed by the *curé* of Lévis on the occasion of Sarah Bernhardt's glittering visit to Quebec City, just across the river, in 1881. The *curé* mounted his pulpit that Sunday to fulminate against the godless Sarah and her troupe: 'Suffice it to say that, Mass having begun at 9:30, the *curé* only climbed down from his pulpit on the stroke of noon. It was the noonday cannonshot that made him decamp, reminding him that the world still turned. No need to be surprised, after that, if Sarah is a phenomenal box-office success in Quebec City: forbidden fruit is always so attractive!'[6]

The Church's stand against indiscriminate performance of public theatre was consistently based upon moral, not political grounds. It was the danger to the immortal soul of its flock that galvanized the tribunes of the clergy to preach or write against the stage. And since in French Canada the danger to the soul has traditionally been perceived primarily in the danger to family bonds arising from sexual prurience, it was against the Parisian repertory of the *théâtre de boulevard*, with its predilection for humorous treatment of adultery, desired, attempted, or committed, and against the 'immoral' dress and deportment of its actresses, that these spokesmen thundered. In this curious way, at this juncture, the Catholic Church in Quebec was in effect taking a strong stand against cultural colonialism. On the other hand, the 'political' theatre of foreigners such as Prud'homme, Leblanc de Marconnay, or even Voltaire, did not normally arouse the Church to public reaction. And the whole long history of dramatic and paradramatic dialogues and playlets seems not to have elicited one hostile comment of an official nature in the period examined. Public, social theatre was perceived as the danger; and it was public theatre which was most vulnerable to the types of pressure the Church could bring to bear.

The second, positive, form of influence the Church exerted upon the evolution of theatre, through the encouragement of drama as a pedagogic or propaganda tool, is not necessarily contradictory to the attitude just described with regard to public performances. But it is here that individual institutions and individual leaders of the Church may be accused of sometimes disconcerting inconsistency. It was the Church (again, ignoring Lescarbot's play) which introduced the first dramatic performances in New France. It was the Jesuits and the Ursulines who made dramatic sketches, debates, and recitations an integral part of the educational fabric of the country. It was the latter (and, perhaps, unobtrusively, the former) who kept a spark alive in their schools in the dead years of the eighteenth century and who eventually kindled a flame in the heart of a young Petitclair, a Gérin-Lajoie, a Fréchette. It was clergy like Gravé de la Rive who acted as critics; like Father Ferland who served as spiritual progenitors for works such as *Le jeune Latour*; who themselves composed plays in the 1850s and 1860s, and who set out to adapt (some might say, subvert) the medium for their own purposes. It was the same Church which withdrew its approbation of theatre in the schools in the late 1850s in the wake of foreign contagion: for a short time only, in the case of the *collèges* which only males attended; for the rest of the century, in the case of the Ursulines' convent. Times change, and tactics with them.

In the absence of a viable public theatre, because of demographic, economic, and social factors as well as the Church's vigilance, it is, I propose, to Quebec's political theatre that we should look for evolution. That is the genre which is a true mirror of the social and political climate of its time.

For all nations, as we know, literary history is also social history. In the case of political theatre examined here, the reverse is just as true: political history is literary history. History in the present tense: ephemeral, but continuously regenerative of itself, it is the healthiest aspect of drama in French Canada in the nineteenth century. We have seen it evolve from the roughly sugared pills contained in Lescarbot's masque, D'Argenson's *réception*, and Saint-Vallier's *pastorale*, from the pale dialogues of the 1760s to the robust playlets of 1834 and 1848. We have seen it progress from staid solemnity (*Le Canadien et sa femme*) to bitter partisanship, from unalleviated diatribe to light, humorous, and musically assisted satire. We have seen the Church and its supporters enlist it as well (for works such as *Les Soirées de village* and *Contrepoison* are political in intent), and we have seen it begin to invade the realm of social theatre, a trend that the next generation would see accelerate in Quebec. Its first full maturity occurred in 1867, for no one before Elzéar Labelle had managed to blend so brilliantly the historical, contemporary, political, entertaining, and musical elements of theatre as he did in his *Conversion of a Nova Scotia Fisherman*. That genre continued to evolve in the direction in which he had pointed it: towards another distinctive product of French Canada, the satirical revue, already a standard in Montreal at the turn of the century, a form that endured through the teens, twenties, and difficult thirties of the twentieth century. For as the Status Quo Comedies are demonstrably forerunners of *La Dégringolade* and Labelle's bright composition, so also did they underlie the thriving modern tradition skilfully adapted, successively, to the new media of music hall, radio, and television. This is why I feel confident in affirming that 1867 represents, for public, social theatre, the end of its most precarious period. In the course of the next dozen years some fifty plays were composed in French Canada, many falling under that description. As many, in other words, as in the entire period preceding Confederation, in all genres. The last two decades of the nineteenth century saw that quantitative trend continue and increase in the domain of public theatre, the 1880s representing the high season of visiting Parisian troupes and their direct and indirect influence on repertoire and local activity, while the 1890s witnessed the birth of those first local professionals I have mentioned, with the first professional theatres to house them, more and more often supplied by local playwrights working in a greater variety of genres.

    In closing, let me underline one point again, without belabouring it: although there were difficult times ahead, French-language theatre was, in most senses, better off than its anglophone equivalent in Canada by the 1860s. This was particularly true with respect to the local composition of dramatic texts, and in this context another point must be reiterated: at no time, in the entire period here examined, was there any sign of opposition by the Church to native dramaturgy. There was no such opposition that I know of before 1880, and on that occasion the Church seems to have been reacting more against the author (Fréchette) than against his play (*Le Retour de l'exilé*). As to theatrical activity in its extended sense, French Canada was arguably better off as well, due to what Lower Canadians often perceived as the principal disadvantage of francophone theatre: its almost exclusive reliance upon amateur players. Esthetic achievements may have been inconsistent, and rarely higher than the pragmatic expectations of an audience long accustomed to that form of entertainment. But out of the darkest periods the stage would face in French Canada, its salvation and eventual rebirth, time and again, would come from those stubborn amateurs.

Perhaps the firmest testimony to an organism's maturing is its capacity to reproduce itself elsewhere. The 1870s saw a theatre strikingly similar to that of the Province of Quebec transpose itself west to the banks of the Red River, there to flourish for a time, as the admirable study by Annette Saint-Pierre, *Le Rideau se lève au Manitoba*, amply demonstrates. The 1880s saw its expansion to the Ottawa-Hull area, and to francophone New Brunswick. Theatre seems to have become as much a part of traditional French-Canadian culture as its cherished folk-songs, or its ancestral methods of tilling the soil.

Notes

CHAPTER ONE: THEATRE IN NEW FRANCE

1 Pierre Erondelle, *Novia Francia* 115. Erondelle, a Huguenot teaching French in London, was persuaded to undertake his translation of the most important parts of Lescarbot's text (excluding *Les Muses de la Nouvelle-France*) by Richard Hakluyt.

2 From the dedication ('A Monseigneur Messire Nicolas Brûlart, Seigneur de Sillery, Chancelier de France et de Navarre') to Lescarbot's *Muses de la Nouvelle-France*, in *Histoire de la Nouvelle-France*. Quoted also by H.T. Richardson in the introd. to her trans., *The Theatre of Neptune in New France* xiv.

3 The translation used is that of R. Keith Hicks, *Marc Lescarbot's Theatre of Neptune*, with an introd. by Principal W.L. Grant, as originally published in *Queen's Quarterly* (Lower Granville, NS: The Abanaki Press [nd]) 5, since it seems to me better to reflect the spirit as well as the versification of the original than Richardson's version (see preceding note), or that of Edna B. Polman, *Neptune's Theatre*. Another excellent translation appeared after completion of this chapter, by Eugene and Renate Benson, in *Canadian Drama / L'Art dramatique canadien*, with a brief preface. Their translation reappears in vol. IV of *Canada's Lost Plays*, edited by Anton Wagner 36-43.

4 Jacques Bouchard, 'Du Théâtre français et occitan en Nouvelle-France en 1606'

5 The historian Marius Barbeau concluded that the melody to which these words were sung was that of a popular 15th-16th century song still known in Quebec, 'La petite Galiotte de France.' The French words and music are to be found in Richardson's text, p 16. But Willy Amtmann in his *Music in Canada, 1600-1800* refutes this conclusion rather convincingly (p 265).

6 The word 'Rabelaisian' is here used advisedly, for his great prose epic is the certain source and inspiration of lines such as:
Qu'on baille à ces gens ci chacun sa quarte pleine
Ie les voy alterez *sicut terra sine acqua*
Garson depeche-toy, baille à chacun son K.

Cf. Rabelais, *Œuvres complètes*, in the Garnier (ed. by P. Jourda 1962) edition, esp. *Gargantua*, ch. 5, 'Les propos des bien yvres,' I, 22-9.

7 Lescarbot's masque, in Richardson's translation, was re-enacted to celebrate the 350th anniversary of the original performance, on 15 Aug. 1956, on the same waters where the original presentation had taken place, opposite Champlain's restored Habitation. The Hicks translation had been performed as early as Apr. 1927 in Toronto, and repeated there in May 1954, as reported by Anton Wagner in the text mentioned in 3 above, p 36. Yet curiously, apart from a brief excerpt of the play performed in Montreal in 1938, no second French-language performance of this text appears to have taken place to date.

8 See below, pp 49-51, 84-5, 130-7.

9 Roméo Arbour, '*Le Théâtre de Neptune* de Marc Lescarbot' 23

10 Lewis P. Waldo, *The French Drama in America*... 22

11 Antoine Adam, *Histoire de la littérature française au XVIIe siècle* I, 165-6

12 The 'political' aspect of the play has been treated very usefully by Hanna Fournier, 'Lescarbot's *Théâtre de Neptune*: New World Pageant, Old World Polemic.' Apart from her analysis and that of H.T. Richardson, the most useful studies of this work in general are Roméo Arbour's (see n 9 above); the brief article by Gilles Girard, '*Le Théâtre de Neptune en la Nouvelle-France* de Marc Lescarbot,' in *Dictionnaire des œuvres littéraires du Québec*, the article by Monique Baillet and Renée Lelièvre, 'Une entrée triomphale en Acadie en 1606'; Anton Wagner's introduction to vol. IV of *Canada's Lost Plays* 6-10, 36-7; and the carefully researched thesis by David Gardner, 'An Analytical History of the Theatre in Canada: The European Beginnings to 1760' 155-97. Gardner has also pointed out the curious coincidence that the first known performance of a play in English in Canada also took place at Annapolis Royal, in 1743-4 (pp 199-208).

13 L.P. Waldo, in the work quoted in n 10 above, interprets the passage in the *Relations* as indicating that the *mistère* was interpolated into the text of the tragi-comedy, and speculates that the latter may have been written by the great Corneille himself (pp 23-4). He offers no evidence in support of this speculation.

14 R.G. Thwaites, ed., *The Jesuit Relations and Allied Documents: Travels and Allied Documents: Travels and Explorations of the Jesuit Missionaries in New France, 1610-1791* XVIII, 87. Future references will be abbreviated to 'Thwaites,' the vol. and page no. This is the most accessible and most useful edition for our purposes, with French and English translation on facing pages.

15 *Les Ursulines de Québec, depuis leur établissement jusqu'à nos jours* I, 337-8. My translation. It has now been established that this uniquely helpful history was compiled by two Ursuline nuns, Catherine Burke and Adèle Cimon, on the basis of manuscript materials in the Order's archives. See *Dictionnaire des œuvres littéraires du Québec* I, 743-5.

16 Jean Laflamme and Rémi Tourangeau, *L'Eglise et le théâtre au Québec* 74; Auguste Gosselin, 'Un Episode de l'histoire du théâtre au Canada (1694).'

17 For some of these performances, very sketchy information is available, and these figures are based on that information.

18 To sidestep some of the friction that had resulted, the Vatican, when François-Xavier de Laval de Montigny was first consecrated Bishop, made him directly dependent upon Rome in designating him Bishop of Petraea (one of the ancient Holy Land dioceses no longer accessible to Catholics).

19 Thwaites, XXVIII, 250

20 Ibid., 251. Gabriel Lalemant was Jérôme's nephew; 'defretat' is Father Amable Defretat, who had been in Canada only a few months at this time.

21 Baudoin Burger, 'Les Spectacles dramatiques en Nouvelle-France (1606-1760)' 43. My translation.

22 Thwaites XXXVI, 149; XXXVII, 95

23 Although there is some doubt about the interpretation of female roles in the plays staged in Quebec in the 1690s under Frontenac's patronage (see below), it appears certain that women were not tolerated on stage (apart from private performances in the Ursuline's convent, where all participants were female) throughout the entire period of French rule. Apart from occasional, unclear references to a female performer (see John Lambert, *Travels through Lower Canada, and the United States of North America, in the years 1806 and 1808* I, 302, 304), such roles were played normally by men or boys. It would not be until the 1880s, in fact, that the presence of female actors was generally accepted in Montreal (see Jeanne Corriveau, *'Jonathas' du R.P. Gustave Lamarche et le théâtre collégial'* 40-1).

24 Thwaites, XXXII, 131

25 Thwaites, XXXVI, 147

26 Thwaites, XLIV, 103

27 It is primarily on this basis that Angus J. MacDougall has identified the author as being, in all probability, Father Paul Ragueneau, author of the *Relations* for 1645-50 ('A Historical Sidelight: Quebec 1658,' in *Culture* 11 (Jan. 1950) 15-28, esp. pp 19-21). Collaborative authorship is supported by Luc Lacourcière, in his excellent reproduction and emendation of the text in *Anthologie poétique de la Nouvelle-France* 58-9 (introduction and notes), 60-4 (text). Lacourcière significantly improves the version of the text published by Pierre-Georges Roy, *La Réception de Monseigneur le vicomte d'Argenson par toutes les nations du païs de Canada...*

28 Lacourcière, *Anthologie poétique* 60. I have used my own translation, for the only other version is that of A.J. MacDougall (cited in preceding note), which seems to me imprecise in some respects, particularly in his decision to add *gestures* to the spoken text. His article preceding that translation is, however, very useful. Apart from this, and the brief commentaries by Roy and Lacourcière in their respective editions (see preceding note), the only significant treatment of this text is in *Dictionnaire des œuvres littéraires du Québec* I, 626-7, a short summary by Aurélien Boivin.

29 Thwaites, XLV, 107

30 Thwaites, XLVI, 161-3
31 Thwaites, LI, 145
32 Henry Carrington Lancaster, *A History of French Dramatic Literature in the Seventeenth Century* II, 674. There is a useful commentary on the text also in Waldo's *The French Drama in America* 29-30. The play itself is reproduced in *Modern Language Association of America: Collection of Photographic Facsimiles* Part II, vol. IX, no 115.
33 Thwaites, XLIV, 234
34 *Les Ursulines de Québec* I, 483
35 Margaret M. Cameron, 'Play-Acting in Canada during the French Regime' 14. Her reference to 'disorders' in 1685 appears to stem from Bishop Saint-Vallier's *Avis donnés par Mgr de Saint-Vallier au gouverneur et à la gouvernante du Canada sur l'obligation où ils sont de donner le bon exemple au peuple*, published in *Mandements, lettres pastorales et circulaires des évêques de Québec* I, 169-74. But that text had been composed for the new governor, Denonville, and his wife, apparently aboard ship, *before* Saint-Vallier's first arrival in the colony; and a careful reading of the context of his *Avis* (he has been counselling them against allowing their daughter to participate in public spectacles, and explains: 'ce serait renouveler ici l'usage du théâtre et de la comédie, ou autant ou plus dangereuse que le bal et la danse, et contre laquelle *les désordres qui en sont arrivés autrefois* [my emphasis] ont donné lieu d'invectiver avec beaucoup de véhemence,' 172), makes it well-nigh certain he is talking about problems that had arisen in former times, *in France*.
36 William J. Eccles, *Frontenac: The Courtier Governor* 296. Auguste-H. Gosselin, in *L'Eglise du Canada depuis Mgr de Laval jusqu'à la conquête* I, 105ff., confirms this aspect of Saint-Vallier's temperament. The preceding quotation on his *bigoterie* comes from *Mgr de Saint-Vallier et l'Hôpital Général de Québec*, by an anonymous author 28. Perhaps most illustrative of all of the Bishop's crotchety disposition is another incident reported by the same chronicler when Saint-Vallier, on his deathbed in 1727, had been administered the Last Sacrament, with appropriate rites, by Father Lotbinière. This unfortunate cleric had the misfortune of forgetting some minor part of the ritual, which was immediately pointed out to him by his moribund superior (p 273).
37 Frontenac, it is known, was personally acquainted with Molière in the 1660s and was at least an occasional spectator at dramas staged for the French court (see *Mémoires de Mlle de Montpensier* [Paris: Chéruel 1859] III, 270-1). As Luc Lacourcière remarks, 'chez Frontenac, il y avait donc un homme de lettres sous l'écorce du militaire et de l'administrateur' (*Anthologie poétique* 108). His wife, who never accompanied her husband to Canada, was an intimate friend of Mme de Sévigné and is frequently mentioned in her letters. The only 'literary' effort by Frontenac himself which has survived (and is of somewhat dubious attribution) is a saucy ballad on one of the king's mistresses, entitled 'Chanson sur Madame de Montespan et Louis XIV,' published by Lacourcière in the text cited, pp 108-9.

38 Corneille's play dates from 1651, Racine's from 1673. For their current popularity in Paris, see Baudoin Burger's article in vol. v of *Archives des lettres canadiennes*, 'Les Spectacles dramatiques en Nouvelle-France' 44. *Mithridate*, the only one of Jean Racine's plays known to have been staged in New France, exemplifies the 'virile' qualities generally associated with his rival Corneille's theatre, and perhaps this fact had something to do with its choice in a pioneering colony.

39 Albert Reyval, *L'Eglise, la comédie et les comédiens* 28. Marion's observation is in his chapter, 'Le *Tartufe* et Mgr de Saint-Vallier,' *Lettres canadiennes d'autrefois* VIII, 24. Another French-Canadian researcher, in the same year, put it rather differently: 'En définitive,' Alfred Rambaud wrote, 'il est peut-être permis de voir dans *Tartuffe* une attaque, non contre l'esprit essentiel du catholicisme, mais seulement contre la forme que le catholicisme avait temporairement revêtue au XVIIᵉ siècle' 'La Querelle du *Tartuffe* à Paris et à Québec' 426).

40 *Avis donnés au gouverneur et à la gouvernante sur l'obligation où ils sont de donner le bon exemple au peuple*, in *Mandements ... des évêques de Québec* I, 169-74. See n 35 above.

41 Waldo, *The French Drama in America* 32; R.L. Séguin, *La Vie libertine en Nouvelle-France au XVIIᵉ siècle* 221-2. Séguin speculates as to the identity of the 'deux filles d'un taillandier' who were purported to perform in *Tartuffe*.

42 *Mandements ... des évêques de Québec* I, 302-4. My translation

43 Reyval, *L'Eglise, la comédie et des comédiens* 88-96

44 Herman Prins Salomon, *Tartuffe devant l'opinion française* 105

45 Eccles, *Frontenac: The Courtier Governor* 303-4. It has been affirmed that the governor immediately distributed this windfall among the poor of Quebec (Salomon, p 10 of text cited in preceding note).

46 A.-H. Gosselin, *L'Eglise du Canada depuis Mgr de Laval jusqu'à la conquête* I, 110-11; Marjorie Ann Fitzpatrick, 'The Fortunes of Molière in French Canada', xiv, note

47 See above, pp 14-15, 22.

48 Margaret M. Cameron, in the article cited in my n 35, p 17; Eccles, *Frontenac* 304. Apart from the texts mentioned to this point, the most useful treatment of the whole *affaire Tartuffe* is in A.-H. Gosselin's 'Un Episode de l'histoire du théâtre au Canada' IX, Sect. I, 43-72.

49 *Rapport de l'Archiviste de la Province de Québec* (1928-9) 276. My translation. The quotation continues:

> Si M. l'évêque avait voulu me croire et suivre les conseils que l'amitié qu'il me témoignait alors me donnait souvent la liberté de lui donner sur toutes les choses que lui ou ses ecclésiastiques entreprenaient tous les jours, et à la connaissance desquelles je lui representai qu'il était impossible qu'à la fin on ne s'opposât, il n'aurait pas fait tant de fausses démarches. Mais vous devez le connaître assez pour savoir qu'il ne suit pas toujours ce que ses amis luis conseillent.

50 *Rapport de l'Archiviste de la Province de Québec* (1923-4) 80-93. My translation
51 Léopold Houlé, *L'Histoire du théâtre au Canada* ... 26: see also Camille Roche-
    menteix, *Les Jésuites et la Nouvelle-France au XVIIe siècle* III, 327-9, 559-60;
    Bertrand de Latour, *Mémoires sur la vie de Mgr de Laval*, in Œuvres com-
    plètes de Latour (Paris: Migne 1855) IV, 36-7. Salomon, in the work cited in
    n 44 above, has a plausible explanation of how Latour, probably confused in
    his notes, mistook reference to one incident for another (pp 114-19).
52 Jean Laflamme and Rémi Tourangeau, *L'Eglise et le théâtre au Québec* 71-5
53 *Ibid.* 69 note. It is apparent that Saint-Vallier's interdiction did not apply to
    similar practices in the Ursuline's convent.
54 A.G. Doughty and N.-E. Dionne, *Quebec under Two Flags* 14
55 Guy Frégault, 'Politique et politiciens au dêbut du XVIIIe siècle'
56 L'abbé Glandelat à Mgr de Saint-Vallier, Archives du Séminaire de Québec,
    Lettres, carton P, no. 9. My translation. Glandelet was not the only churchman
    to harbour misgivings about the Raudots. Father Jean-Henri Tremblay, a
    member of the Seminary stationed in France as its agent-general, wrote to his
    superiors in Quebec the following year:
    Vous ne nous escrivez rien de ce que l'on nous a dit icy (c'est Mr. et
    Mad. D'Auteuil) que Messrs les Intendans ont eus pendant tout le
    caresme de l'année passée deux grandes tables également couvertes, l'une
    en gras et l'autre en maigre, où estoit bien voulu [*sic*] qui vouloit se
    mettre à l'une des deux tables. Je m'estonne que Mr. Raudot le Père qui
    scait qu'on ne souffriroit pas cela à Paris, le fait en Canada, lui qui doit
    donner l'exemple (*ibid.*, *Lettres* M, no. 38, p 39; 25 juin 1707).
57 *Monseigneur de Saint-Vallier et l'Hôpital Général de Québec* (Québec: Darveau
    1882) I, 262. The text of the *réception* is also reproduced in this vol., pp
    263-9, but is defective in part. I have used the ms version made by Jacques
    Viger, found in his *Saberdache rouge* (Archives du Séminaire de Québec, vol.
    J2, pp 197-211), with the emendation offered by Beaudoin Burger in his bib-
    liography to *L'Activité théâtrale au Québec (1765-1825)* 387. The translation
    provided on the following pages is my own.
58 *Monseigneur de Saint-Vallier et l'Hôpital Général de Québec* 269. As a sample of
    the original, here is the last stanza:
    Les tables sont rangées,
    Les viandes desja se trouvent partagées;
    C'est assez déclamer, car les pauvres ont faim,
    Et je croy qu'il est tems de faire leur festin;
    Et laissant loin d'icy les vers et la musique,
    De leur donner un mets qui davantage applique.
    Servons-les, et pensons à l'extrême bonheur
    Que nous avons en eux de servir le Sauveur.(*Saberdache* 211)
    This is not the only occasion on which Saint-Vallier attended similar perfor-
    mances. The chronicler of the Ursuline Order in Canada reports that he came

to their convent frequently, sometimes for purely religious exercises (first communion, confirmation), but also:

Tantôt encore, c'était un exercice moins utile en apparence, mais dont on sent l'avantage, pour habituer les élèves à parler correctement et avec facilité, à se présenter avec grâce, et à se former, comme dit la règle, aux mœurs honnêtes des plus sages et vertueuses chrétiennes qui vivent honorablement dans le siècle (*Les Ursulines de Québec* I, 483).

59 Elisabeth Bégon, *Lettres au cher fils: Correspondance d'Elisabeth Bégon avec son gendre (1748-1753)* 83 (14 Feb. 1749). My translation

60 R.-L. Séguin, *Les Divertissements en Nouvelle-France* 13

61 Burger, *L'Activité* 346 note

62 Craig R. Thompson, *The Colloquies of Erasmus* (Chicago: University of Chicago Press 1965) 312-57

63 Gardner, 'An Analytic History of the Theatre in Canada' 375-80

64 Max Fuchs, *La Vie théâtrale en province au XVIIIe siècle* 46; Pierre Larthomas, *Le Théâtre en France au XVIIIe siècle* 20-1

65 *Journal du marquis de Montcalm durant ses campagnes au Canada de 1756 à 1759* 169. This is vol. VII of *Collection des manuscrits du maréchal de Lévis* (Quebec: Demers & Frère 1895), pub. under the general editorship of H.-R. Casgrain. Burger, *L'Activité* 42

66 *Peter Kalm's Travels in North America...* II, 473

67 As the charmingly malicious Berthelot Brunet remarked, 'nos pères avaient d'autres chats à fouetter qu'à rimer des vers galants ou qu'à composer des discours historiques' (*Histoire de la littérature canadienne-française* 19). A more recent (and more solemn) observer, speaking on the absence of dramatic production, explains it as 'la tragédie vécue à la place de la tragédie écrite' (Gustave Lamarche, *Le Théâtre québécois dans notre littérature* 17).

CHAPTER TWO: NEW BEGINNINGS AND NEW TRIALS

1 This chapter makes much use of Baudoin Burger's brilliant study, *L'Activité théâtrale au Québec (1765-1825)*, in synthesis with unpublished theses by Marjorie A. Fitzpatrick, 'The Fortunes of Molière in French Canada' and Clovis Demers, 'Concerts et représentations dramatiques à Québec, 1764-1800'. I have attempted also, in dealing with anglophone theatre in Lower Canada in this chapter, to form a bridge with Murray T. Edwards's *A Stage in Our Past: English-Language Theatre in Eastern Canada from the 1790s to 1914*, a work that, unfortunately, seems far too little known in French Canada.

2 *The Quebec Gazette / La Gazette de Québec* proclaimed itself bilingual (it never got around to buying complete French typefaces, so its readers had to supply some of their own accents), but didn't know where to stop at times, witness its translation of the innkeeper's name, and of the title of the play here referred to (the 'pierre' in that title is the stone memorial statue of the man whose

death Don Juan had caused, and whom he mockingly invites to a dinner, the 'festin') as 'Peter's Feast.' The paper had been founded by William Brown, a Scot living previously in Philadelphia (June 1764). The article is on p 3 of the issue for 11 Apr. 1765. The *Gazette* did not appear between 31 Oct. 1765 and 29 May 1766, so we learn nothing further about the performances.

3 Fitzpatrick, in her thesis mentioned in n 1 above, speculates that the play is probably the significantly moderated version made popular by Thomas Corneille (p 5); John Hare disagrees, pointing out that editions of Molière published in the eighteenth century attach both titles to this play ('Panorama des spectacles au Québec: De la Conquête au XXe siècle,' in Archives des lettres canadiennes V, 61). Although the political situation of the Church in Quebec in 1765 was precarious enough for it to risk no intervention in a sensitive public domain (and in any case the Bishop, Mgr Briand, was still in London, pleading the case for the very existence of the Roman Catholic Church in the new province), this was much less so in 1795. Indeed, as we shall see, the clergy there had already reacted vigorously, in 1790-1, against the performances of *Le Malade imaginaire* and *L'Avare*, plays so innocuous in comparison with this one. Finally, how could one explain the performance – seemingly unopposed – of this play in Molière's version in Montreal in 1804, when the formidable Octave Plessis was coadjutor bishop? Perhaps Fitzpatrick's interpretation seems more logical.

4 *Quebec Gazette / Gazette de Québec*, 24 Oct. 1765

5 For a listing and general history of these journals, see A. Beaulieu and J. Hamelin, *Les Journaux du Québec, de 1764 à 1964*.

6 *Quebec Gazette / Gazette de Québec*, 3 Aug. 1775

7 Burger, *Activité* 61 note

8 See above, pp 20-1.

9 Burger, *Activité*; Antoine Adam, *Histoire de la littérature française du XVIIe siècle* V, 287 note

10 Reproduced by Marie Tremaine, *A Bibliography of Canadian Imprints, 1751-1800* 97-8, item 214. The receipt reads: '1775, Aug. 5. Printed for C.F. Bailly 700 coarse and 100 on fine Paper, Play Bills making a folio page – £1.15.' The individual mentioned, C.F. Bailly de Messein, was a professor at the Séminaire in the 1770s, later tutor to Governor Carleton's children. As Tremaine reports, 'both were interested in a plan for higher education in Quebec.'

11 Gravé de la Rive had come to Canada in 1755 at the age of 25, and never returned to France, remaining with the Seminary until his death 47 years later.

12 The most obvious borrowing from *Le Bourgeois gentilhomme* is in III, 1-3, where Poussefort and De la Gavotte attempt to instruct Nigaudière, as in *Le Bourgeois*, II, 1-4. The whole tradition of assigning names consonant with character is a long-standing characteristic of the *commedia dell'arte*, but here the influence of Regnard appears to predominate, especially in the form 'nigaud' (simpleton), recalling Nigaudin, the cuckold in Regnard's *Augmenta-*

tion de la Baguette, as well as Nigaudin and Nigaudinet in his *La Coquette ou l'Académie des dames* and *La Foire Saint-Germain* (in the same way, 'Rudanière' is based on French *rude*: 'uncouth, unpolished'; 'Dandinet' recalls Molière's George Dandin and French *dandin*, synonym of *nigaud*; the dancing master is M. de la *Gavotte*, the fencing master *Poussefort* ('Thrust-hard'), and so on). Thematically, the whole question of paternal indulgence and its negative effects upon education is a frequent subject for Jesuit college theatre, especially that of Father Du Cerceau in works such as *L'Ecole des pères*, long popular in France, and *Grégoire, ou les Incommodités de la grandeur*, performed in Montreal in 1782 (see Burger, *Activité* 182).

13 Eg, p 2: 'Suffit que je sçavons ce que je sçavons, et que je sommes ce que je sommes, et que je ne sommes pas un sot, et que j'y menons joyeuse vie, dieu merci, et le bon dieu.' The manuscript is Sém. 34, no. 135, Archives du Séminaire de Québec. My translation is used throughout.

14 I, 5 (p 11):

DANDINET

Tenés. mr. le doux, vous ne me ferés Jamais croire que mon cher papa ait fait ce qu'il falloit faire pour me bien élever: Je ne suis pas si sot, que je ne me sois déja bien apperçu que mes chers oncles me regardent en pitié –

15 I, 8 (p 15):

LE COMTE

je veux qu'on me parle toujours a cœur ouvert et qu'on m'explique nettement sa pensée.

PHILEMON

vous avés raison –

LE COMTE

Et je ne hais rien tant que ces faux amis, qui ne disent jamais ce qu'ils pensent.

PHILEMON

Je suis comme vous sur cet article.

LE COMTE

La police y devroit mettre ordre.

PHILEMON

cela est vrai –

LE COMTE

Je voudrois qu'on en pendit une demie douzaine pour l'exemple.

16 II, 6 (p 28):

LE COMTE (*en entrant*)

[Rodrigue, as-tu du cœur?

LE MARQUIS

tout autre que mon pére l'éprouveroit sur l'heure.

LE COMTE

agréable colére! ... viens mon fils, viens mon sang (*il l'embrasse*) oh! ça,

mon fils nigaudiére, nigaudiére mon fils; il faut soutenir l'honneur de ta
famille; il faut consoler mes cheveux blancs, il faut...
LE MARQUIS
eh! bien, achevés.
LE COMTE
il faut prendre le parti des armes.
LE MARQUIS
le parti?...]
LE COMTE
va, ne réplique pas; Je connois ta poltronnerie, je sçais que tu n'as Jamais
tiré l'épée que pour faire peur a nos servantes; Je sçais qu'un jour aiant
reçu un soufflet d'un Jeune gentilhomme de nos voisins, tu t'en fus
pleurer dans l'écurie – mais en fin voici le tems où il faut te montrer digne
fils d'un pére tel que moi – [Car, qui peut vivre infame, est indigne du
jour – va donc a l'armée] –

17 III, 9 (p 45):
vous me contenterés, mon cher neveu, si vous travaillés solidement pour
vous. vous voiés dans votre frère les suites funestes d'une éducation
négligée; il ne peut entrer ni dans la robe, ni dans l'épée sans s'exposer a
deshonnorer sa famille, et le voila réduit a passer le reste de ses jours dans
une honteuse obscurité, le ciel qui vous a conduit heureusement ici m'a
inspiré le dessin de prévenir dans vous des suites si facheuses ...

18 Sém. 34, no. 135. My translation. This is the only part of Gravé de la Rive's
letter which has ever been reproduced. The entire text reads:
J'ay lu cette comedie de leducaõn negligée en 1780. elle me paroit pitoy-
able; on ny voit ni intrigue ni dénouëment ni jeu de theatre.
    Le caractere Niais de la Nigaudière heros de la piece est asses suivi,
mais cela ne conduit a rien qui interesse son pere et lui sen retournent en
poitou cõe ils etoient venu. aucun d'eux ne fait naitre lenvie de donner de
L'Educaõn aux enfants. un jeune hõe aussi profondement bete que la nig-
audiere en est incapable et on doit se feliciter de navoir perdu ni son tems
ni son argent a éduquer un pareil personage. ce seroit autre chose si on lui
avoit presté quelques unes des bonnes qualités de Dandinet.
    La piece n'excite aucune passion* elle n'est remarquable que par les
manieres de parler basses et populaires dont elle est tissüe; fades et sans
sel ces dictons ne sont capable de faire rire que des païsans. je trouve de
plus que ces dictons sont plus canadiens que poitevins.
    Il paroit encore singulier que ce soit aux valets a qui [sic] la nigaudiere
developpe le plus son caractere tandis que cest Straton et philemon qui en
portent leur jugemĩt. sans en avoir communiqué avec leurs valets ni leur
avoir donné commission de faire cette Enqueste.
    La scene de Poussefort et de la Gavotte a 2 déffauts tous deux se reti-
rent apres avoir fait tomber leur eleve: cette monotonie deplait: de plus
comment ce fait il qu ils aient tant denvie de se procurer des Eleves et que
des la Ire leçon ils agissent a leur egard avec tant dinsolence.

Les sentiments de Dandinet dans la 4e et 5e scene du Ier acte sont assés bien; lesperance qu ils font naitre de lui interesse (cest la seule passion quexcite la piece) mais la 6e scene est une repetition des deux precedente, philemon auroit du sy trouver

Jignore l'autheur de cette comedie et Mr Boivet qui la transcrit a pris plus de peine quelle ne merite. &c. &c. &c.

G.

*G. de la Rive is apparently using 'passion' in its Latin sense, as was common in seventeenth-century criticism. I translate: 'dramatic interest.'

19 Archives du Séminaire de Québec, Sém. 12, no. 6. My translation throughout. Again, since no part of this text seems to have been published I shall provide the French original for each passage cited:

PAVANE

je me garderois bien de leur faire la cour.

quils critiquent, he bien: je critique à mon tour.

j'oppose vers a vers, et rime contre rime,

et je prétends par là mériter leur estime. (I, 1, p 3)

20 As observed with regard to *L'Education négligée* (see n 12 above), characters' names are assigned according to the character traits they display. Thus 'Pavane' suggests *pavaner*: 'to strut, to peacock'; one of his rivals is 'Longue-haleine' ('long-wind'); the soldier is named Fierabras ('bully'), and we shall soon meet De la Hablerie (*hablerie*: 'braggadocio'), and so on.

21 II, 10 (p 76):

FIERABRAS

Carmagnol, clinquand verd

DE LA HABLERIE

il vous demande un siège,

et vous donne en présent un almanach de liege,*

ce livre en son pays est beaucoup estimé,

et par ordre du roi, tous les ans imprimé

PAVANE

je reçois ce présent avec reconnoissance.

FIERABRAS

croc, broc, mouq, brouq, crac, brac.

DE LA HABLERIE

il dit que la science est au dessus de tout.

et que deux de vos vers valent mieux qu'auprintems

cent boisseaux de poids verds.

PAVANE

c'est trop aimable à lui.

*'almanach de liège' could mean an almanach printed on, or bound in, cork; or, more probably, one of the well-known ones printed in Liège (Belgium).

22 It is in a small copy-book with the handwritten title, 'Analyse de Sermons,' and indeed that is what one finds, in another hand, in the interstices between the completed parts of the play. No doubt it is because of these short para-

phrases and commentaries that the copy-book has survived, and the play with it. The analyses are of sermons delivered between 1781 and 1786 (several of them, incidentally, by Gravé de la Rive), which confirms the approximate dating of the text in the annotation by the archivist at the Seminary, 'written towards 1780.' Since the analysis of sermons and the study of their structure is and was an integral part of seminary studies, one can safely assert that this is a student's copy-book, not an instructor's. One assumes the author began the draft in full confidence (indeed, he has written in the names of the student actors he had in mind, beside the list of characters in the play), but never finished it; and the unused portion of his copy-book was then used by another student in preparing his classwork.

23 See above, pp 40-1.
24 Molière's works were probably in the Seminary's library. They are not mentioned specifically by Antonio Drolet in his 'La Bibliothèque du Séminaire de Québec et son catalogue de 1782,' nor in his monograph, *Les Bibliothèques canadiennes, 1604-1960*, but in the article first mentioned he lists Voltaire's *Henriade*, the complete works of Voltaire and Machiavelli, Milton's *Paradise Lost*, 'sans nommer toutes les grandes œuvres des classiques anciens et modernes' (p 265).
25 Certainty is not absolute in this case. Documents discovered by E.-Z. Massicotte in the Château de Ramesay (Montreal) and published by him in *Bulletin des recherches historiques* in 1917 refer to the plays cryptically as *Le Bourgeois* and *Le Médecin* ('Un Théâtre à Montréal en 1789'; 'Le Premier Théâtre à Montréal').
26 Fitzpatrick, 'The Fortunes of Molière in French Canada' ii; Burger, *Activité* 188
27 *Les Ursulines de Québec* III, 160. My translation
28 Brumoy (1688-1742), who never set foot in Canada, was the author of several such works. The Collège Saint-Raphaël had been founded in 1773.
29 *Jonathas et David ou Le Triomphe de l'amitié*. Tragédie en trois actes représentée par les écoliers de Montréal
30 Laflamme and Tourangeau, *L'Eglise et le théâtre au Québec* 82
31 Burger, *Activité* 65. As he points out, 'ce sujet biblique était courant dans les collèges français dès le XVIe siècle.'
32 See John Hare, 'Panorama des spectacles au Québec: De la Conquête au XXe siècle' 62.
33 The letter requesting permission reads:

Montreal, Dec. 11th, 1780

Dear sir,

You will, I dare say recollect, that some of the Young Gentlemen at Montreal entertained us with a Play Last Winter, we are going to sett about fiting up a Play House in Earnest this winter; all the Profit to go to the Poor. Our greatest Loss is Want of Women and of a House to perform in. Application has been made to me, for the use of the Jesuit Old Vestibull, I had not the least difficulty in according their request, but I post-pon'd it, until I should have His Excellencys consent not from any appre-hension of a refusall, but lest the Old Jesuit here should say something about it, and represent that we had made a *Den of Thieves* of the Old Temple, I thought it best to write you that you might mention it to the Commander in Chief, then *toute* [*sic*] *ira en règle* ... I therefore intreat you will mention it to His Excellency, and that we shall be much obliged to him for his Consent it will be of real service to the Building whatever use it may be converted to afterwards, at Present its in a Ruinous condition.

> I have the Honor to be Dear Sir,
> Your most obedient & most
> Humble Servt.
> Allan MacLean

The addressee of General MacLean's letter, Haldimand's adjutant, replied:

> Quebec, 14th December 1780

Dear Sir,

Having laid [?] your letter requesting the sanction of His Excellency the Commander in chief to make use of the Jesuit old vestibull as a Theatre, I have the honor to acquaint you that His Excellency has no objection thereto, particularly as it has been employed on various occasions and as the purpose of that in question is so very laudable.

> I am Sir,
> &c,
> B. Mathews.

These letters were first published by E.-Z. Massicotte in 'Recherches histo-riques sur les spectacles à Montréal, de 1760 à 1800.' They are quoted also by Lewis P. Waldo, *The French Drama in America* 44-5.

34 Burger, *Activité* 134
35 Marine Leland, 'Joseph-François Perrault, années de jeunesse, 1753-1783' 815. My translation. Quoted by John Hare in article mentioned in n 32 above, p 62
36 Burger, *Activité* 134
37 See subsection on English-language theatre before 1825, pp 77-82.
38 *Gazette de Montréal / Montreal Gazette*, 9 Mar. 1789. See Fitzpatrick, 'The For-tunes of Molière in French Canada' 58. Some of the works presented in Eng-lish translation (with or without recognition of the source) are discussed in Waldo's book, mentioned in n 33 above.
39 Jean-Pierre Claris de Florian (1755-94) was Voltaire's grand-nephew. *Les deux Billets*, presented in Montreal on 24 Nov. 1789, had first been performed in Paris 10 years earlier and published in 1780. Jean-François Renard, known to posterity simply as 'Regnard,' lived from 1655 to 1709 and was the most popular light dramatist in the late seventeenth and early eighteenth centuries. *Le Légataire universel*, his most popular play, was performed on 29 Dec. 1789 and again on 9 Feb. 1790, the second time in conjunction with Quesnel's *Colas et Colinette*.

40 Alexandre-Louis Bertrand Robineau, *dit* Beaunoir (1746-1823). *Jérôme Pointu* had been performed in Paris in 1781.

41 See Pierre Larthomas, *Le Théâtre en France au XVIIIᵉ siècle* 22-3; Jacques Truchet, *Théâtre du XVIIIᵉ siècle* I, xx; and Léo Claretie's somewhat dated *Histoire des théâtres de société, passim.*

42 For a solid, but brief, treatment of Quesnel's dramatic production, see David M. Hayne, 'Le Théâtre de Joseph Quesnel,' in *Archives des lettres canadiennes.* Quesnel's activities have also been studied by Baudoin Burger, in *Activité*, esp. pp 199-215, 'L'Œuvre franco-canadienne de Quesnel'; and by Fitzpatrick in 'The Fortunes of Molière in French Canada,' but this important figure in the history of Canadian literature is still awaiting a monograph devoted to his not inconsiderable activities. Members, besides Quesnel and Dulongpré, of the Théâtre de Société were Pierre-Amable de Bonne, later to be a repeated victim of paradramatic publications (see pp 89-90 below), Jacques Hersé, Jean-Guillaume Delisle, Joseph-François Perrault, and François Rolland.

43 Burger, *L'Activité* 187; Willy Amtmann, *Music in Canada, 1600-1800* 242. Amtmann corrects the obvious misprint in the original advertisement, which ascribes the music to Anseaume and the text to Duni, instead of the reverse.

44 Hare, 'Panorama des spectacles au Québec' 63

45 Quoted in *Rapport de l'archiviste de la Province de Québec* (1947) 114, and by Laflamme and Tourangeau, *L'Eglise et le théâtre au Québec* 85

46 Fitzpatrick, 'The Fortunes of Molière in French Canada' 60-1. It is unfortunate that this excellent thesis is still unpublished.

47 Mgr Hubert to M. Brassier, 30 Nov. 1789. See Laflamme and Tourangeau, *L'Eglise et le théâtre au Québec* 86-7.

48 Pierre Larthomas, in the work cited in n 41 above, p 53. My translation

49 Clarence D. Brenner and Nolan A. Goodyear, eds, *Eighteenth-Century French Plays* (New York: Appleton-Century-Crofts 1927) xvii. Original quotation from Moissy, *Des Ouvrages du théâtre* (Paris 1770)

50 *Colas et Colinette ou le Bailli dupé.* Comédie en 3 actes et en prose, mêlée d'ariettes (Quebec: John Neilson 1808). Despite the date of imprint, it seems certain the text was not published until 1812. There is an interesting series of 8 letters from Quesnel to the printer, Neilson, in the Public Archives of Canada, Ottawa (Neilson Collection, MG 24 B1, vol. II) the first from 18 Mar. 1807 and the last, 10 Apr. 1809, dealing with the progress of this edition. We learn that it was a certain M. Vassal de Boucherville who served as go-between, that Quesnel lost a copy of one of the proofs on one occasion, that he wants it to appear he has had nothing to do with the edition ('Je suis loin d'avoir la sotte vanité d'aller montrer d'avance un ouvrage qui doit être sensé [*sic*] ne paraitre que presque à mon insçu, quoiqu'avec ma participation' 70 b-c, 15 June 1808), and so on. The last letters, written just before Quesnel's death, are full of hopeful queries as to when the work may be finished. As to the date of publication, see also Beaudoin Burger, in *Aspects du théâtre québécois*, conférences colligées par Etienne-F. Duval (Université de Québec à Trois-Rivières 1978), 3.

51 (Montreal: Réédition-Québec 1968). The text was also published in both editions of James Huston's *Répertoire national* (1848, 1893); the recording is by Select, CC15001. Finally, we have *J. Quesnel: Colas and Colinette, or The Bailiff Confounded*, English translation of the dialogue by Michel Lecavalier and that of the songs by Michel Lecavalier and Godfrey Ridout (Toronto: Thompson 1974). I shall quote from this latter edition.

52 Burger, *Activité* 214. The play in question was *Le Père des amours* by Eugène Lapierre. See Edouard G. Rinfret, *Le Théâtre canadien d'expression française...* II, 300-1.

53 See D.M. Hayne's article in *Archives* V, 113.

54 *Colas and Colinette* (Toronto: Thompson 1974) II, 5 (p 29)

55 Most of these are in the speech of Colas and his social equal, Dolmont's valet, L'Epine (his name is identical with that of the valet in Florian's *Jeannot et Colin* (1780)). Colas speaks of something happening 'drès l'premier coup' (Réédition-Québec 1968, p 9), uses 'pus' (*plus*), 'et pis,' 'vot' bonté,' 'seroit-t'y possible,' 'amiquié' (*amitié*), 'l'engeoleuse,' 'alle' (*elle*), 'c'est t'y ben vrai,' employs the preposition 'à' regularly to indicate possession ('la fête à Mr. Dolmont'), and so on. Quesnel has made an effort to reproduce the local *parler*; perhaps also, in order to render it more acceptable in terms of a shared literary past, he decided to blend in the 'je sommes' form as well, still artificially retained in the speech of many stage peasants in France at the time. That form was not unknown in Lower Canada, of course, but apparently pretty well restricted to the North Shore (and to Acadia).

56 II, 7 (pp 36-7)

57 Hayne, *Archives* V, 63 note

58 *Quebec Gazette / Gazette de Québec*, 21 Jan. 1790. Quoted at length by Hayne, *Archives* V, 64. My translation. Gravé de la Rive's letter on *L'Education négligée* is dramatic criticism also (see pp 45-6 above), but had of course not been published.

59 Burger, *L'Activité* 204

60 Willy Amtmann, *Music in Canada, 1600-1800* 246. It is obvious, however, that he has overstated the case, for Quesnel's play demonstrably *did* exert some influence on subsequent playwrights, particularly in the twentieth century (see nn 51 and 52 above); and his pioneering role in introducing the music of *The Marriage of Figaro* and of other light operas then current in France (see below, p 62) cannot totally be discounted.

61 Despite many affirmations to the contrary (F.-M.-U.-M. Bibaud, *Le Panthéon canadien* 239; James Huston, ed., *Le Répertoire national...* I, 19 note; Claude Savoie in his brief introduction to the re-edition of *L'Anglomanie* 113; E.-G. Rinfret, *Le Théâtre canadien d'expression française* III, 182), it seems certain that *Les Républicains français* was never performed and it remained unpublished until 1970 (*La Barre du jour* [Summer] 1970 60-88), when the edition by Baudoin Burger appeared in a faithful reproduction of the ms text in Jacques Viger's *Saberdache rouge* (Archives du Séminaire de Québec, vol. P,

pp 114-19). It is from Burger's text, collated with Viger's ms (there are no significant variations) that I here quote, in my own translation.

Apart from Burger's introduction to that edition, the most useful studies of the play are the same critic's treatment of it in *L'Activité* 210-12; the brief analysis by Jean Du Berger in *Dictionnaire des œuvres littéraires du Québec* I, 653; D.M. Hayne in *Archives des lettres canadiennes* V, 114-15; and, most recently, Louise Forsyth's translation, with an introduction, in vol. IV of *Canada's Lost Plays*, ed. Anton Wagner, 94-110.

62   Sc. 2 (pp 69-70 and 73-4)

63   P 79. Jacques Cotnam, in his *Le Théâtre québécois, instrument de contestation sociale et politique*, assumes that Desvignes is a Catholic priest because he is referred to as 'le père Desvignes.' But 'père' in this context refers rather to age than profession. Desvignes' speech makes it abundantly clear he has received no education whatever.

64   Amtmann affirms (p 232) that 'Beaumarchais' *Barbier de Séville* received its first Canadian performance only a few years after its *première* in Paris in 1775, while his *Mariage de Figaro* of 1784 was played only one year later in Montreal.' He offers no proof of this affirmation, and I have nowhere found corroboration of it. *Le Barbier de Séville* had already been performed at least 5 times in French Canada (first performance, Feb. 1791 in Quebec City) by the date generally ascribed to *Les Républicains français*.

65   *L'Activité* 211-12. 'Catau' had a long tradition for serving women in French comedy, going back at least as far as Molière's *La Jalousie du Barbouillé*. There appears to me to be an influence as well of Beaumarchais' *La Mère coupable* (1792), especially on attitudes towards divorce observable in both plays.

66   See Hayne, *Archives* V, 115. Jean Du Berger, in the article cited in 61 above, is thus doubly mistaken in affirming that 'cette petite comédie en un acte et en vers fut composée et créée en 1802,' for the play was never staged. Apart from these studies, the play has been usefully treated by Camille Roy in *Nos Origines littéraires* 133-8; Burger, *Activité* 207-10; Savoie, in his introd. to the re-edition of the text in *La Barre du jour* 113-16; John E. Hare, 'Joseph Quesnel et l'anglomanie de la classe seigneuriale au tournant du XIXe siècle,' in *Co-Incidences* 23-31. Savoie's text, being the most accessible, is the basis for my translation, after collation and correction from the manuscript in Viger's *Saberdache rouge* (Archives du Séminaire de Québec, vol. P, 69-113).

67   P 119

68   In his poem, 'Le P'tit Bonhomme vit encore' (*Saberdache rouge* 28-31), this personage is mentioned, in a variant spelling, in stanza 4:

Orgon, né fourbe et sans esprit,
A d'un trompeur le caractère;
La mort dit: – j'en fais mon affaire,
Et la fièvre aussitôt le prit.
Il s'adresse au Docteur *Pancrève* –

C'est tout dire – il faut bien qu'il crève –
Eh bien, il a trompé la mort!
Le p'tit bonhomme vit encor! (*ter*)
The context highlights the explicit pun (*pan*: 'all,' plus *crève*: 'die'). Thus Claude Savoie's reading of the ms as 'Pennkrène' is incorrect.

69 See the article mentioned in 66 above. The article is described as an extract from the critical edition of Quesnel's works which is being prepared by Professor Hare, and which, if the promise tendered by this sample is kept, will be an outstanding contribution to the history of Canadian literature.

70 P 132-3

71 P 137

72 *Saberdache rouge*, vol. P, 156-76. The poem is analysed briefly by John Hare, in *Dictionnaire des œuvres littéraires du Québec*, I, 596.

73 Some of these poems are discussed by Hare, in the article mentioned in the preceding note.

74 *Quebec Gazette / Gazette de Québec*, 7 Feb. 1805. My translation

75 Only the incomplete voice score for the music of *Lucas et Cécile* has been found (Archives du Séminaire de Québec, fol. Verreau, no. 3. See Hayne, Archives V, 116; Burger, *Activité* 206-7). From what is extant, the projected work would have been more similar to *Colas et Colinette*, both in format and theme, than to other works by Quesnel which have survived. It appears that this unfinished 'opera' was undertaken originally about 1789, just after completion of *Colas et Colinette*.

76 One question that has been debated far beyond its merit is the relative 'Canadian-ness' of Quesnel. Obviously he is more deserving of the appellation 'Canadien' than was, say, Marc Lescarbot, particularly in his poetry and in a work such as *L'Anglomanie*. By the time of his death in 1809 at the age of 63, Quesnel had spent almost half his life in this country. He was certainly sensitive to its problems, even if he felt constrained in his liberty to express himself fully with regard to them. *Les Républicains français* is as political a play as has ever been written in French Canada: the fact of its being targeted upon international politics should not obscure that fact. In its basic strategy, vigour, and venom it foreshadows the sturdiest dramatic hybrid that nineteenth-century Quebec produced. Pierre Petitclair, half a century later, and whether he was aware of *L'Anglomanie* or not, reworked its basic theme in his *Une Partie de campagne*. One sometimes suspects that the very conservative nature of Quesnel's social and political views has led more than one critic, in our day, to refuse citizenship, influence, or relevance to this quaint founder of a certain type of theatrical tradition in Canada.

77 As with most amateur theatrical groups with which I shall deal in this period, 'Les Jeunes Messieurs Canadiens' are a discontinuous company, with the name, and no doubt some of the personnel, changing, for example, to 'Théâtre Canadien' in 1792; then (it seems to have been largely the same group) reappearing as the 'Jeunes Messieurs Canadiens' in 1795-6. Moreover, given

the loose usage of capital letters in French (as in English) at the time, one is never certain that an appellation such as 'Jeunes Messieurs Canadiens' is not merely a *description* of the group.

78 The play by Brueys was his *Avocat Pathelin*, on 11 Jan. 1793; by Regnard, *Le Retour imprévu* (25 Jan. 1793), *Le Légataire universel* (7 Jan. 1795), with the same plays repeated in the autumn of the latter year; by Hauteroche, *Crispin médecin* (30 Dec. 1795), and by Rousseau, *La Ceinture magique* (18 Jan. 1796, with at least one performance *before* that date). At the end of Burger's *L'Activité* 356-64, there is an invaluable, almost exhaustive listing of known francophone performances in the years 1765-1825.

79 Archives du Séminaire de Québec, *Journal*, 19 Jan. 1789. The entire text reads, 'On délibère sur la conduite d'un écolier qui est allé à la Comédie. On s'en rapportera à l'Evêque, Mgr Jean-Frs. Hubert.'

80 The article is in the *Gazette* for 20 Jan., p 2, and has often been reproduced elsewhere, most recently by Laflamme and Tourangeau, 97. My translation

81 Laflamme and Tourangeau, *L'Eglise et le théâtre au Québec* 100-1. My translation

82 *Mrs Simcoe's Diary*, ed. Mary Quayle Innis 51. In a previous letter (13 Feb. 1792, p 50) she had also mentioned performances by the officers.

83 *Quebec Gazette / Gazette de Québec*, 17 Mar. 1791. Philippe Aubert de Gaspé, writing in his *Mémoires* when he was 80 years old (Ottawa: Desbarats 1866), recounts also what a brilliant success the performance of Beaumarchais' play was, and how De Salaberry, not long returned from Paris where he had seen the same play performed by the best professional actors, had reluctantly consented to go see the amateur production, of which one of the chief performers was an actor by the name of Ménard:

> Dès la première scène, entre le comte Almaviva et le B., M. de Salaberry, emporté par l'enthousiasme qu'il éprouvait pour les talents de son jeune compatriote, M. Ménard, se lève de son siège et s'écrie de sa belle voix sonore et retentissante: 'Courage, Figaro! on ne fait pas mieux à Paris!'
>
> Les assistants électrisés par ces paroles se lèvèrent de leurs sièges en criant: 'Courage, Figaro! on ne fait pas mieux à Paris!' Et ce fut des hurrahs pour S. à n'en plus finir (pp 462-3).

It was about this time also that Prince Edward, Duke of Kent (Queen Victoria's father) was stationed in Quebec, where his presence and encouragement galvanized local thespians and audiences. See John Hare, 'Panorama des spectacles au Québec,' in Archives V, 72.

84 See Hare's article, preceding note, pp 73-4. More detailed information on theatres and buildings may be found in E.-Z. Massicotte, '1800 à 1850: Vieux théâtres de Montréal.'

85 *La Sérénade* dates from 1695; *Le Tambour nocturne*, which remained very popular in French Canada, from 1736.

86 *Le Tambour nocturne* (see preceding note) has been referred to as a 'revolu-

tionary' play. Joseph Quesnel used it satirically as a basis for his *Républicains français*. See Burger, *Activité* 211-12.

87 Laflamme and Tourangeau, *L'Eglise et le théâtre au Quebec*, 101

88 The original letter is in the collection of John E. Hare of the University of Ottawa, who has kindly corroborated its authorship. A copy exists in the Archives du Séminaire de Québec, Lettres Y, no 71. This is the version reproduced by Laflamme and Tourangeau, *L'Eglise et le théâtre au Québec* 102, and which they impute to Father Bernardin Robert, then Director of Teaching at the Seminary. A third copy is in the Archives de l'Archevêché de Québec, Registre des lettres 6, no 290, p 338 (see Fitzpatrick, 'The Fortunes of Molière in French Canada' 23-4). My translation

89 Cf. Laflamme and Tourangeau, *L'Eglise et le théâtre au Québec* 103; Burger, *Activité* 141-2.

90 Burger, *Activité* 141

91 Marcel Trudel, *L'Influence de Voltaire au Canada* 120. The announcement of the performance appeared in *Le Spectateur canadien*, 20 Nov. 1815.

92 27 Nov. 1815, p 3. My translation

93 The list is given by Burger, *Activité* 361-2.

94 *Montreal Gazette / Gazette de Montréal*, 20 Jan. 1817, p 3. My translation. Quoted also by Baudoin Burger, *Activité* 370-1

95 *Activité* 143-4

96 *Les Ursulines de Québec* ... III, 161. My translation

97 Clovis Demers, 'Concerts et représentations dramatiques à Québec, 1764-1800' 27. My translation

98 See Owen Klein, 'The Opening of Montreal's Theatre Royal,' in *Theatre History in Canada / Histoire du théâtre au Canada*.

99 *The Siege of Quebec*, according to Franklin Graham, had been performed at Southwark in 1770 (*Histrionic Montreal* [Montreal: Lovell 1906] 11). B.R. Schneider's *Index to the London Stage, 1660-1800* lists *The Siege of Quebec; or Harlequin Engineer*, performed on 14 May 1760 at Covent Garden Theatre, and another work, *General James Wolfe*, enacted on 8 Sept. 1760 at the Haymarket and, 10 days later, at Southwark Fair. The problem is that the first of these two plays is described as an 'anonymous Pantomime,' and that neither corresponds to our title, *The Siege of Quebec; or The Death of General Wolfe*.
  Liberty Asserted was written by John Dennis (1704), and is situated vaguely in Canada, with the theme being wars among the Indian nations in North America. It had apparently been updated for contemporary interest.

100 Burger, *Activité* 183. By contrast, Professor Burger points out, *La Bataille de Waterloo*, of which nothing is known but the title (I suspect the play was *The Duke's Coat; or The Night after Waterloo*, a 'Dramatick Anecdote prepared for Representation on the 6th September [1815] at the Theatre-Royal, Lyceum, and Interdicted by the Licenser of Plays' (London: M. McMillan 1815), based, by the anonymous author's own admission, on the French play, *L'Habit de Catinat*), is the 'seul exemple d'une pièce vraiment contempo-

raine jouée sur la scène francophone' (p 184). One wonders whether the jingoistic nature of some of this theatre did not arouse further clerical hostility, after 1790.

101 The papers include a receipt for £1 3s. 4d. paid by William Metchler to the band of the 53rd Regiment 'for playing at his Benefit play' on 11 Apr. 1789; accounts presented by the same Metchler to John Frederick Holland, apparently one of the managers of the theatre, in the amount of £3 16s. 10d. (undated), and to the manager of the troupe of actors concerned, William Moore, in the order of £1 14s. 0d., the account dated 30 Mar. 1789, payment received by Moore on 6 Apr. Things went downhill for Metchler and Holland from that point on it seems, for next is a very curt, undated letter from Holland to the former:

> Mr. Metcler [sic] the Boards of the Stage cannot be given you till the whole expenses of your Benefit is payed, which I understand is not yet done, likewise One Pound Ballanse of Acct. Night of the Miser, two Ticketts of Night of West Indian, and £1. 18. 4 but by me, all which I desire you to send receipts for, or cash, as tomorrow the Theatre will be taken to pieces; when the Materials will be sold to defray these demands unless you send me or bring me the vouchers. Yours.
>
> Jn Fdk Holland.

Last in the sequence is a legal writ in the amount of £7 15s. 10d., served upon the unfortunate Holland on 30 Apr. 1789, in the name of one Thomas Ferguson. Therein Holland is identified specifically as 'one of the Managers of the Theatre at Quebec, Defendant in this Action' (Archives du Séminaire de Québec, Poly. 37, no 27, a-f). The plays mentioned are Shadwell's *The Miser*, based on Molière's *L'Avare*, and Cumberland's *West Indian*.

102 John Ripley, 'Shakespeare on the Montreal Stage, 1805-1826'

103 Jean Béraud, *350 ans de théâtre au Canada français* 26. Prigmore, born in England, had come to North America in 1792, and appeared frequently on stages in the United States thereafter. Béraud's anecdote seems to be based upon an account by another actor from the States, John Durang, perhaps filtered – or distorted – through Franklin Graham's *Histrionic Montreal* (p 22). There has been no confirmation that I know of, of this tale.

104 Burger, *Activité* 248. My translation

105 I, 4 (Oct. 1823) 348

106 I, 3 (Sept. 1823) 224-6

107 Burger, *Activité* 72

108 *Ibid.* 253

109 John Lambert, *Travels through Lower Canada and the United States of North America...* 302, 304. The second half of this passage is omitted in some editions, such as that of 1816 (London: Baldwin, 2 vols). Lambert's account is obviously highly prejudiced. He has little good to say about Canada, and is particularly hostile towards French-Canadian Catholics.

Although francophone actresses were rare, they appeared on the anglophone stage fairly frequently. Female spectators were also usual at anglophone performances, much less so at French-language ones. The *Quebec Gazette*, for example, on 7 Mar. 1793, had to beg ladies intending to be present at performances of the Subscription Theatre not to wear high hairdos, so that those behind might see; and the same paper, on 23 Feb. 1786, had pleaded with them to use discretion in their allocation of the seats assigned to them: 'It is requested, that no Lady in future will dispose of her Tickets to Serving Maids of any class on Subscription Nights, as the seat occupied by one on Monday night last, was fitted up for the use of the Commander in Chief and his Friends.'

CHAPTER THREE: THE BEGINNINGS OF A NATIVE TRADITION IN THEATRE

1 Much of the following two subsections was published in a series of two articles by the author, '*Les Comédies du statu quo* (1834): Political Theatre and Paratheatre in French Canada,' Part I: 'Dramatized Dialogues before 1834'; Part II: 'Les Comédies du statu quo'; and are here reprinted with permission of that journal, *Theatre History in Canada*.

2 L.P. Waldo, in *The French Drama in America in the Eighteenth Century and Its Influence on the American Drama of that Period (1701-1800)* has amply demonstrated the surprising frequency of French-language performances in that country.

3 Cf. Marcel Trudel, *L'Influence de Voltaire au Canada* 42.

4 *Histoire de l'enseignement au Québec, 1608-1840* I, 187

5 Baudoin Burger in *Activité* 228 says that the *Gazette* carries, in these same issues, a dialogue entitled 'Méthode pour recueillir les Grains dans les années pluvieuses, et les empêcher de germer,' but I have found no such series. The only similar sequence is in *Le Canadien*, 9 May-20 June 1834, where six such 'conversations' on agricultural topics appear.

6 Mesplet, while a resident of Philadelphia, had printed the impassioned appeals addressed to French Canadians by the Continental Congress in 1774 and 1775; Jautard was suspected, with good reason, as a supporter of the American cause. These factors no doubt underlay the order from Governor Carleton that they cease publication, and that both leave the country by 15 Sept. that year, although the 'official' reason given was that no formal permission had been sought for the establishment of their newspaper in 1778. When this dialogue appeared, that order had been suspended by Carleton's successor, Haldimand, but its threat no doubt explains the otherwise uncharacteristically moderate stance adopted by the unknown author of our dialogue, which appeared on 21 Oct. 1778.

7 There seems no basis for speculating, as Jean-Paul de Lagrave has done recently, that in this dialogue, 'sous le pseudonyme de l'Admirateur, Mesplet

émet son opinion sur la liberté de la presse,' or that 'l'idéal de Mesplet est la liberté de la presse absolue, tel[le] que la France la connaîtra aux premiers jours de la Révolution' (*Les Origines de la presse au Québec, 1760-1791* 55). First of all, Mesplet himself had little or nothing to do with what actually went into his paper: surviving correspondence demonstrates that he had neither the education nor the commitment for such a task. Second, his editor, Jautard, had almost certainly borrowed – without credit, as was frequently the case – from a French source.

8 *Conversation au sujet de l'élection de Charlesbourg* (Quebec: Samuel Nelson); *Dialogue sur l'intérêt du jour, entre plusieurs candidats et un électeur libre et indépendent de la Cité de Québec* (Quebec: Wm Moore). For full bibliographic descriptions of both see Marie Tremaine, *A Bibliography of Canadian Imprints, 1751-1800* nos 761, 767.

9 John E. Hare, '*Le Canadien et sa femme*: une brochure de propagande politique (1794).' He reproduces the original text on pp 64-73. Baudoin Burger in *Activité* 229 seems to believe there are two such dialogues, the second entitled 'Dialogue entre André et Brigitte.' But the latter is merely the title assigned to the work by Marie Tremaine (see preceding note: her no. 874), before a copy of the work had actually been located by Professor Hare. My translation

10 – Tout cela ira bien ma chère: J'ai les Canadiens pour moi: 'Les Canadiens sont des lurons, biribi,' ah ah ah!
– Quoi! les Canadiens que vous aves tant joué? [*sic*]
– Ne te fache pas, ma chère: je connois les Canadiens, je suis sûr d'eux.
– Quoi! après leur avoir joué tous les tours que vous prenez souvent plaisir à me conter, vous croyez qu'ils n'en auront pas de ressentiment?
– Tu ne connois pas les Canadiens, ma chère: on peut les jouer tant qu'on veut et les ramener ensuite quand on veut; on n'a qu'à leur faire quelques couplets de chanson; leur dire qu'ils sont *des Lurons, biribi*, et d'autres fadaises, on est sûr d'en faire ce qu'on veut, quelques saluts les amadouent, quelques mots contre les Anglois les montent: j'en ferai bien mon affaire.

11 C'est sur le nombre et non sur la qualité des Electeurs que je dirige mes opérations, le vote d'un coquin vaut celui d'un honnête homme; c'est le grand nombre qui fait une élection. Dieu merci, ce n'est pas du côté de ce qu'on appelle les honnêtes gens que se trouve ce nombre!

12 On 26 Mar. that year (1808), for example, there had appeared a brief, untitled dialogue between 'La Redingotte' (representing the British Party) and 'Le Ventre plat' (the Canadiens) on the subject of the latters' problems with the existing legal system. In this one De Bonne is not mentioned directly, but Le Ventre plat, speaking of the courts, observes that 'la plupart de ceux qui y siègent, n'ont pas la moindre teinture de Jurisprudence, ils n'en ont jamais fait aucune étude,' an accusation frequently levelled at him in *Le Canadien*. The campaign had come to a climax of sorts on 21 May, when the same paper published a detailed analysis of the judge's voting record in the Assembly, fol-

lowed by a solid list of 'Raisons pour lesquelles on ne doit pas voter pour M. le Juge De Bonne.'

13 These are the anti-Napoleonic verse dialogue, 'Bonaparte & son Mamluck,' which appeared in the *Quebec Gazette/Gazette de Québec* on 18 Aug. 1814; and the fanciful 'Dialogue: Saint-Just et Machiavel,' in Montreal's *L'Aurore*, 26 Sept. 1818.

14 LE CURÉ
Eh bien, Pierre, quelles nouvelles?
L'HABITANT
J'en ai pas, Mesieu.
LE CURÉ
Tu n'as pas donné d'argent pour la société d'éducation?
L'HABITANT
Non Mesieu. Je n'suis pas riche; et pis quand même je serois aussi riche que vous, j'en aurois pas donné!

15 Published by N.-E. Dionne, *Les trois Comédies du statu quo* (1834). Reprinted with a brief preface by G. Bernier (Quebec: Réédition-Quebec 1969). Both publish, and refer to, the same three *comédies* only, those I have identified here as 1st, 2nd, and 5th.

16 Tout va à merveille. J'ai eu des nouvelles de la Pointe-aux-Trembles, et nos résolutions y ont passé des mieux; j'en ai eu aussi de presque tous les maîtres d'école, dont je fais la visite tous les étés, comme tu sais, et je t'assure que ça va bien. C'est étonnant toutes les signatures d'enfants que l'on va avoir! Ca vient par centaines, par milliers...

17 Bah! des *honorables*! Si vous aviez été à Londres et à Paris comme moi, messieurs – je me trompe, je voulais dire *citoyens* – c'est là que vous verriez combien on y fait peu de cas des honorables, des marquis, des ducs, des princes, des rois, enfin dans ces grandes villes, les ramoneurs sont respectés au plus haut degré, car ils font partie du peuple, c'est-à-dire qu'ils composent partie des masses.

18 Hélas! si quelque *mouchard* allait rapporter la farce qui vient de se passer à l'*Ami du Statu quo*, ce serait bien le reste!
Avouez-le, Monsieur P., en lisant ce que dessus, ne seriez-vous pas tenté de croire qu'il y avait en effet un *mouchard* parmi vous? Eh bien, songez-y, et regardez-vous sans rire, si vous le pouvez, comme Louis-Philippe et Talleyrand, les plus honnêtes gens d'outre-mer.

19 Cf. the long letter covering two columns of the first page of *Le Canadien* on 26 Mar. 1834, captioned 'Gare aux mouchards.'

20 Pp 81-95. Dionne lists six characters in the play, two of them 'B's (Besserer and Bédard) and two 'G's (Grenier and Garneau). In fact, although they are mentioned by the interlocutors, neither Bedard nor Garneau appears in this play, which has only four characters.

21 J. – Oui, certainement, j'apprécie ta façon de voir. Mais comment veux-tu que Son Excellence tienne un pareil langage? C'est impossible, car il parlerait contre lui!

OL. – Eh bien, il le faudrait pour rendre justice à tout le monde: par ce qu'après tout les gouvernements ne sont établis que pour le bonheur de la masse du peuple!

22   Avouons que les gens de mon espèce sont malheureux! ... Ai-je donc MOU-CHARD écrit en toutes lettres sur la figure? Puis, faire un pareil métier, et le faire gratis encore!!! S'il y avait au moins à obtenir quelque place de Secrétaire, d'associé ou même de premier clerc dans quelque boutique de procureur! Nulle part, l'on ne veut de moi; pas même la *Gazette* que je sers – pas le plus petit *bargain* à faire, – pas un prêt à négocier, à peine une redingotte à vendre – et je suis réduit à occuper les longs loisirs que me laisse ma clientèle à errer, espionner, questionner, rapporter et servir de commissionnaire à l'AMI *du statu quo* et à sa *Gazette*.

23   Je m'en vengerai en me débarrassant de la bile que m'a fait faire Papineau et en la vomissant contre nos P., V., H., B., P. et B. Pas besoin de tant de bonne foi envers des gens qui ne m'écoutent pas. Encore une fois, qu'importe la vérité, si je puis perdre cette *clique* dans l'esprit de cette *bande de chiens à potence, les électeurs de la Haute Ville de Québec!*
'V' is Denis-Benjamin Viger, cousin of Papineau and spokesman for the Patriotes in London.

24   Vous alors, oui, bien vous, JOHN DUVAL, Ecuyer, M.P.P., lisiez à haute et intelligible voix, l'écrit qui parut le mardi suivant adressé à *M. l'Editeur du Canadien, bibliothécaire salarié de la Chambre d'Assemblée*, signé UN AMI *du Statu quo*. N'exposez pas votre foi, car l'écrit en question lu par vous JOHN DUVAL, Ecr. M.P.P. a été si bien entendu, si bien compris, que plus d'une personne savaient, *lundi* que l'écrit paraîtrait *le lendemain* dans la *Gazette* du mardi 6 Mai, et en connaissaient le contenu.

25   Eh bien, étourdi, le voici: Bédard est le dernier homme sur qui vous auriez dû faire retomber le soupçon. Il a été, lui, un des plus maltraités dans nos écrits, et de quel droit voudriez-vous qu'il eût gardé le secret? C'est bonne guerre pour lui de profiter de la découverte, et vous ne pouvez raisonnablement le lui reprocher.
A. – C'est assez vrai. Mais que vouliez-vous que nous fissions? Nous étions découverts, il fallait bien dire quelque chose, et le seul moyen c'était de crier à la honte, au déshonneur; enfin jeter de la poudre aux yeux des gens!

26   HAMEL (*se promenant dans son étude*)
Oh! Oh! que l'honneur est une belle chose! Qu'il est glorieux d'être homme d'Etat, et de se voir, dans les occasions les plus difficiles, le bras droit et l'*aviseur* de celui qui gouverne! ... Est-il bien vrai que je suis avocat du Roi? Si je rêvais, quel désappointement! Mais non, ce n'est point le cas, je sens bien que je suis un grand homme. Les grandes idées, les vastes plans, les *beaux avis*, tout ça roule dans ma tête...
Souvenir cruel! barre, admonition, orateur discourtois, que vous me pesez sur le coeur! Non, non, jamais je ne l'oublierai, cette affaire ... C'était la

première fois qu'on requérait mes services, j'en étais fier, je m'étais piqué d'honneur, je l'avais travaillé nuit et jour, ce funeste *avis*; et voilà comme la chose est tournée!

27   Mais non, restons; il faut que je me venge; il faut que je les calomnie, il faut que je les persécute, ces Patriotes. *Les Amis du Statu Quo* s'assemblent ici ce soir; je le jure, je me vengerai, je me vengerai –

28   HAMEL

Avancez, Messieurs, que je vous fasse une admonition.

JOHNNY DUVAL (*grimaçant pour le coup de toute sa figure*)

Oh! certes, vous en devez savoir le style et la forme.

THOMAS AMIOT

Mais il n'y a point de motion, pour que ce soit au moins régulier!

JOHNNY DUVAL

Laissez-le donc faire; il va nous dire quelque chose de beau, tant en anglais qu'en français.

HAMEL (*d'un ton à la fois solennel et majestueux*)

Vous, Johnny Duval, écuyer, avocat, membre du Parlement Provincial, ami du *Statu quo*, et reviseur de nos écrits, et vous qui les colportez, sieur Thomas Amiot, aussi avocat et marchand, pour avoir, le 5 mai courant, en plein jour, quand c'était l'ordre de n'agir que le soir et dans le secret, écrit, lu et colporté une certaine pièce adressée au Bibliothécaire salarié de la Chambre d'Assemblée, et ce faisant, vous être laissé prendre sur le fait, et nous avoir trahis tous –

DUVAL

Il aura de la peine à sortir de sa période.

HAMEL

– pour ces raisons, dis-je, mon devoir m'oblige de vous censurer et admonéter. Cette circonstance est d'autant plus pénible que vous étiez ceux sur lesquels on comptait le plus –

DUVAL (*bas*)

Oh! Oh! il parle comme l'Orateur!

HAMEL

– et ceux qui montriez le plus d'acharnement contre les Patriotes. Puisqu'il en est ainsi, pour sauver notre honneur et faire un exemple, je vous censure donc et je vous gronde, et vous êtes par le présent censurés et grondés.

29   Préparez-vous donc à écrire sous mille et mille autres noms; allez suggérer ce plan à nos amis qui viennent de sortir; moi, je vais travailler aussi de mon côté. Il faut se venger – Frappez, frappez, et surtout contre Papineau!

The verses quoted read:

Car si vous avez terni le barreau
C'est la faute à Papineau!

The *vaudeville* about Papineau, apparently sung to the tune of a current song, 'Voilà l'effet de l'argent,' seems to have been widely known at the time. *Le*

Canadien had quoted a few lines in support of an editorial position on 30 Apr. 1834 (p 1, col. 3); Jacques Viger, writing to his wife on 17 Feb. that year, had included a printed copy ('revue, corrigée, augmentée et finalement complète') of sixteen stanzas, six lines to a stanza. A sample:

Si les Français Sulpiciens
Trahissent les Canadiens,
S'ils vendent à l'Angleterre
Tous les biens du Séminaire,
S'ils emportent le magot –
C'est la faute à Papineau! (*ter*)

Si je Juge Jonathan [ie, Sewell]
Nous fut donné par Satan,
Et si sa chère famille
Les deniers du public pille,
Du Juge jusqu'au Bourreau –
C'est la faute &c.

Si Mond'let est renégat
Et Cuvillier apostat,
Si John Neilson le Jésuite,
Héney, Quesnel et leur suite
Nous prêchent le *statu quo* –
C'est la faute &c.

(Archives du Séminaire de Québec, *Saberdache bleue* 246)

30 Thus Dionne's résumé of *Le statu quo en déroute* (p 40), 'cette dernière pièce était plutôt une prétendue représaille des écrits très spirituels publiés dans la *Gazette de Québec*,' is repeated verbatim by T. Ouellet in her 'Bibliographie du théâtre canadien-français avant 1900' (Quebec: typescript 1949) 11; and by E.-G. Rinfret in his *Le Théâtre canadien d'expression française* (I, 58).

31 *La Minerve*, 30 Apr. 1827

32 M.A. Fitzpatrick, 'The Fortunes of Molière in French Canada,' 76-81

33 *La Minerve*, 1, 8, 15 Dec. 1831; Fitzpatrick, 'The Fortunes of Molière in French Canada' 84

34 *Napoléon à Sainte-Hélène* 7. One short scene (4) was reproduced by E.-F. Duval in his *Anthologie thématique du théâtre québécois au XIXe siècle* 92-4. Since the text itself is extremely rare, I provide the French original for my translations. This passage reads:

Au lever du rideau, le théâtre représente une partie de l'Ile Sainte-Hélène, la mer est au fond, un énorme rocher est sur la droite, la gauche est occupée par une maison, stylée à la manière des colonies, à droite, un banc de gazon ombragé par un arbre.

Une musique militaire, prêtant à la mélancholie, se fait entendre un peu avant le lever du rideau, et elle continue jusqu'à ce que *Napoléon* et *Bertrand* soient arrivés en scène.

35 P 12:

Je ne devais pas mourir sur le trône; l'adversité manquait à ma carrière –
ils me tueront ici, qu'importe! – ma mémoire restera – et la France, libre
un jour, pourra me pleurer – Si Ste. Hélène était la France, j'aimerais cet
affreux rocher – Mais non, la France est morte pour moi, je la trouble-
rais – je ne lui demande qu'un souvenir – Un seul souvenir – Ah! (*Il
s'assied et prend un des livres qu'il ouvre*) Corneille! – quel homme, c'est le
plus beau génie du théâtre. S'il eût vécu de mon tems, je l'aurais fait
prince! – (*Prenant l'autre volume*) Racine! il me rappelle Talma – qu'il était
beau! – si je n'avais craint de sots préjugés, je l'aurais décoré (*ouvrant le
livre*) Andromaque! – c'est la pièce des pères malheureux (*il lit*):

Je passais jusqu'aux lieux où l'on garde mon fils,
Puisqu'une fois le jour, vous souffrez que je voie
Le seul bien qui me reste et d'Hector et de Troie,
J'allais, seigneur, pleurer un moment avec lui,
Je ne l'ai point encore embrassé d'aujourd'hui!

François-Joseph Talma (1763-1826) was universally considered the greatest
actor of his generation in France. A long stay in England led to his lifelong
passion for Shakespeare, and he was largely responsible for the introduction of
the latter's works to France.

36 Duval, *Anthologie thématique du théâtre québécois au XIXe siècle* 92

37 John E. Hare, 'Panorama des spectacles au Québec: De la Conquête au XXe
siècle,' v 68-9. It may have been the same Prud'homme who published, in
Toulouse in 1843, *Quelques mots sur la doctrine de Samuel Hahnemann suivis de
deux observations du Docteur Prud'homme*, although this is doubtful. See
Duval, *Anthologie thématique* 92. Another work, *Première épître aux hommes de
bonne volonté*, published in Paris in 1848, seems to me more certain of attribution.

38 J.E. Hare, in the article mentioned in the preceding note, p 76. In its edition
of 15 Mar. 1832, *La Minerve* reprinted several articles from newspapers in the
capital, on the subject of Prud'homme's 'affected' style.

39 *L'Hôtel des Princes*: opéra-comique en un acte, paroles de MM. de Ferrier et
de Marconnay, musique de M. Eugène Prévost. Représenté pour la première
fois, sur le Théâtre de l'Ambigu-Comique, le Samedi 23 Avril 1831 (Paris:
'chez tous les Marchands de nouveautés, et chez Martinet, Libraire, rue du
Coq-Saint-Honoré' 1831). The play is set in 1320, and deals with the struggle
for power between Philippe v of France and Eudes, Duke of Burgundy. As
the imprint suggests, it is a light, rosy work, fleshed out with solos and duets,
relying heavily on coincidences and disguises (Philippe is travelling in Burgundy incognito, hoping to patch up the longstanding quarrel between himself
and Eudes). The text is rare, and the copy I consulted in the Bibliothèque
Nationale, Paris, is the only one I have found.

40 See *Relation historique des événements de l'élection du comté du Lac des Deux
Montagnes en 1834*: Episode propre à faire connaître l'esprit public dans le

Bas-Canada (Montreal 1836). The copy in the Bibliothèque Nationale, Paris, has a ms note on title-page: 'Par H. Leblanc de Marconnay, Ecuyer, membre honoraire de la Société française de Statistique Universelle, Président de la Société Française en Canada, rédacteur en chef du Journal La Minerve, imprimé à Montréal (Bas-Canada).' The same note appears on another work, '*La petite Clique dévoilée*, ou Quelques explications sur les manoeuvres dirigées contre la minorité patriote, qui prit part au vote sur les subsides dans la session de 1835 à 1836; et, plus particulièrement contre C.C. Sabrevois de Bleury, Ecuyer, avocat du barreau de Montréal, membre de la Chambre d'Assemblée du Bas-Canada. Etat-Unis; Rome, (N.Y.), 1836,' although this work is attributed also to Sabrevois de Bleury himself, as is the third text, '*Réfutation de l'écrit de Louis-Joseph Papineau, ex-Orateur de la Chambre d'Assemblée du Bas-Canada, intitulé Histoire de l'insurrection du Canada, publiée dans le recueil hebdomadaire, La Revue du Progrès, imprimée à Paris*. Imprimerie de John Lovell, rue St. Nicolas, à Montréal, Bas-Canada. Octobre, 1839.' It seems certain the latter text was, in fact, composed by Sabrevois de Bleury. I suspect the confusion as to attribution of authorship comes at least in part from a brief note Leblanc de Marconnay sent to 'Monsieur le Conservateur-administrateur de la Bibliothèque Royale, Paris,' bound in with *La petite Clique dévoilée*:

Monsieur,
   Je me fais un devoir de vous transmettre quelques écrits imprimés en Canada, veuillez les déposer à la bibliothèque royale. Eloigné de ma patrie, son souvenir agite toujours mon coeur.
   Daignez agréer, Monsieur, l'hommage de mon profond respect.
                  Votre très humble serviteur
                  H. Leblanc de Marconnay
Montréal ce 10 Avril 1836

One assumes this note accompanied copies of all three texts, plus Marconnay's plays. The recipient of the letter then assumed (perhaps Marconnay intended that he assume) that all were from his correspondent.

41 *Nina; ou la Folle par amour*, comédie en un acte, en prose, Mêlée d'ariettes. Par M. M.D.V. Musique de M. Dal[ayrac]. Représentée pour la première fois, par les Comédiens Italiens ordinaires du Roi, le 15 Mai 1786 (Paris: Brunet 1786). Félix Gaiffe, in *Le Drame en France au XVIIIe siècle* (Paris: Colin 1910), has pointed out that 'les opéras-comiques purement tragiques et larmoyants, comme *Nina ou la Folle par amour*, sont extrêmement rares' (p 479).

42 There is no equivalent to Prainville in Marsollier's play, for example; nor is there any semblance of the secondary plot which Marconnay has used so well, the love of St-Léon for Mme Derbois. There is no 'comedy' in the first play, as the quotation from Gaiffe (see preceding note) attests, apart from the stereotyped peasant speech and rustic ways of the villagers.

43 *Valentine, ou la Nina canadienne*, par H. Leblanc de Marconnay, Ecuyer.

Montreal: De l'Imprimerie de l'*Ami du peuple* 1836, sc. 1 (p 7). My translation. The only useful treatment of this play which I have found is the brief article by Reine Bélanger, in *Dictionnaire des œuvres littéraires du Québec* I, 746. Having examined *Nina ou la Folle par amour* in detail, it is my opinion that Bélanger, in this article, has greatly overstated the extent of 'borrowing' from Marsollier's text. The original edition of 1836 was reprinted by Réédition-Québec in 1968.

44 Jean-Baptiste refers to his master as *not' bourgeois*, frequently uses the prevalent Canadianisms, *pas en toute* ('pantoute'), *c'est-t-y pas d'valeur*, etc.; he pronounces *pardu* ('perdu'), *all' part* ('elle part'), deforms 'le steamboat de Montréal' to *le squinebote de Moral*, and so on. Even his *j'fesions l' berdas* (p 9) is *half* right.

45 Sc. 11 (pp 31-2). My translation

46 Pp 44-5. My translation

47 As shown below, the native Canadien Pierre Petitclair has as good an ear for rural Québécois speech, but would have been unable to produce the sophisticated, *mondain* patter of the upper class.

48 *Le Soldat*: Intermède en deux Parties mêlé de chants. Exécuté sur le Théâtre Royal de Montréal (Bas-Canada) en 1835 et 1836. Arrangé par Mr. Leblanc de Marconnay. Montréal: De l'Imprimerie d'Ariel Bowman, Rue St. François-Xavier 1836. The text consulted was in the Bibliothèque Nationale, Paris. I know of no study of this play.

49 Hare, *Archives* (see note 37 above) 77

50 Since the text is rare, and has not been re-edited, here is the original passage (p 3):

> On a beau dire, c'est un bien bel état que celui de soldat; après le laboureur, qui arrose de ses sueurs les champs qu'il féconde, on doit ranger celui qui verse son sang pour la défense de sa patrie. Je n'étais propre à rien dans mon village, je ne me sentais aucuns goûts pour l'étude; les arts et les sciences m'étaient insensiblement inférieurs et je voyais le moment où je resterais dans une obscurité complète. Je me suis engagé, en sorte que maintenant j'espère faire du bruit dans le monde en filant mon chemin. Je suis nourri, habillé et blanchi aux frais du gouvernement; c'est un plaisir car pour tout cela je n'ai qu'à monter ma garde, me trouver à la manœuvre, exécuter la charge en 12 temps 18 mouvements, patiner assez proprement mon fusil et me faire tuer à la première occasion. Je sais qu'il y a des gens qui ne s'amuseraient point de cette perspective; mais cette vie me charme et je trouve qu'elle forme merveilleusement la jeunesse.

51 P 7:

> Le médecin qui m'a fait l'opération prétend qu'y a pas d'resources et qu'il faut m'attendre à faire bientôt le grand voyage – C'est tout d'même embêtant d's'en aller comme ça du monde quand on a l'envie d'y rester. Ah! bah! faut s'attendre à tout dans notre état; l'ennemi a été repoussé, nous avons gagné la bataille et ça fait qu'on s'décide à finir plus doucement.

52 Cf. his letter to the Librarian of the Bibliothèque Nationale in Paris, reproduced in note 34 above.
53 Cf. his 'A la Mémoire de Napoléon,' pub. in *Le Fantasque* on 20 Aug. 1838, reprinted by J.-P. Tremblay in *Napoléon Aubin* 27-8.
54 *Quebec Gazette / Gazette de Québec*, 15 Aug. 1831; *Le Canadien*, 4 Sept. 1833. See also Fitzpatrick, 'The Fortunes of Molière in French Canada' 45. Actually, Voltaire's *Mort de Jules César* is in itself relatively innocuous and had in fact been offered by the author to the principal of the Jesuit Collège de Harcourt as 'une pièce toute propre pour un collège où l'on n'admet point de femmes sur un théâtre' (L.-V. Gofflot, *Le Théâtre au collège du moyen âge à nos jours* 177. Quoted by Jeanne Corriveau, 'Le Théâtre collégial au Quebec: L'apport de Gustave Lamarche,' in *Archives* v, 183)
55 *Quebec Gazette / Gazette de Québec*, 25 Oct. 1839. The other three plays were Destouches' *Tambour nocturne* and two plays attributed to Aubin, *Le Soldat français* (but see above, p 112) and *Le Chant des ouvriers* (see J.-P. Tremblay, *A la Recherche de Napoléon Aubin* 183).
56 An announcement in *Le Canadien* on 7 Nov. 1836 asks for contributions towards the publication, not of this play, but one entitled *Qui trop embrasse mal étreint*, by the same author. This is the only reference to that title. But perhaps instead of speaking of a 'lost' play, one should speculate that Petitclair may have changed its title to *Griphon*, since the former title could appropriately apply to the activities of old Griphon himself.
57 In his thesis, 'Pierre Petitclair, premier dramaturge canadien-français' 32-3
58 Jean-Claude Noël, 'Le Théâtre de Pierre Petitclair,' in *Archives des lettres canadiennes* v, 128-9. Apart from Noël's thesis and this article, plus the brief study by Jean Du Berger in *Dictionnaire des œuvres littéraires du Québec*, I, 299-300, the only other source I have found useful is Baudoin Burger's 'Théâtre, littérature, et politique en 1837-1838,' in Etienne-F. Duval, *Aspects du théâtre québécois au XIXe siècle* 1-23.
59 *Griphon, ou la Vengeance d'un valet*. Comédie en trois actes. Par P. Petitclair. A Québec: chez William Cowan, imprimeur, no. 9, rue la Fabrique. 1837. Pp 15-18. My translation
60 P 86
61 For example, the short first scene of Act II:

    CITRON
    Qu'a-t-il donc le bon homme?

    FLORETTE
    Bin dame, j'sé pas. I'm'fé peur avec sés gins. Il é blême comme la chaux de la muraille, pi i vomit, pi i dit qu'il a la colique, pi s'plaint d' son coup.

    CITRON
    Comment? Quel coup?

    FLORETTE
    Quoé donc? I te l'a pas dit? Il a timbé, à s'en r'venant de l'église. J'cré qu'siment qu'il a quoqu'chose de démanché.

CITRON

Il te l'a dit?

FLORETTE

Bin oui. Il é d'ane himeur, d'ane himeur. J'en é peur, quand i m'parle. Ah! mon gueu! L'v'la-ti-i pas!

62 *Lord Durham's Report on the Affairs of British North America*, II, 294-5

63 In Etienne-F. Duval, *Aspects du théâtre québécois au XIXe siècle* 3

64 *Ibid.*, 10-12. My translation

65 Murray D. Edwards, *A Stage in Our Past* 3

CHAPTER FOUR: TOWARDS THE DEVELOPMENT OF A FRENCH-CANADIAN DRAMATURGY

1 The Advertisement in Quebec City's *L'Artisan* for 7 Nov. 1842 announces that 'La partie dramatique consistera en une comédie inédite en deux actes, intitulée *La Donation*, tout dernièrement composée pour les Amateurs Typographes, par M.P. Petitclair.' The play was performed on 16 and 19 Nov. and published in *L'Artisan* in the issues of 15, 19, 22, 26, and 29 Dec. 1842. Published in full in James Huston's *Répertoire national* (both editions, 1848 and 1893). The play was revived for two performances in Oct. 1851, and once on 28 Sept. 1858.

2 *Le Répertoire national* (Montreal: Valois, 4 vols, 1893) II, 269. My translation throughout

3 J.-C. Noël, 'Pierre Petitclair, premier dramaturge canadien-français' 91-2. My translation

4 Delorval says (II, 5, p 285), 'il doit même *m'introduire* un de ses amis'; on the same page Caroline responds, 'je ne suis pas de votre opinion,' etc. See J.-C. Noël's article in *Archives* V, 134.

5 For example, it is not until II, 8 that Petitclair seems to realize that the expulsion of Auguste without his being told why he is fired, needs some preparation. But Delorval's brief monologue (the following is the entire scene) only serves to heighten the confusion:

DELORVAL

Ce qui me chagrine, c'est la promesse que j'ai faite à Auguste de ne lui pas dire la cause de son expulsion. C'est bien tyrannique de se voir condamner sans pouvoir être entendu. Il est vrai que cela se voit assez souvent de nos jours, mais je ne puis m'habituer à ce mode, moi. (p 287)

Did Petitclair mean to say, 'la promesse que j'ai faite à *Bellire*?' or is the logic as twisted as it sounds? A similar problem arises in II, 12 (p 281), where Martel explains (through Bellire, to the reader) how he has prepared the false documents incriminating Auguste. Again, why would Delorval not confront Auguste with the 'evidence'? Bellire responds, 'oh! je ne crains rien de ce côté-là. Il m'a juré qu'il ne montrerait les papiers qu'à sa nièce, et je viens de te dire que l'honneur est son dieu.' A curiously unconvincing conception of 'honneur'!

6 Baudoin Burger, 'Théâtre, littérature et politique en 1837-1838,' in *Aspects du théâtre québécois* 3-4, commenting on the fact that Petitclair, although he had the prospectus of *Qui trop embrasse mal étreint* published in *Le Canadien* (7 Nov. 1837), none the less had his first play printed by William Cowan:
Le changement reste important pour nous à cause du choix de l'imprimeur: l'auteur n'a pas choisi l'imprimeur du *Canadien* qui est pro-patriote et qui sera arrêté en décembre 1838 pour être accusé de haute trahison, mais un imprimeur de deux périodiques, le *Morning Herald and Commercial Advertiser* et le *Literary Transcript*, qui défendent la politique coercitive de Londres dans le Bas-Canada, sans être cependant extrémistes ... En 1837, tout comme aujourd'hui, le choix de l'éditeur est politique.
But in the light of *La Donation*'s preparation for Aubin (and its printing in *L'Artisan*, for that matter), does that choice of Cowan seem significant? May one not rather speculate that Petitclair's advertisement for assistance in *Le Canadien* had not found the support he needed (the economic situation, following the cholera epidemics of the early 1830s, along with the virtual cessation of government funding, was poor at the time), and that he had turned to the first printer willing to accept his copy?

7   Oh! non, monsieur – c'est tout d'vant c't'endroite qui r'présente l'Canada, parc'qu'il y a des chaînes autour – comment qu'ils appellent ça donc – Ah! la Place d'Armes – tout à l'opposition de la Place d'Armes – une grande maison qui fait l'encoignure (p 295).

8 Jeanne Corriveau, '*Jonathas* du R.P. Gustave Lamarche et le théâtre collégial' 38; M.A. Fitzpatrick, 'The Fortunes of Molière in French Canada' 45; René Dionne, *Antoine Gérin-Lajoie, homme de lettres* 327

9 Jeanne Corriveau, 'Le Théâtre collégial au Québec: l'Apport de Gustave Lamarche,' in *Archives* V, 175

10 Dionne, in the work mentioned in note 8 above, p 104

11 *Quebec Gazette / Gazette de Québec*, 15 Aug. 1831; *Le Canadien*, 4 Sept. 1833

12 The music and words, in French with English version, are in *Chansons de Québec / Quebec Folk Songs*, ed. Edith Fulton Fowke and Richard Johnston 16-17.

13 Quoted by Léon Gérin (Antoine's son), in *Antoine Gérin-Lajoie: La Résurrection d'un patriote canadien* 14. My translation. Gérin-Lajoie adds, significantly, 'on m'a toujours découragé de cultiver ce talent, comme on fait généralement dans les établissements d'éducation de ce pays.'

14 Jacques Cotnam is mistaken in situating the action of *Le jeune Latour* in Quebec at the time of the Conquest (*Le Théâtre québécois: Instrument de contestation sociale et politique* 24). In fact, of course, it is situated in Acadia, 130 years earlier.

15 A marriage is a 'doux hymen'; any strong desire is a 'flamme'; any distress calls for invocation of 'les cieux'; the characters are constantly conscious of their 'gloire', etc.

16   Il n'a qu'une parole, et quand il dit: je veux,
N'espérez rien de plus; car la terre et les cieux,
L'univers croulerait, ou changerait de place,
Il redirait encore: oui, je veux qu'on le fasse.
Le jeune Latour was published initially in *L'Aurore des Canadas*, in three
instalments (7, 12, and 17 Sept. 1844); the same month (16, 18, and 20
Sept.) in *Le Canadien*; in a limited separate edition (Montreal: Cinq-Mars
1844); in both editions (1848 and 1893) of James Huston's *Répertoire
national*; by Séraphin Marion, in *Les Lettres canadiennes d'autrefois* (IV,
143-92); and, in 1969, by Réédition Québec, with a brief introduction by Baudoin Burger. It is from this last edition, assumed to be the most accessible,
that I quote (p 12). My translation
     The most useful treatments of the play are René Dionne's excellent mono-
graph, *Antoine Gérin-Lajoie, homme de lettres* 103-17; the same author's '*Le
Jeune Latour* d'Antoine Gérin-Lajoie (31 juillet 1844)'; Séraphin Marion's
article accompanying his re-edition, *Les Lettres canadiennes d'autrefois* IV,
91-107; Baudoin Burger's introduction to the reprint by Réédition-Québec
(Montreal 1969); and Louvigny de Montigny's somewhat dated *Antoine
Gérin-Lajoie* (Toronto: Ryerson c1925).

17   AIR: *Un jour pur éclairait mon âme*
           Je ne recherche que ta gloire
           Et ton bonheur, ô mon pays,
           Que les palmes de la victoire
           Couronnent le front de tes fils!
           Jeune guerrier, l'amour m'enflamme,
           Mais connaissez-vous mon amour?
    bis { Ah! j'aime, tu le sais, mon âme,
           Le sol où j'ai reçu le jour.

           Qu'un autre chante sa folie
           Et les attraits de son Iris,
           Moi, je chanterai ma patrie.
           Elle seule aura mes souris.
           Je veux lui conserver ma flamme
           Et lui faire à jamais la cour,
    bis { Car j'aime, tu le sais, mon âme,
           Le sol où j'ai reçu le jour.

18 P 24
19 There is a curiously anachronistic note to the patriotism at times, as when the
unseen singer who opens the play recalls, speaking of his native soil:
        Pour elle autrefois *dans les plaines* [my emphasis]
        Nos aïeux ont versé leur sang. (p 5)
20 'Souvenirs de collège,' quoted by Léon Gérin, *Antoine Gérin-Lajoie...* 25. My
translation

21 *Lettres canadiennes d'autrefois* IV, 6-7

22 R. Dionne, in the work cited in note 16 above, p 112

23 Cf. Jeanne Corriveau, 'Le Théâtre collégial au Québec: L'Apport de Gustave Lamrache,' in Archives V, 179-80. She goes on to point out that 'l'année scolaire qui s'étendait alors de septembre à août, sans congé de Noël, pouvait accorder plus de temps à ces activités non réglées par le programme d'étude' (p 180).

24 Fitzpatrick, 'The Fortunes of Molière in French Canada' 91 note

25 *L'Eglise et le théâtre au Québec* 128

26 PAUL
Et où vous appelle-t-elle (*Après quelques instants de silence.*) Enfin vous vous déclarez: vous voulez quitter le monde.

BILINSKI
Traîner votre misérable existence dans un couvent!

PAUL
Vous serez la honte de notre père.

BILINSKI
L'opprobre de votre famille.

PAUL
Voilà donc vos généreux désirs, votre noble ambition: vous faire la risée des gens sensés, le rebut des hommes comme il faut!

STANISLAS
Mon frère, j'aspire au ciel! (p 27)

All quotations are from the edition which does not bear the author's name, *Stanislas de Kostka* (Montreal: Aux bureaux de la Revue de Montréal 1878). Little has been written on the play itself, the most useful study I have found being that of Reine Bélanger in *Dictionnaire des œuvres littéraires du Québec* I, 691-2. See also the short, anonymous article, 'Le drame de "Saint-Stanislas" par l'abbé H.A. Verreau,' in *Bulletin des Recherches Historiques* XXIII (1917) 160.

27 PAUL
...J'allais l'atteindre, quand les chevaux s'arrêtent tout-à-coup. En vain le guide les presse de la main et de la voix: une barrière insurmontable semble s'élever devant eux; une force invisible les a cloués au sol.

AUGUSTE
Merci, ô mon Dieu!

PAUL
Lorsque j'ai voulu reprendre la route de Vienne, mes chevaux ont re-trouvé leur liberté et leur vigueur. J'ai compris que le ciel se déclarait pour mon frère. (pp 55-6)

28 John E. Hare, 'Le Choix d'un répertoire théâtral et le goût du public: Recherche d'une méthode sociologique' 61-2. My translation

29 *La Minerve*, 9 July 1859. Almost every issue of this paper carries ads for opera, circuses, and theatre by touring players.

30 *Mandements, lettres pastorales et circulaires des évêques de Québec* IV, 14. Quoted also by Laflamme and Tourangeau, *L'Eglise et le théâtre au Québec* 130
31 Some of his underlying reasons are presented, with excellent insight, in Laflamme and Tourangeau, *L'Eglise et le théâtre au Québec* 132-4
32 Mason Wade, *The French Canadians, 1760-1967* I, 350
33 Laflamme and Tourangeau, *L'Eglise et le théâtre au Québec* 134-5. The authors reproduce quotations from *Le Pays* (26 May 1860) to show the basis for the Bishop's accusation.
34 *Les Soirées du village, ou Entretiens sur le protestantisme.* Ière Partie: *Les Saints protestants.* Ière Soirée: *Saint Luther.* The second volume is *Les Soirées du village, ou Entretiens sur le protestantisme.* 2me Soirée: *Jean Calvin.* The first volume is mentioned in the excellent Bibliographie Générale at the end of vol. I of *Dictionnaire des œuvres littéraires du Québec* 806. I have never found reference anywhere to the second volume, nor comment upon either one.
35 Pp 3-4. My translation throughout
36 See p 146 below. At the top of the first page of this text are the initials 'J.M.J.' But it is less probable that they represent the author's than those of 'Jésus, Marie et Joseph,' an invocation to the Holy Family with which students in schools or colleges operated by the clergy were (and no doubt still are) encouraged to begin every written task.
37 *La Comédie infernale, ou Conjuration libérale aux enfers*, en plusieurs actes, par un illuminé. Montréal, Imprimerie du *Franc-Parleur*, 9 rue Sainte-Thérèse. Ancienne place autrefois occupée par le *Pays.* 1871; and *Contre-poison: Faussetés, erreurs, impostures, blasphèmes de l'apostat Chiniquy; Dialogue sur l'Eucharistie.* Montréal. Typ. Le *Franc-Parleur*, 1875. The latter, bearing the author's name and the imprimatur of Bishop Bourget of Montreal, has five characters: 'un Instituteur, un Menuisier, un Forgeron, un Cultivateur,' and, most significantly, 'un Membre de l'Institut-canadien.' It is the latter who serves as devil's advocate, and against him the Instituteur marshals his overwhelmingly convincing arguments, with long, verbatim quotations from Scripture and from Catholic commentators. The 'play' comprises some forty pages subdivided into ten scenes, with titles such as (Sc. 1): 'Les schismes prouvent que l'apostat Chiniquy a parlé contre la vérité, en affirmant que la croyance à la présence réelle est une nouveauté dans l'Eglise catholique, apostolique et romaine'; (Sc. 7): 'Que les chefs protestants ne s'entendent pas sur le sens à donner à ces paroles de Notre Seigneur: Ceci est mon corps. Ceci est mon sang. Que les grands génies protestants ont interprété ces paroles comme le font les catholiques.' The structure and the method of exposition are remarkably close to those of *Les Soirées du village*, and the characters similar. The piece ends with all concerned, even the Member of the Institut, on their knees reciting a long litany, the 'Prose du *Lauda Sion*' (pp 79-81). A note is attached: 'Le prochain dialogue sera sur les *Indulgences* et sur les *Jubilés*,' an apparent reference to other such texts that, if they were in fact published, are unknown to us. It is hardly likely that Alphonse Villeneuve was the author of

Les Soirées du village, however, if the date 1860 is correct: born in 1843 in Montreal, he would have been a mere 17 years old.

38 *Les Anciens Canadiens*. Drame en trois actes tiré du roman populaire de P.A. de Gaspé (Montreal: C.O. Beauchemin & Fils, Libraires-imprimeurs. 256 et 258. rue Saint-Paul 1894). Useful studies of this play may be found in *Dictionnaire des œuvres littéraires du Québec* I, 38-9, by Reine Bélanger; and, anonymously, in *Bulletin des Recherches Historiques* IX (1903) 249-53.

39 JULES (*avec force*)
Quoi! Arché porter les armes contre le Canada qui l'a accueilli au jour de son infortune! – Arché, trahir mon père, me trahir, moi, son ami, son frère – Si cela était, autant je l'ai aimé, autant je le détesterais, le malheureux!
ARCHÉ
...Faut-il vous supplier? – Me voici à vos genoux. Je vous en prie, dites-moi que vous me pardonnez –
JULES (*avec émotion*)
Relevez-vous, Archibald de Locheill!

Scène VIII: Les précédents, MONTGOMERY

MONTGOMERY
Que vois-je! Quoi! Archibald Cameron de Locheill, un officier de sa Majesté Britannique aux genoux d'un méprisable ennemi!!...
JULES (*tirant son épée*)
Major Montgomery, qui vous a donné le droit de m'insulter ici? Si vous n'êtes pas aussi lâche qu'insolent, défendez-vous.
ARCHÉ
Que viens-tu faire ici, vil espion? (p 46)

JULES
Arrête, Arché. (*Il se détourne*.) Non, il ne peut être aussi coupable qu'il le paraît, celui qui sacrifie ainsi de coeur joie les espérances les plus belles et les plus légitimes aux sentiments de l'amitié et de la reconnaissance. (*Lui tendant les bras*.) Arché, mon ami, je te pardonne!!! (*Arché se précipite dans ses bras en disant*:) Mon frère!!! (pp 48-9)

40 An English translation of the novel, titled *The Canadians of Old*, was published in New York (Appleton 1890) and Toronto (Hart 1891), with several subsequent editions. For useful studies of the work, see P.-G. Roy, *A travers 'Les Anciens Canadiens' de Philippe Aubert de Gaspé* (Montreal: Ducharme 1943); the incisive but brief article by Maurice Lemire in *Dictionnaire des œuvres littéraires du Québec* (I, 17-23); the thesis by Verna I. Curran, 'Philippe-Joseph Aubert de Gaspé: His Life and Works.'
At least two other plays were drawn from Aubert de Gaspés novel, one of them published with the title *Blanche d'Haberville* (the name of the heroine excised from Caisse and Laporte's version), by Georges Monarque (Montreal:

Librairie d'Action canadienne-française 1931), the other entitled *Les Sorciers de l'Ile d'Orléans*, to which the only reference I have found is in *La Minerve*, 22 Jan. 1867, p 3, where an announcement for a performance to take place on 31 Jan., 'A la Salle Académique du Collège Ste Marie,' is inserted, the work being described as a 'drame tiré des *Anciens Canadiens* de M. P.A. de Gaspé.' A brief and unrevealing report of the program appears in the same newspaper on 5 Feb. 1867, the correspondent reporting, 'Tous les figurants, en un mot, ont fait merveille, et nous aurons rarement vu un programme aussi bien composé et aussi bien exécuté. Nous souhaitons que cette séance se répète.'

41 An exceptionally detailed account appears in the Montreal paper *L'Ordre* for 23 Jan. 1865, comprising most of p 2, but is devoted mainly to the ceremonies accompanying consecration of a new altar in the college's chapel, for which the performance of the play was obviously a sidelight. The reporter observes:

La pièce et le dénouement que les acteurs ont amené à l'admiration de tous les assistants, étaient bien choisis pour couronner l'acte de piété et de reconnaissance des donateurs du magnifique autel en marbre qui enrichit aujourd'hui le choeur de l'élégante chapelle du collège de l'Assomption.

42 Much of Aubert de Gaspé's speech is reproduced in the anonymous article, 'Les Anciens Canadiens,' in *Bulletin des Recherches Historiques* IX (1903) 249-53.

43 *La Minerve*, samedi matin, 16 juillet 1685, p 1, col. 5. My translation

44 Parts of the following subsections appear, in French, as a long article in vol. V of *Revue d'histoire littéraire du Québec et du Canada français* under the title, 'Théâtre, parathéâtre et politique, 1847-1868.'

45 *Le Populaire*. Journal des intérêts canadiens. Léon Gosselin, propriétaire, H. Leblanc de Marconnay, éditeur en chef. (P 1, col. 1):

Pour le *Populaire*

CONVERSATION ENTRE DEUX HABITANS CANADIENS

JEAN

Dis donc, voisin, je viens d'apprendre une nouvelle qui m'étonne beaucoup.

PIERRE

Oui donc, qu'est-ce que c'est?

JEAN

On dit que Mr. Papineau vient de tourner casaque, c'est à dire qu'il abandonne le poste honorable où il était placé pour s'adonner au plus vil des métiers –

PIERRE

Bah! c'est une calomnie! Pourrais-tu douter de l'honneur et de la probité de Mr. Papineau!

46 Ne sais-tu pas que les Américains détestent notre religion, nos lois et nos usages. Après avoir brûlé le couvent de Boston, que n'ont-il pas fait pour flétrir le caractère et la moralité de nos prêtres et de nos dignes religieuses

de Montréal! N'a-t-on pas vu, il y a cinq ou six mois, présenter au congrès des Etats-Unis une pétition demandant une loi par laquelle le territoire de ce pays serait interdit à tout individu qui ne renoncerait pas à la croyance catholique? Voilà ce que Papineau nous représente comme un modèle des idées libérales! (pp 1-2)

47 *L'Echo des campagnes*. Journal religieux, politique et industriel. Samedi, 7 novembre 1846, p 1, col 1:
Pour la plupart des ouvriers des villes, la vie se passe dans l'atelier et dans le cabaret, enlevée comme par un tourbillon; mais pour les habitants de la compagne, la paroisse est la petite patrie, la seconde patrie, la véritable patrie presque. Or, qui représente la paroisse? Est-ce la maison d'école, est-ce la mairie? Non, c'est l'église.
Cf. *Des Caisses d'épargne*. Extrait des *Entretiens de village*, par Timon. A. M. D. C. (Montréal: Des Presses à vapeur de John Lovell, rue St Nicolas 1853).

48 *L'Avenir*, samedi 18 décembre 1847, p 4:
La Dissolution
Le Gouverneur en conseil
(*Chant en cinq voix*)
LE GOUVERNEUR OUVRE LA SÉANCE
Moi, lord Elgin de Kincardine,
L'ami du brave Canadien,
Au peuple en proie à la rapine
Je veux faire le plus grand bien.
PAPINEAU.
Ciel! C'en est fait du ministère.
DALY.
Quel démon trouble mon repos!
BADGLEY.
Grand Dieu! quelle nouvelle amère!
UNE VOIX INCONNUE
Oh! vous tremblez, messieurs les sots.

LE GOUVERNEUR
Oh! ciel enfin, me voici libre!
Dieu j'ai chassé ces nigauds.
Les ministres de ce calibre
Ne sont bons que pour les tripots.
PAPINEAU
Comptant j'ai quatre mille livres.
DALY
J'en ai presque deux fois autant.
BADGLEY
Pour l'an à peine j'ai des vivres.
LA VOIX
Nigaud, va vivre en pénitent.

Ceux qui vous opprimaient naguères
Se trouvent sans force aujourd'hui.
Allez, que vos chefs populaires,
Elus, m'aident de leur appui.

49 *Ibid.*, samedi 15 janvier, 1848, p 1:

LE GOUVERNEUR
Comment! vous voilà de retour?
Qui, diable, a donc pu vous élire?
Messieurs, c'est un très mauvais tour,
Quoi! le peuple est-il en délire?

BADGLEY
En vrai joueur de gobelets
J'ai fait cent tours de passe-passe;
Milord, c'était tous des anglais
Vous comprenez que j'eus ma passe.

DALY
A tous j'ai fait bien des promesses;
Aux anglais j'ai montré de l'or,
Aux romains j'ai promis des messes.

50 *L'Avenir*, 2 août 1848, pp 1-2: 'Une Scène d'intérieur, ou Relation d'une séance du comité chargé de surveiller la rédaction des lettres d'un célèbre Dr. Guerrier':

GEORGES
Allons! ça n'est pas comme ça – tu dois comprendre, Octave, que dans une bataille on a une avant-garde et un corps d'armée. Tu es l'avant-garde. *La Minerve* est le corps d'armée. Or si tu te lances quelquefois étourdiment, tu ne peux pas exiger que nous compromettions le corps d'armée pour te soutenir?...

OCTAVE
Oui, mais avec tout cela je passe pour un imbécile!

GEORGES
Tiens, tu cherches bien à faire passer ce maudit Papineau pour un fou, un furieux, un maniaque.

HECTOR
C'est un moyen de polémique cela: d'ailleurs allez-vous le lui reprocher? C'est par votre ordre.

LE DR
Voyons, mon petit Octave, un moyen – car si je sais bien me battre –

OCTAVE
Invitez M. Papineau à aller voir chez vous la preuve écrite. – Lui, sait bien qu'elle n'existe pas, et il n'ira pas – et les neuf dixièmes des lecteurs de *la Minerve* seront satisfaits.

LUDGER (*battant des mains*)
Bravo, bravo! Octave; tu es un homme de mérite; je te vote un dîner.

HECTOR
Hourra pour Octave! – c'est un matois celui-là.
LE DR
Le moyen est bon, où mettre la phrase?
OCTAVE
Parbleu! ici! (*montrant le manuscrit*)
LE DR
C'est bien – avez-vous encore des changements à faire?
GEORGES
Ma foi! oui, corrigeons les fautes de français!
OCTAVE
Y pensez-vous? Cette sotisse que vous allez faire là! Il faut les aug-
menter et non les diminuer!
LUDGER
Pourquoi?
OCTAVE
Mais c'est bien simple, pourtant. Comment voulez-vous qu'on croie que
c'est notre brave Dr. qui écrit, s'il n'y a pas de fautes de français?

51   *L'Avenir* du 2 août courant, contenait une communication en forme de
dialogue signé 'Tuque Bleu' [*sic*] où les interlocuteurs ne sont désignés
que par prénoms. Je recontrai hier matin un de mes amis qui me dit
qu'un intime de l'*Avenir* insinuait que l'on fesait allusion à moi dans ce
dialogue sous le prénom de Georges... Comme cette communication, dans
le cas où réellement on aurait voulu faire allusion à ma personne, n'était
quant à moi qu'un tissu d'insinuations et d'allégations fausses et menson-
gères, j'étais en droit d'obtenir des éditeurs et colloborations [*sic*] qui pub-
lient et rédigent l'*Avenir*, une déclaration formelle, pour savoir si oui ou
non l'on fesait allusion à moi dans la correspondance anonyme, et dans le
cas d'une réponse affirmative, j'étais en droit de m'adresser pour réparation à l'un des collaborateurs dont la position sociale eût pu correspondre
à la mienne ... J'étais aussi en droit d'obtenir le nom du lâche et anonyme
correspondant, pour de même savoir de lui s'il avait voulu faire allusion à
moi, et dans le cas d'une réponse affirmative obtenir de lui réparation
pour la publication de ses mensonges. Hier matin vers onze heures, je fus
accompagné de mon ami M. Hubert, avocat de cette ville, au bureau de
l'*Avenir*, où je recontrai M. J. B. E. Dorion, qui s'affuble du titre de *directeur gérant de l'Avenir* et à première vue j'en eus la pitié et la commisé-
ration que l'on a naturellement pour l'adolescence.

Voulant enfin en terminer avec M. Dorion, je lui demandai péremptoire-
ment et pour une dernière fois s'il voulait oui ou non me donner le nom
de son correspondant; il me répondit que non. Là-dessus je lui dis que lui
et son correspondant n'étaient que des poltrons, et que son journal était
conduit sur un système irresponsable de poltronnerie. Je me suis alors re-

tiré avec M. Hubert, passablement indigné, car il y avait matière à soulever l'indignation par suite d'un semblable traitement. Les faits qui précèdent n'ont point besoin de commentaire. Le public est maintenant à même de juger de la portée des insultes de l'*Avenir*.

Votre serviteur très humble,
GEO. ET. CARTIER.

Montréal, 3 août 1848.

J'affirme pour vrais les faits ci-dessus qui pourront en outre être certifiés par M. Lewis Harkin, marchand de cette ville, qui s'est trouvé par hasard présent avec moi.

R. A. R. HUBERT.

52   Le second des faits que je vais rectifier est celui qui tend à faire croire que le petit George E. C. fut brave à la bataille de St.-Denis. Voici, par rapport à ce dernier, le fait tel qu'il est, tel que le Dr. sait qu'il est et le petit George lui-même mieux que qui que ce soit. Figurez-vous, M. le directeur, le petit George revêtu d'un vieux capot d'étoffe du pays fait pour un homme, et couvert d'une immense *Tuque Bleue* qui lui pendait jusque dans le milieu du dos et dont la largeur correspondait à la longueur, de manière, qu'au besoin, il n'y a aucun doute qu'elle aurait pu le contenir tout entier, surtout pas plus gros qu'il était ce jour là.

53 *L'Avenir*, 26 août 1848, pp 1-2: 'Le Diable à quatre: à propos d'une *Tuque Bleue*':

OCTAVE (*court à perdre haleine, un papier à la main*)
George! George! [*sic*]

GEORGES (*se retourne*)
Qu'est-ce que c'est donc, bon Dieu? Te voilà tout effaré! Le feu est-il à ton bureau?

OCTAVE
Non, mais il n'y en a pas moins de quoi courir. Regarde. (*Il lui montre l'Avenir.*)...

GEORGES
Tiens c'est signé *Tuque Bleue*, ça doit être bête.

OCTAVE
C'est plus menteur que bête; pourtant tout n'est pas faux. Il faut absolument que quelqu'un ait parlé. On dirait qu'il a tout entendu!

LE DR
Bonjour, mon cher Georges – Mais quoi donc, tu es tout bouleversé. *What is the matter?*

GEORGES
Tenez, lisez ce s. ... papier: ça vous regarde aussi, on y parle de vous. Bande de petits gueux! ça n'a que l'impudence! Un journal au maillot! des collaborateurs qui devraient y être! Un directeur gérant de trois pieds de haut, et ça s'attaque à vous et à moi: en vérité c'est à n'y rien comprendre. Tout se démoralise.

GEORGES

Je vais tous les souffleter les uns après les autres!

LUDGER

Diable, c'est une sérieuse besogne que tu t'imposes là! Prends-y-garde.
Donner un soufflet à quelqu'un qui est plus faible que soi, c'est lâche; à
quelqu'un qui est plus fort, on en reçoit deux pour un, par exemple, si tu
t'attaques à P... tu pourras à peine lui toucher le menton!

LUDGER

Dans *La Minerve* je vais les écraser de reproches, mais entre nous je dois
dire qu'ils ont raison et que j'aurais fait comme eux.

GEORGES

C'est peut-être vrai, après tout, j'y prendrai garde une autre fois.

LUDGER

As-tu jamais été à la chasse au canard?

GEORGES

A propos de quoi cette question vient-elle?

LUDGER

Réponds toujours!

GEORGES

Eh bien non.

LUDGER

Eh bien mon cher, quand on a manqué son canard il ne revient plus...

54 Aegidius Fauteux, *Le Duel au Canada* 276-7
55 J.-C. Taché, author of the political study, *Des Provinces de l'Amérique du Nord
et d'une union fédérale* (1858) and of *Forestiers et voyageurs*, based on Quebec
folklore (1863), contributed an act to the political play of Hubert La Rue, *Le
Défricheur de langue* (see below, pp 171-6). Loranger, Provincial Secretary in
1857-8 and later a judge of the Supreme Court, is the author of *Commentaires
sur le code civil du Bas-Canada* (2 vols, 1873-9) and of *Lettres sur l'interpréta-
tion de la constitution fédérale, dite l'Acte de l'Amérique britannique du Nord,
1867* (2 vols, 1883-4). I am indebted to my colleague, David M. Hayne, for
first pointing out to me the existence of *La Dégringolade*.
56 See Jacques Monet, *The Last Cannon Shot: A Study of French-Canadian
Nationalism, 1837-1850*.
57   Car voyez-vous, Johnné se prépare à jouer vis-à-vis de moi le rôle de Brutus à l'égard de César. Johnné est mon élève, il me doit toute sa position
politique et il est aujourd'hui avéré qu'il conspire contre moi –
The political songs which end each act of *La Dégringolade* have been reproduced, words and music, in vol. II of *Chansons politiques du Québec*, ed. by
Maurice Carrier and Monique Vachon (Montreal: Leméac 1979) 340-9; and
thus, now being accessible, are not reproduced here.
58   En deux mots, voici ce que je pense. Dans le Haut-Canada, il faudrait
faire disparaître MacNab, Ross, Cayley, et un autre que je ne nomme pas.

Dans le Bas-Canada, il faudrait se débarrasser de Taché, Cartier, Cauchon et Drummond. Taché parce qu'il n'est responsable à personne et qu'il empoche toujours en se moquant de tout le monde, parce qu'il est détesté pour son dernier coup de canon, et enfin parce qu'il est honni pour s'être déclaré fier d'être colon. Cartier parce qu'il n'attire que de l'inimitié et du ridicule sur le ministère, parce qu'il a trop souvent tourné son capot, sans compter sa tuque bleue...

L'Avenir published in its issue of 28 Feb. 1856 half a column of errata to *La Dégringolade*, correcting, for example, E.-P. Taché's song at the end of Act II:

.   (*Sur l'air: 'T'en souviens-tu...'*)
    Vous souvient-il du temps de la révolte,
    Quand j'exerçais les fils d'la liberté;
    J'avais peu l'air d'un ministre en récolte
    D'honneur et d'or, pour trahir enfaîté.
    Depuis dix ans, pour la bonne Angleterre,
    J'ai réveillé mon orgueil de colon;

bis { Pour sa puissance et pour mon gros salaire,
      { Moi, le dernier, j'affûterai l'canon!

59   La réunion qui va bientôt se terminer a fait ressortir deux faits importants à mes yeux: le 1er c'est que le parlement se disloque et nous fait défaut; le 2nd, c'est que l'opinion en dehors nous abandonne également, puisque la presse qui nous représente est nulle quand elle nous fait pas de mal [*sic*]. Le bouquet de ce double fait, vous le sentez comme moi, c'est la dégringolade de chacun de nous.

L'Avenir's corrected version of Cartier's song (errata of 28 Feb. 1856):
    Allons, enfants de la patrie,
    Battez-vous, Montjoie-St. Denis!
    Pour moi, devant l'artillerie,
bis Tout glacé d'effroi, je m'enfuis.
    Tout plein ma tuque à St. Antoine,
    Plomb et balles je trouverai;
    Je sauverai mon péritoine,
    Et près de vous je reviendrai.
       Aux armes, Canadiens!
       Je vais à reculons,
       Fuyons, fuyons,
    Un plomb impur n'atteindra mes talons.

Obviously, the author is here underlining the connection with the *Tuque Bleue* sequence from 1848.

60   See below, pp 179-82. For the history of songs of this nature, see Maurice Carrier and Monique Vachon, *Chansons politiques du Québec* esp. vol. II (1834-58).

61   *L'Avenir*, 30 mai 1856: 'La Crise: petite comédie en un acte':
    M. SPENCE
    Je me moquerais bien de ce vote, s'il y avait moyen de gouverner avec

une majorité Bas-Canadienne. Mais si nous l'essayons, vous allez voir dégringoler tous nos amis dans l'opposition en moins d'une semaine.

M. MacDONALD

Je le sais pardieu bien!

M. SPENCE

Alors que faire? Ce qui me choque, c'est de ne pouvoir pas donner un grand coup de pied dans la plus intelligente partie de Cartier...

62 *L'Avenir*, 5 juin 1856:

M. TACHÉ

Si ça ne payait pas si bien, je jetterais le froc aux orties.

M. SPENCE

Oui, mais £1800, c'est un article.

M. TACHÉ

C'est cela. Pour ma part je ne me résoudrai jamais à déguerpir.

63 *Le Fantasque*, 26 Nov. 1857: 'Le Siège futur du gouvernement, ou la Querelle des cinq villes: Récit peu fantastique d'un songe des plus réels':

Il n'y en a qu'une digne de cette grande distinction: c'est Toronto! Savez-vous pourquoi? D'abord, le Haut-Canada doit l'emporter sur le Bas. Cela est écrit là-haut, et c'est la nature des choses que le veut. Le Haut-Canada est anglais, fichtre! et il en est fier ... C'est pour cela que nous sommes ici la race supérieure et là-bas (*montrant le Bas-Canada*) vous savez – c'est la place où ne se trouvent pas les hommes – supérieurs ... *And moreover*, messieurs, personne d'entre vous n'ignore que Toronto dans tous les cas est la ville par excellence, *the best of all cities*...

64 *Le Fantasque*, 3 Dec. 1857: 'Le Ministère jugé. Aux collaborateurs du *Fantasque*':

Messieurs,

Avant-hier, j'escaladais comme je le pouvais la côte Lamontagne, mon bâton à la main, et j'avançais au petit pas. Deux hommes marchant comme moi dans la direction de la haute-ville me précédaient; l'un était Maxime, le balayeur, l'autre Benjamin, vendeur d'huîtres de ma connaissance. Le dialogue suivant s'établit entre nos deux camarades, et je vous le rapporte presque mot à mot.

BENJAMIN

J'dis seulement que si y a presque pas d'ministres à Québec, ça fait pas l'affaire, car quand y en a plusieurs, ça fait renchérir les huîtres. Ça en mange tant des huîtres c'monde là!

MAXIME

Ça mange et pis ça fait balayer aussi. Quand j'pense qu'y avait un d'ces messieurs là qui m'faisait gagner à lui seul deux trente sous par jour, sans mentir, pour balayer son corridor et son d'vant d'porte!

BENJAMIN

Comment ça donc?

MAXIME

J'vas te l'dire. D'abord j'balayais l'matin. L'midi je r'commençais, car i v'nait ben du monde chez lui pour d'mander des places, et ça en faisait un frottement sur les planchers! J'étais obligé de r'faire l'même ouvrage tous les soirs; ça n'manquait pas.

BENJAMIN

Et tu r'cevais deux trente sous pour tout ça? C'était pas trop, ben sûr!

Puisque Martin-Pêcheur veut connaître notre pensée, nous lui dirons que la résolution qu'il a prise en faveur de M. Alleyn nous semble bonne, et qu'après tout il suffit de se rappeler le proverbe: *Un moineau dans la main vaut mieux que l'oie qui vole!* (pp 22-3)

65 *Le Défricheur de langue.* Tragédie-bouffe, en trois actes et en trois tableaux, par Isidore de Méplats. 1859. Republished in 1870 in Hubert LaRue's *Mélanges historiques, littéraires et d'économie politique* (Quebec: Garant & Trudel, 2 vols) I, 93-112, with an 'Explication' of the play's genesis by LaRue. The name 'Isidore de Méplats' is, given the subject-matter, appropriately sonorous ('Isidore' is from Greek, 'gift of Isis'; 'Méplats' seems to be a dig at the grandiloquent language of Chevalier in the parodied article, for the Frenchman had spoken of 'ce nez grec, taillé sur des méplats arrondis'). There has been, it seems, no detailed study of this text to date.

66 The passages which LaRue and his friends intend to parody are first presented in a prologue, and the quotations given here (in my translation) are from the 1859 text, pp 2-3.

67 1870 edition, p 94. In this text, Taché's contributions are indicated by LaRue with an asterisk. This is the same Taché who is victimized as a 'lackey' in *La Dégringolade* of 1856.

68 *L'Electeur*, Quebec, 25 May 1866, p 3:

LA CONFÉDÉRATION ET JOHN BULL

Derrière les coulisses

La rampe s'illumine – la toile est levée la comédie se joue – Arlequin enlace Colombine et Pantalon fait des pirouettes.

Pendant que le parterre rit à ces arlequinades, pénétrons dans les coulisses.

C'est dans l'ombre de ces coulisses que les destinées des peuples se moulent au creuset des ardentes convoitises, des ambitions avides.

C'est là que les plans se forment – là que se préparent ces gigantesques sauts de tremplin que l'on exécute aux yeux de l'opinion publique ébahie.

John Bull et la Confédération s'entretiennent. Ecoutons.

JOHN BULL

Quel est ce vampire?

LA CONFÉDÉRATION

Je suis la chrysalide d'où sortira une monarchie anglaise implantée sur le Nouveau Monde. Larve à l'heure présente, je deviendrai plus tard une

Gorgone féconde en iniquités. Je ne suis pas une conception démocratique comme on l'a cru d'abord. Non – L'infamie m'a mise au monde. Je mets en vigueur, John Bull, ce système en honneur dans votre politique, j'absorbe les nationalités et les patries, et je sacrifie sur l'autel de l'égoîsme ces choses qu'on dit sacrées. Enfin je suis une grande prostituée.

69   Il est probable qu'il y aura du sang versé. La guerre civile n'a pas dit son dernier mot, au Canada surtout. Demandez aux peuples opprimés ce qu'on leur répond en Europe. Demandez à la Pologne, à la Hongrie, à l'Irlande. – L'échafaud est là.

JOHN BULL

Allons! Je vois que vous comprenez bien les choses, ma fille. (*John Bull et la Confédération se retirent.*)

On the next page of the same issue of *L'Electeur* is a fine example of another direction the dramatized dialogue could take, by the 1860s: advertising. There is a 'Conversation entre deux amis,' which begins:

JACQUES

Ah! bonjour Baptiste, dis-donc, tu étrennes des bottes aujourd'hui, où les a-tu [*sic*] achetées?

BAPTISTE

Chez Jos. Poirier, coin des rues du Pont et des Fossés, à l'enseigne de la grande botte, dans la maison de M. William Venner.

And continues for several more exchanges on the merits of the boots and their purveyor.

70   Cantate. *La Confédération*. Paroles de M. A. Achintre, musique de M. J. Bte. Labelle. Dédiée à L'Hon. George Etienne Cartier Ministre de la Milice. *La Minerve* had informed its readers, on 19 Sept. 1867 (p 2), that 'M. J.B. Labelle, organiste de la Paroisse, est à composer une grande Cantate sur la Confédération. La musique serait, paraît-il, splendide et digne du sujet.' The piece was performed on 7 Jan. 1868, and the first page of *La Minerve* for 11 Jan. provides a long analysis of *La Confédération*, reproducing the entire text. See also Edmond Lareau, *Histoire de la littérature canadienne* 107, and Clément Moisan, '*La Confédération*, cantate d'Auguste Achintre,' in *Dictionnaire des œuvres littéraires du Québec* I, 134-5.

71   *Prière à l'Eternel*
Français, Anglais, enfants d'un même père,
Demandons tous, en ce jour solennel,
Que le Très-Haut bénisse notre terre...
L'Acadienne. Air
Perdue, errante en ce désert sauvage
autrefois:
Je pleure, hélas, sur mon triste destin!...
Larmes séchez! La douce *Evangeline*
De l'Acadie exprima le malheur.
aujourd'hui:

Le passé meurt sous le temps qui le mine
Et l'avenir m'offre paix et bonheur...
QUATUOR
Sur notre honneur sur la foi de nos pères,
Chacune ici nous jurons devant vous
De soutenir, défendre contre tous,
Le Canada, ses provinces prospères...

72 *La Conversion d'un pêcheur*. Opérette canadienne. Paroles de Elzéar Labelle,
musique de J.B. Labelle, organiste à l'église de Notre Dame, auteur de la
Cantate à la Confédération. Montréal. Prix $1.00. This is the 186[9] version,
with both words and music. The better known (and more accessible) edition is
in *Mes Rimes* par Elzéar Labelle. Québec, P.G. Delisle, imprimeur, 1, rue
Port Dauphin, 1876, where the title is extended to 'La Conversion d'un
pêcheur (de la Nouvelle-Ecosse), opérette en un acte' (pp 117-47. It is from
this second edition that I quote, in my own translation:

Et dire qu'c'est pour ces *originals-là* qu'j'ai quitté ma province, et pi ma
chère Anastasie; par'cqu'i Z'ont empêché l'poisson d'mordre; ah! les
misérables! les pirates! eh! ben oui! les *pirates*! puisque nos vaches mêmes
ne donnent plus d'lait depuis leur fameuse Confédération; tous les *pis* ont
raté; et on viendra m'dire que ça n'est pas dû à leur changement d'Constitution!...
PIERRICHON
Quel commerce, bonté! quel commerce! J'suis t'arrivé c'matin sur le
marché aux grosses bêtes, avec trois boeufs, six moutons, une vache,
deux dindons, ma femme et moé. Eh ben! vous m'*crairez* si ma figure
vous en dit: mais, tout ça est parti si vite, que j'en suis t'encore à chercher
ma femme qu'a disparu avec tout l'reste (pp 120-1).

73   En chantant ce duo, tous deux s'avancent à reculons; l'un la figure tournée vers la droite des auditeurs, et l'autre vers la gauche, jusqu'à ce que,
venant à se rencontrer, ils se heurtent l'un sur l'autre; après quelques
secondes d'attente et d'étonnement, ils chantent (p 126).

Tout allait à pleine voile, et j'vivais ben heureux entre mes morues, ma
femme et mes enfants, déjà au nombre de dix-sept, quand v'la ti pas
qu'c'te gueuse de politique est venue agiter si fort not'e Province, que les
eaux du golfe s'en ressentirent, et qu'tous les poissons, au lieu d'mord'e à
la ligne, prirent le mord aux dents, et s'enfuyèrent du pays (p 129).
MORUFORT
Au vieux père Howe, avec ivresse,
Je boirais du matin au soir;
C'est lui qui combat la détresse
Où nous a mis votre Pouvoir.
PIERRICHON
A la santé de George Etienne

Je bois ce verre avec transport!
De la race Canadienne,
C'est le défenseur le plus fort! (p 131)

PIERRICHON

Si c'est *quinqu'ça* qui vous inquiète, soyez pas en peine. J'avons justement
parlé à not'e Député pour placer mon *filleau* dans les affaires du gouvernement, et i m'a dit, hier, qu'la place était sûre, malgré qui z'en aient pas besoin; mais, voyez-vous, ces gens-là aiment à encourager l'commerce; – eh!
ben, mon *filleau* attendra une aut'e chance, et vous prendrez la sienne.

MORUFORT

Comment! moé une place! – mais ça s'peut pas, Monsieur Perrichon; moé
qu'a tant dit d'bêtises cont'e vot' gouvernement.

PIERRICHON

Pas si bête d'aller l'dire.

MORUFORT

C'est vrai que c'était entre nous aut'es, et pi qu'la colère du moment m'a
fait dire des choses – enfin; vous comprenez! – on s'excite – on
s'excite – on s'monte – et pi on finit par d'v'nir injuste (pp 143-4).

74 *Mes rimes* 27. My translation
75 Eg, the sequence in Morufort's first monologue, p 119:
    ...Mon portrait est si peu répandu, pour une bonne raison, c'est qu'voyez-
    vous, en ma qualité d'pêcheur, j'ai toujours *pris* sans jamais m'laisser
    prendre; et t'nez! j'vous dirai ben franchement: j'ai jamais été ben fort sur
    ces bêtises-là; y'a toujours assez d'nos hommes politiques qu'ont la fureur
    de s'faire *pendre*, pour avoir le plaisir de s'faire *prendre* à la porte de tous
    les *Poteaugraphes* ... Faut avouer qu'y en a un grand nombre qu'on f'rait
    ben mieux d'tirer au *blanc* plutôt qu'les tirer en *couleurs*, parc'que, voyez-
    vous, moé j'crai qu'les *Couleurs* les gâtent.
76 My own intensive (but not exhaustive) examination of Montreal newspapers
    for 1867-8 has revealed no reference to *La Conversion d'un pêcheur*. The first
    mention I have found is in *La Minerve* for 29 May 1869, p 2, where an adver-
    tisement appears for a 'Concert et opérette: Grande Fête musicale, donnée au
    profit des pauvres, dans la vaste Salle de la Maîtrise Saint-Pierre, Faubourg
    Québec, jeudi, le 10 Juin 1869.' The advertisement informs us that 'L'opérette,
    La Conversion d'un pêcheur, paroles de M. Elzéar Labelle, musique de J.B. La-
    belle, actuellement sous presse, sera jouée pour la dernière fois avant sa publi-
    cation,' which implies this is not to be its *first* performance (and also negates
    the asseveration frequently made, incidentally, that the undated first edition of
    the work [see note 72 above] appeared in 1867). The same ad reappears on 31
    May, 1, 2, 3, 4, 7-10 June, and on 11 June there is a brief report on the per-
    formance, ending:
    Dans la seconde partie, MM. J. Boucher et O. Labelle, si bien connus par
    leurs talents comme acteurs comiques, exécutèrent la célèbre opérette de

M. E. Labelle, *La Conversion d'un pêcheur*. Encore une fois mise en scène, cette opérette canadienne fut applaudie on ne peut plus! Another series of ads appears in *La Minerve*, beginning on 19 Apr. 1870, announcing that the same actors would perform again, on 22 Apr. On 26 Apr. there is an even briefer résumé, ending, 'L'opérette comique de M. Elzéar Labelle a eu un nouveau succès. MM. Boucher et O. Labelle ont dit leurs rôles respectifs avec un rare talent qui leur a valu bien des applaudissements' (p 3).

77 *Histoire de la littérature canadienne* 109. Apart from this brief reference, the most useful treatments of *La Conversion* are the introduction by A.N. Montpetit to *Mes Rimes* (see note 57 above), Jeanne d'Arc Lortie's entry on *Mes rimes* in *Dictionnaire des œuvres littéraires du Québec*, 492-3, which includes a paragraph on this play; Laurent-Olivier David, in *Souvenirs et biographies, 1870-1910* 24-9; and Marie-Claire Daveluy, 'Deux Pionniers du théâtre canadien' (the other being R.-E. Fontaine).

78 A performance is mentioned in *Le Canard*, 21 Feb. 1880, p 2, and in Quebec's *Le Soleil*, 22 Mar. 1899, p 6. I am indebted to Lucie Robert of the Faculté des Lettres, Université Laval, for these two references.

79 Apart from *Qui trop embrasse mal étreint*, he is purported to have written a play called *Le Brigand*. No trace survives of either.

80 *Une Partie de campagne*. Comédie en deux actes par M. Pierre Petitclair. Représentée pour la première fois, à Québec, par les Amateurs canadiens-français, le 22 avril 1860. Québec: Imprimé et publié par Joseph Savard, typographe. 1865

81 Jean-Claude Noël, in his thesis, 'Pierre Petitclair, premier dramaturge canadien-français,' points out that the author may have based his character 'William' on a real person, since a son of the Labadie family to which he served as tutor in Labrador and on the North Shore, although baptised 'Guillaume,' had changed his name to 'William' by 1858 (p 170, note).

82 Pp 26-7. Since this play has never been reprinted, I provide a sample of the original:

WILLIAM
I hope you had a pleasant morning walk.

MALVINA
Extremely pleasant, Sir. The country looks so beautiful! But why don't you speak french, Mr. William? – Pourquoi donc ne me parlez-vous pas français. Vous n'ignorez pas que cette langue me plaît infiniment.

BROWN (*imitant sa sœur*)
Vous n'ignorez pas – Mon soeur parlé oune piou miou qué moâ, jé croâ – But c'est moâ apprendre bientôt – Vous n'ignorez pas, hem!

MALVINA (*à Flore*)
Je pense que monsieur votre cousin voudrait oublier sa langue, mademoiselle.

FLORE

Il voudrait aussi oublier bien d'autres choses, et il en oublie beaucoup.

WILLIAM (*à Malvina*)

En votre présence, mademoiselle, j'oublie tout pour n'admirer qu'un ange. – Et d'ailleurs, l'anglais, vous le savez, est plus fashionable.

MALVINA (*riant*)

Ha! ha! ha! ha! – Fashionable de mépriser sa langue! Je pensais qu'il n'y avait que certains messieurs de l'Assemblée Législative qui eussent ce privilège.

WILLIAM

Toujours satirique.

FLORE

Il est aussi de mode de n'avoir plus de cœur. (*William jette un coup d'œil sévère à Flore*.)

83 Jean-Claude Noël, 'Le cas Pierre Petitclair.' 28; Louis-Michel Darveau, *Nos hommes de lettres* 61-74

84 Thesis (see note 81 above) 169

85 Eg, p 10:

JOSEPH

Imagine-toi que le bonhomme Charlot à Jean-Marie-Pierriche Thibeau s'adonnait à me parler, accoudé sur une pagée de clôture. Notre jeune homme, donc, M. Brown, était avec moi, le cigare au bec. Je le vis bien tournailler autour de Charlot, mais je ne soupçonnais rien, dites donc. – Je me retourne – Charlot se sauvait à toutes jambes, tandis qu'il lui sortait du feu du corps, et puis une minute après, flaque! – la tête la première dans un rigolet. Quand il se releva, il avait l'air d'un monstre – le visage noir de boue. Mon boindre d'Anglais était pâmé de rire. C'était des pétards, comme il appelle ça, qu'il avait mis à Charlot.

It is perhaps true that, as J.-C. Noël has pointed out (Archives V, 134), the literary praeterite used here ('il se releva') is inappropriate (although the form, 'je vis,' reflects regional Quebec usage); but in general, Joseph's diction is convincing.

86 *Archives* V, 134-5

87 *Le Canadien*, 27 Apr. 1857; see also *le Journal de Québec*, 21 and 25 Apr. 1857.

88 This performance was preceded by an unusually lengthy advertising campaign in the newspapers, beginning on 12 Apr. 1860 in the *Journal de Québec*. Petitclair's play was to be preceded by a speech from the president of the Saint-Jean-Baptiste Society and by the 5-act comedy, *Grandeur et décadence de M. Joseph Prud'homme*, written by H. Monnier and G. Vaez and first performed in Paris in 1852. There would be comic songs in the intermissions, the entire marching band of the Société Saint-Jean-Baptiste would perform, and 'deux chambres, l'une pour les Dames et l'autre pour les Messieurs, seront à la disposition des personnes qui désireraient ôter leur pardessus.' But even before

the advertising campaign, a reader of the same newspaper had challenged the Amateurs typographes, on 5 Apr., asking if that group, which 's'est acquis une si brillante réputation sur notre théâtre, voudrait bien nous dire, par la voie des journaux, si, à l'exemple des Amateurs Canadiens, il entend, lui aussi, mettre sa main puissante à l'oeuvre si patriotique du monument de Sainte-Foye.' (I have found no evidence that the Amateurs typographes responded.) The same expensive ads began in *Le Courrier du Canada* on 13 Apr., continuing in both papers until the performance on 28 Apr. Two days later this second paper's reporter reported briefly on the plays:

> Nous n'avons pu, à notre grand regret, assister samedi à la soirée dramatique dont le produit sera consacré à l'érection du monument des héros de 1760. Les pièces représentées sont irréprochables au point de vue de la morale, et les acteurs, paraît-il, ont joué avec habileté et entrain. *La partie de campagne*, comédie en deux actes, par M. P. Petitclair, a fait fureur.

The obvious concern for the 'morality' of these plays exhibited in that second-last sentence is indicative of the atmosphere I have described for the late 1850s and early 1860s when visiting French professionals drew fire from ecclesiastical authorities against them and papers like *Le Pays* who dared support them.

89 The reviewer for *Le Canadien* is very favourable, praising the play's humour, its 'style aisé, verve intarissable, gaîté vive' (10 Jan. 1866). According to the advertisements in *Le Journal de Québec*, Petitclair's play was preceded by a performance of the popular melodrama, *Hariadan Barberousse*, and a military band performed (9, 13, 18, 20 Jan. 1866).

90 An unusually long critique of the performance appears in *Le Canadien* for 24 Nov. 1862, p 2. I quote in part:

> Nous sommes trop sincère ami [*sic*] du talent pour ne pas faire écho au sentiment de tous en rendant hommage à ceux qui ont monté la pièce dramatique de *Félix Poutré*, auteur et amateurs. Il y a réellement l'étoffe d'un dramaturge dans M. L.H. Fréchette, le poète déjà connu et aimé du public canadien. Il en a donné la preuve samedi soir dans la représentation de son *Félix Poutré*, cette page si palpitante de notre histoire.
>
> M. Fréchette préluda à la levée du rideau par un petit prologue dans lequel il sut se concilier son public en quelques paroles heureuses et très convenablement adressées du haut de la scène aux auditeurs qui les accueillirent de même.
>
> Nous ne croyons pas que jamais pareille salle, pour la quantité comme pour la qualité, ait encore répondu à l'appel de nos amateurs; ç'a été, de l'aveu de tous, un succès, un triomphe – on se serait cru à un spectacle des *Variétés* pour le moins...
>
> Nous ne voulons rien exagérer dans notre appréciation, où il serait presque ingrat de vouloir placer une critique que l'auteur désarma dès le début. Il s'agit d'un jeune auteur et de jeunes amateurs qui se sont donné la main pour faire au public Canadien l'admirable surprise de samedi soir, et nous ne faisons que notre partie en leur disant à tous que cette pièce

sera redemandée et qu'elle est destinée à être au premier rang du
Répertoire Canadien, quand elle aura reçu son complément.
The anonymous reviewer had his wish, and the play reappeared on 19 Jan. of
the following year. Another long analysis followed in *Le Canadien* 2 days later,
concentrating mainly on the individual actors' performances. The reviewer was
particularly impressed with the lead role:

> Mais celui chez qui se révèle une puissance d'action dramatique vraie, qui
> sait maîtriser son public et se mesurer avec les difficultés et les délicatesses
> de son rôle, c'est incontestablement M. PAUL DUMAS. Celui-là a su se
> tremper dans les sources vives de l'art et son jeu accuse en lui les ressorts
> de la scène dont il a les secrets ... Cette fois ce qu'il y avait pu y avoir de
> tant soit peu exagéré dans son rôle, qui prête à son emphase naturelle,
> s'est effacé au fur et mesure [*sic*] qu'il se familiarisait avec son public. Au
> tomber de la toile celui-ci est sorti à regret, mais enchanté de l'acteur pour
> avoir su si heureusement traduire le rôle si bien conçu par l'auteur de
> *Félix Poutré*.

Such attention to individual performances was quite rare at the time and
underlines what a histrionic vehicle Fréchette had created in this lead role.

91 The most useful studies of Fréchette's theatre in general are those by Paul
Wyczynski, 'Dans les coulisses du théâtre de Fréchette,' in *Archives des lettres
canadiennes* I, 100-28; and 'Louis Fréchette et le théâtre,' which makes use of
much of the material of the preceding article, in the same series, V, 137-65.
For *Félix Poutré* in particular, Pierre Filion's introduction, 'Du Traître au
héros, ou du Drame à la comédie' (pp 9-25) to the Leméac (Montreal 1974)
edition of the play is an admirable résumé of its genesis and history. See also
the useful entry by Reine Bélanger, '*Félix Poutré*, drame de Louis Fréchette,'
in *Dictionnaire des œuvres littéraires du Québec* I, 246-8, and Pierre Gobin, *Le
Fou et ses doubles...Figures de la dramaturgie québécoise* 84-90.

92 *Echappé de la potence: Souvenirs d'un prisonnier d'état canadien en 1838.*
Imprimé pour l'auteur par De Montigny et cie. 1862. English title here given
is that of the translation published in Montreal by Beauchemin and Valois, in
1885.

93 All quotations are from the Leméac (Montreal 1974) edition, in my translation. Since this text is readily available, original French is not provided.

94 Radio-Canada presented an adaptation of this play by Guy Dufresne, in its
radio series, 'Théâtre canadien,' in 1953, but I have been unable to consult
this version. See Reine Bélanger, '*Félix Poutré*, drame de Louis Fréchette,' in
Dictionnaire des œuvres littéraires du Québec I, 246.

95 In the text mentioned in note 91 above Gobin observes (p 87), 'Pour nous
qui connaissons le dessous des cartes, la forme de sa folie est non seulement
l'expression de ses rêves mais aussi la révélation outrée de l'option politique
véritable qu'il doit celer.'

96 Jean Béraud [Jacques Laroche], *350 ans de théâtre au Canada français* 53-4

97 The most conclusive and most devastating case against Poutré was made by Gustave Lanctôt, in *Faussaires et faussetés en histoire canadienne* 201-24.

98 Wyczynski, in the article mentioned in note 91 above, demonstrates conclusively that only *Papineau*, published and performed in 1880, can lay claim to any originality. But one recalls Pascal Poirier's cruel *mot*, the following year, that 'Papineau est de trop dans la pièce. Ce personnage retranché, le 'grand drame historique' n'en vaudrait que mieux' (*La Revue canadienne* XVIII [1881] 363).

99 'Le Sentiment national dans le théâtre canadien-français de 1760 à 1930,' thèse de Doctorat d'Université présentée par Etienne F. Duval devant la Faculté des Lettres et Sciences Humaines de l'Université de Paris en 1967; *Anthologie thématique du théâtre québécois au XIXe siècle*, by Etienne-F. Duval

100 One would like to know what modifications to Fréchette's text would have been made for later performances in collèges classiques in Quebec. Would the many appeals to Providence, by the hero and the traitor, remain? And what of the solemn oaths on the Bible taken by the conspiring Patriotes in I, 5 (pp 44-5)?

101 The only reference I have found to this play is in *Bulletin des Recherches Historiques* XLII (1936) 215:

QUESTION

Le 18 avril 1863, des amateurs québécois interprétaient, à la salle de Musique, rue St.-Louis, un proverbe en trois actes de J.-F. Gingras, intitulé *A quelque chose malheur est bon*. La scène se passait, paraît-il à Québec même, en 1850. Cette pièce a-t-elle été publiée? Qui était J.-F. Gingras?

The anonymous questioner seems to have received no answer to his query.

102 Laflamme and Tourangeau, *L'Eglise et le théâtre au Québec* 123-4, describe an interesting intervention by Bishop Lartigue and his coadjutor, Ignace Bourget, in 1838, when the college had proposed to perform, among other plays, one dealing with Napoleon.

103 *Un Duel à poudre*. Comédie en trois actes, par R. E. Fontaine. Représentée pour la première fois au Théâtre des Amateurs de St. Hyacinthe, le 30 octobre 1866. St. Hyacinthe. Imprimerie du 'Journal de St. Hyacinthe.' 1868. This is the only known edition of the play. Most useful sources are Reine Bélanger, '*Un Duel à poudre*, comédie de Raphaël-Ernest Fontaine,' in *Dictionnaire des œuvres littéraires du Québec* I, 717-18; Marie-Claire Daveluy, 'Deux Pionniers du théâtre canadien.'

104 Since copies of this text are rare, I provide the original, in my translation:

Le Théâtre représente une cuisine d'auberge; au fonds un poële, au milieu une table de cuisine chargée de plats, assiettes et autres ustensiles. Un plat en ferblanc est rempli de patates. Josephte plume un poulet, assise près de la table, manches retroussées, en mantelet, sans crinoline. Jacob est assis auprès d'elle, chapeau blanc, canne en jonc, culottes jaunes, lorgnon, il se dandine sur une chaise...

JOSEPHTE

N'braillez pas m'sieu, ça serait bien laid. Excitez-vous pas, j'vous cré, j'vous cré. Vous m'faites tout de même un drôle d'effet: i'm'semble qu'vous m'aimez pour tout d'bon. Eh! ben prouvez-moi lé et pis ensuite on verra.

JACOB (*se relevant et gesticulant violemment*)

Te le prouver, o nymphe admirable! O ma Sylphide! Dame de mes rêves, O idéal de mon âme, oui je veux, je jure de te le prouver. Faut-il que j'acquiers (*sic*) sur les champs de bataille une renommé napoléonienne? Faut-il que je délivre mon pays des serres de vautour de la perfide Albion? Faut-il que j'extermine les Feniens? Eh! bien, je suis capitaine dans les armées de Sa Majesté, je verserai le sang humain à flots ... Mon génie exalté par ton amour fera des merveilles dans les arts et les sciences, j'irai fouiller –

JOSEPHTE (*étonnée*)

Fouiller quoi?

JACOB (*continuant*)

J'irai fouiller les entrailles de la terre et en ferai jaillir les trésors qu'elle recèle dans son sein. (*Essoufflé.*) Faut-il? Faut-il?

JOSEPHTE

Non! Non! m'sieu, allez seulement m'charcher un sciau d'eau.

JACOB (*continuant*)

Faut-il anéantir vos ennemis? Vous mettre dans un palais? Vous couvrir de soie, d'or et de pierreries? Dites, je suis votre esclave, votre chien. Prononcez, choisissez, ordonnez.

JOSEPHTE

Eh! ben m'sieu, j'vous ordonne d'aller me cri un sciau d'eau et une brassée de bois de poèle.

105   Cher père.

Quand vous recevrez cette lettre, votre fils aura cessé de vivre. Un Patauville insulté tue l'insulteur, ou meurt en vengeant son honneur, les armes à la main. Adieu, votre fils infortuné

JACOB PÉLO DE PATAUVILLE

106   FLETCHER

Alors, à l'œuvre, Messieurs Pinard et Francoeur, témoins de Monsieur le Bourdon, venez avec moi charger les pistolets et vous, Messieurs Jacob et le Bourdon, veuillez vous retirer à l'écart. (*Le Bourdon et Jacob se retirent, les quatre témoins se réunissent, Fletcher ouvre la boîte, et on commence à charger les armes.*)

SWEENEY

C'est nous prendre les balles rondes ou des balles coniques?

TOUBEAU

Des balles coniques seraient mieux, car elles tuent plus raide!

PINARD
C'est bien, prenons-les car c'est un duel à mort!
JACOB (*lugubre, à part*)
A mort! Seigneur, j'étouffe!
LE BOURDON (*à part*)
Ces imbéciles là sont capables de mettre des balles! (*Francœur lui fait un signe de tête*.)
PINARD
Allons, Fletcher, une seconde balle, il faut au moins que ces messieurs se tuent comme il faut.
JACOB (*à part*)
Mais ils veulent donc me faire cribler. Jésus, je n'en reviendrai pas!
FLETCHER
A dix pas, n'est-ce pas?
FRANCŒUR
Oui!
PINARD
A cinq pas cela serait mieux.
JACOB (*à part*)
Mé, Mé, Mé, il est enragé celui-là!

JACOB
Mon Dieu! je l'ai tué! (*Tous, sauf, Jacob, entourent le Bourdon*.)
FLETCHER & TOUBEAU (*à Jacob*)
Run! Patauville! run!
PINARD & FRANCŒUR (*à Jacob*)
Sauvez-vous Patauville! Sauvez-vous! (*Jacob reste immobile*.)
TOUBEAU (*penché sur le Bourdon, l'examinant et lui tâtant le pouls*)
Il se meurt, les balles lui ont fracassé le cranium, transpercé les temporaux et fracassé l'occiput.
PINARD (*à Jacob*)
Mais, sauvez-vous donc!
SWEENEY (*allant à Jacob et l'entraînant*)
Venez ci, vos suivre moé, courrons! (*Jacob et Sweeney sortent en courant*.)

107 Mgr C.-P. Choquette, *Histoire de la ville de Saint-Hyacinthe* 267. Marie-Claire Daveluy, in the article mentioned in note 103 above, makes use of the information supplied by Choquette.

108 *Le Duel au Canada* 309:
Ceux qui lisent cette pièce aujourd'hui, n'arrivent pas à la trouver aussi spirituelle qu'on le disait autrefois. Elle est bouffonne, et l'esprit n'y est pas de la meilleure qualité. Elle eut cependant un succès immense en son temps, parce qu'on la prétendait basée sur un incident vrai. Mais là encore Raphaël Fontaine avait surtout pour objet de ridiculiser un adver-

saire politique, et c'est assez dire qu'il ne s'est aucunement soucié de respecter la vérité.

109 *Une Partie de tire! Fricot politique en l'honneur de Pierre-Samuel Gendron, M.P. pour le comté de Bagot.* Imprimé aux ateliers de la *Gazette de Saint-Hyacinthe*, 1871

CONCLUSION

1 A.I. Silver, *The French-Canadian Idea of Confederation, 1864-1900* 17; W.L. Morton, *The Critical Years: The Union of British North America, 1857-1873* 1.

2 See Jean-Marc Larrue, *Le Théâtre à Montréal à la fin du XIXe siècle*, esp. ch. 3, 'Le Théâtre canadien' 75-97; and ch. 4, 'Les Troupes professionnelles locales' 115-23.

3 *Le nouveau-Monde* (Montreal) II, no. 11, 28 août 1868, p 2. Quoted by Laflamme and Tourangeau, *L'Eglise et le théâtre au Québec* 146

4 'Graves avertissements donnés aux fidèles par Mgr des Trois-Rivières, à l'occasion des représentations de la Compagnie d'Opéra français, le 19 et le 20 du courant,' in *Le Journal des Trois-Rivières* XVI, 54 (29 Nov. 1880) 4. Quoted by Laflamme and Tourangeau, *L'Eglise et le Théâtre au Québec* 174

5 L'abbé Ricard to Mrg Cooke, 23 Feb. 1861. Quoted by Laflamme and Tourangeau, *L'Eglise et le théâtre au Québec* 140

6 L'abbé Laflamme to Frère Gauvreau, 6 Jan. 1881. Quoted by Laflamme and Tourangeau, *L'Eglise et le théâtre au Québec* 179-80.

Bibliography

Sources cited in this book, or found useful in its preparation

MANUSCRIPTS

Archives Nationales du Québec (Quebec City)
- 4182, M0067-0058, Papers of Louis Le Verrier
Archives du Séminaire de Québec
- *Journal* du Séminaire (*passim*)
- *Saberdache rouge* (30 vols):
  vol. J2, pp 196-211, 'Extrait des Annales [de l'Hôpital Général de Québec]' and 'Reception de Mgr de Saint-Vallier'
  vol. P, 'Poésies et autres œuvres de Mr Joseph Quesnel, tant publiées qu'inédites,' esp. pp 69-113, *L'Anglomanie*; pp 114-49, *Les Républicains français*; pp 177-249, *Colas et Colinette*
- *Saberdache bleue* (13 vols), esp. pp 245-6, 'Lettre à Mme J. Viger (17 février, 1834, soir)' and printed copy of vaudeville, 'C'est la faute à Papineau'
- 'Séminaire 12, no. 6: 'Analyse de sermons,' containing untitled, incomplete verse play from about 1780, principal character named 'Pavane'
- Séminaire 34, no. 135: *L'Education négligée* and critical letter by Gravé de la Rive
- Lettres P, no. 9: l'abbé Charles Glandelet à Mgr de Saint-Vallier
- Lettres M, nos 20, 38: corres. de Jean-H. Tremblay
- Fol. Verreau 45, no. 3: voice score for Quesnel's *Lucas et Cécile*
- Lettres, Y, no. 71, copy of letter from Octave Plessis to Judge Jonathan Sewell
- Poly 37, no. 27, a-f: various documents concerning theatre operated by W. Metchler and J. Holland
Public Archives of Canada (Ottawa)
- MG 24 B1 (Neilson Collection), esp. vol. I, p 384 (activity of John Neilson with Théâtre de Société in 1802); vol. II, pp 7a, 43a-d, 43e-g, 44a-b, 67a-b, 70a-c, 109a-b, 117a-d: Letters of Joseph Quesnel to John Neilson, concerning printing of *Colas et Colinette*

NEWSPAPERS AND PERIODICALS
(most consulted extensively, but not exhaustively)

Berthier

L'Echo des campagnes

Montreal

L'Artisan
L'Aurore
L'Avenir
The Canadian Magazine and Literary Repository
The Canadian Spectator
La Gazette du commerce et littéraire pour la ville et le district de Montréal
La Minerve
The Montreal Gazette / La Gazette de Montréal
The Montreal Herald
Le Nouveau-Monde
L'Ordre
Le Pays
Le Populaire
The Scribbler
Le Spectateur canadien

Quebec City

Le Canadien
Le Courier du Canada
Le Courier de Québec
L'Electeur
Le Fantasque
Le Journal de Québec
The Quebec Gazette / La Gazette de Québec
The Quebec Magazine
The Quebec Mercury

Saint-Hyacinthe

Le Courier de Saint-Hyacinthe
Le Journal de Saint-Hyacinthe

Trois-Rivières

La Gazette des Trois-Rivières

DRAMATIC TEXTS

Achintre, Auguste, *La Confédération*. Cantate. Paroles de M.A. Achintre, musique de M.J. Bte Labelle. Dédiée à l'Hon. George Etienne Cartier Ministre de la Milice

Anon., *Le Canadien et sa femme: une brochure de propagande politique (1794)*, ed. J. Hare, in *Cahiers de la Société bibliographique du Canada* II (1963) 57-73

- *La Confédération et John Bull*, in *L'Electeur* (Quebec), 25 May 1866, p 2
- *Conversation au sujet de l'élection du comté de Québec*, in *Etudes françaises* (Montreal), V, 3 (Aug. 1969) 362-71. Reprinted from *Le Canadien*, 14 May 1808
- *Conversation entre deux amis*, in *L'Electeur*, 25 May 1866, p 3
- *Conversation entre deux habitans canadiens*, in *Le Populaire*, 27 Oct. 1837, p 1
- *La Crise: petite comédie en un acte*, in *L'Avenir*, 30 May 1856, p 3; 5 June 1856, p 3 [Joseph Doutre?]
- *La Dégringolade*, in *L'Avenir*, 1-22 Feb. 1856 [Joseph Doutre?]
- *Le Diable à quatre: A propos d'une Tuque Bleue*, in *L'Avenir*, 26 Aug. 1848, pp 1-2 [Joseph Doutre?]
- *Dialogue entre un curé et un habitant*, in *Le Canadien*, 20 Mar. 1822, p 2
- *Dialogue: Saint-Just et Machiavel*, in *L'Aurore*, 26 Sept. 1818
- *Dialogue sur l'intérêt du jour, entre plusieurs candidats et un électeur libre et indépendent de la Cité de Québec* (Québec: Wm Moore 1792)
- *L'Eglise du village: Dialogue ou entretien de deux cultivateurs*, in *L'Echo des campagnes*, 7 Nov. 1846, p 1
- *Liberté de la presse: Débat en forme de dialogue*, in *Etudes françaises* (Montreal), V, 3 (Aug. 1969) 287-90. Reprinted from *La Gazette du commerce et littéraire de la ville et district de Montréal*, 21 Oct. 1778
- *Le Ministère jugé*, in *Le Fantasque*, 3 Dec. 1857, pp 22-3
- *Napoléon & son Mamluck*, in *Quebec Gazette / Gazette de Québec*, 18 Aug. 1814
- *La Réception de Mgr le vicomte d'Argenson par toutes les nations du païs de Canada à son entrée au gouvernement de la Nouvelle-France*, ed. P.-G. Roy (Quebec: Brousseau 1890); re-ed. (with emendations) by Luc Lacourcière in *Anthologie poétique de la Nouvelle-France* (Quebec: Presses de l'Université Laval 1966) 58-64
- *Le Siège futur du gouvernement, ou la Querelle des cinq villes: Récit peu fantastique d'un songe des plus réels*, in *Le Fantasque*, 26 Nov. 1857, pp 1-15
- *Les Soirées du village, ou Entretiens sur le protestantisme*. Ière Partie: *Les Saints protestants*. Ière Soirée: *Saint Luther*. Montreal: Des Presses à vapeur de Plinguet et Laplante, 11, rue Ste Thérèse. 2ème Soirée: *Saint Calvin*. Montreal 1860
- *The Fourth Comédie du statu quo*, ed. L.E. Doucette, in *Theatre History in Canada / Histoire du théâtre au Canada* III, 1 (Spring 1982) 33-42
- *Le Statu quo en déroute*. Plattsburgh, NY [June 1834]. Re-ed. by G. Bernier (Dionne's text, without his notes), (Réédition-Québec 1969)

- *Les trois Comédies du statu quo*, ed. N.-E. Dionne (Quebec: Laflamme & Proulx 1909)
- *Une Scène d'intérieur, ou Relation d'une séance du comité chargé de surveiller la rédaction des lettres d'un célèbre Dr Guerrier*, in *L'Avenir*, 2 Aug. 1848, pp 1-2 [Joseph Doutre?]
- *Veillée d'un candidat avec sa belle amie*, in *Le Canadien*, 29 Aug. 1807
Berthelot d'Artigny, M.-A., *Conversation au sujet de l'élection de Charlesbourg* (Quebec: Samuel Nelson 1792)
Caisse, Camille and Arcade Laporte. *Les anciens Canadiens* (Montreal: Beauchemin 1894)
Fontaine, Raphaël-Ernest, *Un Duel à poudre* (Saint-Hyacinthe: Imprimerie du Journal de Saint-Hyacinthe 1868)
Fréchette, Louis-Honoré, *Félix Poutré* (Montreal, n.e., n.d. [1871])
Gérin-Lajoie, Antoine, *Le jeune Latour*
- in *L'Aurore des Canadas*, 7, 12, 17 Sept. 1844
- in *Le Canadien*, 16, 18, 20 Sept. 1844
- separately (Montreal: Cinq-Mars 1844)
- in *Le Répertoire national*, ed. James Huston (Montreal: Lovell & Gibson, 4 vols, 1848-50) III, 5-49; (Montreal: Valois, 4 vols, 1893) III, 3-55
- in *Lettres canadiennes d'autrefois*, ed. Séraphin Marion (Ottawa: Presses de l'Université d'Ottawa) IV (1944) 143-92
- (Réédition-Québec 1969), ed. Baudoin Burger
Groulx, Louis-Thomas, *La Dissolution*, in *L'Avenir*, 18 Dec. 1847, p 4
- *Le Retour des ministres*, in *L'Avenir*, 15 Jan. 1848, p 1
Labelle, Elzéar, *La Conversion d'un pêcheur* (Montreal: [n.e., n.d. 1869?])
- *La Conversion d'un pêcheur (de la Nouvelle-Ecosse)*, in *Mes Rimes* (Quebec: Délisle 1876) 117-47
Labelle, Jean-Baptiste. *See* Achintre, A. and E. Labelle.
La Chasse, Pierre-Joseph de, *Réception pour Mgr de Saint-Vallier*, in *Monseigneur de Saint-Vallier et l'Hôpital Général de Québec* (Quebec: Darveau 1882) 263-9
Laporte, Arcade. *See* Caisse, Camille.
LaRue, Hubert, *Le Défricheur de langue*. Tragédie-bouffe, en trois tableaux, par Isidore de Méplats. 1859. Repub. in H. LaRue, *Mélanges historiques, littéraires et d'économie politique* (Quebec: Garant & Trudel 1870) I, 93-112
Lescarbot, Marc, *Histoire de la Nouvelle-France, contenant les navigations, découvertes & habitations faites par les François és Indes Occidentales & Nouvelle-France souz l'avœu et authorité de noz Rois Tres-Chrétiens...* (Paris: Millot 1609), containing *Le Théâtre de Neptune en la Nouvelle-France* (V, 19-29). Repub., in Millot's ed., in *Ecrits du Canada français* XVIII (1964) 267-95
- ed., Edna B. Polman, *Neptune's Theatre* (New York & London: Samuel French 1927)
- ed., Harriette T. Richardson, *The Theatre of Neptune in New France* (Cambridge, MA: Riverside Press 1927)

- transl. Pierre Erondelle, *Nova Francia* (London: Bishop 1609), repub. with introd. by H.P. Biggar (New York & London: Harper & Bros 1928)
- ed. and transl., Eugene and Renate Benson, in *Canadian Drama / L'Art dramatique canadien* VIII, 1 (1982) 87-95

Marconnay, Hyacinthe Leblanc de, *L'Hôtel des princes*. Opéra-comique en un acte, paroles de MM. de Ferrier et de Marconnay, musique de M. Eugène Prévost. Représenté pour la première fois sur le Théâtre de l'Ambigu-Comique le Samedi 23 Avril 1831. Paris, chez tous les marchands de nouveautés, et chez Martinet, Libraire, rue du Coq-Saint-Honoré
- *Le Soldat*. Intermède en deux Parties mêlé de chants. Exécuté sur le Théâtre Royal de Montréal (Bas-Canada) en 1835 et 1836. Arrangé par Mr. Leblanc de Marconnay (Montreal: L'Imprimerie d'Ariel Bowman, rue St-François-Xavier 1836)
- *Valentine, ou la Nina canadienne*. Par H. Leblanc de Marconnay, Ecuyer (Montreal: L'Imprimerie de L'Ami du peuple 1836) Repub. by Réédition-Québec 1968

Méplats, Isidore de. *See* LaRue, Hubert.

Petitclair, Pierre, *Griphon, ou la Vengeance d'un valet*. Comédie en trois actes. Par P. Petitclair. Québec: chez William Cowan, imprimeur, no. 9, rue La Fabrique 1837
- *La Donation*. Comédie en deux actes
- in *L'Artisan* (Montreal), 15-29 Dec. 1842
- in *Le Répertoire national*, ed. James Huston (Montreal: Lovell & Gibson, 4 vols, 1848-50), II, 234-70; (Montreal: Valois, 4 vols, 1893) II, 262-304
- *Une Partie de campagne*. Comédie en deux actes par M. Pierre Petitclair. Représentée pour la première fois à Québec, par les Amateurs Canadiens-français, le 22 avril 1857, et par les Jeunes Amateurs canadiens, le 28 avril 1860 (Quebec: Imprimé et publié par Joseph Savard, typographe, 1865)

Proulx, Jean-Baptiste, *L'Hôte à Valiquet, ou le Fricot sinistre*. Tragi-comédie en trois actes (Montreal: Beauchem & Valois, libraires-imprimeurs 1881)

Prud'homme, Firmin, *Napoléon à Sainte-Hélène*. Scènes historiques, arrangées par Firmin Prud'homme, et représentées pour la première fois sur le Théâtre de Montréal, le 28 de décembre 1831 (Montreal: La Minerve 1831)

Quesnel, Joseph, *Colas et Colinette, ou le Bailli dupé*. Comédie en 3 actes et en prose, mêlée d'ariettes. Les paroles et la musique de M.Q. (Quebec: John Neilson, imprimeur-libraire 1808)
- *Colas and Colinette, or The Bailiff Confounded*, English trans. of the dialogue by Michel Lecavalier and that of the songs by Michel Lecavalier and Godfrey Ridout (Toronto: Thompson 1974)
- *Les Républicains français*, ed. B. Burger, in *La Barre du jour* 25 (Summer 1970) 60-88
- *L'Anglomanie ou le Dîner à l'anglaise*, in *Le Canada français* XX, 4-6 (Dec. 1932-Feb. 1933)
- in *La Barre du jour*, ed. Claude Savoie (July-Dec. 1965) 113-41

/

Verreau, Hospice-Anselme, *Stanislas de Kostka* (Montreal: Aux bureaux de la Revue de Montréal 1878)
Villeneuve, Alphonse, *Contre-Poison: Faussetés, erreurs, impostures, blasphèmes de l'apostat Chiniquy*. Par Alph. Villeneuve, Ptre. Troisième édition. Montreal: Typ. Le Franc-Parleur, no. 22 rue Saint-Gabriel 1875

BOOKS AND MONOGRAPHS

Adam, Antoine, *Histoire de la littérature française du XVIIe siècle* (Paris: Del Duca 1965) 5 vols
Amtmann, Willy, *Music in Canada, 1600-1800* (Montreal: Habitex 1975)
Angers, F.-R., *Révélations du crime, ou Cambray et ses complices*, ed. J. Hare (Réédition-Québec 1969)
Anon., *Monseigneur de Saint-Vallier et l'Hôpital Général de Québec* (Quebec: Darveau 1882)
Archives des lettres canadiennes, I: *Le Mouvement littéraire de Québec, 1860* (Ottawa: Eds de l'Université d'Ottawa 1961); v: *Le Théâtre canadien-français* (Montreal: Fides 1976). Most useful articles were Roméo Arbour, '*Le Théâtre de Neptune* de Marc Lescarbot' 21-31; Baudoin Burger, 'Les Spectacles dramatiques en Nouvelle-France (1606-1760)' 33-57; John Hare, 'Panorama des spectacles au Québec: de la Conquête au XXe siècle' 59-107; David M. Hayne, 'Le Théâtre de Joseph Quesnel' 109-17; René Dionne, '*Le jeune Latour* d'Antoine Gérin-Lajoie (21 juillet 1844)' 119-25; Jean-Claude Noël, 'Le Théâtre de Pierre Petitclair' 127-36; Paul Wyczynski, 'Louis Fréchette et le théâtre' 136-65; Jeanne Corriveau, 'Le Théâtre collégial au Québec: L'apport de Gustave Lamarche' 169-201.
Aubert de Gaspé, Philippe, *Les anciens Canadiens* (Quebec: Desbarats et Derbishire 1863)
– *Mémoires* (Ottawa: Desbarats 1866)
Audet, L.-P., *Histoire de l'enseignement au Québec, 1608-1840* (Montreal and Toronto: Holt, Rinehart & Winston 1971) 2 vols
Ball, J.L. and R. Plant, *A Bibliography of Canadian Theatre History, 1583-1975* (Toronto: Playwright's Co-op 1976)
Beaulieu, André and Jean Hamelin, *Les Journaux du Québec, de 1764 à 1964* (Quebec: Presses de l'Université Laval 1965)
Bégon, Elisabeth, *Lettres au cher fils: Correspondance d'Elisabeth Bégon avec son gendre (1748-53)*, pref. by Nicole Deschamps (Montreal: HMH 1972)
Bellerive, Georges, *Nos Auteurs dramatiques anciens et contemporains* (Quebec: Garneau 1933)
Benson, Adolph B. *See* Kalm, Peter.
Béraud, Jean [pseud. Jacques Laroche], *350 ans de théâtre au Canada français* ([Montreal]: Cercle du Livre de France [1958])
Bernier, Gérard, ed., *Les Trois comédies du statu quo* (Réédition-Québec 1969)
Bibaud, F.-M.-U.-M., *Le Panthéon canadien* (Montreal: Cérat & Bourguignon 1858)

Brenner, Clarence D. and Nolan A. Goodyear, eds, *Eighteenth-Century French Plays* (New York: Appleton-Century-Crofts 1927)

Brumoy, Pierre, *Jonathas et David, ou le Triomphe de l'amitié* (Montreal: Fleury Mesplet & Ch. Berger 1776)

Brunet, Berthelot, *Histoire de la littérature canadienne-française* (Montreal: L'Arbre 1946)

Burger, Baudoin, *L'Activité théâtrale au Québec (1765-1825)* (Montreal: Parti Pris 1974)

– ed., Joseph Quesnel's *Les Républicains français*, q.v.

Burke, Catherine. *See* Ursulines de Québec.

Carrier, Maurice and Monique Vachon, *Chansons politiques du Québec* (Montreal: Leméac) I, 1765-1833 (1977); II, 1834-58 (1979)

Casgrain, H.R. *See* Montcalm de Saint-Servan.

Choquette, C.-P., *Histoire de la ville de Saint-Hyacinthe* (Saint-Hyacinthe: Richer et fils 1930)

Cimon, Adèle. *See* Ursulines de Québec.

Claretie, Léo, *Histoire des théâtres de société* (Paris: Molière [1905])

Costisella, Joseph, *L'Esprit révolutionnaire dans la littérature canadienne-française de 1837 à la fin du XIXe siècle* (Montreal: Beauchemin 1968)

Cotnam, Jacques, *Le Théâtre québécois, instrument de contestation sociale et politique* (Montreal: Fides 1976)

Darveau, Louis-Michel, *Nos Hommes de lettres* (Montreal: Stevenson 1873)

David, Laurent-Olivier, *Mélanges historiques et littéraires* (Montreal: Beauchemin 1917)

– *Souvenirs et biographies, 1870-1910* (Montreal: Beauchemin 1911)

Deschamps, Marcel and Deny Tremblay, *Dossier en théâtre québécois* (Jonquière: Presses collégiales de Jonquière 1972)

Dictionnaire des œuvres littéraires du Québec I (Montreal: Fides 1978)

Dionne, Narcisse-E., ed., *Les Trois Comédies du statu quo (1834)* (Quebec: Laflamme & Proulx 1909)

– and A.G. Doughty, *Quebec under Two Flags* (Quebec: Quebec News Co. 1903)

Dionne, René, *Antoine Gérin-Lajoie, homme de lettres* (Sherbrooke: Naaman [1978])

Doughty, A.G. *See* Dionne, N.-E.

Douville, J.-Antoine-Irénée, *Histoire du collège-séminaire de Nicolet (1803-1903)* (Montreal: Beauchemin 1903) 2 vols

Drolet, Antonio, *Les Bibliothèques canadiennes, 1604-1960* (Montreal: Cercle du Livre de France 1965)

Durham, Lord, *Report on the Affairs of British North America*, ed. with an introd. by Sir C.P. Lucas (Oxford: Clarendon 1912) 3 vols

Duval, Etienne-F., with the collaboration of Jean LaFlamme, *Anthologie thématique du théâtre québécois au XIXe siècle* (Montreal: Leméac 1978)

Eccles, William J., *Frontenac: The Courtier Governor* (Toronto: McClelland & Stewart 1959)

Edwards, Murray D., *A Stage in Our Past: English-Language Theatre in Eastern Canada from the 1790s to 1914* (Toronto: University of Toronto Press 1968)

Erondelle, Pierre, *Nova Francia* (London: George Bishop 1609; re-ed. with introd. by H.P. Biggar, New York and London: Harper & Bros 1928)

Fauteux, Aegidius, *Le Duel au Canada* (Montreal: Editions du Zodiaque 1934)

Forget, Anastase, *Histoire du Collège de l'Assomption* (Montreal: Imprimerie populaire 1933)

Fowke, Edith Fulton and Richard Johnston, *Chansons de Québec / Quebec Folk Songs* (Waterloo, Ont.: Waterloo Music Co. 1973)

Frégault, Guy, *La Civilisation de la Nouvelle-France (1713-1744)* (Montreal: Pascal 1944)

– *Le XVIIIe siècle canadien: Etudes* (Montreal: HMH 1970)

Fuchs, Max, *La Vie théâtrale en province au XVIIIe siècle* (Paris: Droz 1933)

Gaiffe, Félix, *Le Drame en France au XVIIIe siècle* (Paris: Colin 1910)

Gaspé. See Aubert de Gaspé, Philippe.

Gérin, Léon, *Antoine Gérin-Lajoie: La Résurrection d'un patriote canadien* (Montreal: Eds du Devoir 1925)

Gobin, Pierre, *Le Fou et ses doubles: Figures de la dramaturgie québécoise* (Presses de l'Université de Montréal 1978)

Godin, J.-C. and L. Mailhot, *Le Théâtre québécois: Introduction à dix dramaturges contemporains* (Montreal: HMH 1970)

Gofflot, L.-V., *Le Théâtre au collège du moyen âge à nos jours* (Paris: Champion 1907)

Gosselin, Amédée, *L'Instruction au Canada sous le régime français (1635-1760)* (Quebec: Laflamme & Proulx 1911)

Gosselin, Auguste-H., *L'Eglise du Canada depuis Mgr de Laval jusqu'à la Conquête* (Quebec: Laflamme & Proulx 1911-14) 3 vols

– *L'Eglise du Canada après la Conquête* (Québec: Laflamme 1916-17) 2 vols

Graham, Franklin, *Histrionic Montreal* (New York: Blom 1969: reprint of Montreal ed. of 1902)

Hallays-Dabot, Victor, *Histoire de la censure théâtrale en France* (Paris 1862; Slatkine: Geneva 1970)

Hamel, Réginald, John Hare, and Paul Wyczynski, *Dictionnaire pratique des auteurs québécois* (Montreal: Fides 1976)

Hare, John, ed., F.-R. Angers, *Révélations du crime, ou Cambray et ses complices* (Réédition-Québec 1969)

Hicks, R. Keith. See Lescarbot, Marc.

Houlé, Léopold, *L'Histoire du théâtre au Canada: Pour un retour aux classiques* (Montreal: Fides 1945)

Hughes, Glenn, *A History of the American Theatre, 1700-1950* (London & Toronto: Samuel French 1951)

Huston, James, ed., *Le Répertoire national, ou Recueil de littérature canadienne* (Montreal: Lovell & Gibson 1848-50) 4 vols; (Montreal: Valois 1893) 4 vols

Innis, Mary Quayle, ed., *Mrs Simcoe's Diary* (Toronto: Macmillan 1965)

Kallmann, Helmut, *A History of Music in Canada, 1534-1914* (Toronto: University of Toronto Press 1969)

Kalm, Peter, *Peter Kalm's Travels in North America: The English Version of 1770,* rev. from the original Swedish and ed. by Adolph B. Benson (New York: Wilson-Erickson 1937) 2 vols

Klinck, George A., *Louis Fréchette, prosateur: Une Réestimation de son œuvre* (Lévis: Le Quotidien 1955)

Lacourcière, Luc, ed., *Anthologie poétique de la Nouvelle-France* (Quebec: Presses de l'Université Laval 1966)

Laflamme, Jean and Rémi Tourangeau, *L'Eglise et le théâtre au Québec* (Montreal: Fides 1979)

Lagrave, Jean-Paul de, *Les Origines de la presse au Québec, 1760-1791* (Montreal: Eds de Lagrave 1975)

Lamarche, Gustave, *Le Théâtre québécois dans notre littérature* (Centre de Recherches en Lettres québécoises, Université de Québec à Trois-Rivières [nd])

Lambert, John, *Travels through Lower Canada and the United States of North America, in the Years 1806, 1807 and 1808* (London: Gillet 1810) 3 vols

Lancaster, Henry C., *A History of French Dramatic Literature in the Seventeenth Century* (Baltimore: Johns Hopkins University Press 1929-32) 2 vols

Lanctôt, Gustave, *Faussaires et faussetés en histoire canadienne* (Montreal: Eds Variétés [1948])

Lareau, Edmond, *Histoire de la littérature canadienne* (Montreal: Lovell 1874)

Larrue, Jean-Marc, *Le Théâtre à Montréal à la fin du XIXe siècle* (Montreal: Fides 1981)

Larthomas, Pierre, *Le Théâtre en France au XVIIIe siècle* (Paris: Presses Universitaires de France 1980)

LaTour, Bertrand de, *Mémoires sur la vie de Mgr de Laval*, in *Œuvres complètes de LaTour* (Paris: Migne 1855) IV

Lévesque, Eugène and Charles Urbain, *L'Eglise et le théâtre* (Paris: Grasset 1930)

Louvigny de Montigny, ed., *Antoine Gérin-Lajoie* (Toronto: Ryerson [nd])

Mandements, lettres pastorales et circulaires des évêques de Québec, eds Hétu and Gagnon (Quebec: Côté 1869-87) 8 vols

Mandements, lettres pastorales, circulaires et autres documents publiés dans le Diocèse de Montréal depuis son érection (Montreal: Chapleau, vols II and II; Typographie 'Le Nouveau Monde,' vol. III; Plinguet, vol. IV), period 1836-83

Marconnay, Hyacinthe Leblanc de, *Relation historique des événements de l'élection du comté du Lac des Deux Montagnes en 1834: Episode propre à faire connaître l'esprit public dans le Bas-Canada* (Montreal 1836)

– *La petite Clique dévoilée*, ou Quelques explications sur les manœuvres dirigées contre la minorité patriote, qui prit part au vote sur les subsides dans la session de 1835 à 1836; et, plus particulièrement contre C.C. Sabrevois de Bleury, Ecuyer, avocat du barreau de Montréal, membre de la Chambre d'Assemblée du Bas-Canada. Etats-Unis: Rome, N.Y. 1836 [text also attributed to C.C. Sabrevois de Bleury]

Marion, Séraphin, *Les Lettres canadiennes d'autrefois* (Ottawa: Eds de l'Université d'Ottawa 1939-54) 8 vols

Marsollier des Vivetières, Benoît-Joseph, *Nina, ou la Folle par amour*. Comédie en un acte, en prose, mêlée d'ariettes. Par M. M.D.V. Musique de M. Dal. Représentée pour la première fois par les Comédiens Italiens ordinaires du Roi, le 15 mai, 1786. Paris: Brunet 1786

Maurault, Olivier, *Le Petit Séminaire de Montréal* (Montreal: Derome 1918)

Modern Language Association of America: Collection of Photographic Facsimiles (New York 1929)

Monet, Jacques, *The Last Cannon Shot: A Study of French-Canadian Nationalism, 1837-1850* (Toronto: University of Toronto Press 1969)

Montcalm de Saint-Servan, Louis-Joseph de Montcalm-Gazon, marquis de, *Journal du marquis de Montcalm durant ses campagnes en Canada de 1756 à 1759*. Vol. VII of *Collection des manuscrits du Maréchal de Lévis*, ed. H.-R. Casgrain (Quebec: Demers 1895)

Montpensier, Mlle de, *Mémoires de Mlle de Montpensier, petite-fille de Henri IV, collationés sur le manuscrit autographe, avec notes biographiques et historiques par A. Chéruel* (Paris: Charpentier 1859)

Morton, W.L., *The Critical Years: The Union of British North America, 1857-1873* (Toronto: McClelland & Stewart 1977)

Neatby, Hilda, *Quebec: The Revolutionary Age, 1760-1791* (Toronto: McClelland & Stewart 1966)

Parizeau, Gérard, *La Société canadienne-française au XIXe siècle* (Montreal: Fides 1975)

Plant, Richard. *See* Ball, John L.

Polman, Edna B. *See* Lescarbot, Marc.

Pontaut, Alain, *Dictionnaire critique du théâtre québécois* (Quebec: Leméac 1972)

Poutré, Félix, *Echappé de la potence: Souvenirs d'un prisonnier d'état canadien en 1838* (Imprimé pour l'auteur par De Montigny et cie 1862)

– *Escaped from the Gallows: Souvenirs of a Canadian State Prisoner in 1838* (Montreal: Beauchemin & Valois 1885)

Prince-Falmagne, Thérèse, *Un Marquis du grand siècle: Jacques-René de Brisay de Denonville* (Montreal: Leméac 1965)

Reyval, Albert, *L'Eglise, la comédie et les comédiens* (Paris: Spes 1953)

Richardson, Harriette Taber. *See* Lescarbot, Marc.

Rinfret, Edouard-G., *Le Théâtre canadien d'expression française: Répertoire analytique des origines à nos jours* (Montreal: Leméac 1975-8) 4 vols

Rochementeix, Camille, *Les Jésuites et la Nouvelle-France au XVIIe siècle* (Paris: Letouzey & Ané 1895-6) 3 vols

– *Un Collège de Jésuites au XVIIe et XVIIIe siècles* (Le Mans: Leguicheux 1889) 4 vols

Roy, Camille, *Nos Origines littéraires* (Quebec: L'Action Sociale 1909)

Roy, Pierre-Georges, ed., *La Réception de Monseigneur le vicomte d'Argenson par toutes les nations du païs de Canada à son entrée au gouvernement de la Nouvelle-France* (Quebec: Brousseau 1980)

- *A travers les Anciens Canadiens de Philippe Aubert de Gaspé* (Montreal: Ducharme 1943)
- *Toutes petites choses du régime français* (Quebec: Garneau 1944) 2 vols
Rumilly, Robert, *Monseigneur Laflèche et son temps* (Montreal: Zodiaque [1938])
Sabrevois de Bleury, C.C., *La petite Clique dévoilée. See* Marconnay, H. Leblanc de.
- *Réfutation de l'écrit de Louis-Joseph Papineau, ex-Orateur de la Chambre d'Assemblée du Bas-Canada, intitulé Histoire de l'insurrection du Canada, publiée dans le recueil hebdomadaire, La Revue du Progrès, imprimée à Paris* (Imprimerie de John Lovell, rue St Nicolas, à Montréal, Bas-Canada octobre 1839)
Saint-Pierre, Annette, *Le Rideau se lève au Manitoba* (Saint-Boniface: Eds des Plaines 1980)
Salomon, Herman Prins, *Tartuffe devant l'opinion française* (Paris: Presses Universitaires de France 1962)
Savoie, Claude, ed., Joseph Quesnel's *L'Anglomanie*, q.v.
Schneider, B.R., *Index to the London Stage, 1660-1800* (Carbondale: University of Southern Illinois Press 1979)
Séguin, Robert-Lionel, *La Vie libertine en Nouvelle-France au XVIIe siècle* (Montreal: Leméac 1972)
- *Les Divertissements en Nouvelle-France* (Ottawa: National Museum, Bulletin 227, 1968)
Silver, A.I., *The French-Canadian Idea of Confederation, 1864-1900* (Toronto: University of Toronto Press 1982)
Thompson, Craig R., *The Colloquies of Erasmus* (Chicago: University of Chicago Press 1965) 2 vols
Thwaites, Reuben Gold, ed., *The Jesuit Relations and Allied Documents* (New York: Pageant 1959) 73 vols
Toupin, Paul, *L'Ecrivain et son théâtre* (Montreal: Cercle du Livre de France 1964)
Tourangeau, Rémi. *See* Laflamme, Jean.
Tremaine, Marie, *A Bibliography of Canadian Imprints, 1751-1800* (Toronto: University of Toronto Press 1952)
Tremblay, Jean-Paul, *A la Recherche de Napoléon Aubin* (Quebec: Presses de l'Université Laval 1969)
- ed., *Napoléon Aubin*, in Collection Classiques Canadiens, no. 43 (Montreal: Fides 1972)
Truchet, Jacques, *Théâtre du XVIIIe siècle* (Paris: Gallimard 1972) 2 vols
Trudel, Marcel, *L'Influence de Voltaire au Canada* (Montreal: Fides 1945)
Les Ursulines de Québec depuis leur établissement jusqu'à nos jours (Quebec: Darveau 1863-6) 4 vols [compiled by Catherine Burke and Adèle Cimon]
Vachon, Monique. *See* Carrier, Maurice.
Wade, Mason, *The French Canadians, 1760-1967*, rev. ed. in 2 vols (Toronto: Macmillan 1968)
Wagner, Anton, ed., *Canada's Lost Plays*, IV: *Colonial Quebec: French-Canadian Drama, 1606 to 1966* (Toronto: Canadian Theatre Review Publications 1982)
Waldo, Lewis P., *The French Drama in America in the Eighteenth Century and Its*

Influence on the American Drama of that Period, 1701-1800 (Baltimore: Johns Hopkins University Press 1942)

ARTICLES AND CHAPTERS

Arbour, Roméo, '*Le Théâtre de Neptune* de Marc Lescarbot,' in *Archives des lettres canadiennes* v, *Le Théâtre canadien-français* 21-31

Baillet, Monique and Renée Lelièvre, 'Une Entrée triomphale en Acadie en 1606,' in *Revue d'histoire du théâtre* (Paris, Apr.-June 1969) 134-41

Bélanger, Reine, '*L'Hôte à Valiquet ou le Fricot sinistre*, comédie de Johannes Iovhanné (pseudonyme de l'abbé Jean-Baptiste Proulx),' in *Dictionnaire des œuvres littéraires du Québec* I, 379-80

- '*Valentine, ou la Nina canadienne*, comédie d'Hyacinthe Leblanc de Marconnay,' in *Dictionnaire des œuvres littéraires du Québec* I, 746

Boivin, Aurélien, '*La Réception de Monseigneur le vicomte d'Argenson*, drame anonyme,' in *Dictionnaire des œuvres littéraires du Québec*, I 626-7

Bouchard, Jacques, 'Du Théâtre français et occitan en Nouvelle-France en 1606,' in *Bulletin du Centre de recherche en civilisation canadienne-française* 20 Apr. 1980) 5-7

Burger, Baudoin, 'Les Spectacles dramatiques en Nouvelle-France (1606-1760),' in *Archives des lettres canadiennes* v, Le Théâtre canadien-français (Montreal: Fides 1976) 33-57

- 'Théâtre, littérature et politique en 1837-1838,' in *Aspects du théâtre québécois*, conférences colligées par Etienne-F. Duval (Université du Québec à Trois-Rivières 1978) 1-23

Cameron, Margaret M., 'Play-Acting in Canada during the French Regime,' in *Canadian Historical Review*, XI, 1 (Toronto, Mar. 1930) 9-19

Chartier, Yves, 'La Reconstitution musicale de *Colas et Colinette* de Joseph Quesnel,' in *Bulletin du centre de recherche en civilisation canadienne-française* (Ottawa, April 1972) 11-24

Corriveau, Jeanne, 'Le Théâtre collégial au Québec: L'Apport de Gustave Lamarche,' in *Archives des lettres canadiennes* v, 169-201

Daveluy, Marie-Claire, 'Deux Pionniers du théâtre canadien,' in *La Revue moderne* (Montreal, no 3, janvier 1933, p 7). (The 'deux pionniers' are E. Labelle and R.-E. Fontaine.)

Dionne, René, '*Le Jeune Latour* d'Antoine Gérin-Lajoie (31 juillet 1844),' in *Archives des lettres canadiennes* v, 119-25

Doucette, Leonard E., 'Les Comédies du statu quo (1834): Political Theatre and Paratheatre in French Canada,' Part I: 'Dramatized Dialogues before 1834,' in *Theatre History in Canada / Histoire du théâtre au Canada* II, 2 (Fall 1981) 83-92; Part II: 'Les Comédies du statu quo,' *ibid.* III, 1 (Spring 1982) 21-33

Drolet, Antonio, 'La Bibliothèque du Séminaire de Québec et son catalogue de 1782,' in *Le Canada français* XXVIII, 3 (Nov. 1940) 261-6

Du Berger, Jean, '*Griphon ou la Vengeance d'un valet*, comédie de Pierre Petit-clair,' in *Dictionnaire des œuvres littéraires du Québec*, I 299-300

- '*Les Républicains français, ou la Soirée du cabaret*, comédie de Joseph Quesnel,' *ibid*. I, 653

Fitzpatrick, Marjorie A., 'La Présence de Molière au Canada,' in *Archives des lettres canadiennes* V, 399-416

Fournier, Hannah, 'Lescarbot's *Théâtre de Neptune*: New World Pageant, Old World Polemic,' in *Canadian Drama / L'Art dramatique canadien* VII, 1 (1981) 1-12

Frégault, Guy, 'Politique et politiciens au début du XVIIIᵉ siècle,' in *Ecrits du Canada français* XI (1960) 180-91

Galarneau, Claude, 'Recherches sur l'histoire de l'enseignement secondaire classique au Canada français,' in *Revue de l'Histoire de l'Amérique française* XX, 1 (June 1966) 18-27

Girard, Gilles, '*Le Théâtre de Neptune en la Nouvelle-France* de Marc Lescarbot,' in *Dictionnaire des œuvres littéraires du Québec* (Montreal: Fides 1978) I, 699-702

Gosselin, Auguste, 'Un Episode de l'histoire du théâtre au Canada (1694),' in *Mémoires de la Société royale du Canada* series I, vol. IV (1898) 56-7

Hare, J.E., 'Le Choix d'un répertoire théâtral et le goût du public: Recherche d'une méthode sociologique,' in *Aspects du théâtre québécois*, conférences colligées par Etienne-F. Duval (Université du Québec à Trois-Rivières 1978) 57-69

- 'Panorama des spectacles au Québec: De la Conquête au XXᵉ siècle,' in *Archives des lettres canadiennes* V, 59-107
- 'Joseph Quesnel et l'anglomanie de la classe seigneuriale au tournant du XIXᵉ siècle,' in *Co-Incidences* (Ottawa) VI, 1 (Jan.-Feb. 1976) 23-31
- 'Poèmes épars de Joseph Quesnel,' in *Dictionnaire des œuvres littéraires du Québec* I, 596-7
- 'Le Théâtre de Société à Montréal, 1789-1791,' in *Bulletin du Centre de Recherche en civilisation canadienne-française* 16 (Apr. 1978) 22-6

Hayne, David M., 'Le Théâtre de Joseph Quesnel,' in *Archives des lettres canadiennes* V, 109-17

Klein, Owen, 'The Opening of Montreal's Theatre Royal,' in *Theatre History in Canada / Histoire du théâtre au Canada* I, 1 (Spring 1980) 24-36

Leland, Marine, 'Joseph-François Perrault, années de jeunesse, 1753-1783,' in *Revue de l'Université Laval* XIII, 9 (1959) 804-20

Leymarie, A.-Léo, 'Une Tragédie de Racine, en Nouvelle-France, en 1694,' in *Blancheflor: Revue régionale de folklore* 4 (June 1939) 15-17

MacDougall, Angus J., 'An Historical Sidelight: Quebec 1658,' in *Culture* 11 (Jan. 1980) 15-28

Marion, Séraphin, '*Le Tartufe* et Mgr de Saint-Vallier,' in *Lettres canadiennes d'autrefois* (Université d'Ottawa) VIII (1954) 15-37

- 'Notre première tragédie,' in *Origines littéraires du Canada français* (Eds de l'Université d'Ottawa) VII (1951) 13-29

Massicotte, Edouard-Zotique, '1800 à 1850: Vieux théâtres de Montréal,' in *La Revue populaire* 7 (July 1909) 63-9

- 'Un Théâtre à Montréal en 1789,' in *Bulletin des recherches historiques* XXIII, 12 (1917) 373-6

- 'Le Premier Théâtre à Montréal,' *ibid.* XXIII, 6 (1917) 191-2
- 'Recherches historiques sur les spectacles à Montréal, de 1760 à 1800,' in *Mémoires de la Société royale du Canada* 3ᵉ série, XXVI (1932) 113-22
Noël, Jean-Claude, 'Le Théâtre de Pierre Petitclair,' in *Archives des lettres canadiennes* V, 127-36
- 'Le Cas Pierre Petitclair,' in *Bulletin du Centre de recherche en civilisation canadienne-française* 19 (Dec. 1979) 27-9
Pichette, Robert, 'Marc Lescarbot et son *Théâtre de Neptune*,' in *Cahiers de la Société historique acadienne* 8 (May 1965) 21-32
Rambaud, Alfred, 'La Querelle du *Tartuffe* à Paris et à Québec,' in *Revue de l'Université Laval* VIII, 5 (Jan. 1954) 421-34
Ripley, John, 'Shakespeare on the Montreal Stage, 1805-1826,' in *Theatre History in Canada / Histoire du théâtre au Canada* III, 1 (Spring 1982) 5-6
Roy, Pierre-Georges, ed., 'Lettre de M. de Lamothe-Cadillac (28 septembre 1694),' in *Rapport de l'archiviste de la Province de Québec* 1923-4, pp 80-93
- *ibid.*, 'Lettre de M. Bochart Champigny au ministre (27 octobre 1694)' 94-6
Wyczynski, Paul, 'Louis Fréchette et le théâtre,' in *Archives des lettres canadiennes* V, 136-65

THESES

Corriveau, Jeanne, '*Jonathas* du R.P. Gustave Lamarche et le théâtre collégial' (Université de Montréal 1965)
Curran, Verna I., 'Philippe-Joseph Aubert de Gaspé: His Life and Works' (University of Toronto 1957)
Demers, Clovis, 'Concerts et représentations dramatiques à Québec, 1764-1800' (Université Laval 1955)
Duval, Etienne-F., 'Le Sentiment national dans le théâtre canadien-français de 1760 à 1930' (Université de Paris 1967)
Fitzpatrick, Marjorie Ann, 'The Fortunes of Molière in French Canada' (University of Toronto 1968)
Gardner, David, 'An Analytical History of the Theatre in Canada: The European Beginnings to 1760' (University of Toronto 1982)
Noël, Jean-Claude, 'Pierre Petitclair, premier dramaturge canadien-français' (Université d'Ottawa 1973)
Ouellet, Thérèse, 'Bibliographie du théâtre canadien-français avant 1900' (Université Laval 1949)

Index

Titles of French-Canadian plays are cross-indexed to name of author, where known. Titles of non-Canadian plays appear under name of author only, except where author is unknown.

UNIVERSITY OF TORONTO ROMANCE SERIES

UNIVERSITY OF TORONTO ROMANCE SERIES

UNIVERSITY OF TORONTO ROMANCE SERIES